SUPERSONIC
VISUALS FOR MUSIC

Die Gestalten Verlag

Featuring interviews with Big Active, Stylorouge, Emek, Voodoo Rhythm Rec. and Gomma Rec.

BECK
BECK
BECK
BECK
BECK
BECK

BIG ACTIVE for Beck "The Information" *(Album) on Interscope in 2006* - Pop -

BECK
MOTORCADE
NAUSEA
the horrible fanfare-landslide-exoskeleton
ELEVATOR MUSIC
new round
MOVIE THEME
Strange Apparition
THE INFORMATION
no complaints
WE DANCE ALONE
BECK

BECK
INFORMATION
THE INFORMATION
BECK
NEW ROUND
think I'm in love
Strange Apparition
ELEVATOR MUSIC
NO COMPLAINTS
INSIDE
NAUSEA
MOTORCADE
SOLDIER JANE
DARK STAR
CELL PHONE'S DEAD
THE HORRIBLE FANFARE/ LANDSLIDE/ EXOSKELETON
WE DANCE ALONE

BIG ACTIVE for Beck "The Information" *(Album) on Interscope in 2006*

BIG ACTIVE *Answers by Gerard Saint, Creative Director*

Founded by Gerard Saint, Mark Watkins and Paul Hetherington in 1990, London-based design agency Big Active has been going from strength to strength ever since its inception.

Not unlike a record company in spirit and make-up, the trio soon began to scour the capital for like-minded talents from music and visual arts to develop their striking visual concepts, campaigns and entire CIs for artists from the emerging Brit Pop scene. 'Collaboration allowed us to work on bigger ideas, with people whose creative and optimistic irreverence we shared. Plus, you could turn up to meetings after a heavy night out and everyone else would be in the same state as you.' Thriving on this creative exchange, the founders decided to expand their business by representation for some of their favourite contributors from photography and illustration – a unique and uniquely successful approach for a commercial design agency. To this day, the Big Active gang (now expanded by designer Mat Maitland) entertains strong ties to the music and clubbing scene, a fact reflected in their mischievous, powerful and most of all seductive graphics for music and magazines.

A few words on what Big Active is all about?

Big Active is a London design based studio that believes in creative networks. Our aim is to produce creative design and commercial art based on ideas with an accessible common touch. What makes our studio unique is that we also represent other commercial artists and illustrators, many of whom were involved in the artwork for Beck's 'The Information'.

How do you approach the actual 'branding' of a band or artist - considering that a discipline like pop music thrives on unpredictability and perceived subversion?

Music design is all about creating the defining image. These days, the idea that it's in any way subversive just sounds like some sort of woolly idealistic hippy nonsense from the late1960's. All good design is unpredictable in some way and all forms of design are about creatively solving problems and improving on the way things work. Music design has always been about packaging another person's creative work – which just happens to take the form of a piece of music. The work of some musicians may be more subversive, pretentious or worthy, others may be more glamorous, pop or mainstream or whatever – in the end, it's the designer's role to translate this visually and package the product appropriately.

It's very arrogant of designers to assume that their artwork is more important than the work they are packaging – at best the two work in synergy to create a complete experience.

When it comes down to it, we don't work in a vacuum. We respond to a brief, and all sorts of people - from the band or artist themselves to their management and the record label - are going to be involved in defining the objectives of that brief. But we always try to come back with a route that feels appropriate to the spirit of the artist or band. Every project is really different and some artist chose to be involved in the process more than others. At the end of the day, it's worth bearing in mind that music design can be very subjective. A great sleeve is visually inseparable from the music – imagine trying to repackage 'Dark Side Of The Moon' or 'Never Mind The Bollocks' etc.

Would you say that musicians have become more aware of their own image, the overall design and available marketing tools?

Artist management and record labels have always been aware of this - that's why they employ art directors, designers, stylists, video makers, PRs and a whole raft of other creatives to seamlessly create and develop a tangible image for their artists. Great songs sell records, but visibility brings definition in the market place.

To what extent does the shift towards digital and web-based releases affect your work?

Right now is an extremely exciting time for music design. Both CDs and downloads are essentially delivering the same digital information - so the challenge in selling physical product is to define the format in a way that gives it a reason to exist outside the digital content it carries. Arguably, everything is in a state of flux, but the potential possibilities are enormous. Music design is becoming a much broader discipline and that can only be a good thing for designers in the future. It's just the medium of delivery that is changing. Hopefully physical product and digital formats can work side by side in the future, maybe not to the same degree as we've become accustomed to, but perhaps in a way that each can make the most of it's own particular strength. I particularly like the analogy of the hard back and the soft back book idea – both can co-exist whilst satisfying different parts of the market. Certainly, it could be argued that the traditional, larger record labels have been quite lazy when it comes to producing physical products that really deliver value for money, whilst being slow to fully embrace the possibilities of the digital age. Nowadays, the average CD offers little more than a 5" plastic disc and at best a well-designed booklet. In a world where you can cherry-pick tracks online from an album, the album format as a 'collective work' of songs is almost becoming obsolete. If the packaging is poor, why spend extra money to own that format? You might as well download the digital 'soft- back' version or just buy your favourite songs online.

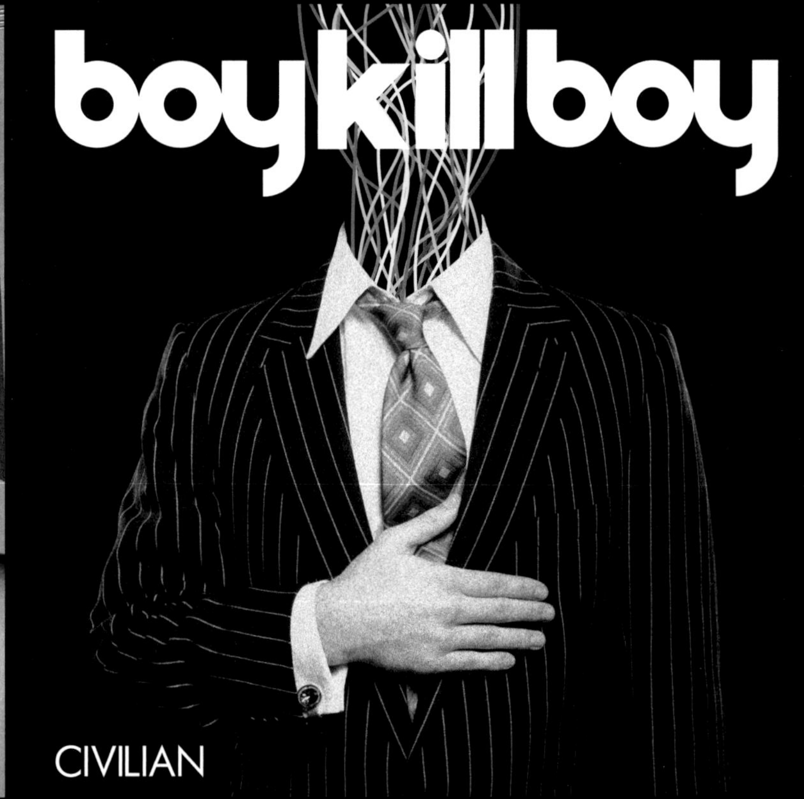

BIG ACTIVE for **Garbage** „Bleed Like Me“ (Album) *on WEA in 2005. Art Direction: Big Active, Design/Montage: Mat Maitland @ Big Active.* - Pop - **& for Boy Kill Boy „Civillian“** (Album) *on Mercury in 2006. Art Direction: Big Active, Design: Markus Karlsson @ Big Active.* - Pop -

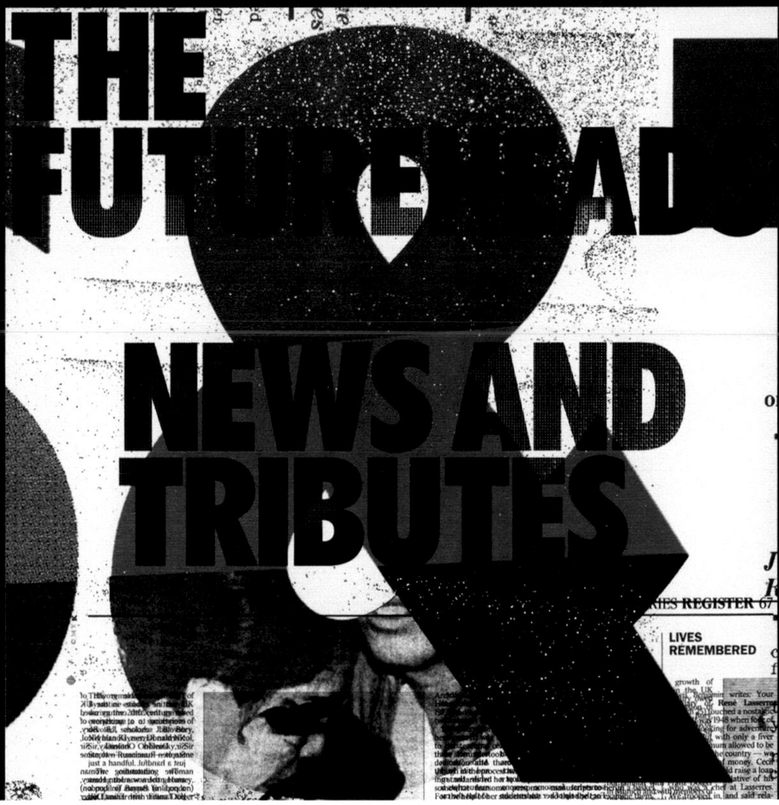

BIG ACTIVE for **The Futureheads** “The Futureheads” & “News & Tributes” (Album) *on 679 Recordings in 2004 & 2006. Art Direction & Design: Big Active.* - Pop -

However, if the packaging is integral to the experience of physically owning the album, then the idea of a physical format is still relevant and I'd like to think that we've really achieved this with design on the Beck album - the packaging completes the experience.

So, how did this unique collaboration come about?

Beck was keen to work with Big Active and is a fan of many of the artists we represent. Likewise, we really admired his music and creative approach, especially the theatre of his live shows. So, Mat Maitland and I were invited to spend a few days in LA with him to work out a plan for the artwork.

Could you explain the idea behind it? How did you arrive at the final concept?

The first thing we talked about was whether the package was even relevant and how we could give it a context as a physical form. We had been toying with an idea that threw the whole idea of creating a singular definable image for the release on its head – a sticker-based DIY approach using stickers more akin to homemade mix tapes and CDs. Beck had been thinking along similar lines and, as it turned out, was also big fan of sticker art.

There is no 'front cover' as such - the CD contains one of four different sticker sheets, each featuring original images by 20 different artists commissioned and curated by Big Active and Beck. The package itself is simply about participation and as such a good example of the invisibility of good design. Given a blank canvas of graph paper, the listener is encouraged to get creative and design their own cover or customize the package using the kit of stickers supplied within. We wanted to make the packaging experience integral to the physical CD format and I definitely think we've achieved that.

Why was it so important to involve the user in the whole cover design experience?

It was more a case of re-engaging the fan with the idea of what the experience of a physical album can be. Beck is more than happy to embrace downloads as a way of accessing music, but he wanted to give his audience something more when they buy the complete physical form of the album. After spending so long recording 'The Information', he didn't feel like it could be summed up with one image.

Our aim was to create a package that would be highly reflective of Beck's individual and creative approach to his art. It's simply about being part of the experience and as a result giving the listener the opportunity to express their own individuality - bringing them closer to the spirit of what Beck is about.

What about the artists involved? Who selected them and how did you co-ordinate the overall creative process for the artwork?

Beck was keen for us to work with many of the artists represented by Big Active, and as the project developed we all invited additional artists to achieve the right variety and eclectic balance we were after. We gave them a lot of creative leeway as long as each image would make a good sticker. To really make this work, it was vital to create more imagery than we would actually need so this could be curated by ourselves and Beck. During this process, Mat Maitland also created a number of specific stickers as we saw themes evolving across the sticker sheets. We ended up with different 250 stickers by a total of 20 artists as well as Beck himself. This was certainly the most artists we've ever commissioned for one project - maybe we've even set a world record for artists collaborating on one album sleeve! I hope so.

Sounds like a very ambitious undertaking – any particular pitfalls or setbacks?

The UK very nearly didn't release the album in the sticker format that we'd envisaged as they were worried that it didn't comply with the BPI's chart eligibility rules which do not allow stickers and the like. However, because the stickers are so legitimate to the credibility of the overall idea, the record label and Beck decided to release the record regardless.

Did people submit or publish their own creations?

The response has been phenomenal. Fans have been sharing their customized covers on Beck fan sites, websites like flickr.com or uploaded them to the dedicated website www.beckgallery.co.uk. The main feedback we have been getting is that many fans who buy pretty much all of their music online felt that this package has given them a reason to actually want to own the physical album - which is exactly what we set out to do. There's never been an album that's invited participation on this scale before.

BIG ACTIVE for **Snow Patrol** "Eyes Open" (Album) *on Fiction in 2006. Art Direction: Big Active, Design/Imagery: Mat Maitland @ Big Active.* - Pop -

BIG ACTIVE for Keane "Under the Iron Sea" (Album & Single Campaign) *on Island Records in 2006. Art Direction: Richard Andrews & Gerard Saint @ Big Active, Design: Richard Andrews @ Big Active, Illustrations: Sanna Annukka @ Big Active.* - Pop -

BIG ACTIVE for Keane "Under the Iron Sea" (Album & Single Campaign) *on Island Records in 2006. Art Direction: Richard Andrews & Gerard Saint @ Big Active, Design: Richard Andrews @ Big Active, Illustrations: Sanna Annukka @ Big Active.* - Pop -

STYLOROUGE LTD, D: MIKKEL LUNDSAGER HANSEN for The Brilliant Things "Stronger than Romeo" (CD) *on Spokes Records in 2006* - Electronic Pop -

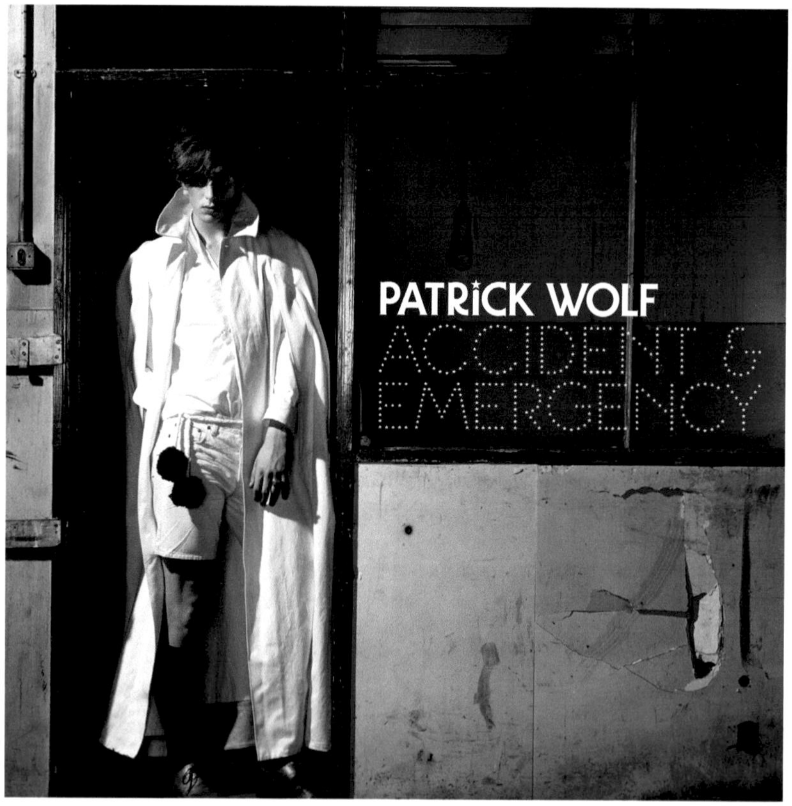

TRAFFIC for Patrick Wolf "Accident & Emergency" (7" Single) *in 2006* - Indie/Alternative -

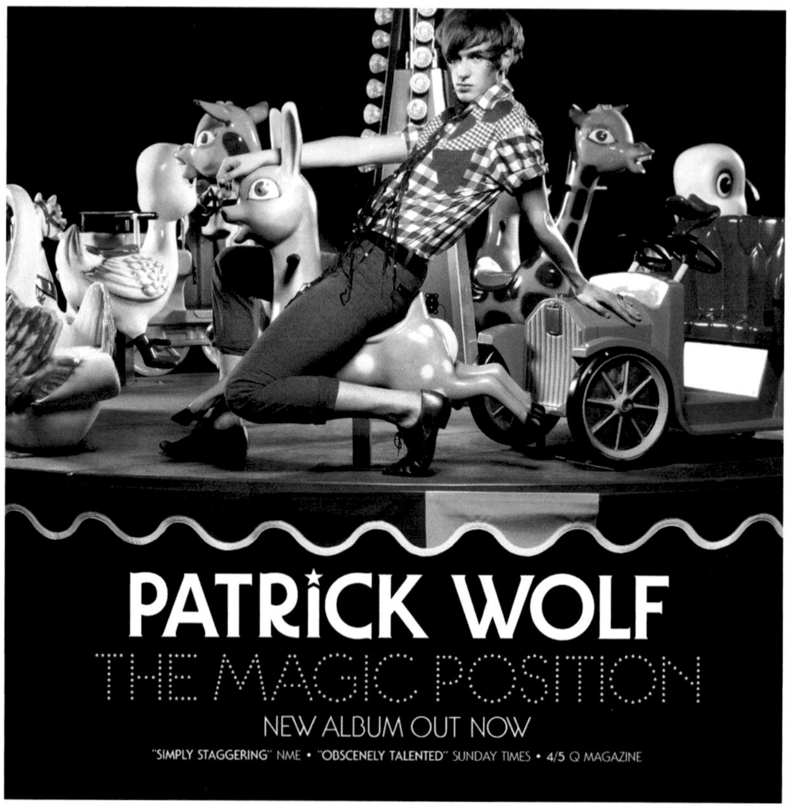

TRAFFIC for Patrick Wolf "The Magic Position" (7" Single & Promotional 12 x 12) *on Loog/Polydor in 2007* - Indie/Alternative -

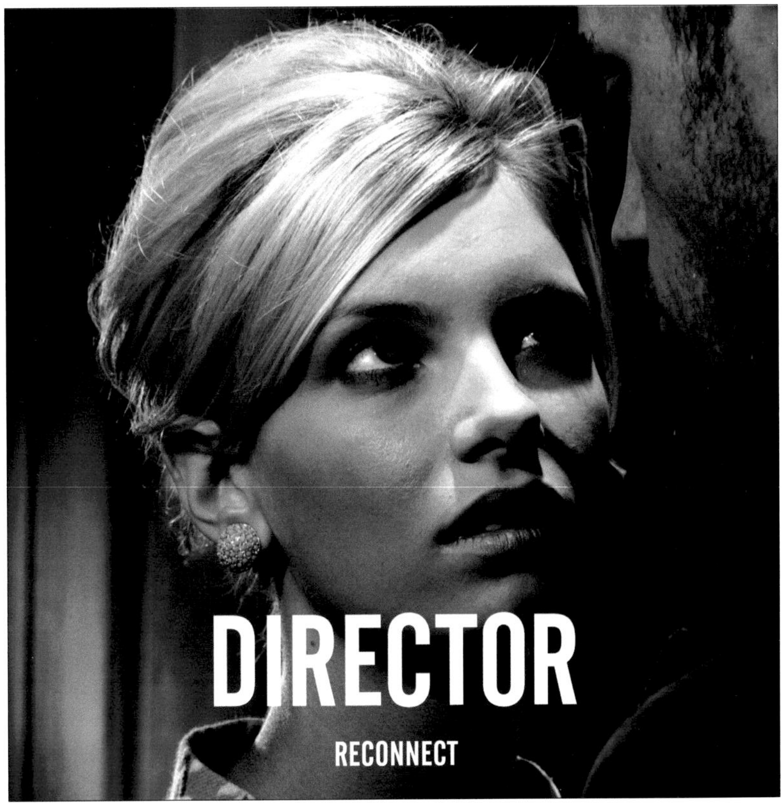

RED DESIGN for Director "Easy to me" & "Reconnect" (7" / CD) *on Atlantic in 2006* - Indie / Alternative -

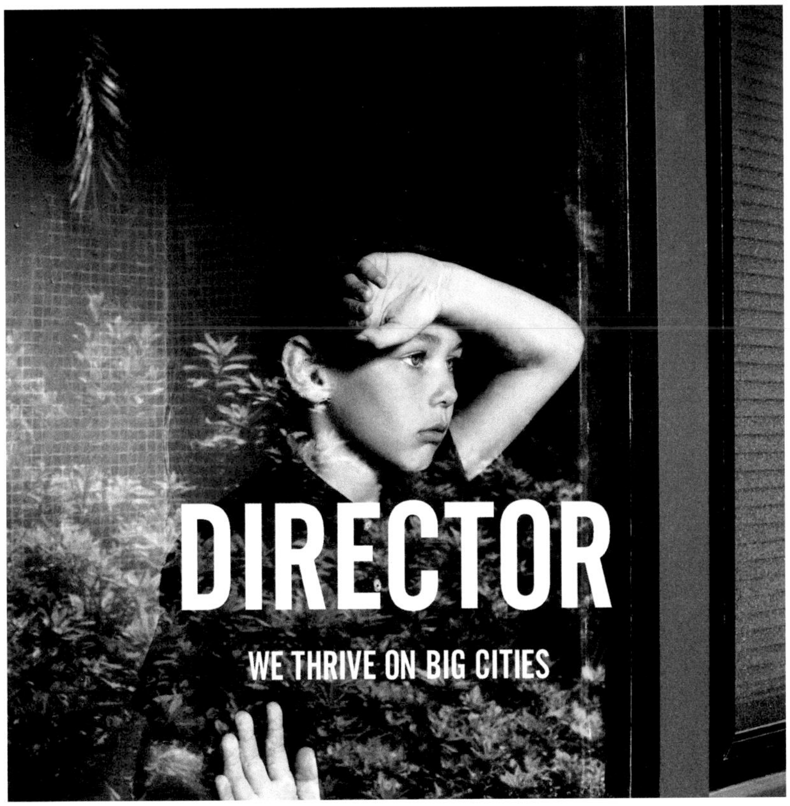

RED DESIGN for Director "We thrive on big cities" (CD) *on Atlantic in 2006* - Alternative / Indie -

ZION GRAPHICS for Melody Club "Destiny Calling" (Single) *on EMI Music Sweden in 2006* - Pop -

FORM DESIGN for Ministry of Sound "Sessions" (compilation series, CD) *on Ministry of Sound in 2006.*

FORM DESIGN for Ministry of Sound "Sessions" (compilation series, CD) *on Ministry of Sound in 2006.*

ZIP DESIGN, D.: DAVID BOWDEN "12"/80's" (3 jcards, 3 onbodies, slipcase and sticker) *on Family Recordings in 2005*

ZIP DESIGN, D.: DAVID BOWDEN "12"/80's" (3 jcards, 3 onbodies, slipcase and sticker) *on Family Recordings in 2005*

ZIP DESIGN, D.: NEIL BOWEN "In The House Miami 2007 Compilation 1-2" (Digipack, 2 onbodies 3 x 12" sleeves and labels) *on Defected Records in 2007*

ZIP DESIGN, D.: DAVID BOWDEN **for Cicada** "You Got Me Feeling" (12" Bag and labels) *on Critical Mass Recordings in 2006*

ROCK INSTRUMENT BUREAU, D.: ROY GARCIA **for Don Adams** "Don Adams" (CD Inlay) *on Ozone3 in 2006* - Rock&Roll -

ZION GRAPHICS for Steve Angello & Laidback Luke "Otherwize Then" (12" vinyl) *on Refune in 2006* - House -

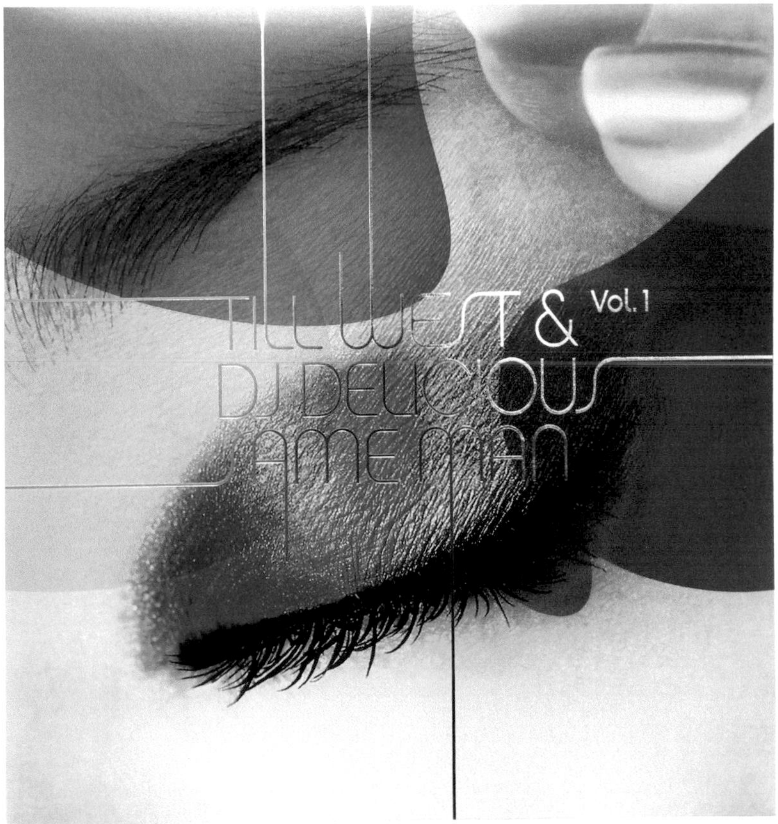

ZION GRAPHICS for Till West & DJ Delicious "Same Man" (12" Vinyl) *on Refune in 2006* - House -

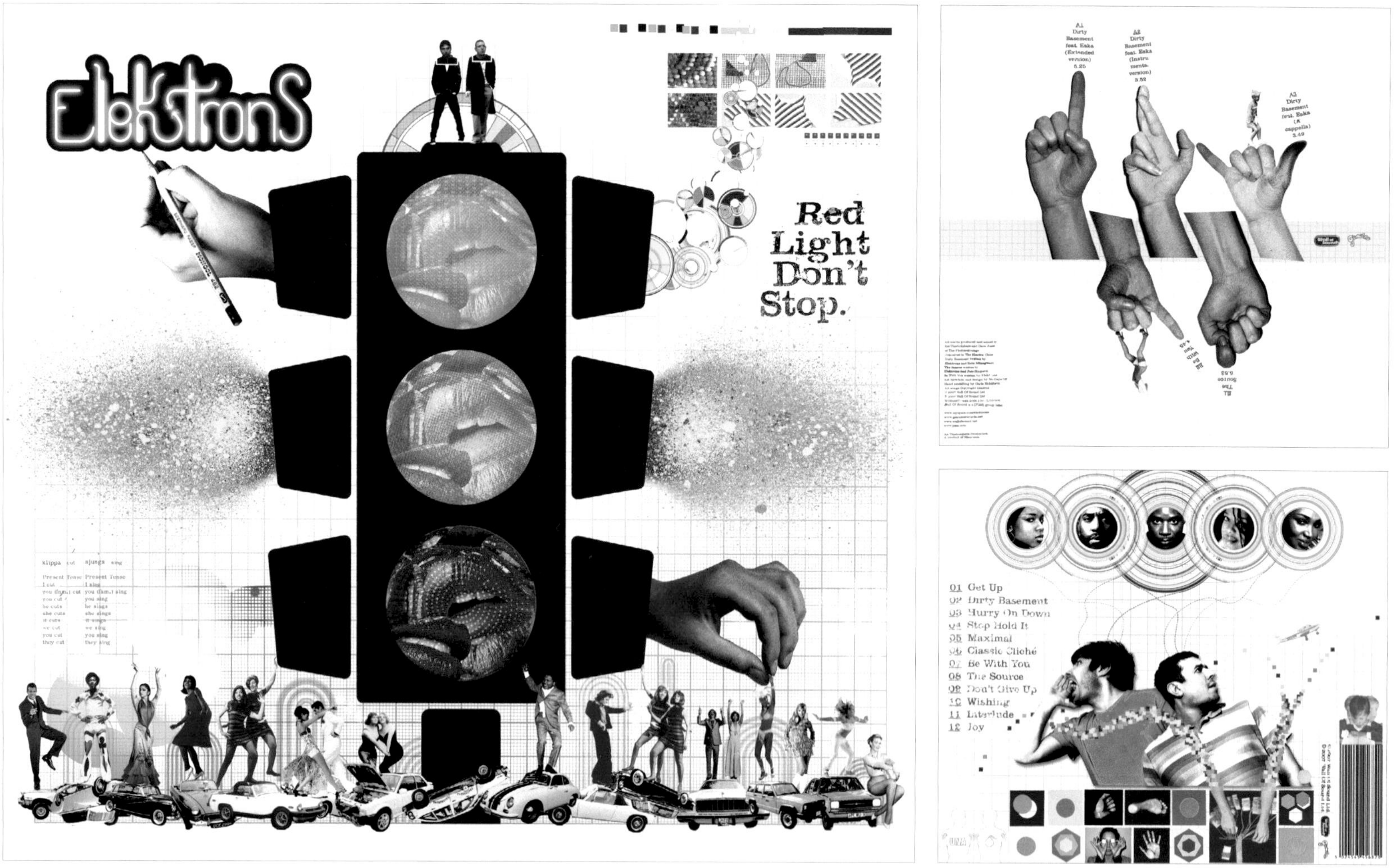

NO DAYS OFF, D.: PATRICK DUFFY **for Elektrons** "Red Light Don't Stop" (6 panel digipak printed on uncoated stock) *on Wall Of Sound in 2007* - Dance -

ZIP DESIGN, D.: JAMES WHITE **for Kiko Navarro** "Perceptions of Pacha" (Digipack, onbodies and sticker) *on Swank Recordings in 2007*

NO DAYS OFF, D.: PATRICK DUFFY **for Elektrons** "Dirty Basement" (12 inch sleeve printed on uncoated board) *on Wall Of Sound in 2007* - Dance -

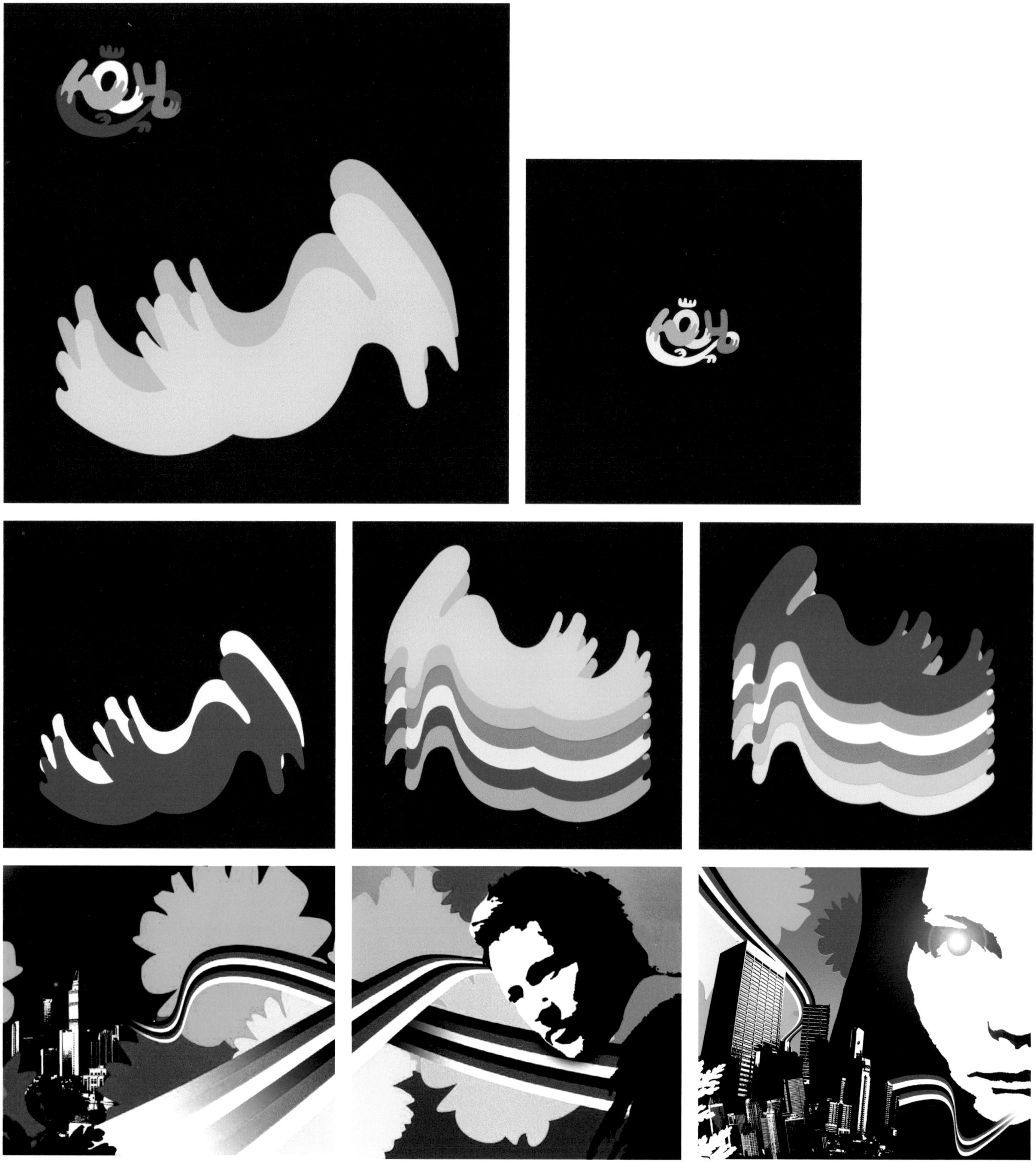

SKIN DESIGN for Amerika "The Good Luck" (6 panel CD Digifile) *on Columbia/Sony BMG in 2005* - Electronic Pop -

NO DAYS OFF, D.: PATRICK DUFFY **for Basement Jaxx** "The Singles" & "The Videos" (CD, Digipak, Jewel Case, Super Jewel Case, Gatefold card wallet w/ silver foil blocking) *on XL in 2006* - Dance

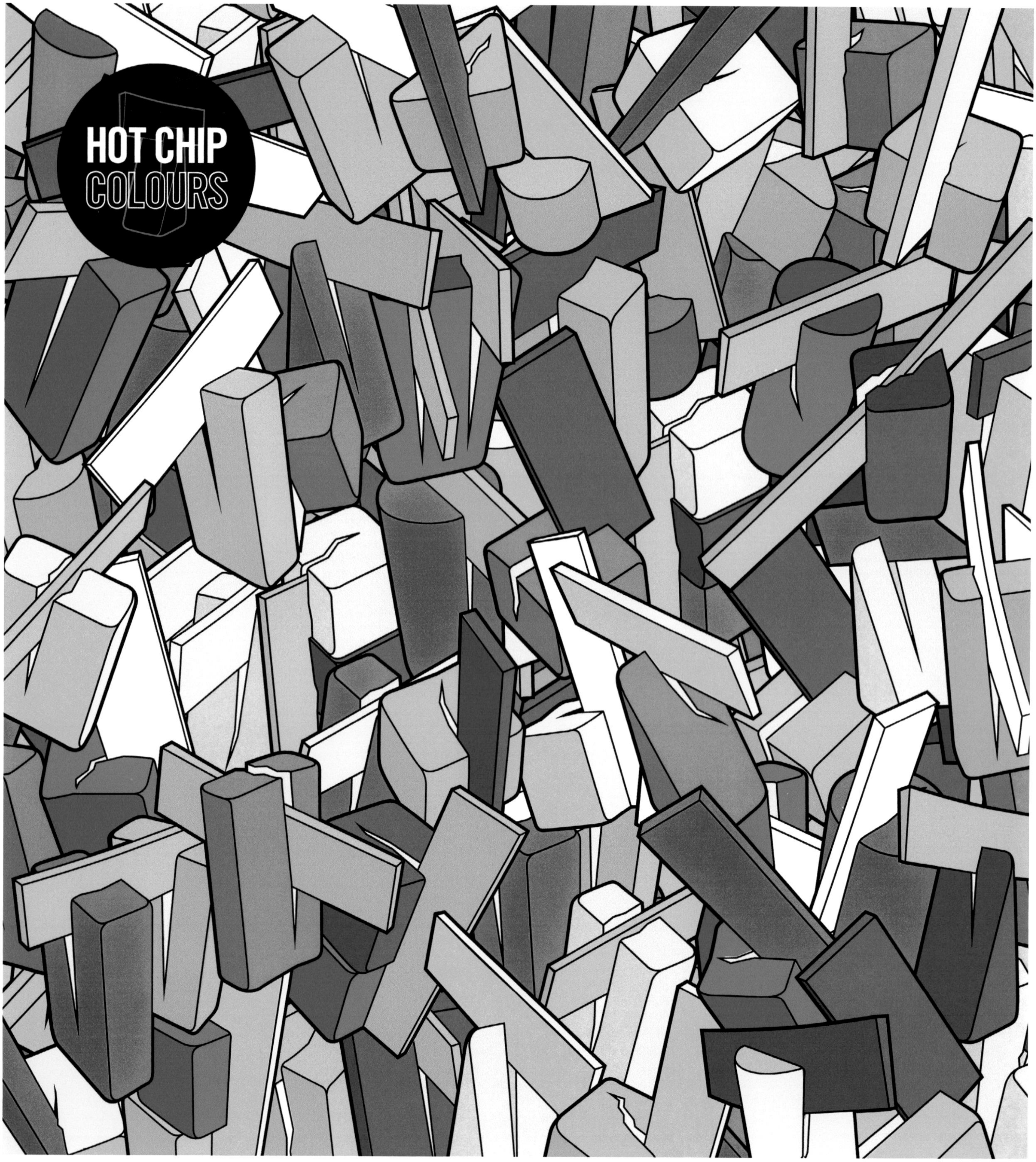

WALLZO, D.: DARREN WALL **for Hot Chip** "Colours" (12") *on EMI in 2006* - Pop -

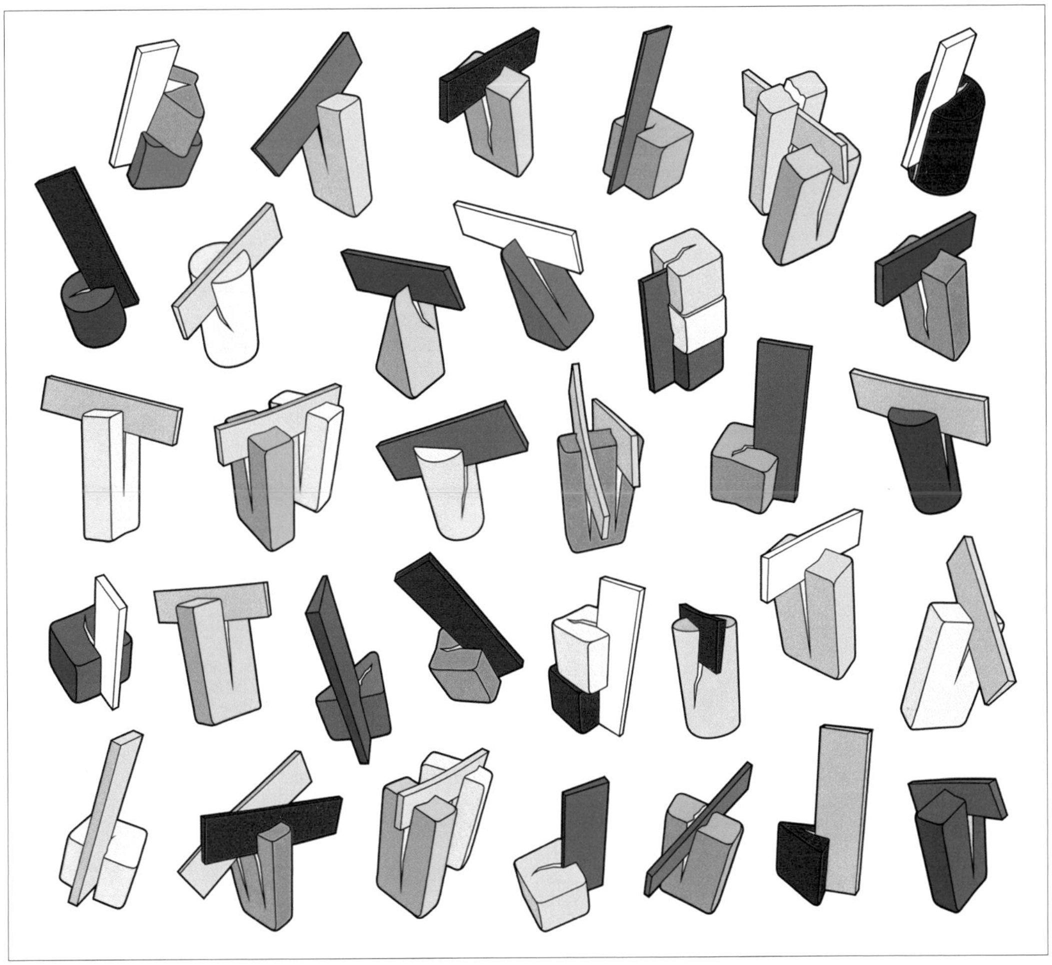

WALLZO, D.: DARREN WALL **for Hot Chip** "The Warning" (CD) *on EMI in 2006* - Pop -

JDK PETER SUNNA for RAQ/DJ Charles Smooth (Hand screen printed Poster.)

JDK PETER SUNNA for Fiery Furnaces/Deerhoof (Hand screen printed Poster.) *in 2006*

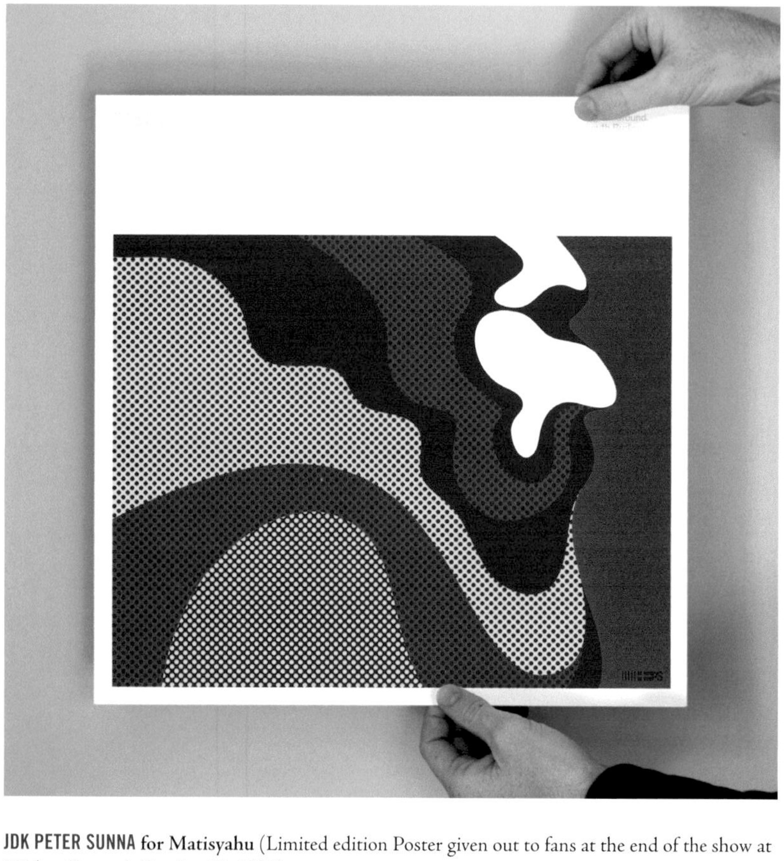

JDK PETER SUNNA for Matisyahu (Limited edition Poster given out to fans at the end of the show at Higher Ground, October 22, 2005)

LA BOCA, D. SCOT BENDALL for Tom Tyler "Forward Going Backward" (12" Vinyl & CD) *on DC Recordings in 2005* - Downtempo -

TWOPOINTS.NET, D.: MARTIN LORENZ **for Palau de la Música Catalana** (Poster) *in 2006* - Classic -

SELDON HUNT for Conrad Schnitzler "Trigger Trilogy" (3 CD box set) *on Important Records in 2006* - Experimental/Ambient -

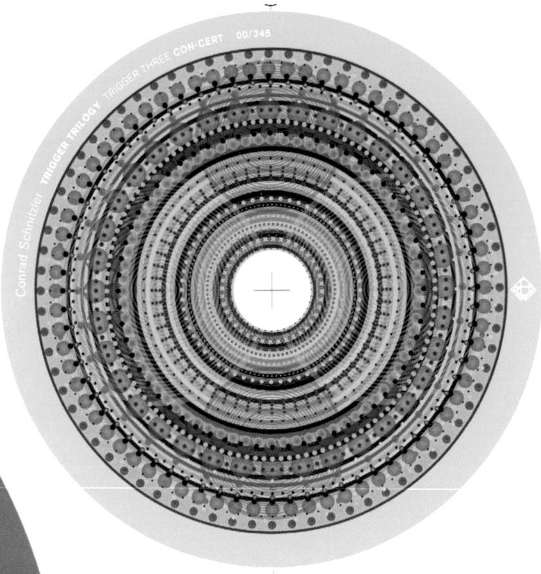
Conrad Schnitzler TRIGGER TRILOGY TRIGGER THREE CON-CERT 00/345

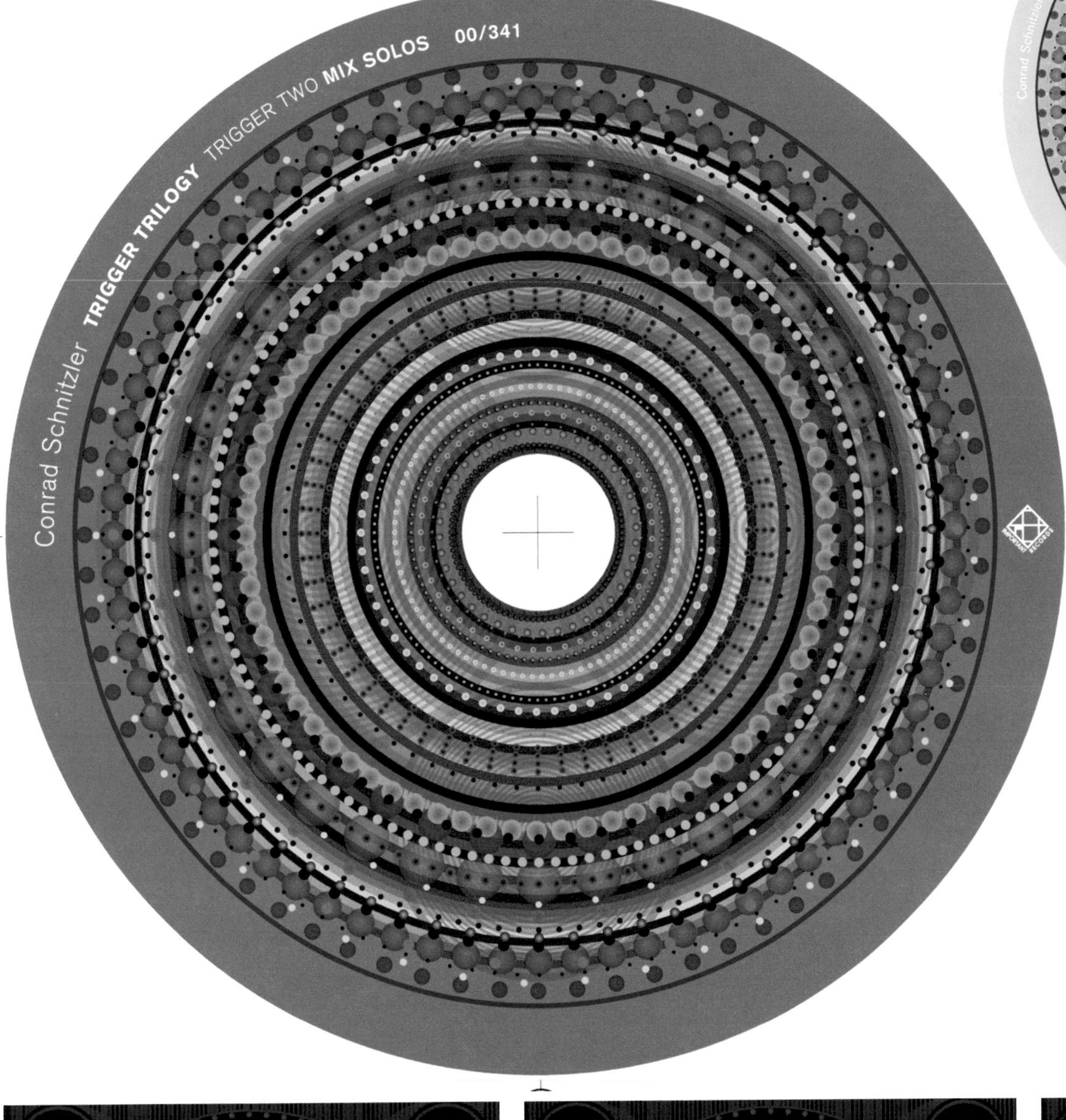
Conrad Schnitzler TRIGGER TRILOGY TRIGGER TWO MIX SOLOS 00/341

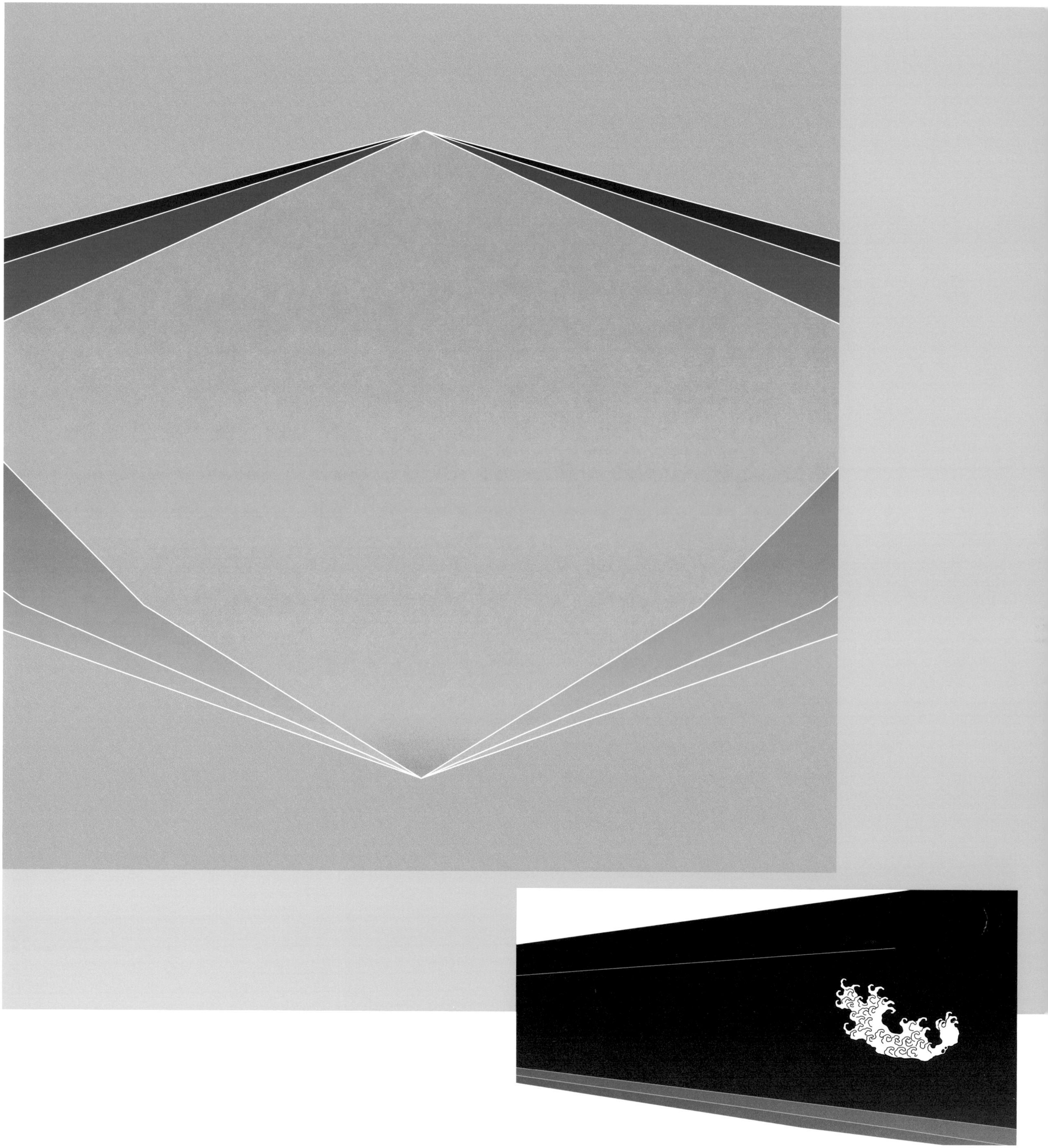

KIM HIORTHØY for Tussle "Telescope Mind" (CD) *on Smalltown Supersound in 2006*

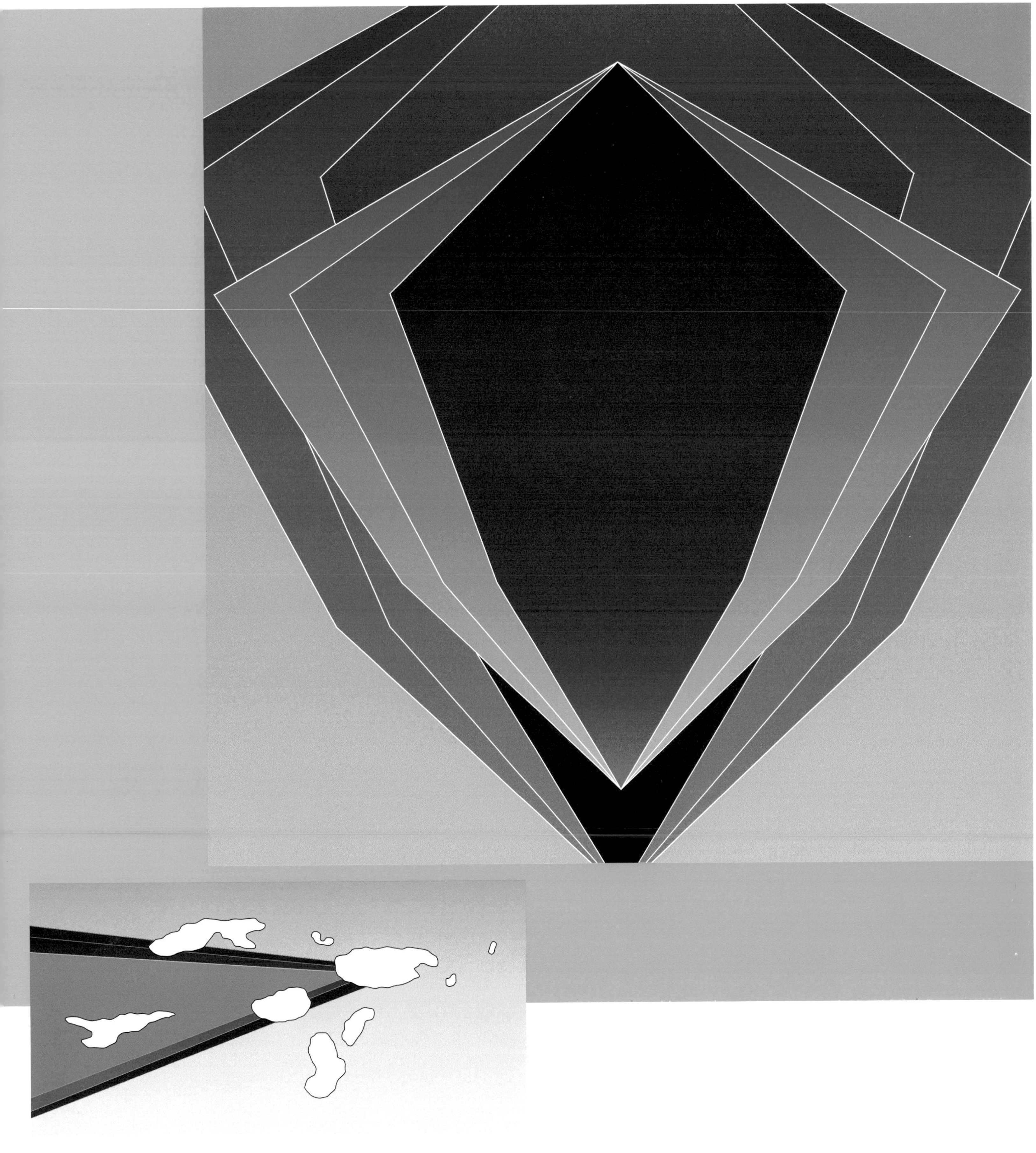

ZION GRAPHICS for **The Virtues** "Where Were You?" (CD) on Zip Records *in 2005*

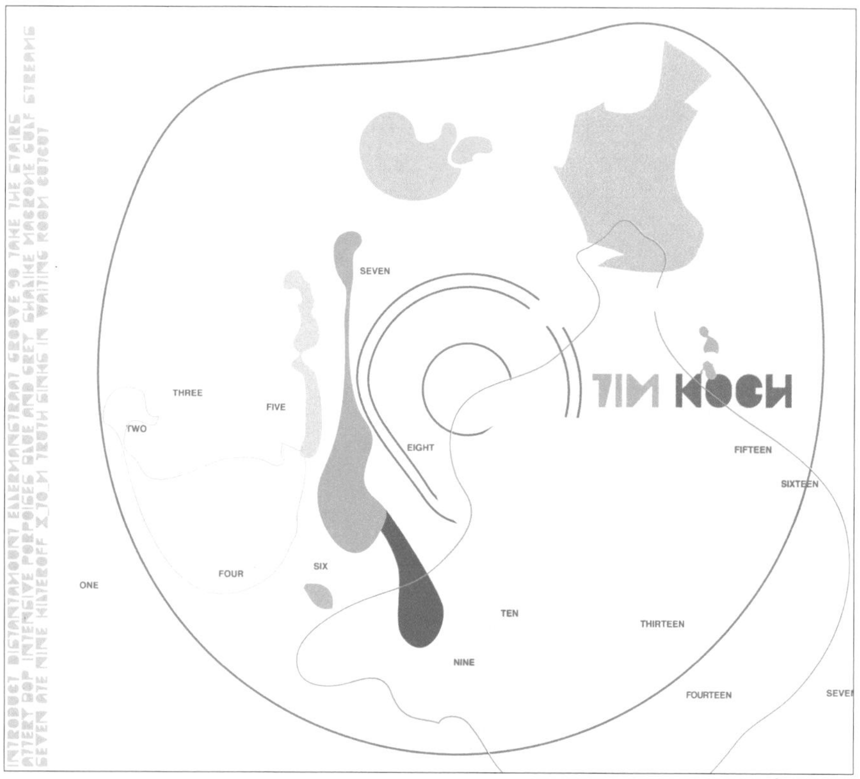

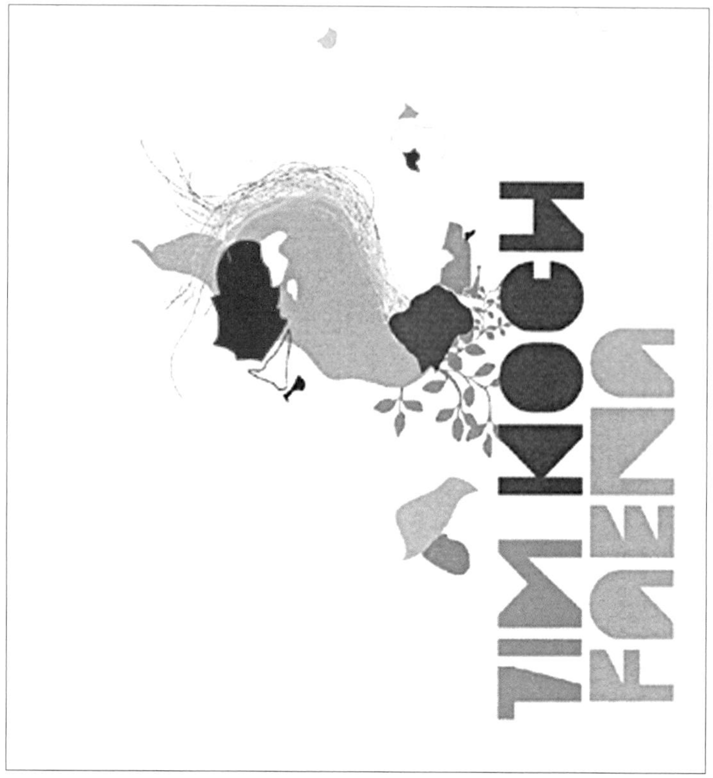

JOE A. SCERRI for **Tim Koch** "Faena" (CD) *on Merck Records in 2006* - Electronica -

SLANG SLANGINTERNATIONAL.ORG for Snowdrop "Fueradeserie! presents: Snowdrop" (CD) *on Fueradeserie! in 2005* - Electronic -

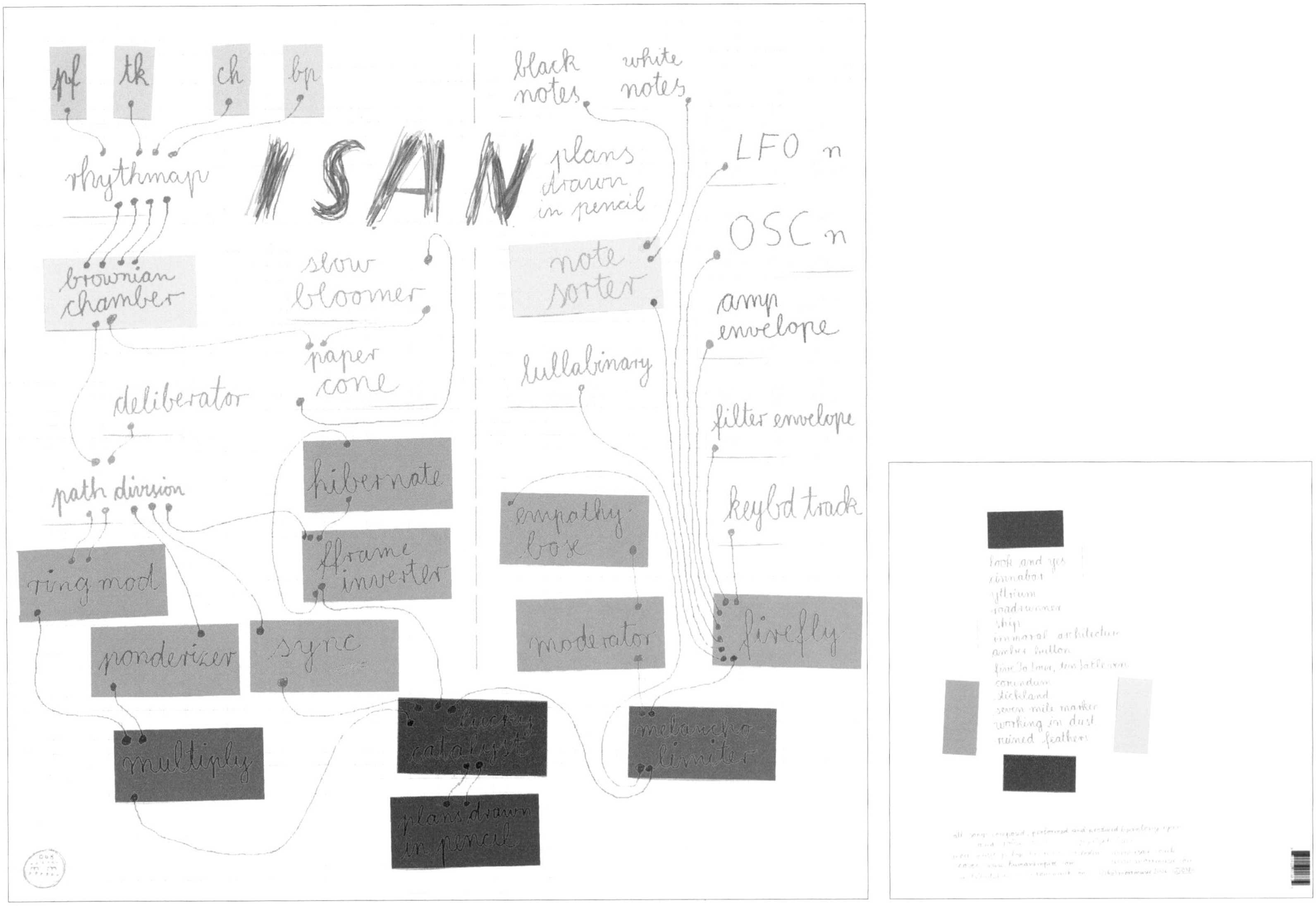

HUMAN EMPIRE, D.: JAN KRUSE **for Isan** "Plans drawn in pencil" (LP) *on Morr Music in 2006*

JAWA AND MIDWICH, D.: NILS DAVEY AND SIMON DOVAR **for Jimpster** "Amour Remix Two" (12" Single sleeve) *on Freerange Records in 2006* - House -

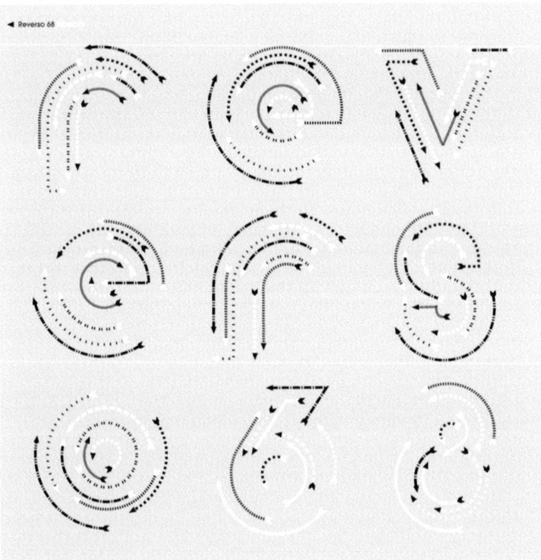

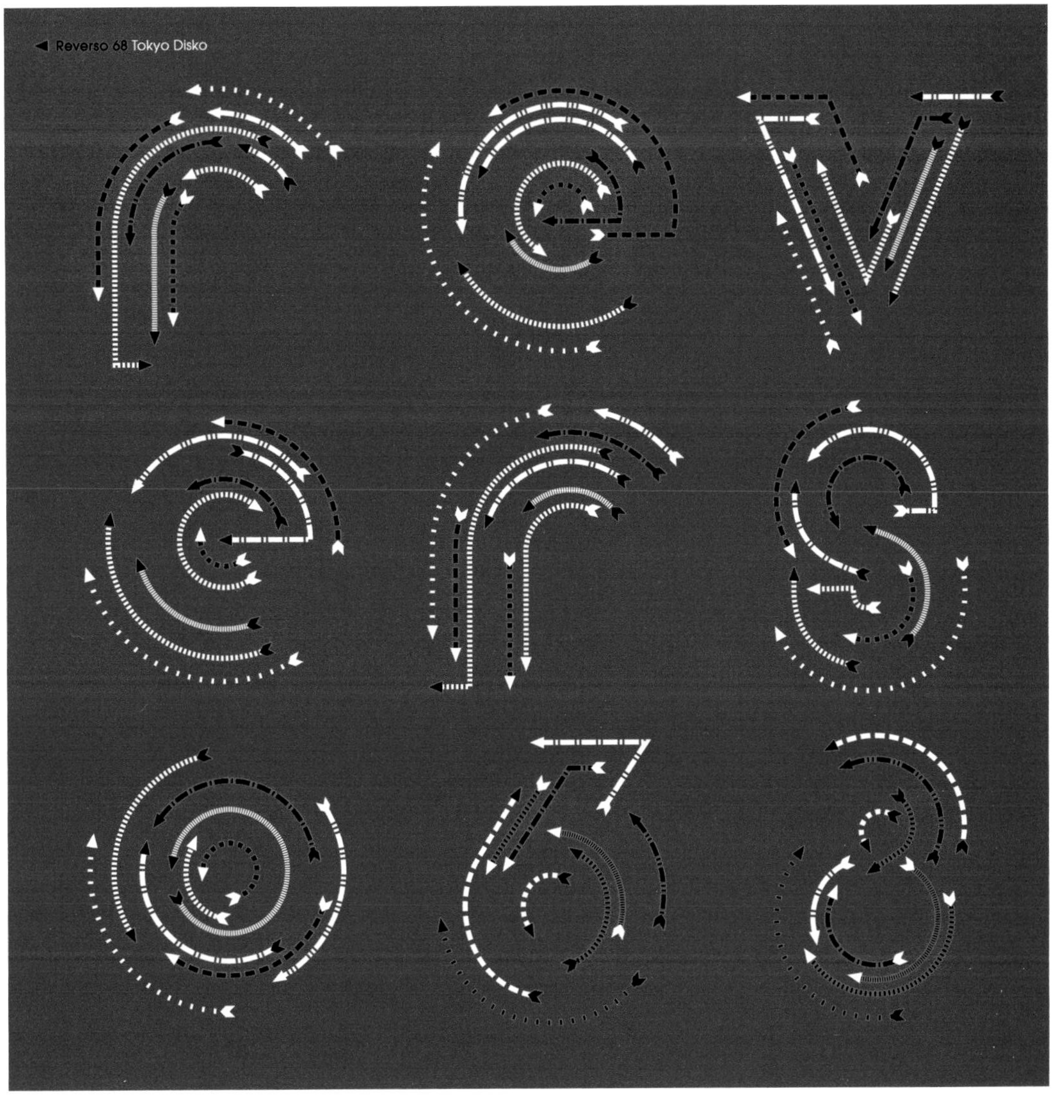

CHRIS BOLTON for Reverso 68 "Tokyo Disko" & "Especial" (12inch Sleeve) *on Eskimo Recordings in 2006* - Electronic -

BÜRO DESTRUCT, D.: LOPETZ for Dave Clarke "Remixes & Rarities" (Double CD and Double Vinyl Sleeve) *on Music Man, News Distribution, Belgium in 2006* - Techno -

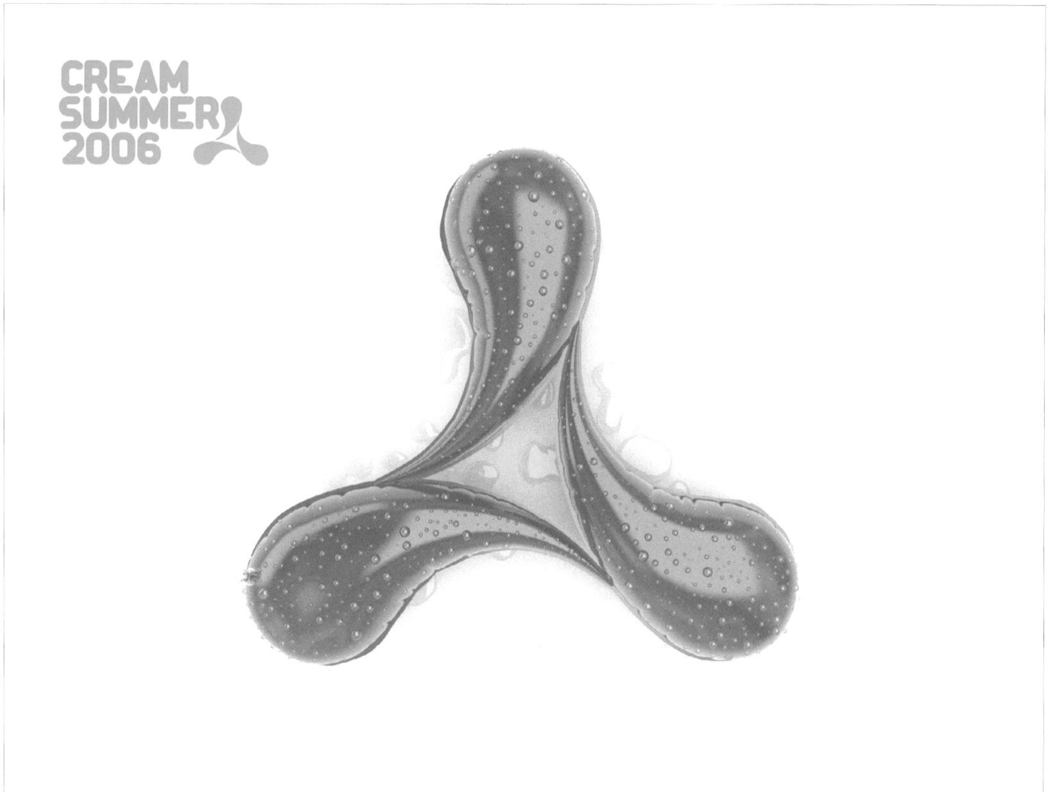

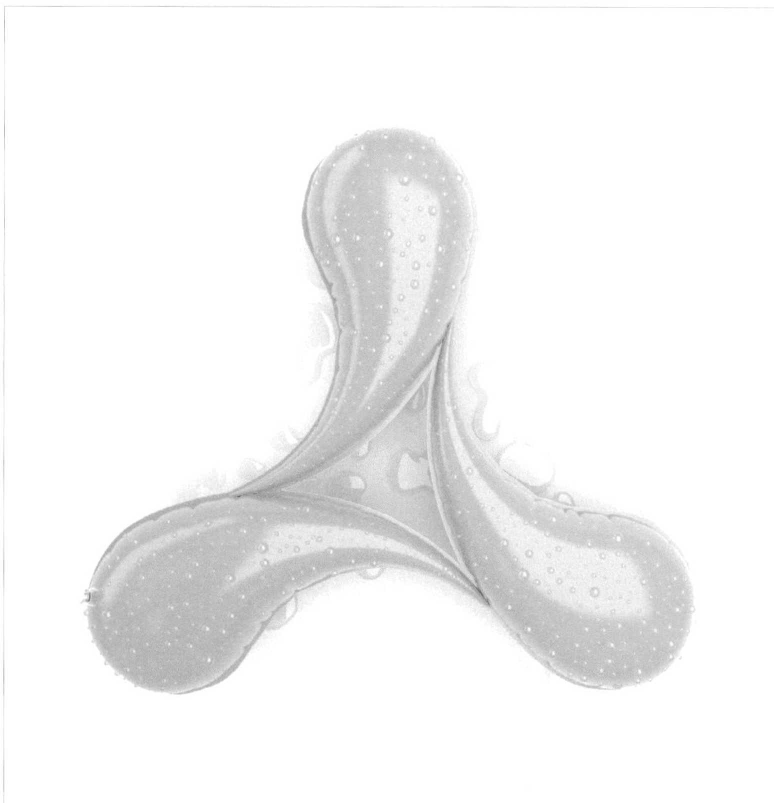

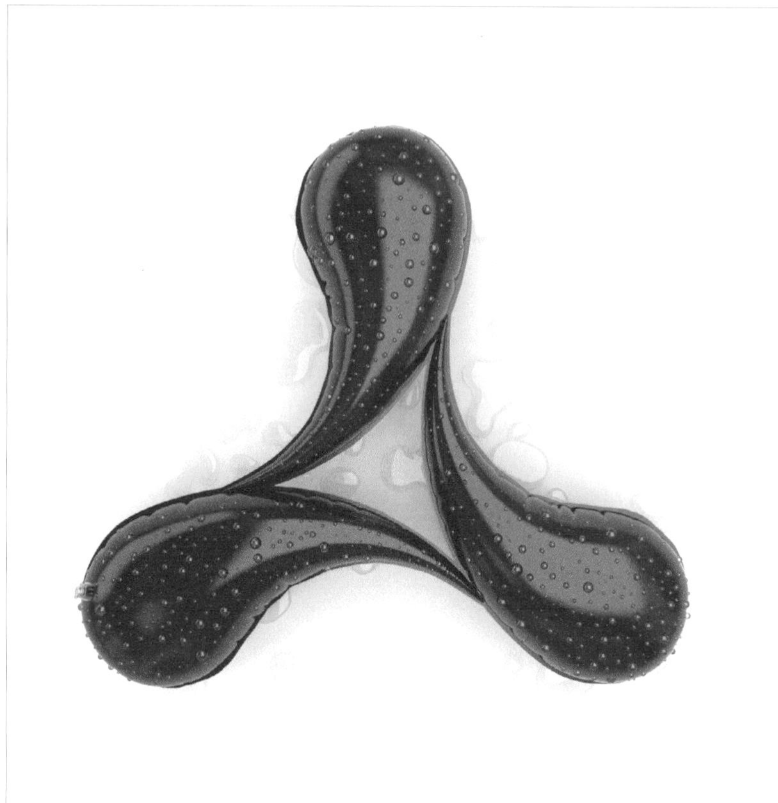

ZIP DESIGN, D.: DAVID BOWDEN **for Cream Summer 2006 compilation series** "Cream Summer 2006" (3 j-cards, 3 onbodies, slipcase and sticker) *on Ministry Of Sound Recordings in 2006* - Dance -

ZION GRAPHICS for Who's Who? "Sexy F**k" (12" vinyl),
for Steve Angello "Teasing Mr. Charlie" (12" vinyl)
& **for MBG & SDS** "TNew Jack" (12" vinyl)
on Size in 2006 - House -

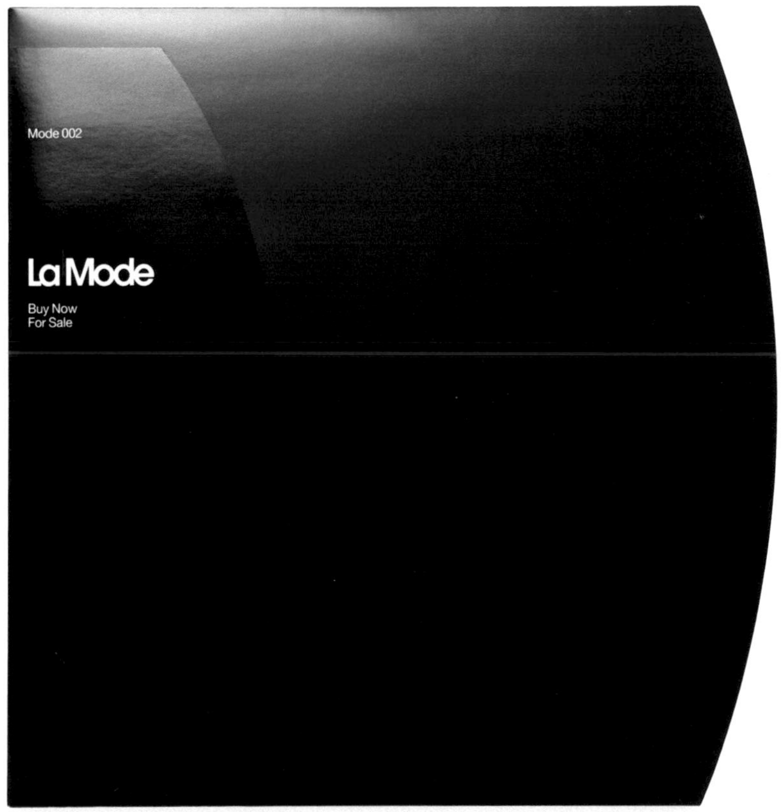

ZION GRAPHICS for La'Mode "Yeah" & "Buy Now For Sale" (12" vinyl) *on La'Mode in 2005* - House -

LORENZO GEIGER for Matt Darriau's Paradox Trio "Paradox Trio" (Poster 42 x 52.5 cm) *in 2006* - Jazz -

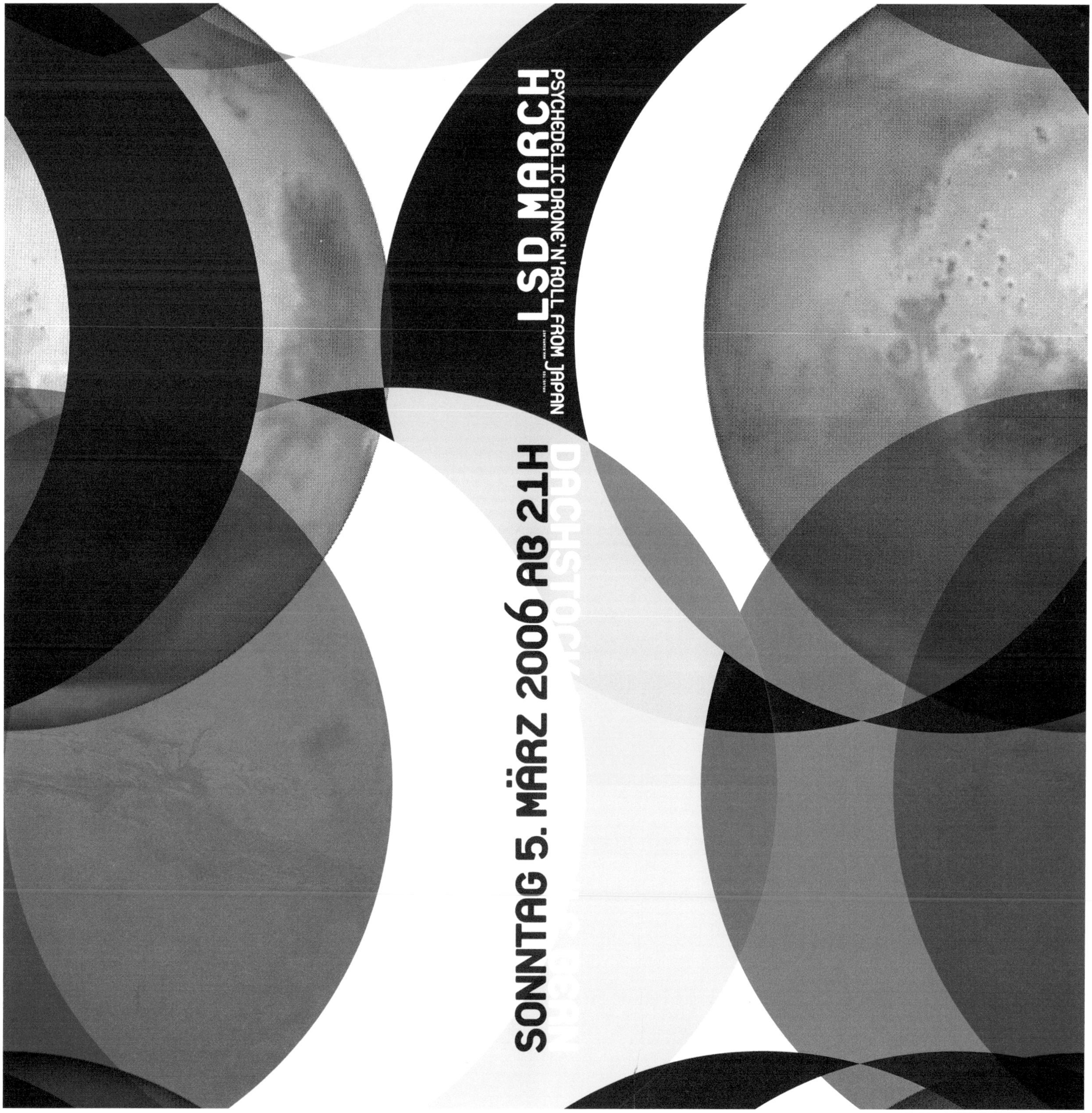

LORENZO GEIGER for LSD March "LSD March" (Poster 42 x 42 cm) *in 2006* - Psychodelic Drone-Roll -

CHRIS BOLTON for Optimo "Optimo Presents Psyche Out" (CD Fold Out Poster & 12inch Sleeve/Cd Slipcase Cover) *on Eskimo Recordings in 2005* - Compilation Album -

MULTIFRESH, D.: **DAVID NAKAMOTO for Kid606** "Sugarcoated" (10" vinyl sleeve) *on Audraglint in 2005*

ANGELA LORENZ for White Hole "Snow" (12") *on KYO in 2005*
- Electronic -

BHATOPTICS for SKAYP001 "Skam year planner" (LP) *on Skam in 2004*

CHRIS BOLTON for Optimo "Optimo Presents Psyche Out" (CD Fold Out Poster & 12inch Sleeve/Cd Slipcase Cover) & **for Hiem** "Clubscene Popscene" (12inch Vinyl) *on Eskimo Recordings in 2005-2007* - Electronic -

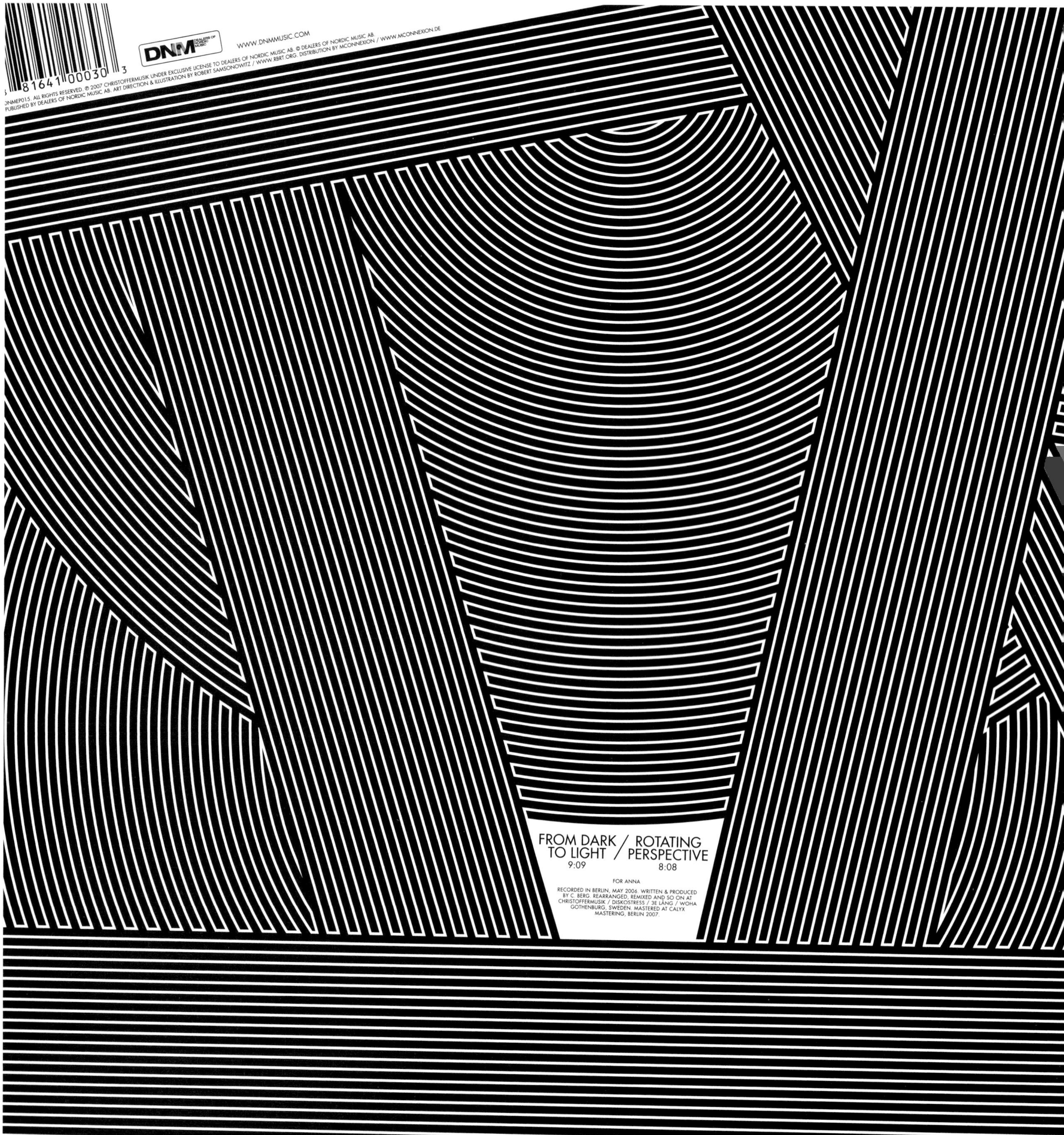

ROBERT SAMSONOWITZ for Hird "From Dark To Light / Rotating Perspective" (12" vinyl) *on Dealers of Nordic Music in 2007*

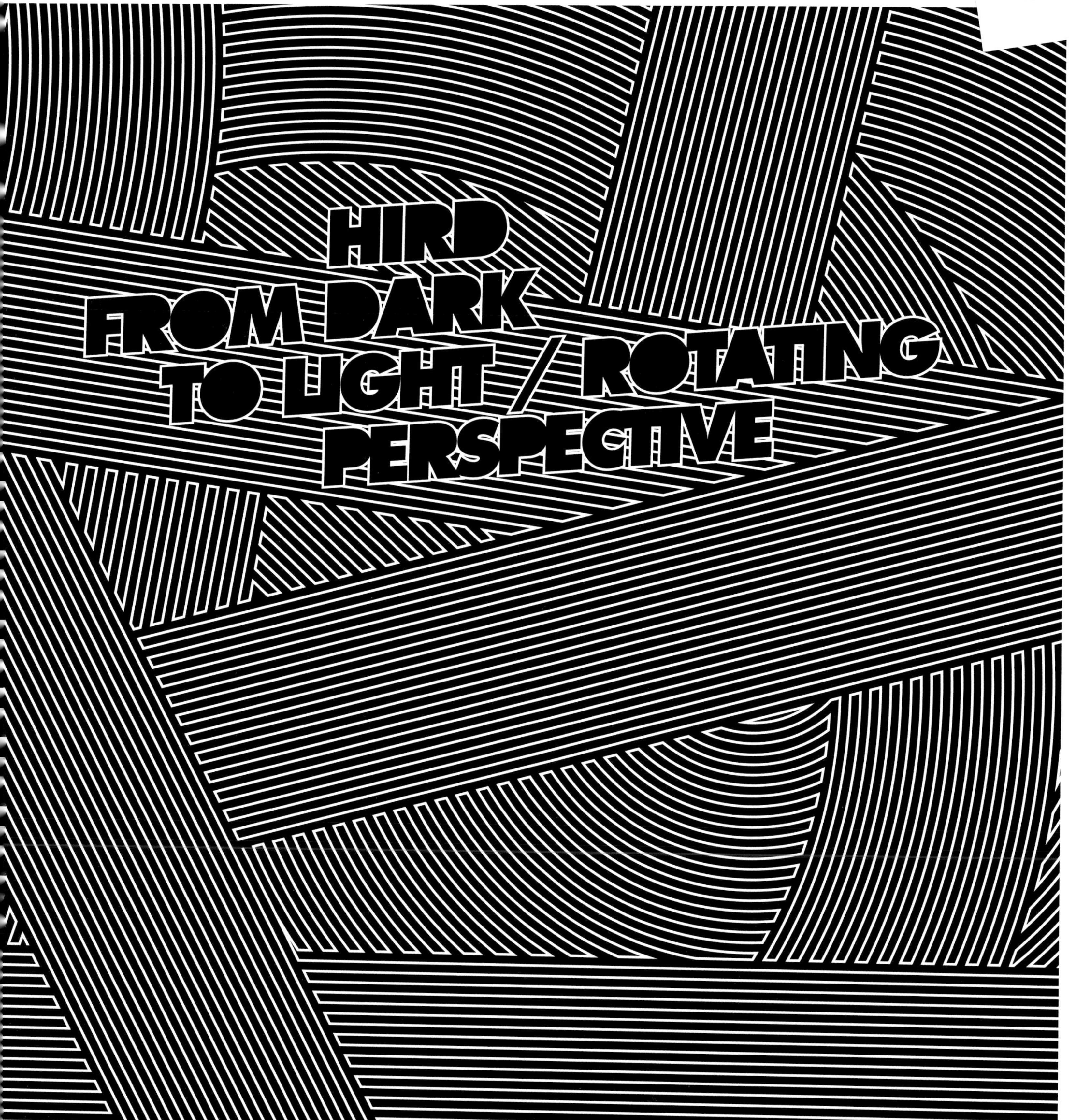
HIRD
FROM DARK
TO LIGHT / ROTATING
PERSPECTIVE

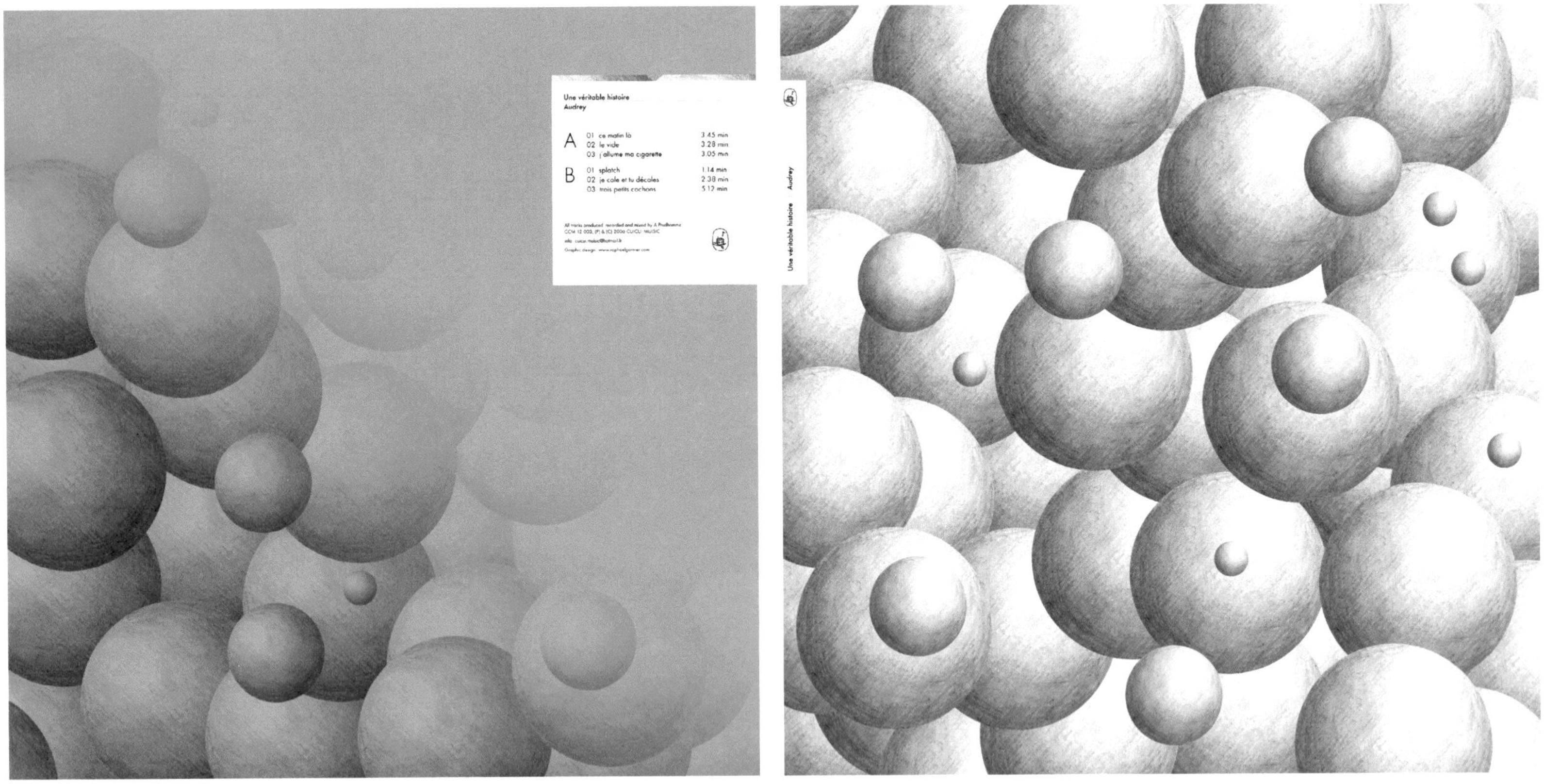

RAPHAEL GARNIER for Audrey "Une véritable histoire" (12") *on Cuicui Music in 2006* - Pop / Electro / New Wave -

RAPHAEL GARNIER for Tutu Pointu "La vie de château" (12") *on Cuicui Music in 2006* - Pop / Electro / New Wave -

RAPHAEL GARNIER for Mobile "UMTKZT" (12") *on Cuicui Music in 2006* - Pop / Electro / New Wave -

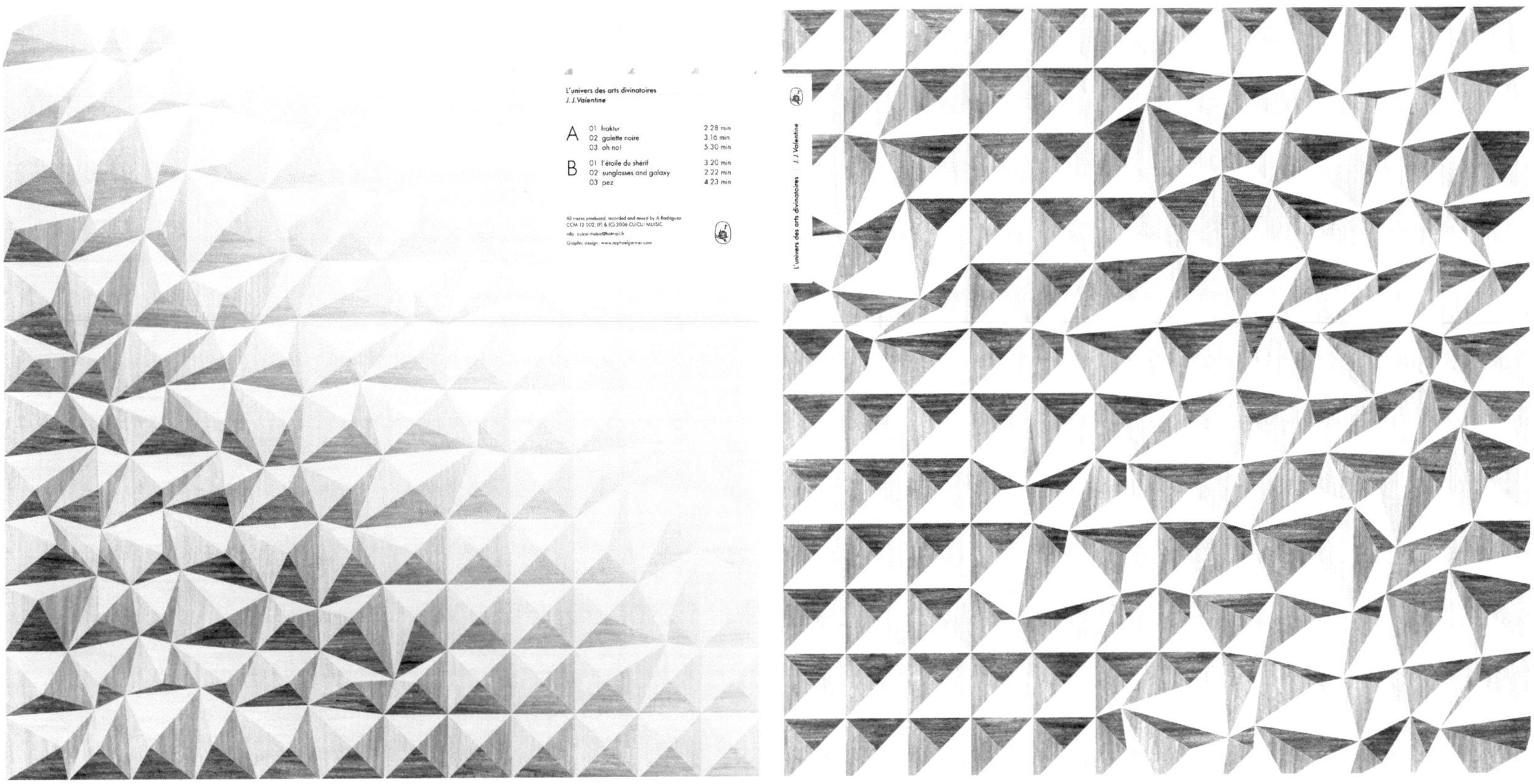

RAPHAEL GARNIER for J.J.Valentine "L'univers des arts divinatoires" (12") *on Cuicui Music in 2006* - Pop / Electro / New Wave -

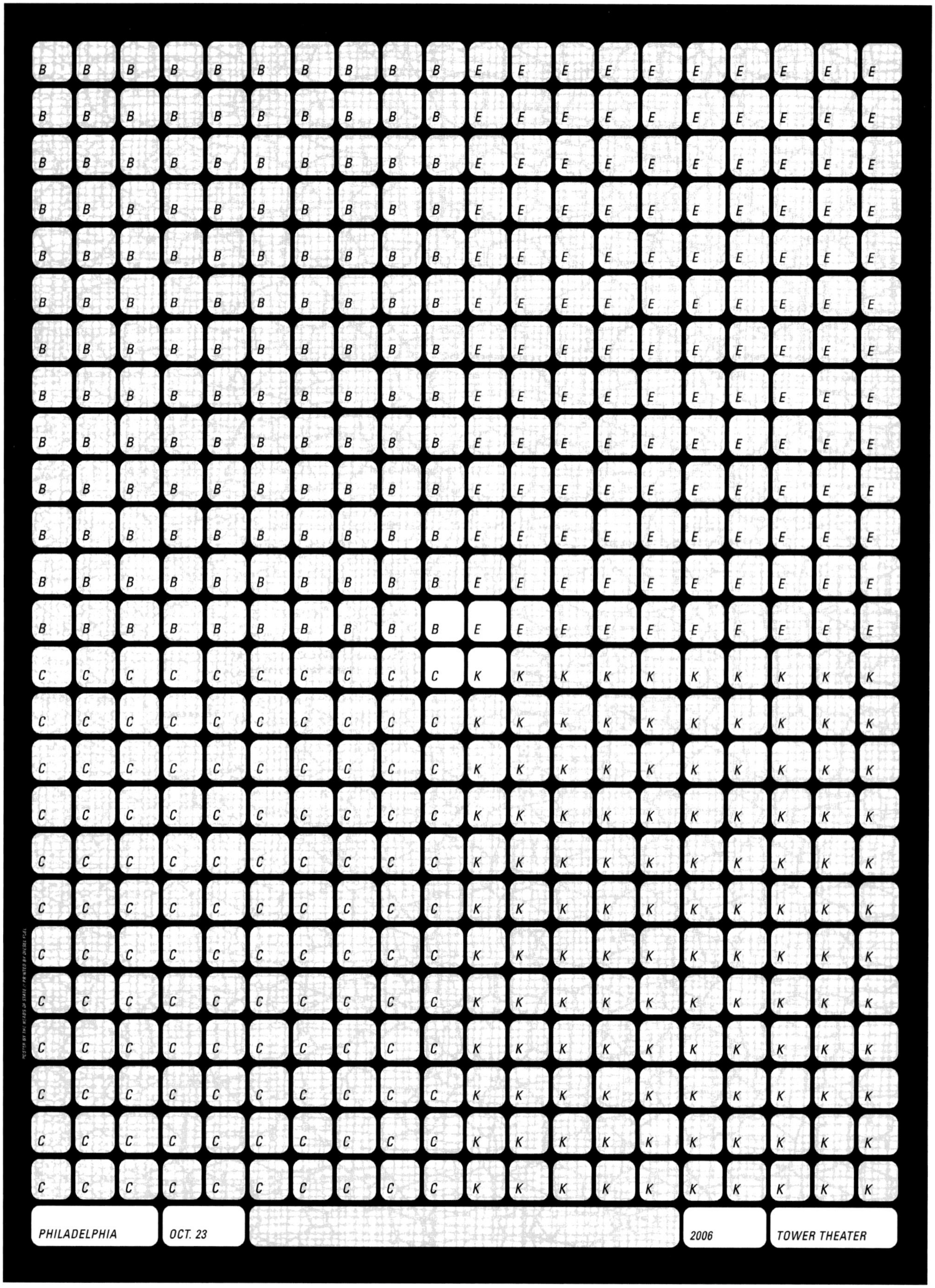

THE HEADS OF STATE, D.: DUSTIN SUMMERS **for Beck** (Poster 18x24 silksceen) *on in 2007*

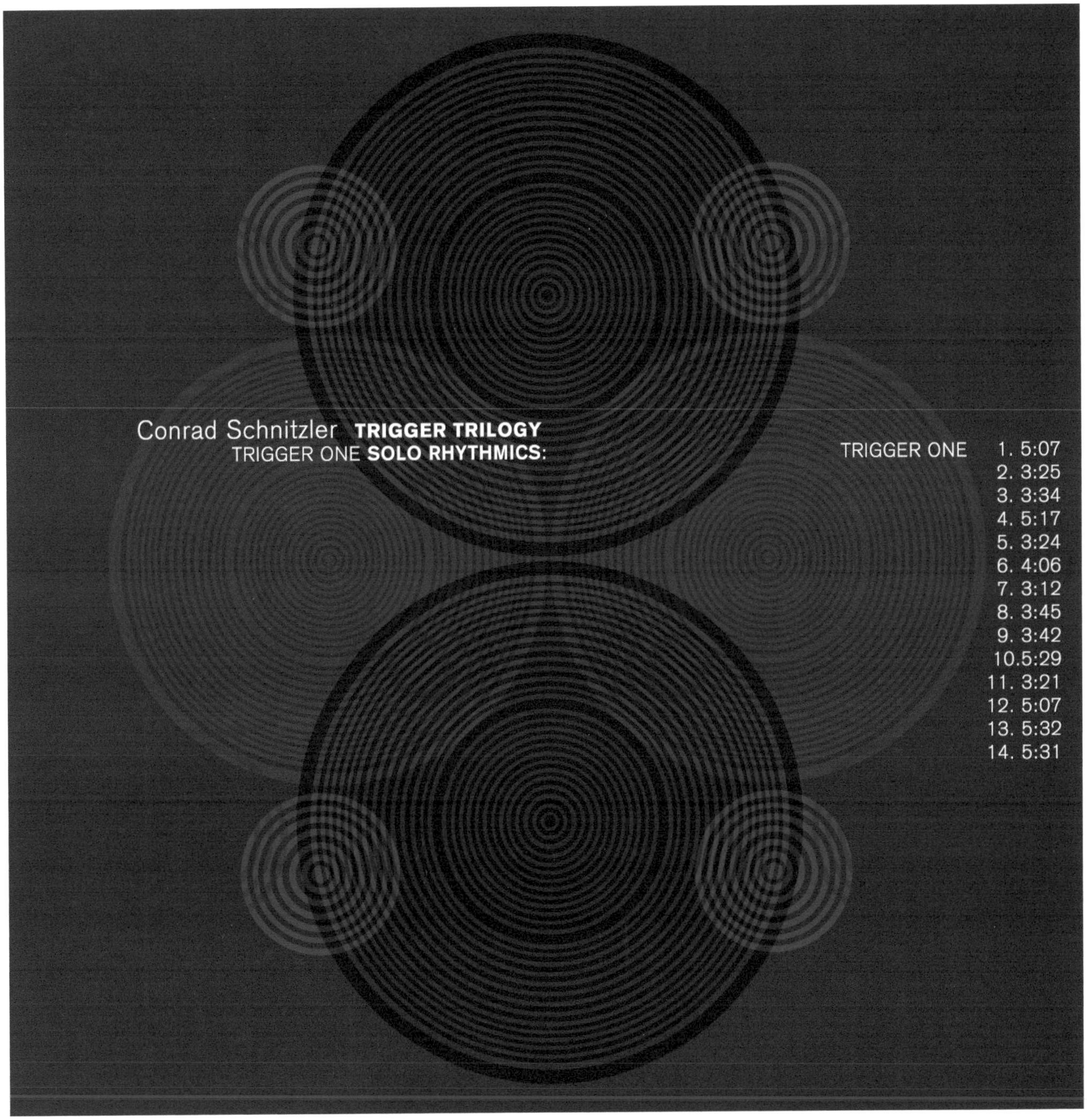

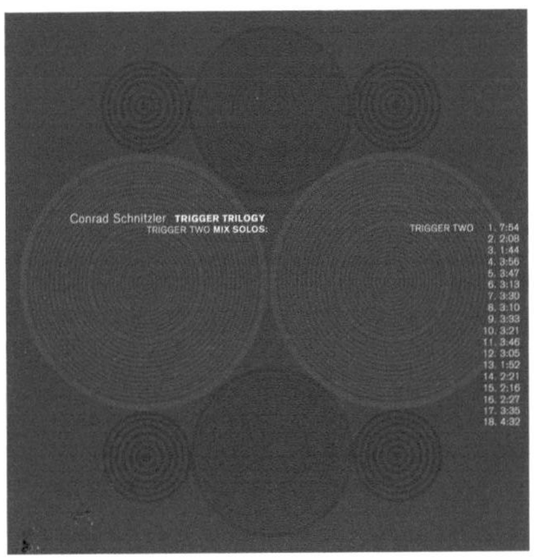

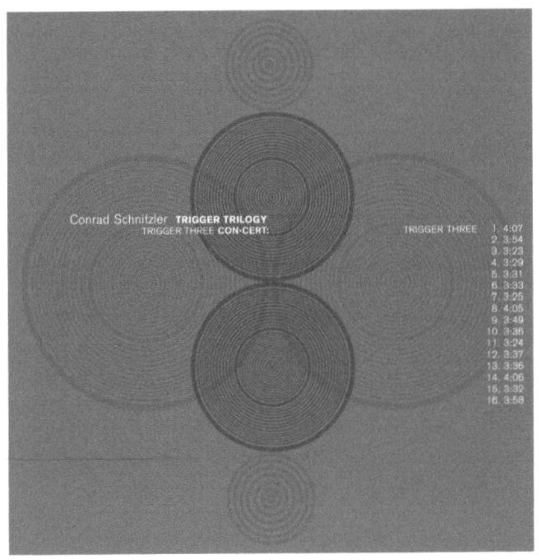

SELDON HUNT for Conrad Schnitzler "Trigger Trilogy" (3 CD box set) *on Important Records in 2006* - Experimental/Ambient -

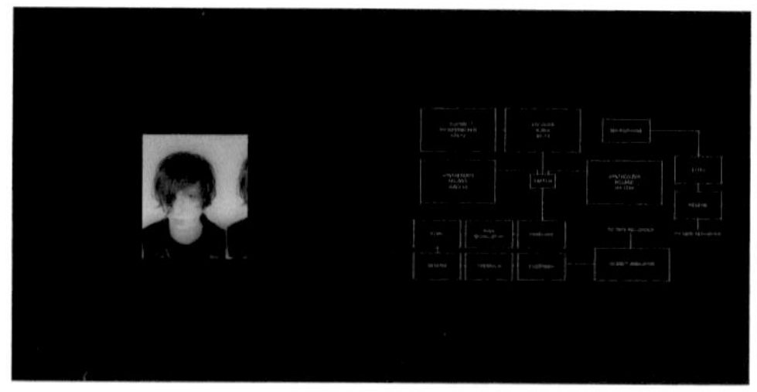

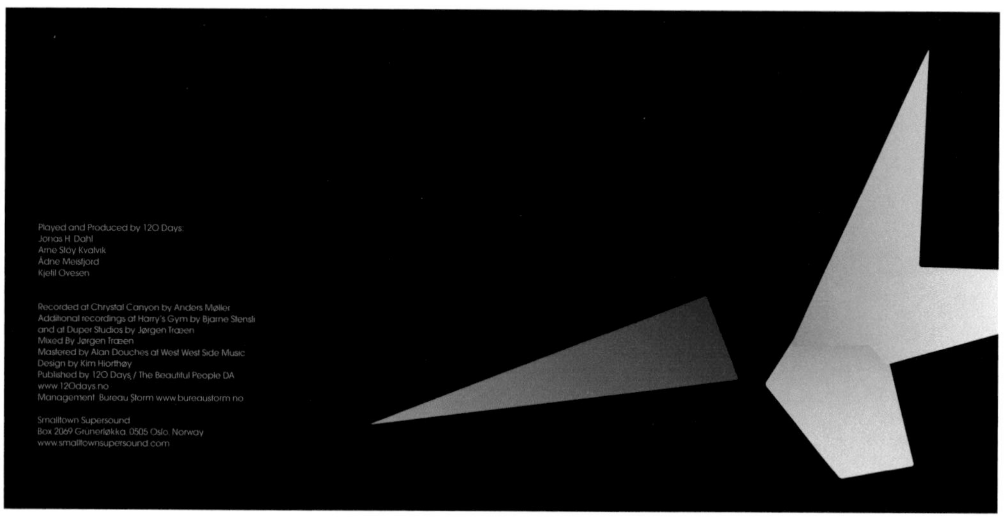

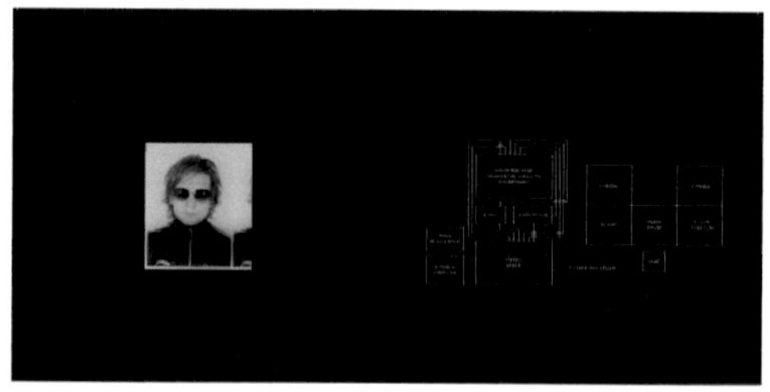

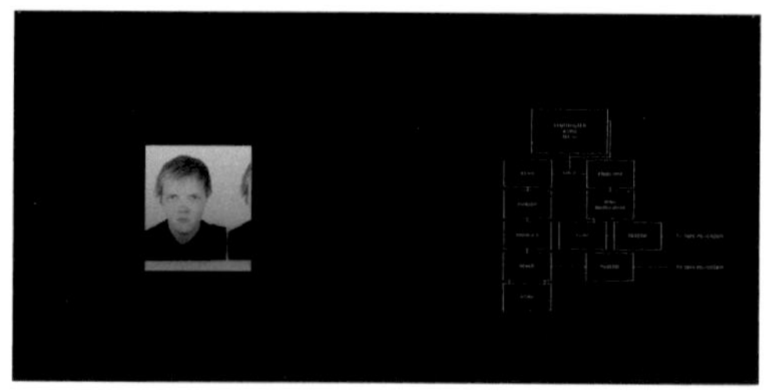

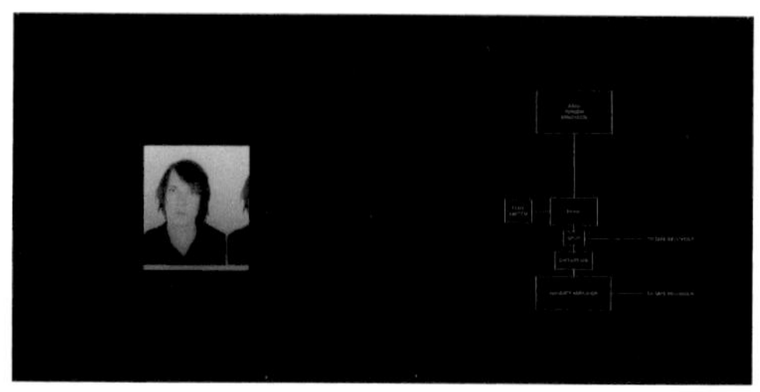

KIM HIORTHØY **for 120 Days** "120 Days" (CD) *in 2006*

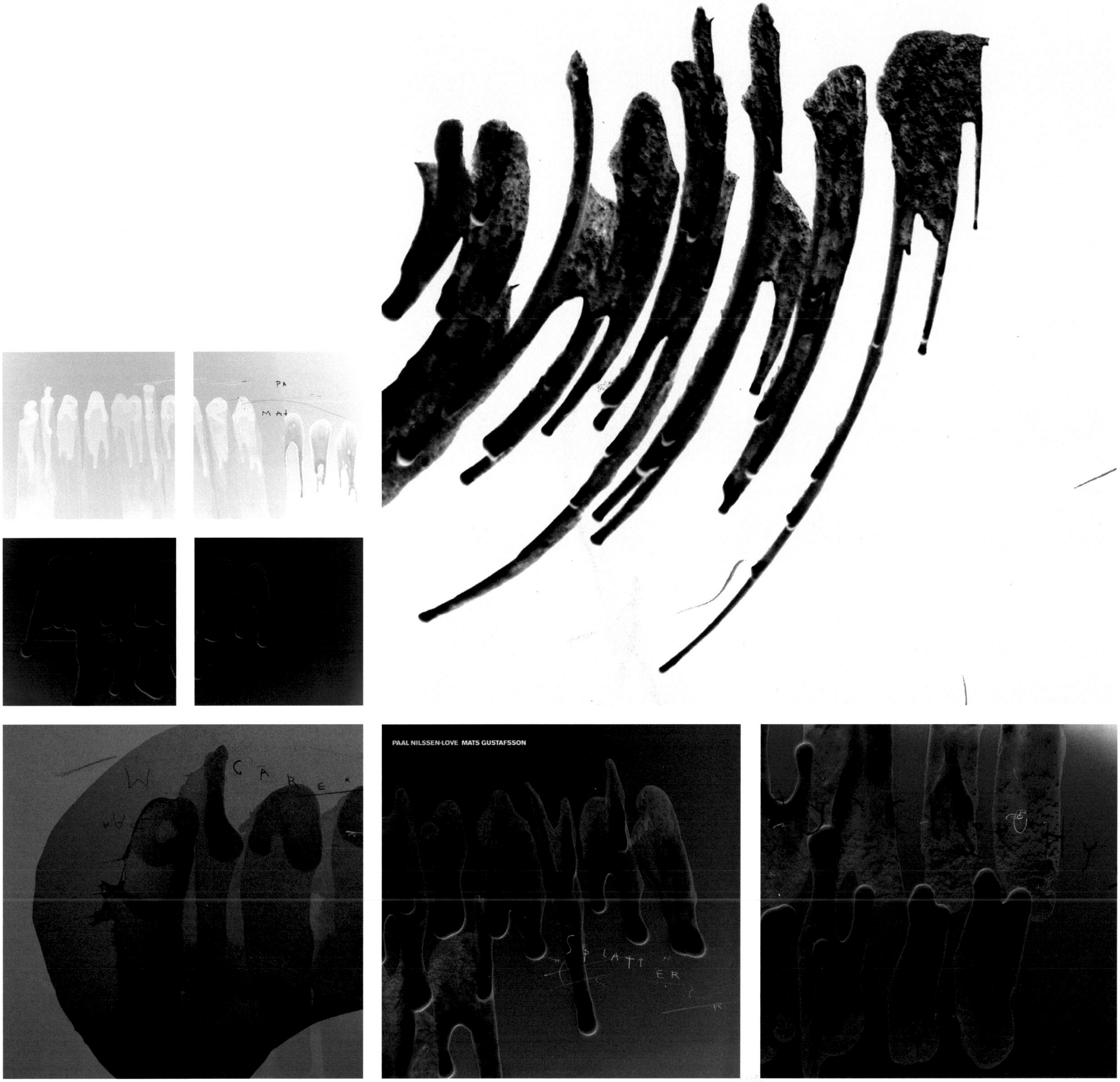

RUNE MORTENSEN for Mats Gustafsson / Paal Nilsen-Love "Splatter" (CD) *on Smalltown Superjazzz in 2007* - Freejazz -

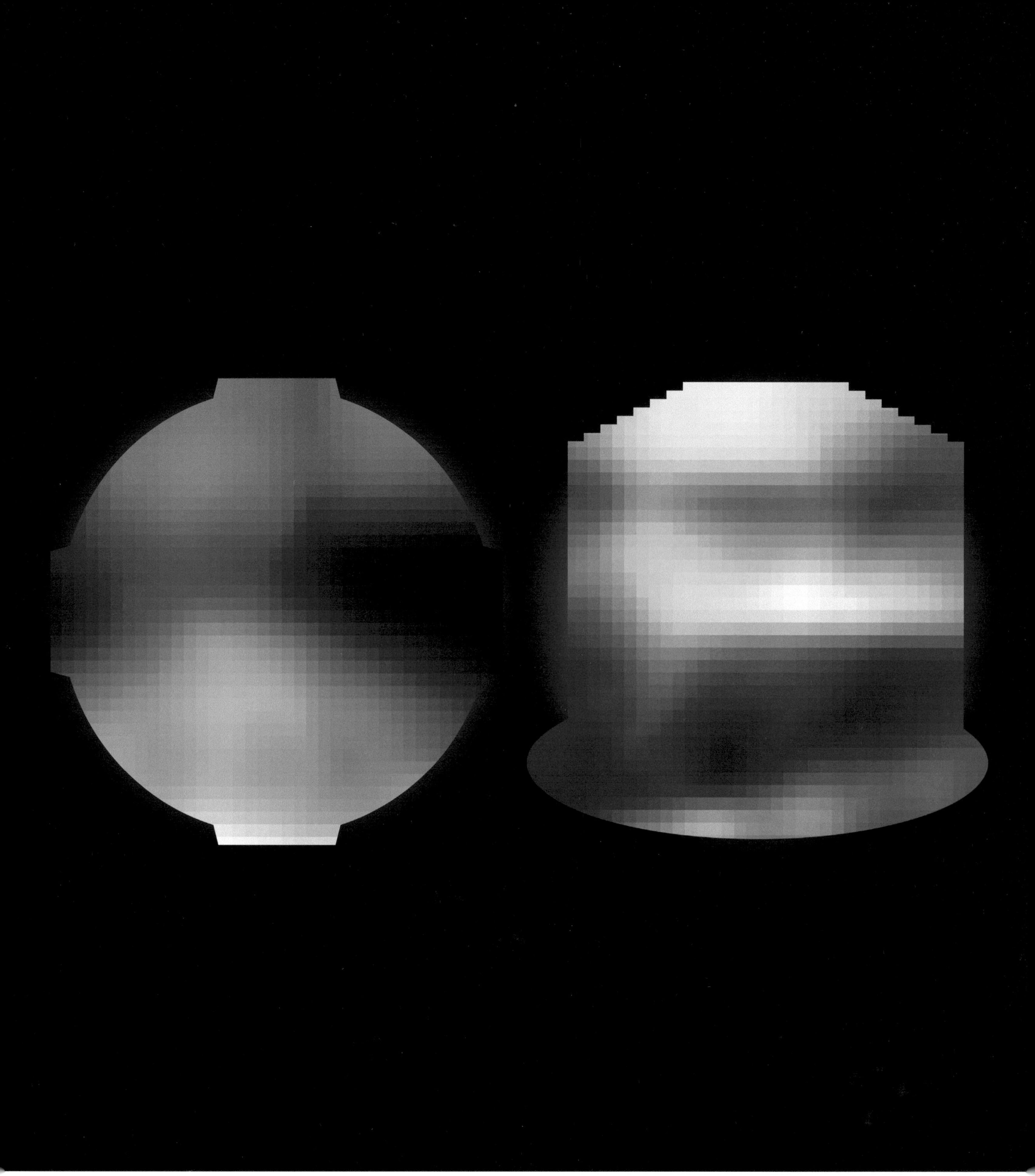

KARLSSONWILKER INC. for Claudia Quintett "For" (CD) *on Cuneiform in 2007* - Jazz -

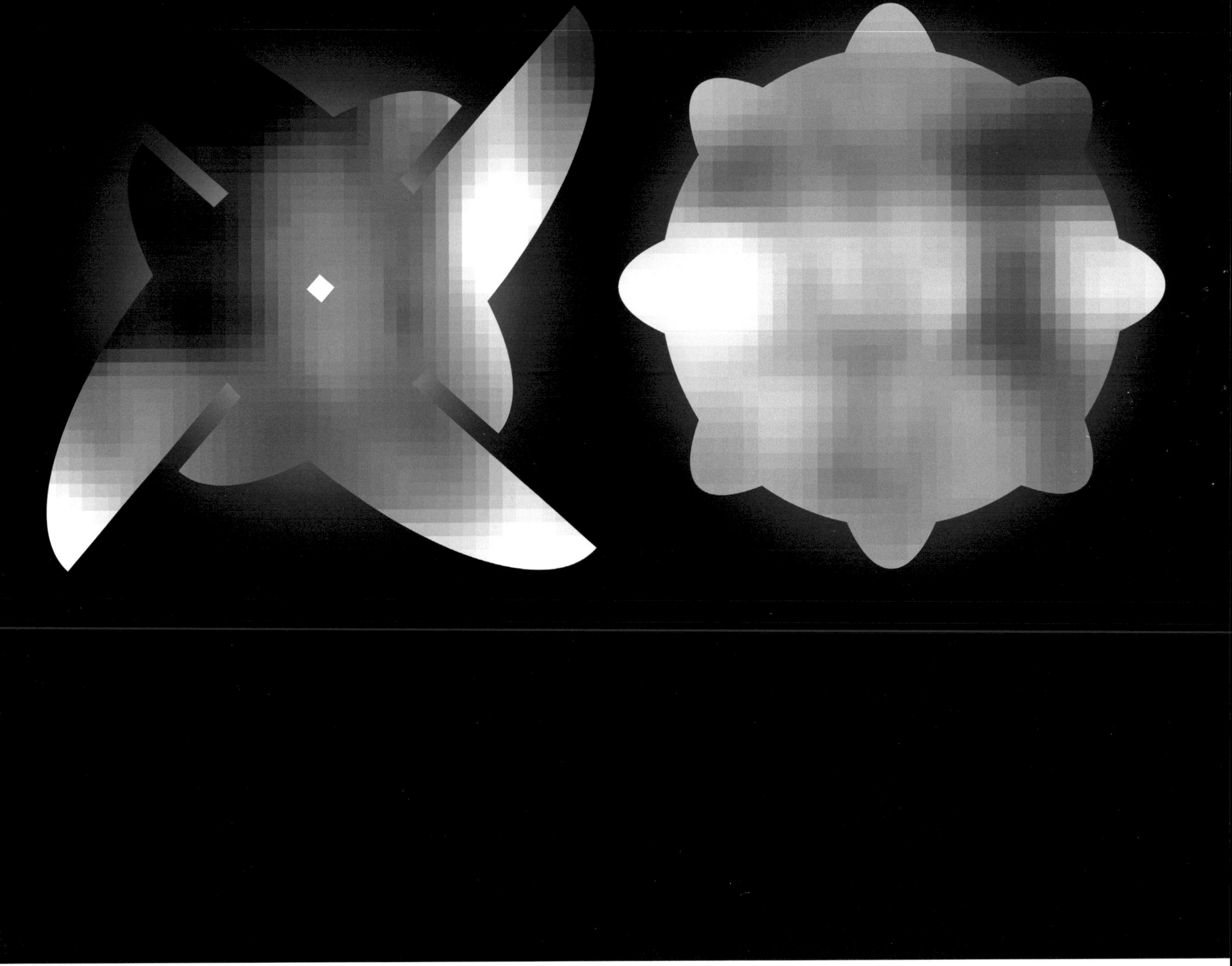

STYLOROUGE LTD, D.: MARK HIGENBOTTAM **for Illegal King** "Popkomm festival EP" (promo CD) *on Como Park Music in 2006* - Electronic -

RICHARD CHARTIER for Various Artists "ColorField Remix event" (4 color Poster) *on Washington Project for the Arts in 2007* - Experimental / Electronic -

LA BOCA, D.: SCOT BENDALL **for The Emperor Machine** "Vertical Tones & Horizontal Noise" (12")
on DC Recordings in 2007 - Electronica -

LA BOCA, D.: SCOT BENDALL for **The Orichalc Phase** "Respond In Silence" (12") *on DC Recordings in 2006* - Electronica -

SKIN DESIGN AS, D.: ARE KLEIVAN **for The Cumshots** "Just Quit Trying" (CD Jewelcase) *on Big Dipper in 2006* - Metal -

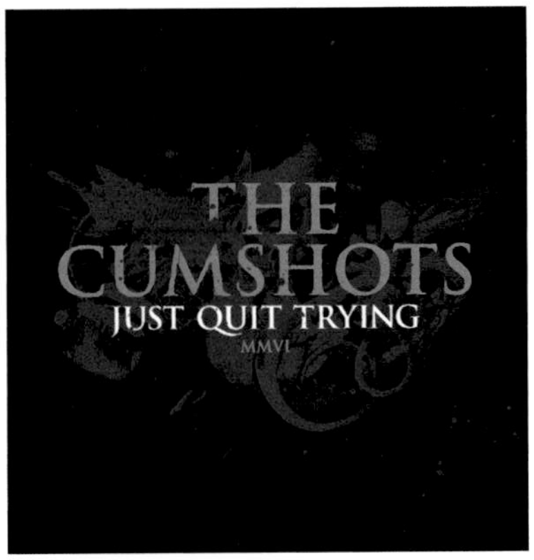

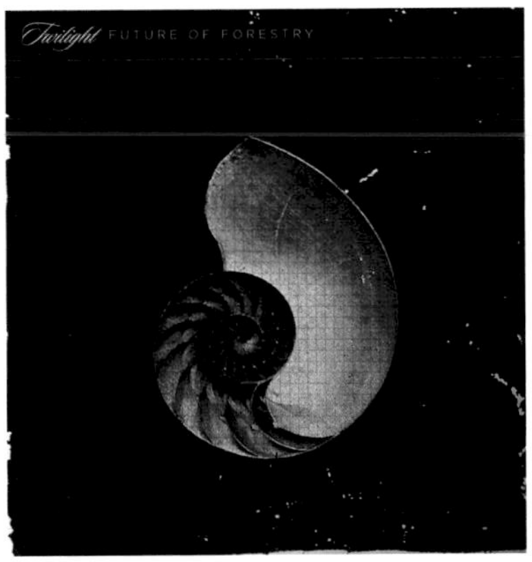

THE HEADS OF STATE, D.: DUSTIN SUMMERS **for Future of Forestry** "Twilight" (Jewel Case) *on Credential Recordings in 2007*

LA BOCA, D.: SCOT BENDALL **for White Light Circus** "Rocaket Ride" (12" Vinyl)

GRANDPEOPLE **for Arne Nordheim / Draumkvedet**
"Draumkvedet" (27x19 cm) *on Simx in 2006*
- Contemporary Music -

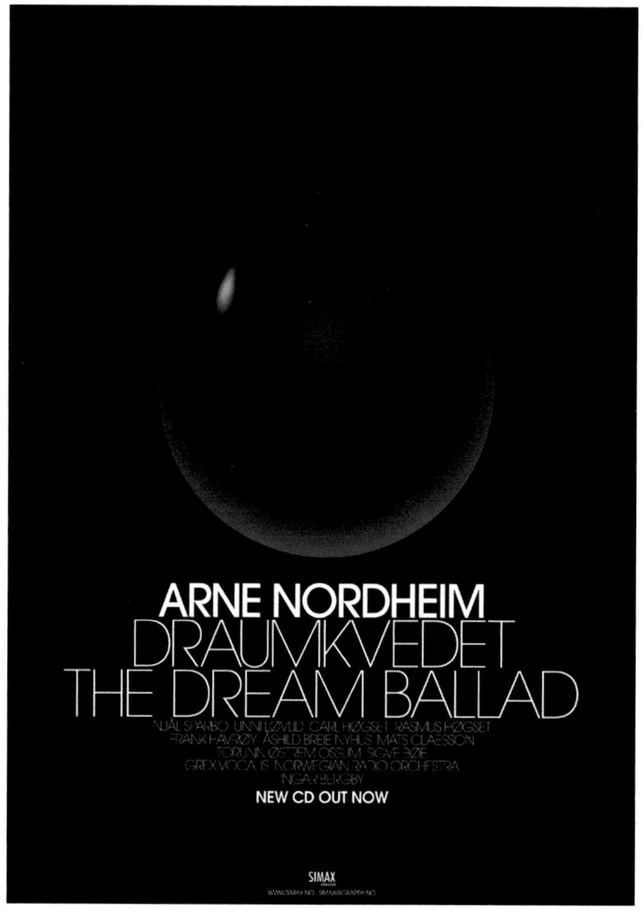

GRANDPEOPLE **for Alog** "Islands of Memory" (sticker 9x9 cm) *on Creaked records in 2006* - Experimental / Electronic -

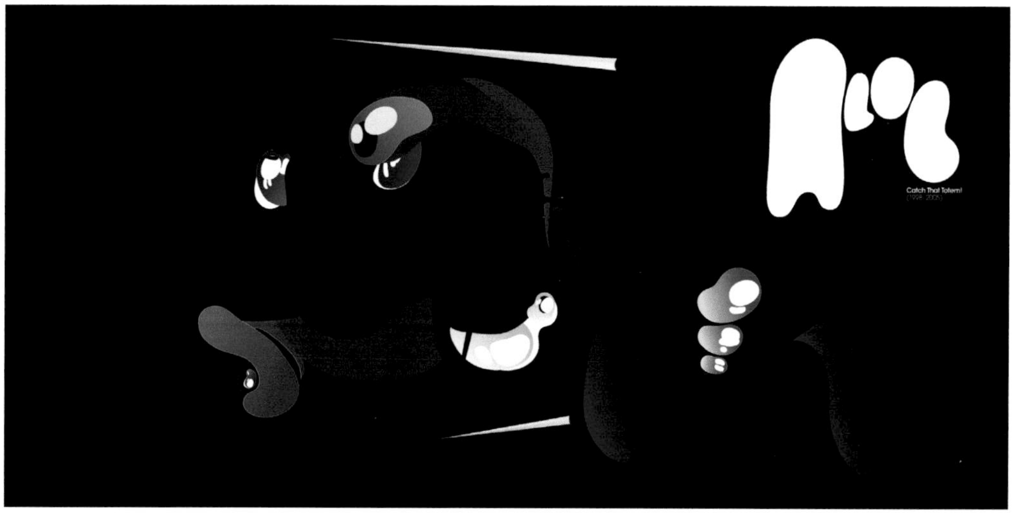

GRANDPEOPLE for Alog "Catch that totem" (14,9x13,5 cm) *on Melektronikk in 2005* - Experimental / Electronic -

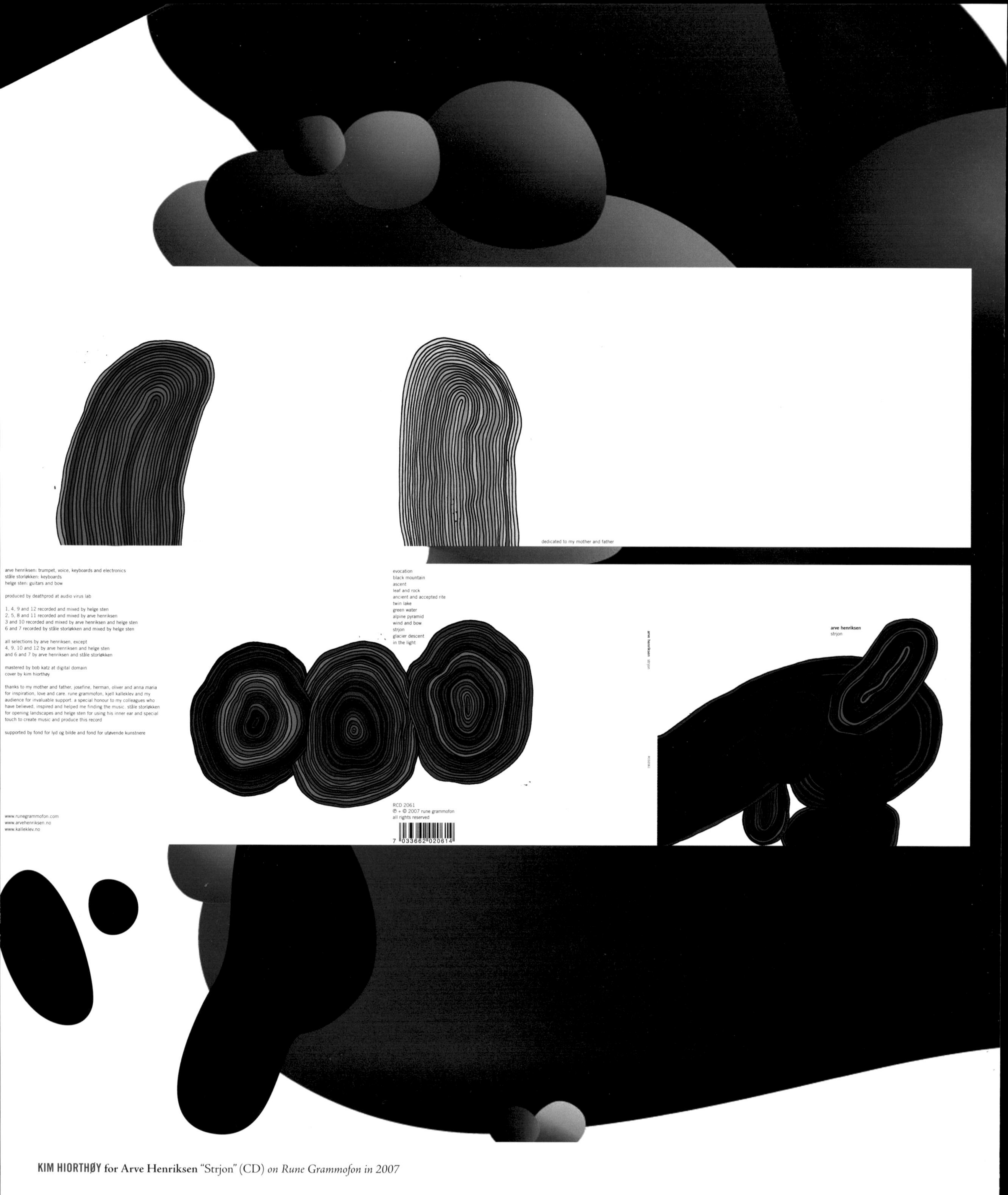

KIM HIORTHØY for Arve Henriksen "Strjon" (CD) *on Rune Grammofon in 2007*

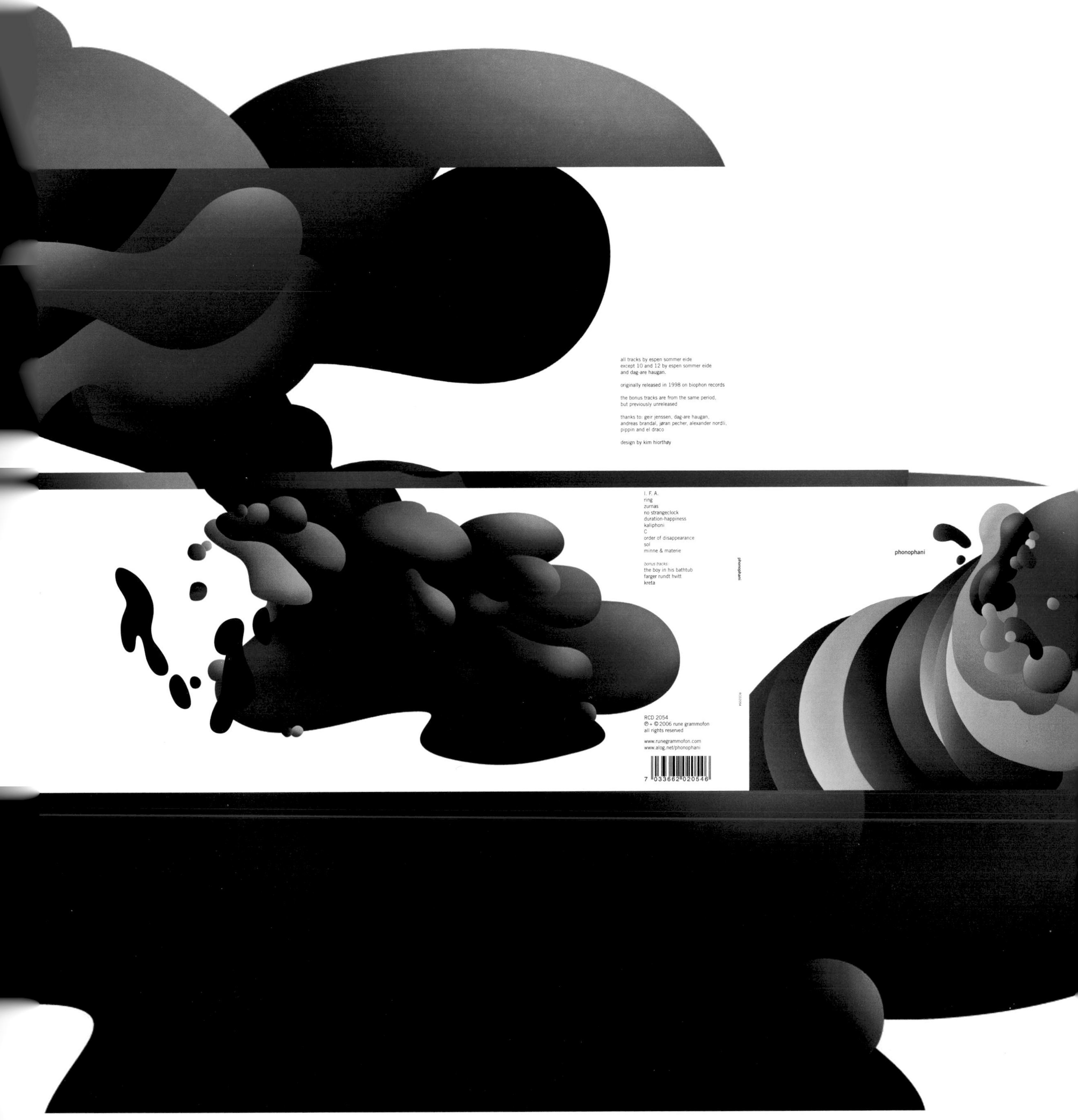

KIM HIORTHØY for Phonophani "Phonophani" (CD) *on Rune Grammofon in 2006*

BUFFET FÜR GESTALTUNG for Hp.stonji "Metic ep" (12") & "mélaina chloé" (CD) *on Spezialmaterial in 2004 & 2005*

BUFFET FÜR GESTALTUNG, for Hp.stonji "Syntonum" (CD) *on Konkord in 2006* - Electronic -

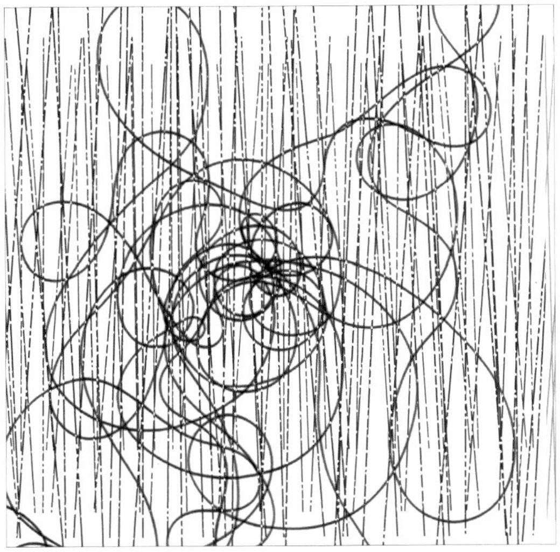

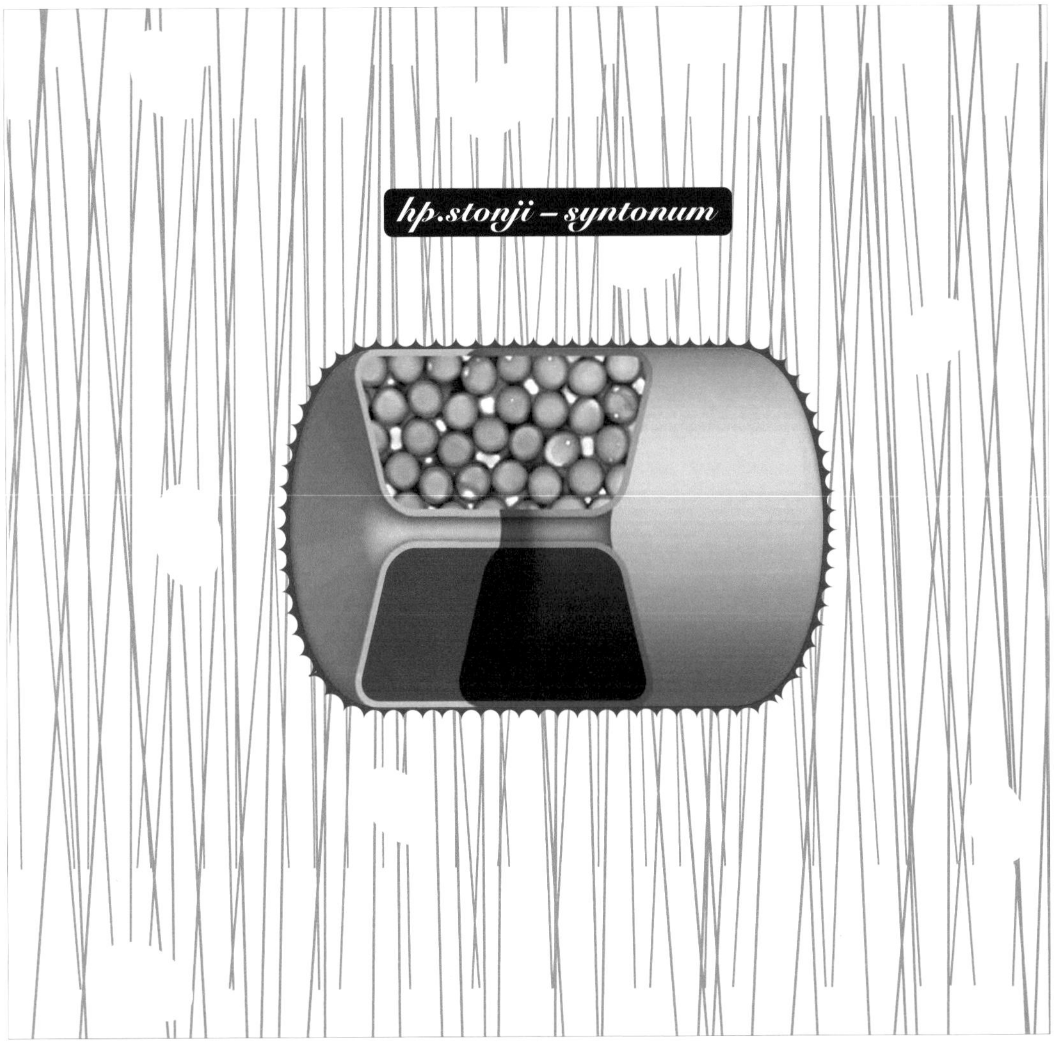

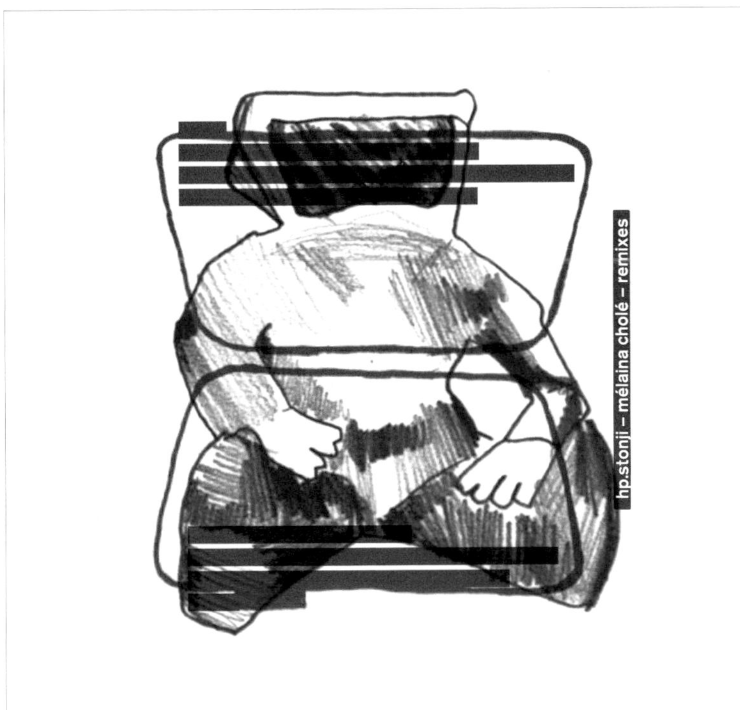

BUFFET FÜR GESTALTUNG for Diverse / Hp.stonji - Mélaina chloé "Remixes" (12") *on Phantomnoise records in 2005* - Electronic -

JAWA AND MIDWICH, D.: NILS DAVEY AND SIMON DOVAR **for Mowgly** "Solar System EP" (12") *on Freerange Records in 2006* - House -

JAWA AND MIDWICH, D.: NILS DAVEY AND SIMON DOVAR **for Kirk Degiorgio** "Kirk Degiorgio Presents Esoterik – Alcyone EP" (12") *on Freerange Records in 2005* - House -

KIOKARMA, D.: YVES FAES-DUPONT **for Dr Monster** "Propeller EP" (CD) *in 2004* - Alternative Rock -

JAWA AND MIDWICH, D.: NILS DAVEY AND SIMON DOVAR **for Jake Childs** "The pain" (12") *on Freerange Records in 2006* - House -

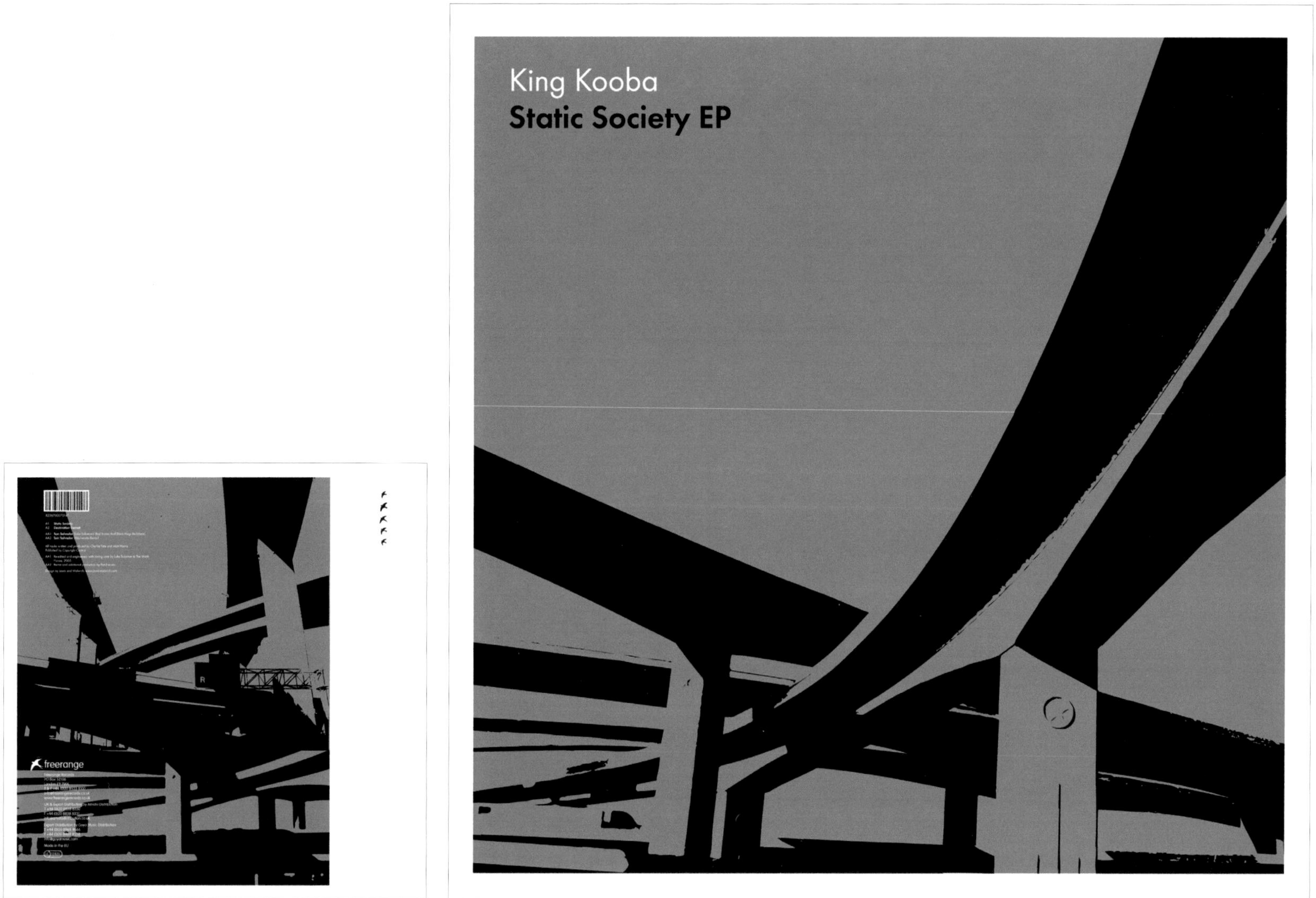

JAWA AND MIDWICH, D.: NILS DAVEY AND SIMON DOVAR **for King Kooba** "Static Society EP" (12")
on Freerange Records in 2006 - House -

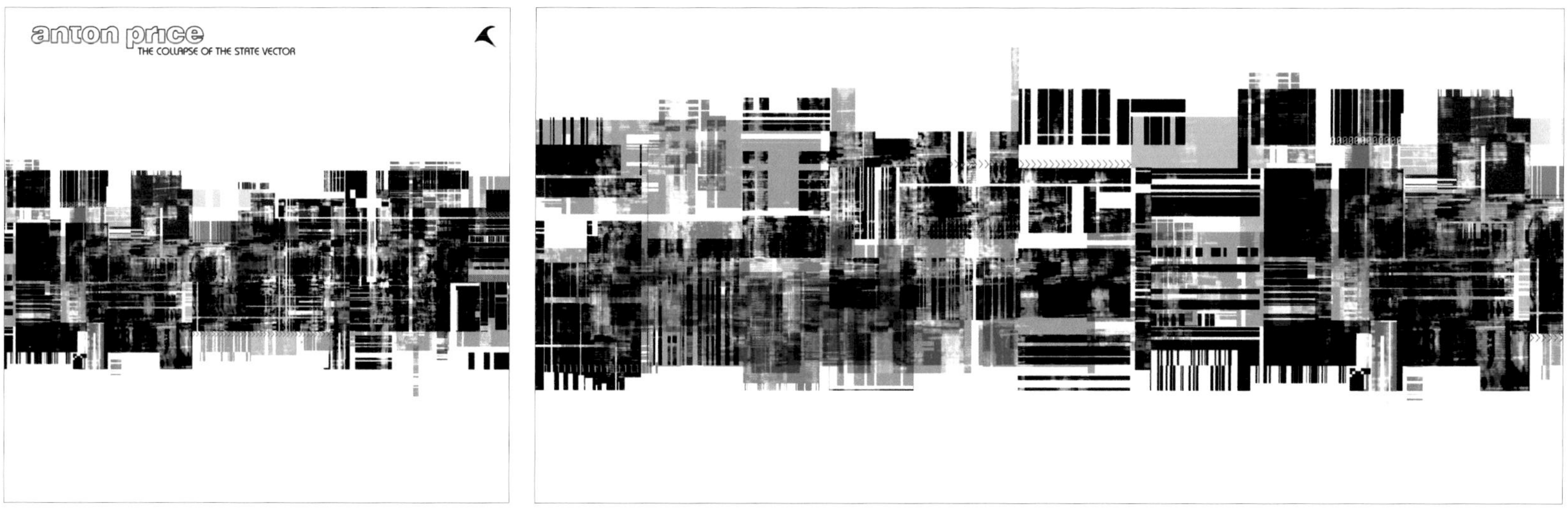

KIOKARMA, D.: YVES FAES-DUPONT **for Anton Price** "Collapse of the State Vector" (12", CD)
on Lowlands/Audioview in 2003 - Electro -

JAWA AND MIDWICH, D.: NILS DAVEY AND SIMON DOVAR **for BC400** (12") *on Buttercuts Records in 2005* - Hip-Hop -

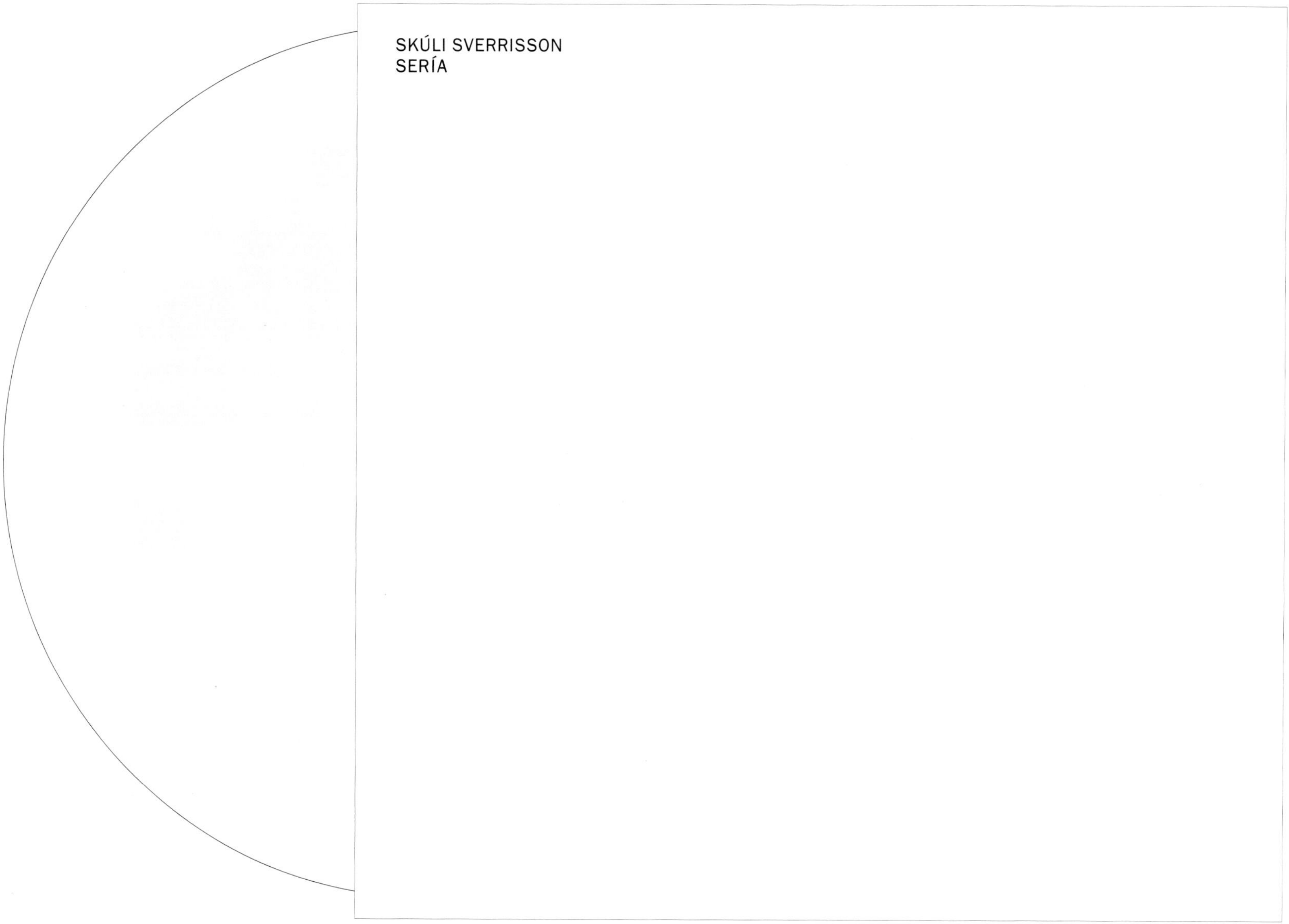

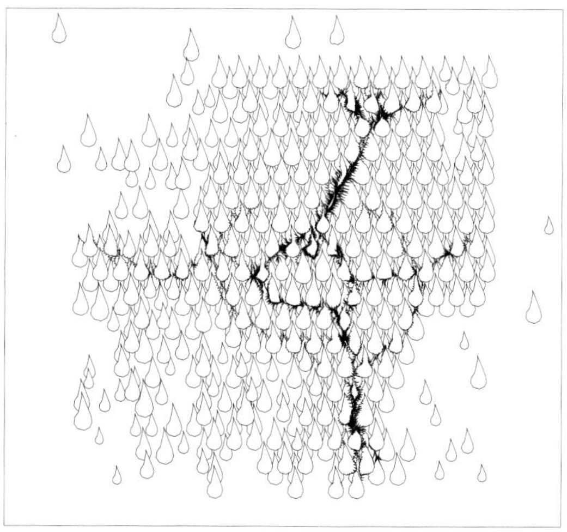

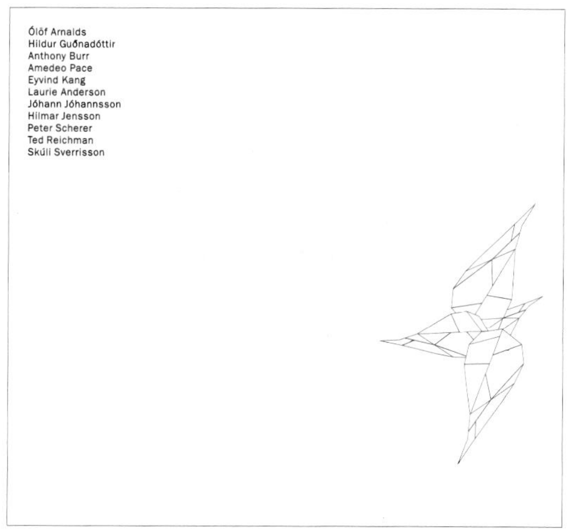

KARLSSONWILKER INC. for Skuli "Seria" (CD) *on 12tonar in 2006* - Various -

WEISSRAUM.DE(SIGN)°, D.: BERND BRINK **for U73 Club** "U73 Shaky Underground Travelling" (Flyer) *in 2006 - 2007* - Techno/Electro -

STRUGGLE INC. **for Bitter:sweet** "The Mating Gmae" (CD) *on Quango in 2006* - Downtempo -

HUMAN EMPIRE, D.: JAN KRUSE **for Morr promo sleeve** (CD) *on Morr Music in 2006*

WEISSRAUM.DE(SIGN)°, D.: BERND BRINK & LUCAS BUCHHOLZ **for Karl Bartos** "Communicaion" & "I'm The Message" (Vinyl Album) *on Home Records/Sony in 2004*

MASA for Venezuelan Electronic Compilation "Dance Venezuela" (CD) *on Gozadera Records in 2006* - Electronica -

MASA for Los Amigos Invisibles "Super Pop Venezuela" (CD) *on Gozadera Records in 2005* - Dance -

MORDANT MUSIC, D.: GARY MILLS **for Mordant Music** "Dead Air" (Special CD album packaging outer graphic) *on Mordant Music in 2006* - Electronica -

MORDANT MUSIC, D.: GARY MILLS **for Mordant Music** "Dead Air" (Album CD front label & Philip Elsmore Badge) *on Mordant Music in 2006* - Electronica -

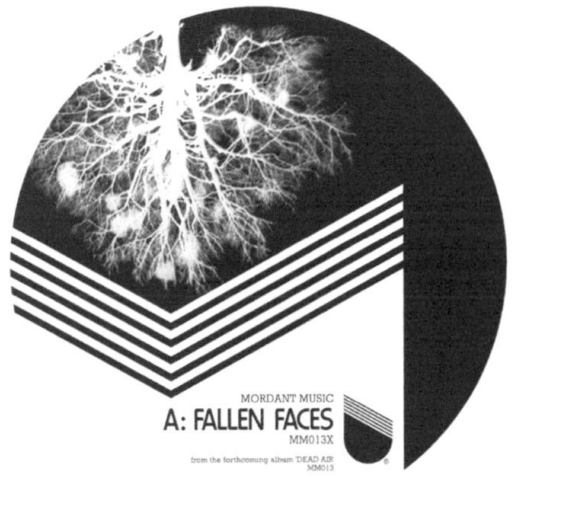

MORDANT MUSIC, D.: GARY MILLS **for Mordant Music** "Fallen Faces (Dead Edit)" (7" vinyl picture disc single) *on Mordant Music in 2006* - Electronica -

KIM HIORTHØY for Opsvik & Jennings "Commuter Anthems" (CD) *on Rune Grammofon in 2007*

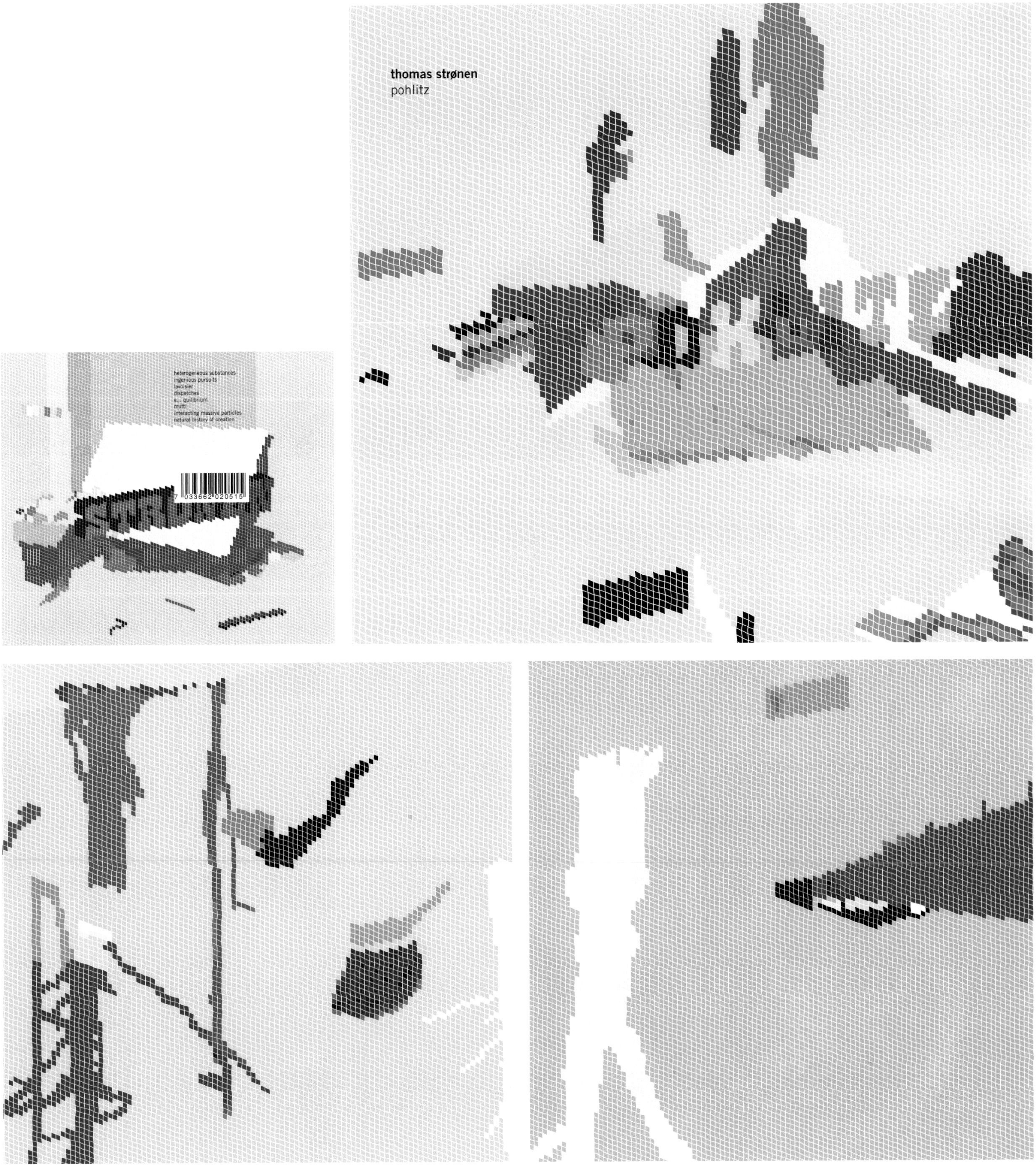

KIM HIORTHØY for Thomas Strønen "Pohlitz" (CD) *on Rune Grammofon in 2005*

MADEWITHHATE **for Pop Dylan** "Give chance a piece" & **for Lassie & Chris** "Lassie & Chris" (LP) *on Esel in 2004 & 2006* - Optical Electronica -

MADEWITHHATE **for Gaumen** "Patcher, Panels, Brass" & **for James Din A4** "Karl der Käfer" (LP) *on Esel in 2004 & 2007* - Electronica -

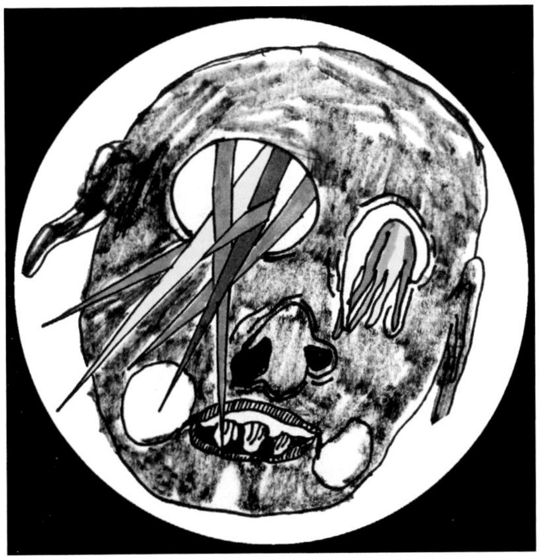

MADEWITHHATE for **James Din A4** "Karl der Käfer" & **for Pop Dylan** "Take me to the slaughterhouse, I will wait there with the lamb" (LP) *on Esel in 2004 & 2006* - Electronica -

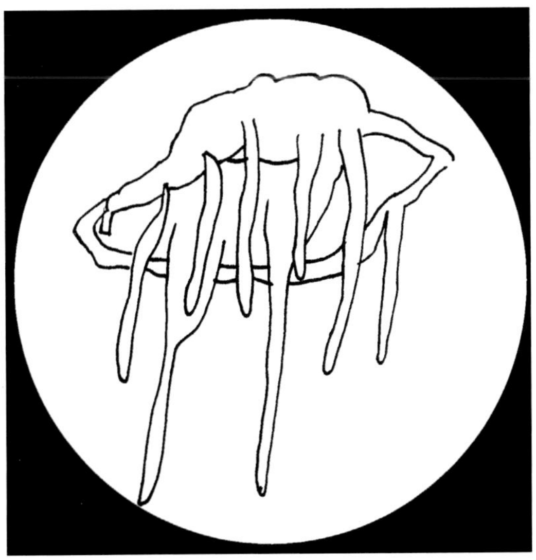

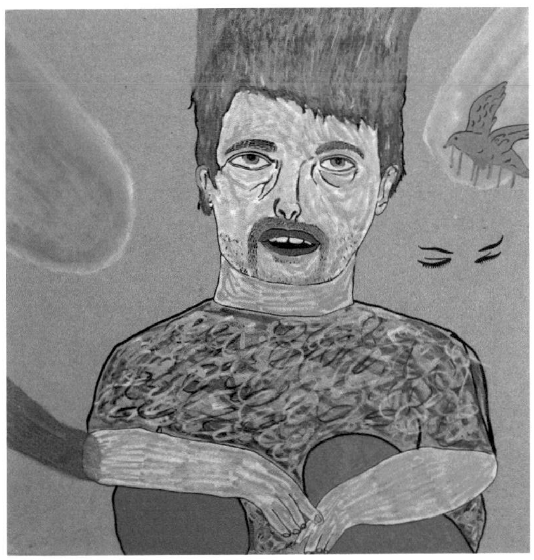

MADEWITHHATE for **Pop Dylan** "Take me to the slaughterhouse, I will wait there with the lamb" & **for Lassie & Chris** "Lassie & Chris" (LP) *on Esel in 2006* - Electronica -

GOMMA *Answers by Mirko Bosche*

The brainchild and musical outlet of Jonas Imbery and Mathias Modica, Gomma represents a truly rare breed – a label unafraid to shed its skin every few releases.

Since its inception in 2001, when their 'Anti NY' sampler helped to kick-start the latest New Wave/Electro craze and put the label on the map, the two label founders, otherwise known as Karl Lagerfeld favourites Munk and a myriad of other pseudonyms that account for a hefty chunk of the label's 100+ back catalogue, have been championing idiosyncratic talents and constant reinvention – an attitude that is also reflected in their genre-defying artwork.

Confrontational, challenging and never dull, the label found its perfect match in designers Mirko Bosche (former art director of seminal youth supplement jetzt and currently responsible for the award-winning SZ Magazin by German broadsheet Süddeutsche Zeitung) and Süddeutsche regular Thomas Kartsolis.
Flitting between beats, blips and genres like there's no tomorrow, Gomma's music and artwork throws up a wild, unpredictable and always challenging mix that has become part of the label's unspoken code.

How did you get sucked into the label's extended universe?

At the time, around five or six years ago, I was art director at jetzt and already doing the odd sleeve or poster on the side. One night, Matthias approached me about doing some flyers for their label. I mean, I really appreciated their music, but I wasn't wild about doing just odds and ends. Soon enough, Thomas Kartsolis and I had taken over the label's entire artwork, from posters to sleeves, and we haven't looked back since.
Thomas and I go way back, we both come from a graffiti background and met during a spraying spree at the tender age of 17. Sometimes we work together, sometimes it's just one of us; whichever makes more sense. Over the years, we've developed our own, peculiar style and visual language – distinctive, yet impossible to pin down. Even the sleeves feature a curious, peculiar mix of German, English, Italian and Bavarian to reflect Gomma's collective, convoluted roots.

An ambitious mix – many releases feature a range of different, seemingly disjointed styles and elements ...

We tend to treat each element of the artwork separately. For example, a lot of our work and attention goes into the design of the actual CD itself. Call us sticklers, but this is something that is very important to us – when you take it out of the case, the CD itself should always look great. The design might be totally different from the rest of the artwork, but it's almost more important than the cover itself. In addition, each of our releases comes with a four-page booklet that doesn't usually feature any information on the release, but rather yet another motif that might have started out as a cover sketch for an entirely different release ...

Considering the breadth of styles on display, it's virtually impossible to pin you down. What is the prime intention behind this approach?

We want to make sure that the kids don't get bored. Ideally, nobody should ever get bored by either the music or the artwork. And naturally, it should also have some kind of entertainment value. Most of all, we don't want people to file the label under a certain style or genre, but rather keep surprising ourselves and the listeners with every release. What holds it all together is never a specific style, but our collective taste – it works like a mix tape that has a certain attitude, but brings together many different, varied and surprising tracks. Mathias and Jonas, the musical minds behind the label, are responsible for the pick and mix approach - and quality is their only selection criterion. To us, Gomma is less of a label than an aesthetic framework that encompasses far more than posters, sleeves and music.

So, what else is part of the Gomma realm?

A lot of what we do starts out as a spontaneous idea and then develops a life of its own.

Our experimental spin-off magazine Amore, for example, came out of a 12" sleeve design for Princess Superstar. At the time, we weren't quite sure about which angle to explore. The record had this special Latin/Electro feel and we needed to come up with an unusual advertising spin that would do it justice and stand out in a business that thrives on an extremely fast, aesthetic turnover, where anything remotely innovative immediately attracts a gaggle of copycats.

So, in order to reinvent ourselves and come up with new ideas, we often go through quite a few sketches and false starts before we hit on the right one. And even if we love the result, Jonas and Matthias might reject it, which is only fair because they also give us equal say when it comes to the music.
So, with tricky releases we might end up with something like 40-60 artwork alternatives, and the ones that don't make it are usually just as good and definitely not for the trash can. Some are recycled for 12-inches, flyers and posters, but the rest, and this is what came out of the Princess Superstar designathon,

the
PORTO
FINO
MOSH

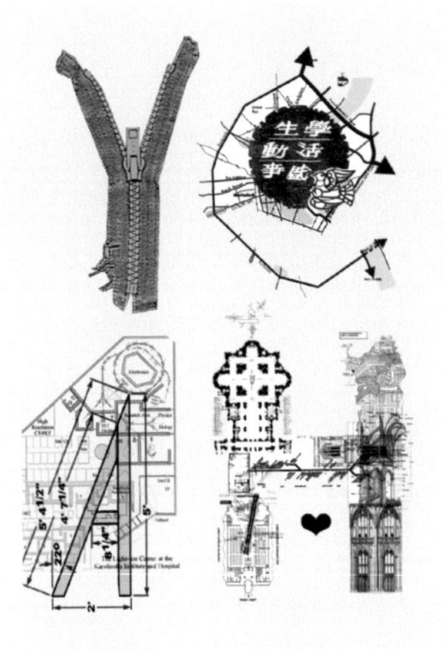

GOMMAGANG
START
TOM
BOY
SERIØS

L.i.d.o.
Disco
GOMMAParty!
1.+3. Do im MO
Erste Liga

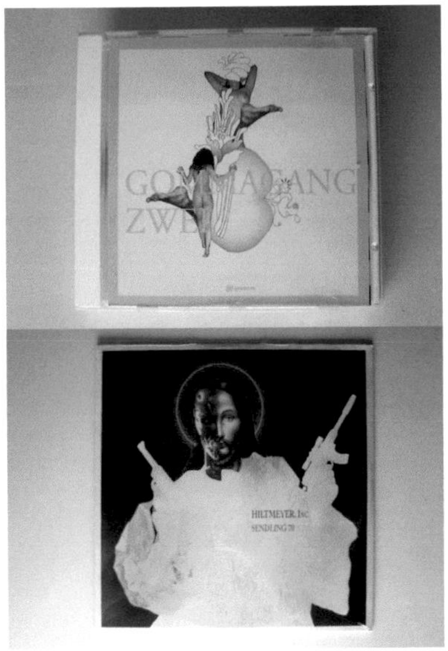
GOMMAGANG
ZWEI

L.i.d.o.
Disco
GOMMAParty!
1.+3. Do im MO
Erste Liga

MUNK
&
JAMES MURPHY
KICK OUT THE CHAIRS!
out in autumn 04

GOMMAGANG
START

NO?
NO.
SMAL
PAZE

3
GOMMA
GANG

THE
PORTO
FINO
MOSH

DRECKIGER
DONNERSTAG

can find a new home in Amore. Initially, we only saw it as an outlet for talented friends and all the odds and ends that didn't make the label's official artwork, but all of a sudden it was picked up by Colette in Paris, Visionaire asked us to participate in an exhibition on up-and-coming magazines in New York, followed by Mondo Gomma exhibitions in Berlin, Milan and Barcelona, even Shanghai and Tokyo ...

It's obviously popular with designers, but what about your fans and buyers – do they ‚get' the design, or does the level of abstraction leave some of them confused? What about the artists themselves?

Interestingly enough, most of the people who buy our releases have no fixed musical taste, but rather a certain spirit, a general willingness to check out new stuff. With the artists, on the other hand, it can be bit of a tightrope walk. Most of the time, they share our tastes and aesthetics, but naturally they also want to have their say and sometimes it takes many, many long discussions to persuade them to drop some fixed idea. You might have to tell them, "this really doesn't work with your music" or that it would mean pandering to a certain style or trend and date very quickly.

The only strong, negative reaction we ever got came from our French distributors who really hated 'Teutonic Disaster', a compilation of rare German funk and disco trash from the late 70s and early 80s culled from Mathias' and Jonas' own record collections. For the cover, I went for an in-your-face Metal font with a martial Norse knight, lance and all, holding a rose between his teeth. Incidentally, they totally loved the follow-up, a tongue-in-cheek montage of a German soldier from the Great War and a French Can-Can dancer. So it's not even worth worrying if something is too strange or over the top as you can't ever second-guess your audience.

What are the dynamics between label and design? Any danger of one side overshadowing the other?

Considering that we rarely ever see each other – we're all really busy and travel a lot – and that most of our exchanges take place via phone, e-mail and the Internet, it's amazing how well it all works out. We have developed a very similar taste in music and while they take a strong interest in the design side of things, they have also come to value our musical input and opinion. Recently, I went back to one of the early Princess Superstar releases and played it at 33 by mistake – it sounded amazing! I told the guys straight away and now they've put it on their release schedule ... Among ourselves, we don't really disagree about taste or music per se, we are much more likely to argue about individual tracks or the tracklisting.

I mean, we've all been close friends for years, so we're almost like two old couples, there's always a shoulder to cry on. If you need to bitch about your personal 'spouse' you can always run to the other two, and if the other team pisses you off, you can tell your label or design partner, "god, we're never going on holiday with those two again" ...

How does all of this fit in with your regular day job? Does it even leave any time or scope for private projects?

Fortunately, I work quite fast. With its strict weekly schedule, my job at SZ Magazin taught me to how to come up with ideas on spec. I found that you can actually force yourself to produce ideas at short notice; it's just a matter of habit and discipline.

Besides the Gomma stuff, I always have a few projects or developments going on, but truly private projects tend to stay in the family. Recently we wasted a huge amount of toilet paper on building a giant palm tree for the Easter bunny – according to my pre-teen son, this particular chocolate-provider would feel much happier in a tropical environment ...

I shouldn't really admit this, but whenever I needed some abstract illustrations for Neon, jetzt or SZ Magazin, it was often his drawings that made the grade. He wields a bold and inspired stroke - and so far, no one's ever noticed!

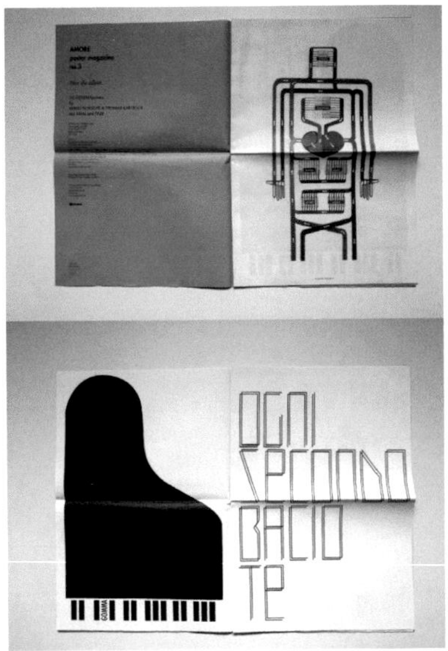
OGNI
SECONDO
BACIO
TE

MY HOME IS MY CASTLE
AND MY HO
IST IN SCHWA

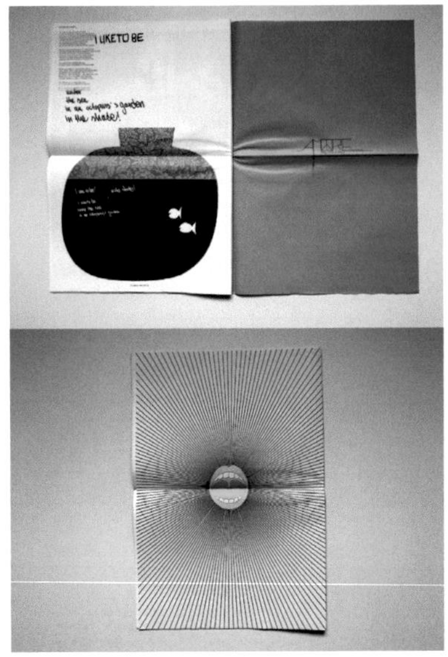
I LIKE TO BE

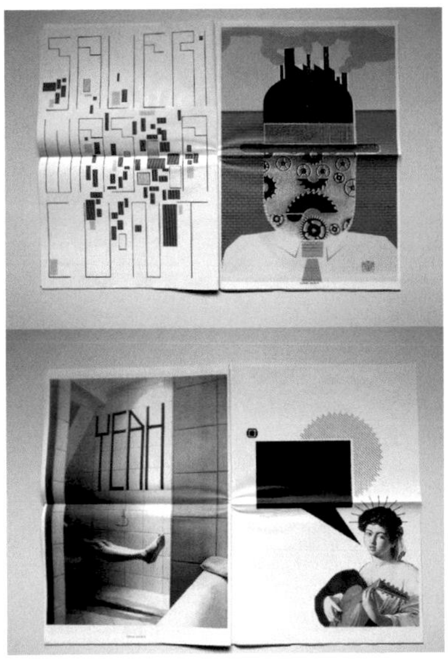
YEAH

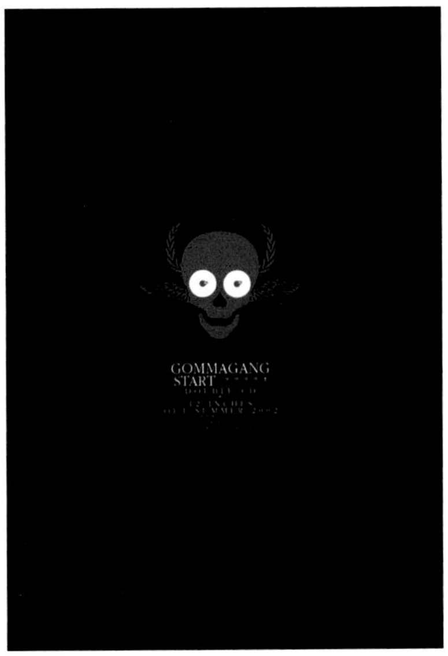
GOMMAGANG
START

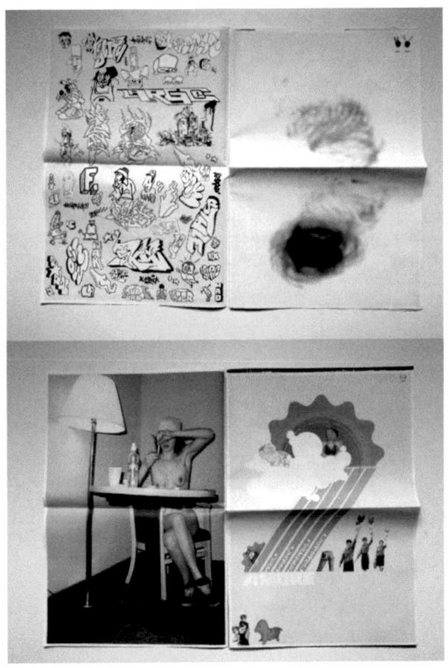

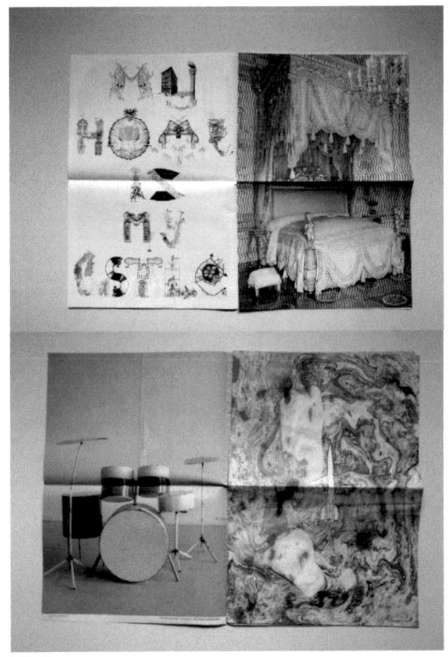

BURN

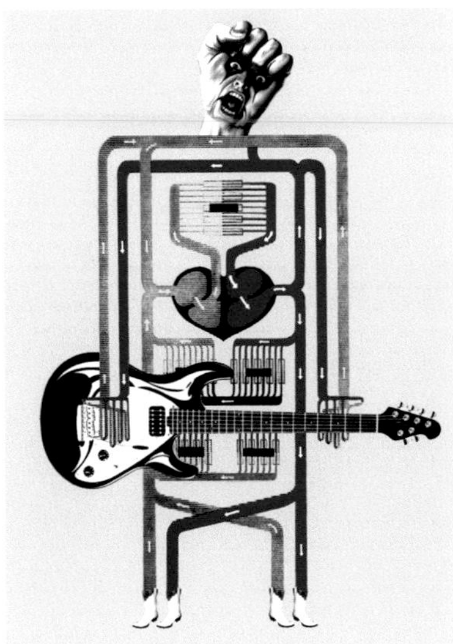

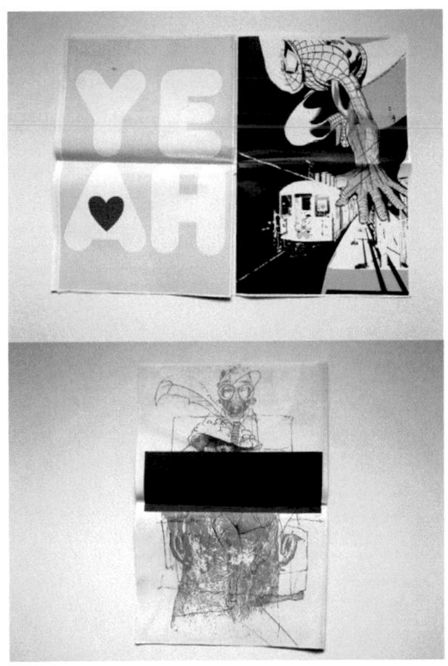
YE
AH

ick
ou
the
ch
rs

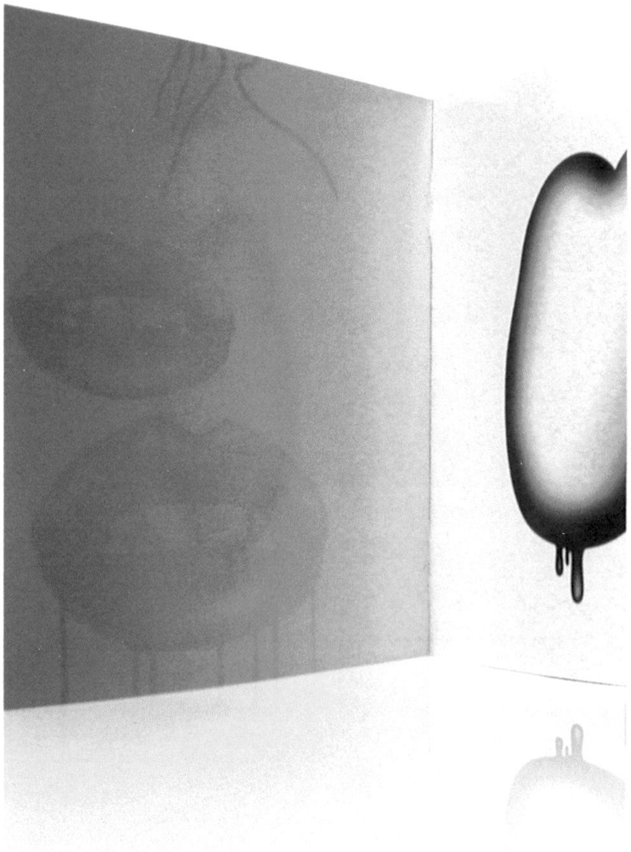

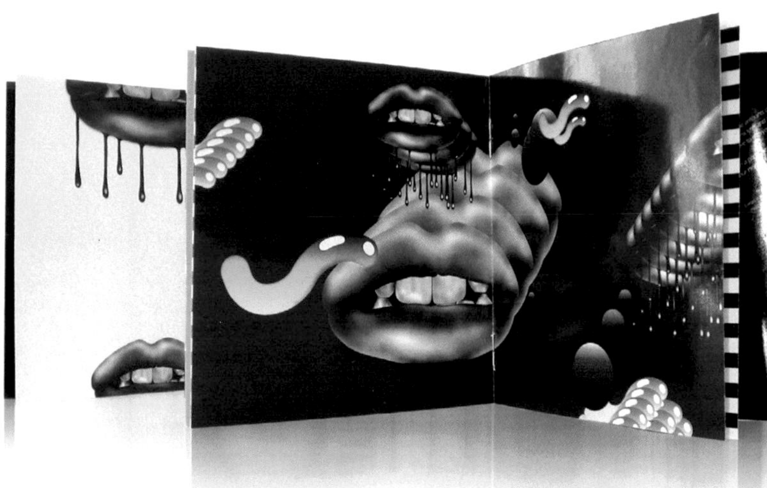

GRANDPEOPLE **for Skatebård** "Midnight Magic" (diverse) *on Digitalo Enterprises in 2006* - Electro / Techno -

DIRK RUDOLPH for Schrottgrenze "Chateau" (CD) *on Motor Music in 2006; Photography by Hadley Hudson* - Rock -

SEB JARNOT for Jesse Harris "Mineral" (CD) *on Secret Sun Recordings in 2006* - Pop -

SEB JARNOT for São Paris "Là" (CD) *on F communications in 2006* - Electronica -

RUNE MORTENSEN for Popface "Teardropper" (CD) *on CCAP in 2006* - Indie -

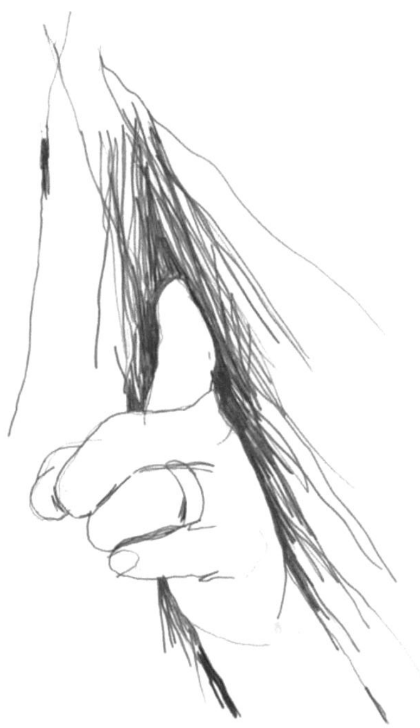

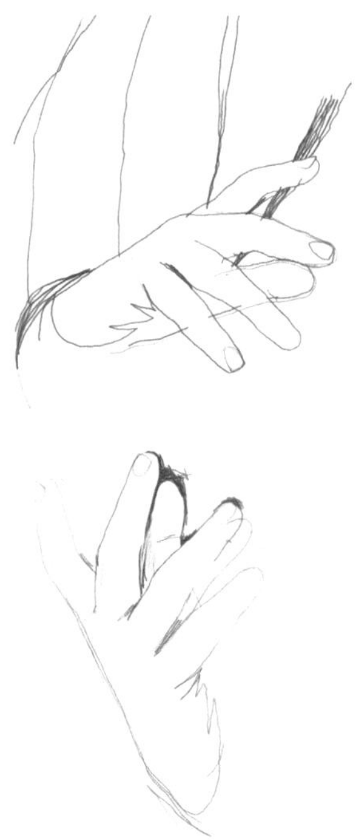

STYLOROUGE LTD, D.: ANTHONY LUI **for Paul McCartney** "Chaos & Creation in the Backyard" (CD) *on Parlophone in 2005* - Pop -

SEB JARNOT for William Sheller "Épures" (CD) *on Mercury France in 2004* - French Songs -

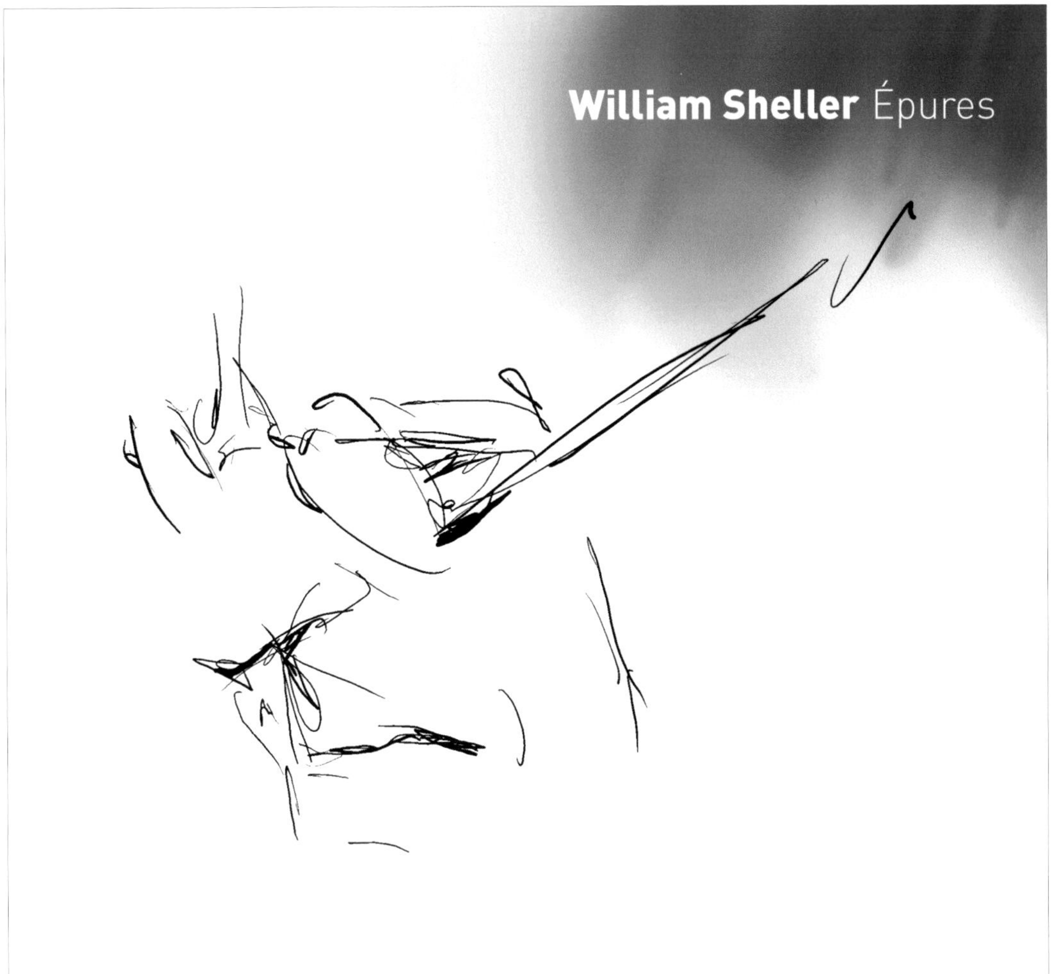

MARIA TACKMANN, D: DIMITRI GRIMM, I: MARIA TACKMANN for the Slapped Eyeballers "Sloppy future manipulations" (12") *on Sonar Kollektiv in 2006*

IO STUDIO for **The Animal Five** (Promotional Poster) *on Univeral Music in 2006* - Pop/Rock -

IO STUDIO for Ben Kaan "Zuhause Wohnen" (CD) *on Lamm Records in 2006*

LAURA VARSKY for Laura Levy "La verdad interior" (CD) *on Independent edition in 2006* - Alternative Pop -

ZIP DESIGN, D.: DANIEL KOCH **for Mozez** "So Still" & "Mozez - Feel Free" (LP & Single, Digi, onbody and sticker) *on Apace Music in 2005* - Pop -

JOTOPIA | VISUAL NOISE, D.: JOHANNES BAYER **for Livingroom** "Displaced Dreamings" & for Benea "Lay Your Weapons Down" (CD) *in 2005* - Alternative -

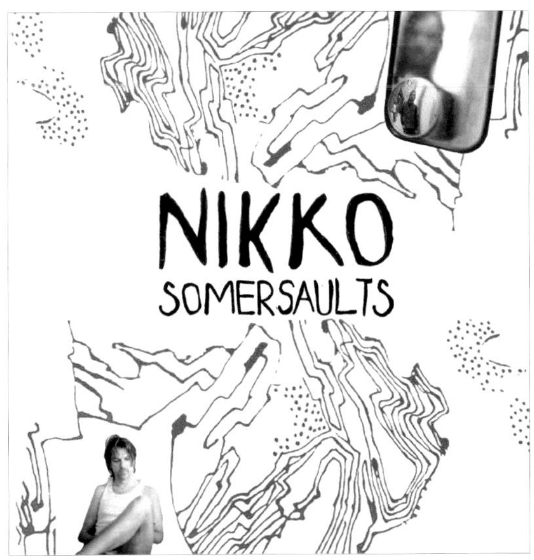

IO STUDIO for Nikko "Somersaults" (CD) *on Couch Records in 2006*

BUFFET FÜR GESTALTUNG for Kate Wax / Safety Scissors / Aster Oh (23 x 35 cm) *on Spezialmaterial in 2005* - Electronic - & for Wevie Stonder (35 x 50 cm) in 2004 - Electronica -

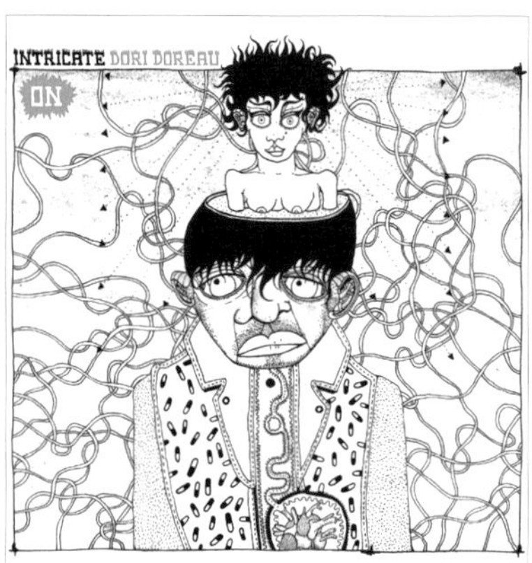

BUFFET FÜR GESTALTUNG for Intricate "Dori doreau" (12") *on Spezialmaterial in 2005* - Electronic -

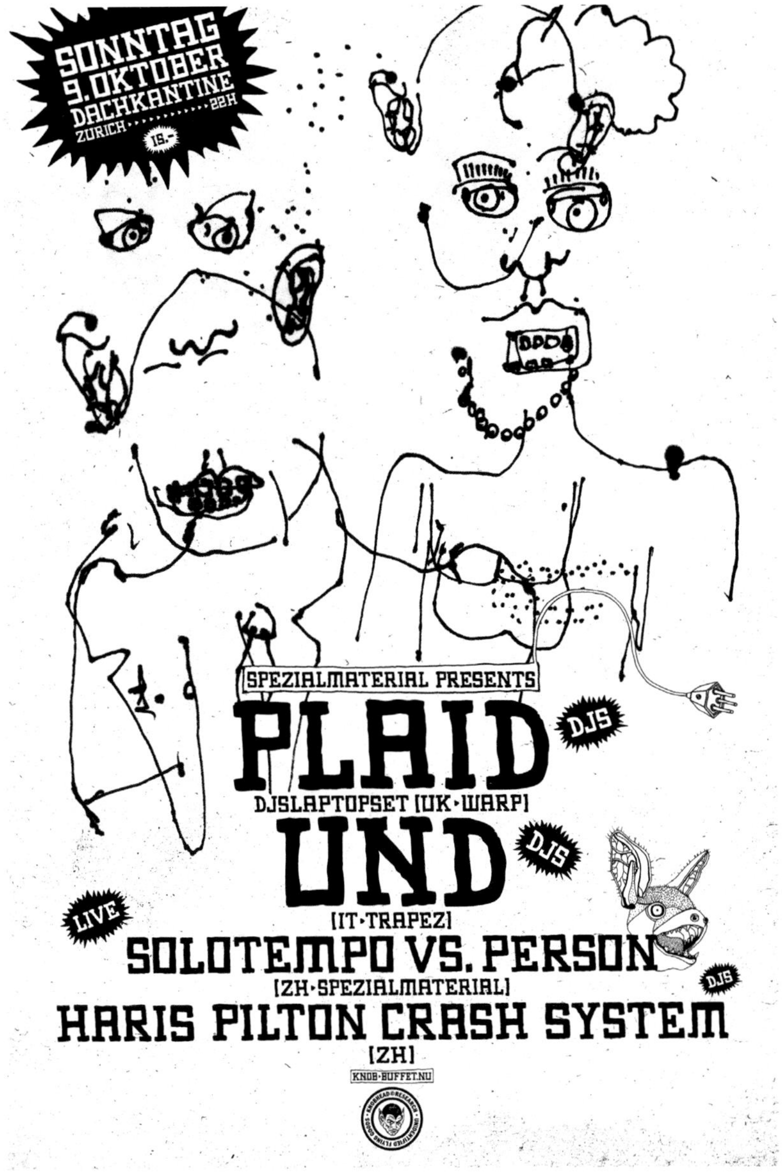

BUFFET FÜR GESTALTUNG **for Candie Hank** "The one man festival" (A3) *in 2005* - Hypnotic Synthscapes - & **for Plaid** (50x33cm) *on Spezialmaterial in 2005* - Electronica -

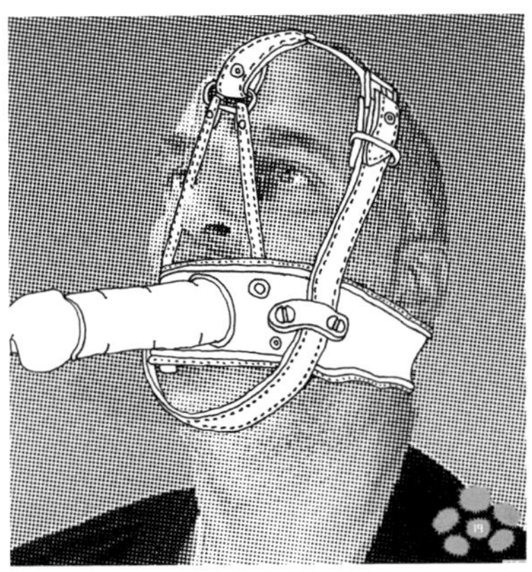

BUFFET FÜR GESTALTUNG **for Nosrep** "Just don't" (12") & **for Intricate** "Captain Trunk" (12")
on Spezialmetrial in 2005-06 - Electronica -

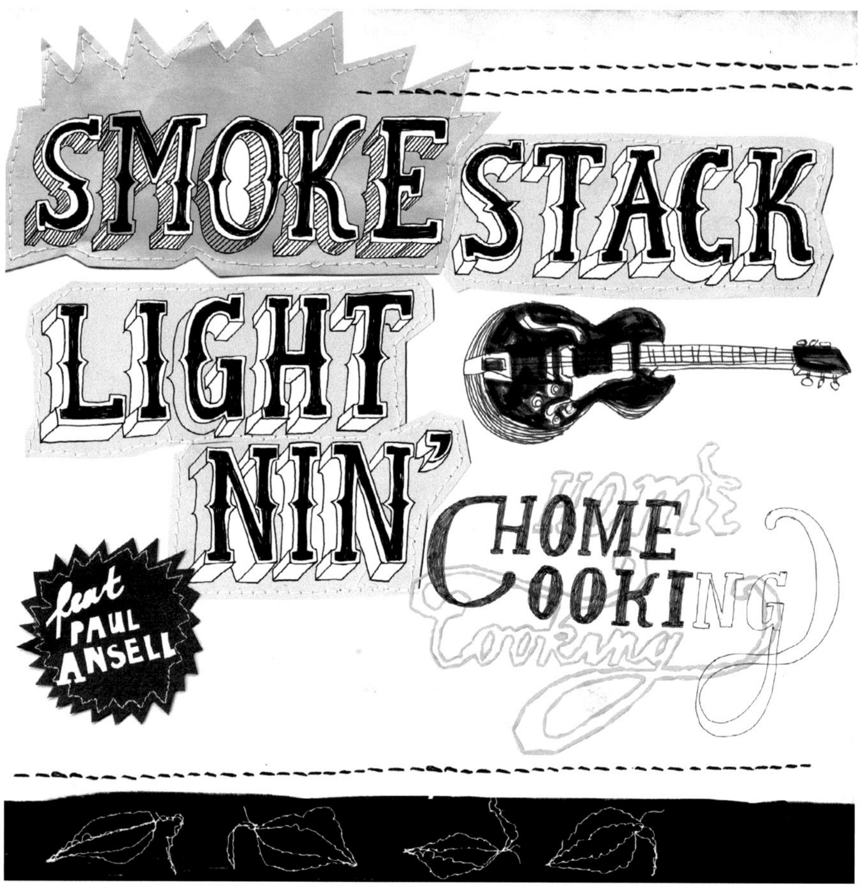

JULIA PFALLER for Smokestack Lightnin' "Home Cooking" (CD) *on Part Records in 2006* - Rockabilly -

BUFFET FÜR GESTALTUNG for Mucke 1-5 "Mucke" (A7) *on Knobhead Research / Freudo Produktion in 2006* - Mixed Grill -

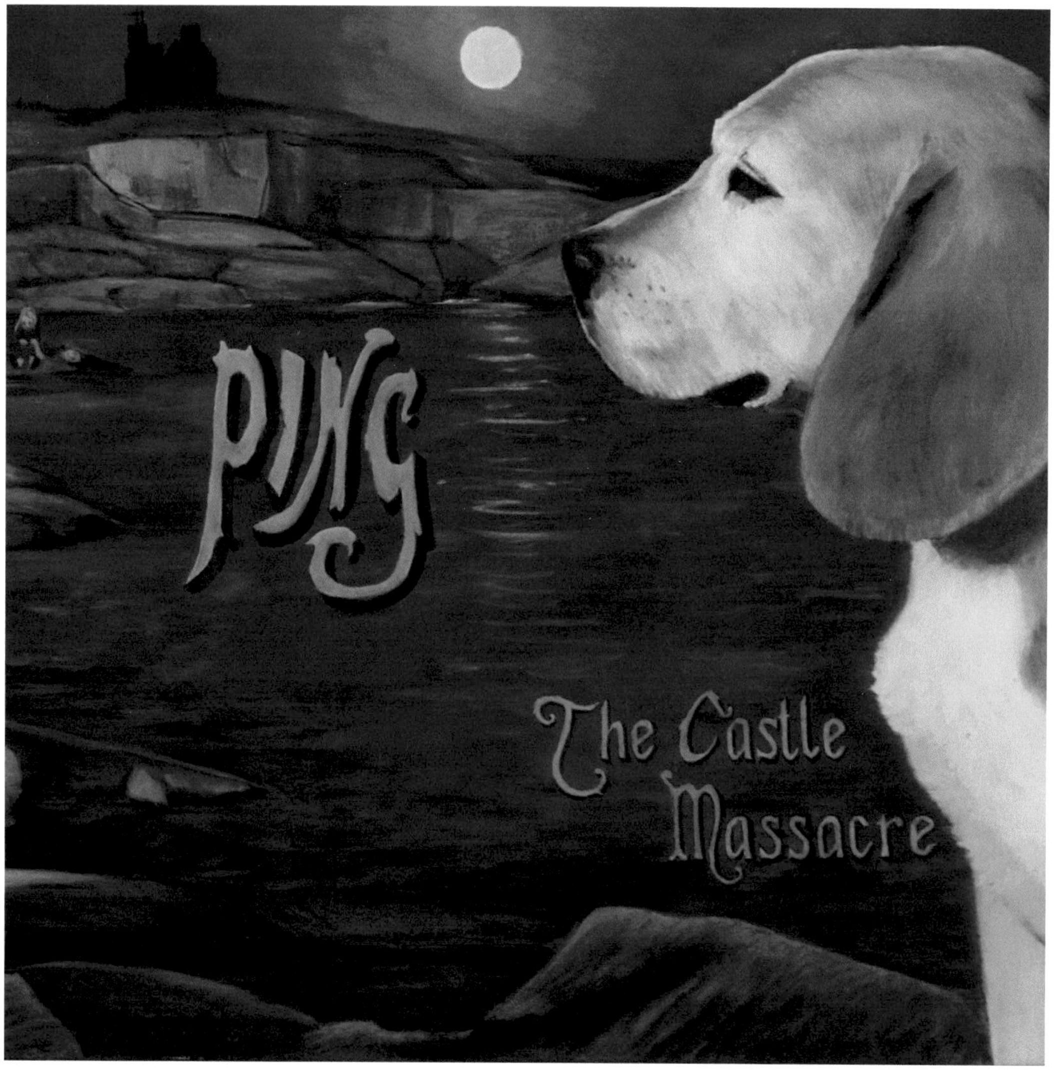

MARTIN KVAMME for Ping "The Castle Massacre" *on Psycadelic Music in 2005* - Alternative -

JOE A. SCERRI for Tim Koch "Elk Meadow" (online mp3 album) *on Monotonic in 2006* - Electronica -

BÜRO DESTRUCT, D.: LOPETZ for Crush "No Right, No Wrong" (CD) *on Echochamber in 2006* - Pop -

ZIP DESIGN, D.: DANIEL KOCH for Beth Orton "Comfort of Strangers" (Album) *on EMI Records in 2006* - Folk Pop -

STEPHAN DOITSCHINOFF for Hot Rod Circuit "The Underground is a Dying Breed" (CD) *on Immortal Records in 2007* - Rock -

STEPHAN DOITSCHINOFF for Sepultura "Dante XXI" (CD, Vinyl album) *on SPV Records in 2006* - Metal -

STEPHAN DOITSCHINOFF for Sepultura "Dante XXI" (CD, Vinyl album) *on SPV Records in 2006* - Metal -

STEPHAN DOITSCHINOFF for Sepultura "Dante XXI" (CD, Vinyl album) *on SPV Records in 2006* - Metal -

CHRIS BOLTON for Radio Slave "Radio Slave Presents Creature of the Night" *on Eskimo Recordings in 2006* - Electronic Compilation -

RINZEN for Ponyloaf "O Complex" (CD) *on Valve Records in 2004* - Electronica -

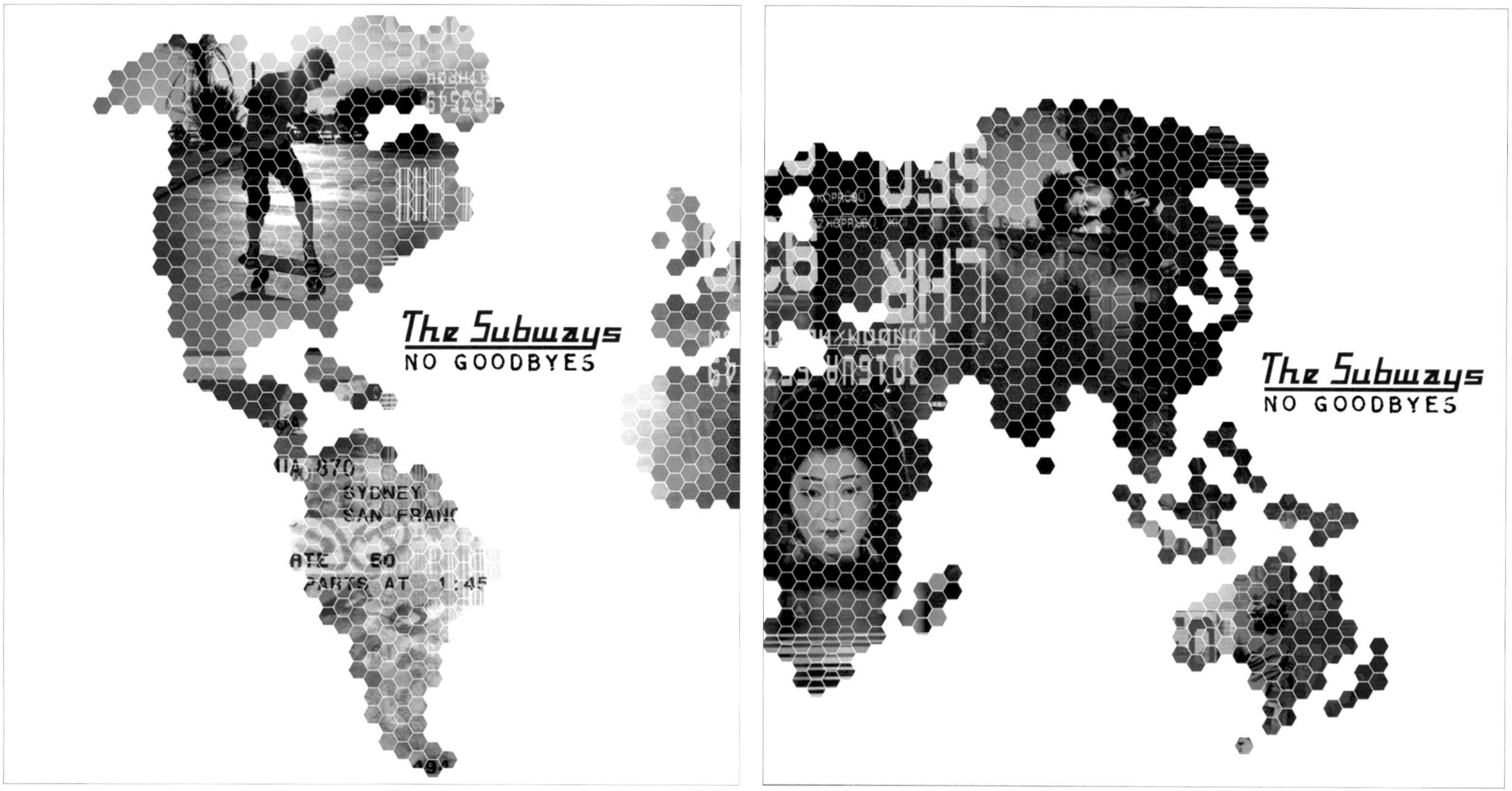

STYLOROUGE LTD, D.: SHARON CHAI **for The Subways** "No Goodbyes" (7"; specifically designed to encourage fans to buy both single formats) *on Infectious records in 2005* - Rock -

THE BACK BURNER, D.: MATT WAGNER **for The Potomac Accord** "Lemmons' Poster" (13 x 19 inch digital poster) *on First Flight Records in 2004* - Rock -

ANDRIO ABERO | 33RPM for Candle Records Showcase Poster (18"x 24" 3-color screen print) *on Candle Records in 2006* - Pop -

BIANCA STRAUCH for Hans Nieswandt "Ich vermiss die Zeit" (12") *on Mute Deutschland in 2005* - Electronic -

ANDRIO ABERO | 33RPM for Karen Pernick (CD) *in 2006*

Spy 51
Play For Your Life

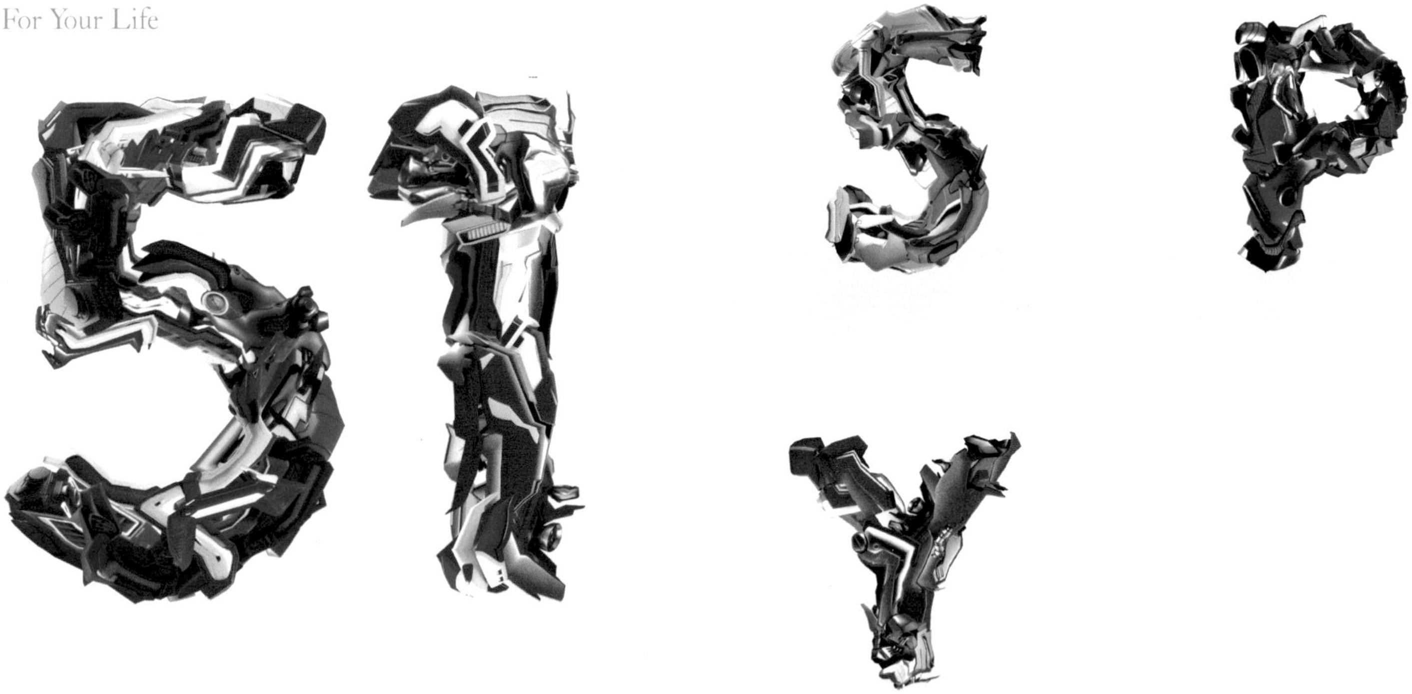

WALLZO, D.: **DARREN WALL for Spy 51** "Play For Your Life" (CD) *on Corporate Risk in 2006* - Pop -

TRAFFIC for Just Jack "Overtones" (Album CD - Booklet roll out) *in 2007* - Pop -

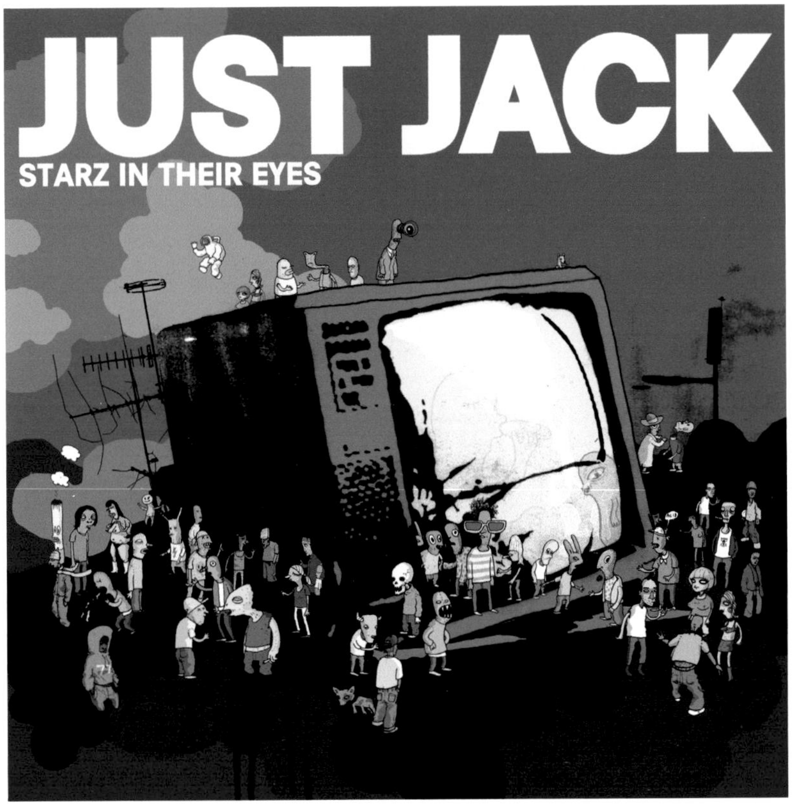

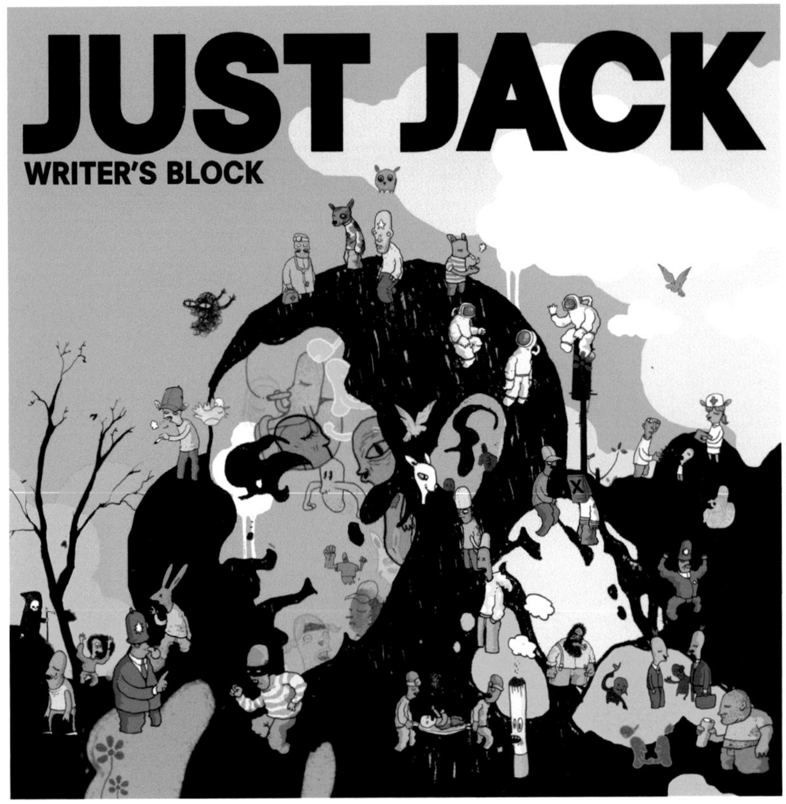

TRAFFIC for Just Jack "Overtones" (CD/ 7") *on Mercury in 2007* - Pop -

SELLOUT INDUSTRIES for Momentan "Soul mates" (24 x 24 cm / CD, LP)

SELLOUT INDUSTRIES for Malente "How can you still stand to stand still" (24 x 24 cm / CD, LP) *on Unique Records in 2006* - Electro / Funky Breaks -

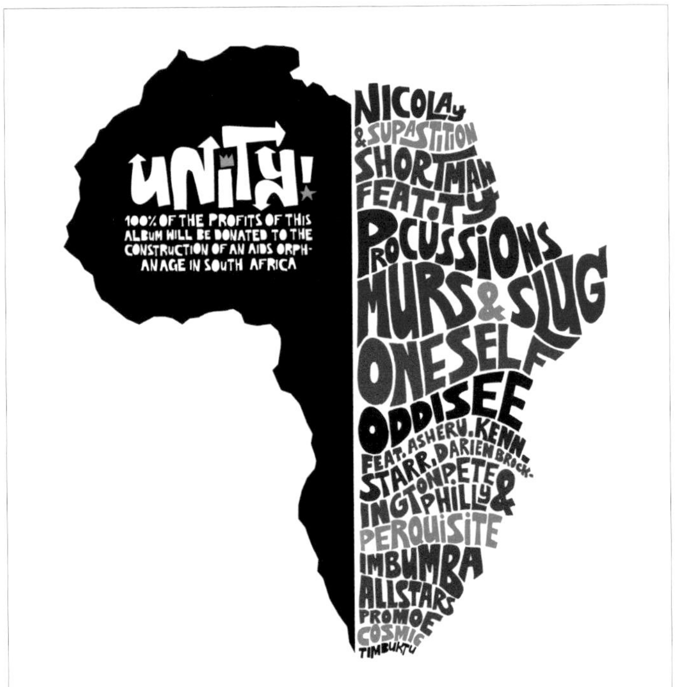

SELLOUT INDUSTRIES for V.A. "Unity" compilation (LP) *on Jakarta records in 2006* - Hip Hop / Breaks -

SELLOUT INDUSTRIES for Hardfloor "Our acid experience" (22.69 x 20 cm, CD) *on HMV Japan in 2005* - Acid Techno -

SELLOUT INDUSTRIES for Momentan "So far so good" (22,69 x 20 cm, CD) *on Mad Flava Music in 2006* - Hip Hop -

SELLOUT INDUSTRIES for Ursula 1000 / Federico Aubele "A night with esl music" (poster 20 x 21,38 cm) *on ESL Music / SSC Concerts in 2005* - Funky Breaks / Electro -

SELLOUT INDUSTRIES for DJ Rafik "Spread the message mixtape" (CD) *in 2006* - Turntableism - & for The Saint "Variety hour" (24 x 24 cm, CD) *on Mad Flava Music in 2006* - Hip Hop -

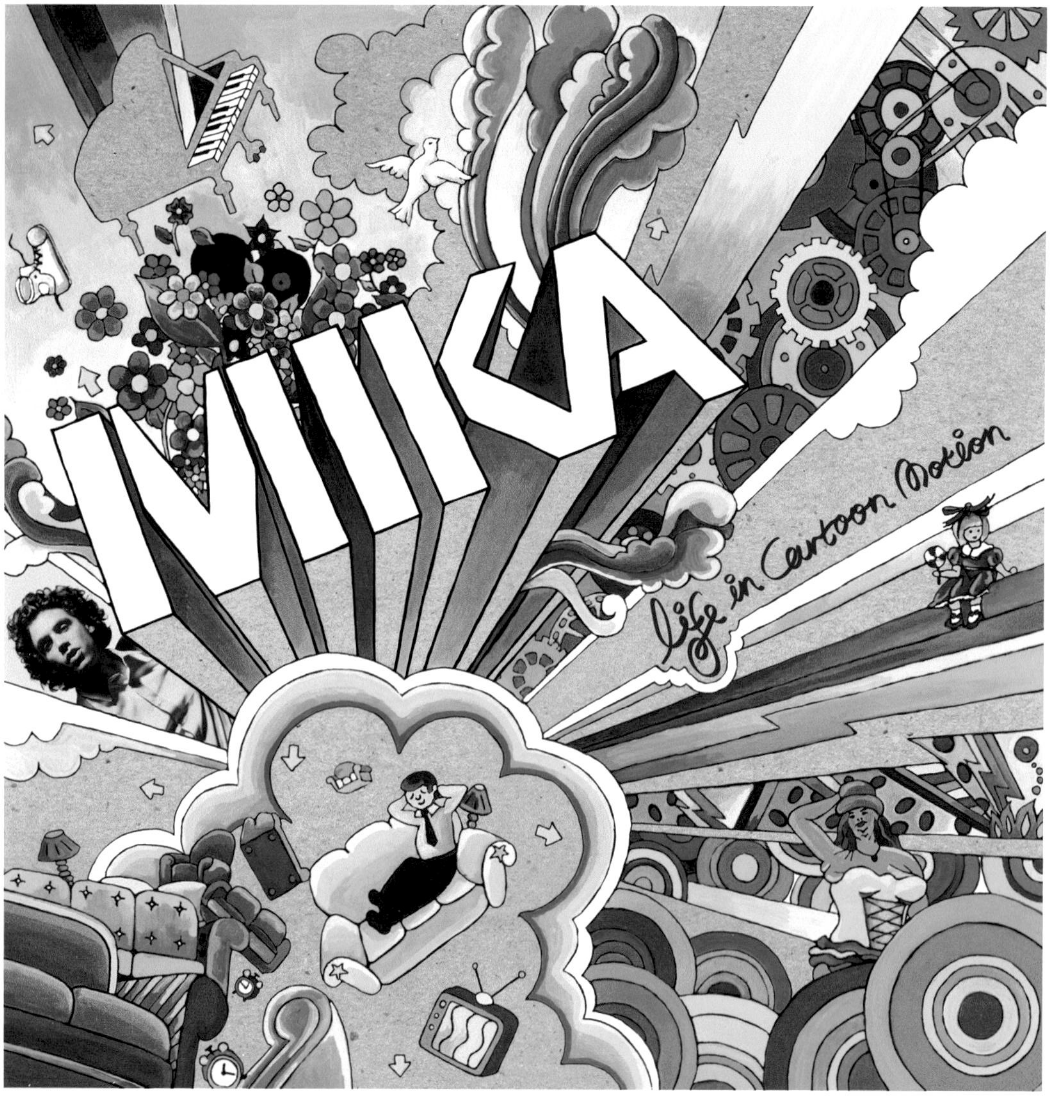

AIRSIDE AND MIKA **for Mika** "Life in Cartoon Motion" & "Relax" (LP & 7")
on Universal Music in 2006 - Pop -

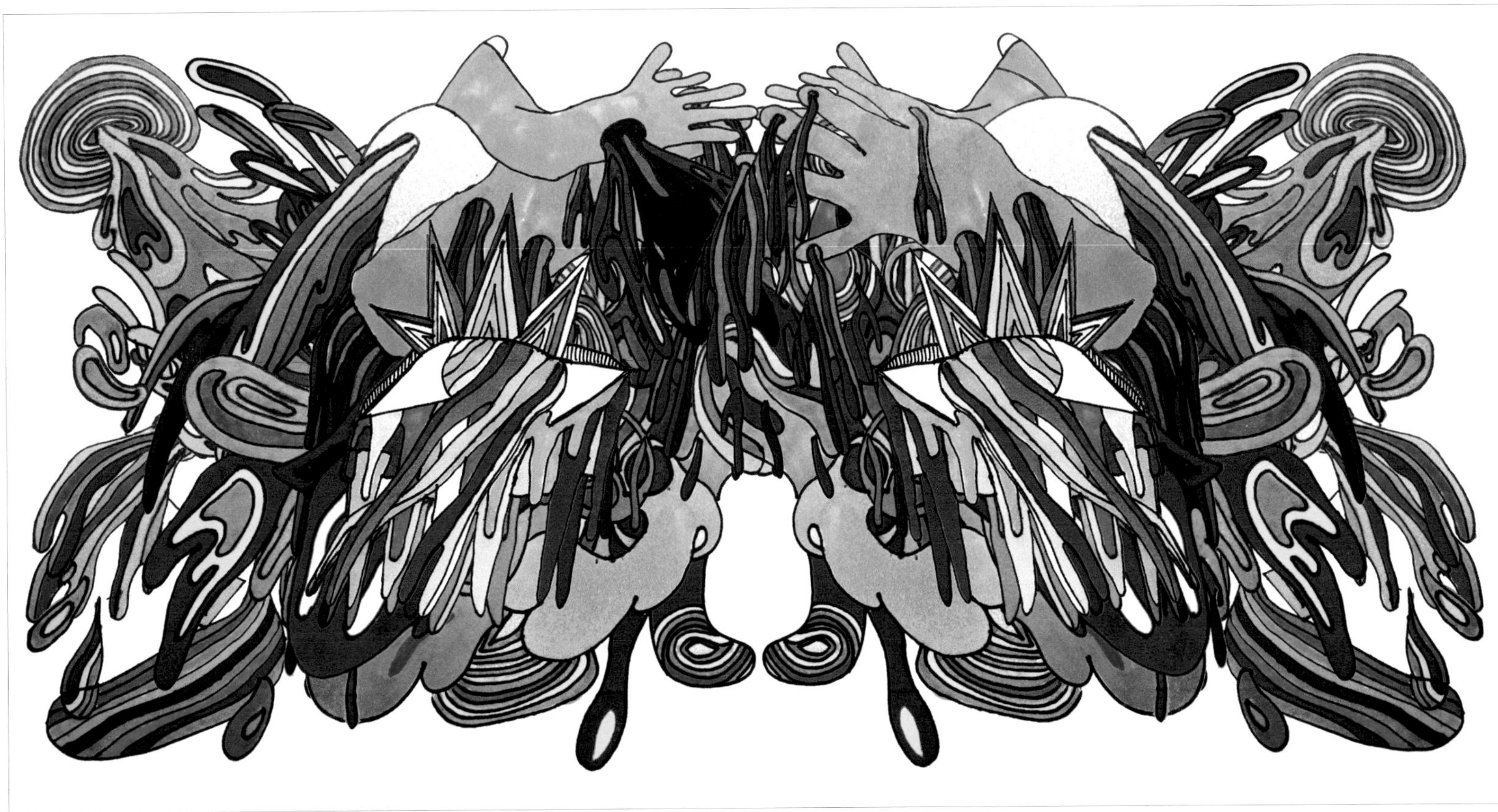

MADEWITHHATE for James Din A4 "Karl Der Käfer" (LP Poster Within Record) *on Esel in 2007*
- Jazzy Gypsy Rondo Metal Folk Minimal -

MADEWITHHATE for Pop Dylan "Take me to the slaughterhouse, I will wait there with the lamb" (LP) *on Esel in 2006* - Electronica -

ANDRIO ABERO | 33RPM for **Death Cab for Cutie** (18"x24" 3-color screen print) *in 2006*
- Indie Rock -

STYLOROUGE LTD, D.: SARAH FOLEY **for The Corrs** "Home" (CD)
on Atlantic in 2005 - Pop -

STYLOROUGE LTD, D.: SARAH FOLEY **for Sound & Vision (Cancer Research music event for charity)**
"Sound & Vision" (Poster) *on Cancer Research UK in 2007*

CHRIS BOLTON / LAURA LAINE for Make-Up Club
(Invitation) *in 2006*

MULTIFRESH, D.: **DAVID NAKAMOTO** for Audraglint fifth anniversary compilation "Silverware"
(CD) *on Audraglint in 2006*

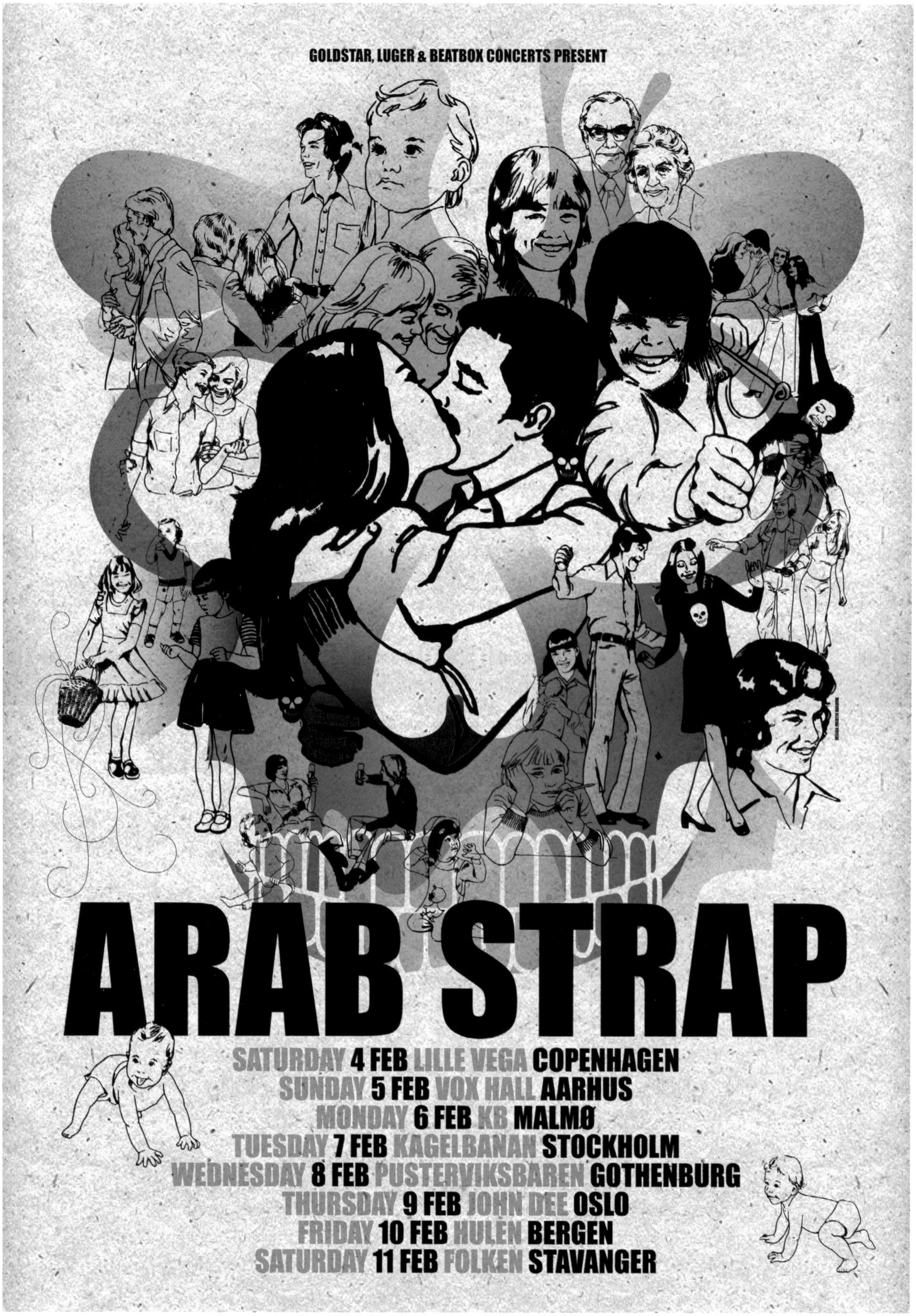

MARTIN KVAMME for Arab Strap (Poster printed on brown paper) *on in 2005*

MARTIN KVAMME / SVEIN KVAMME for Moving Oos "Love & Peace" (CD) *on Kong Tiki Records in 2007* - Rock -

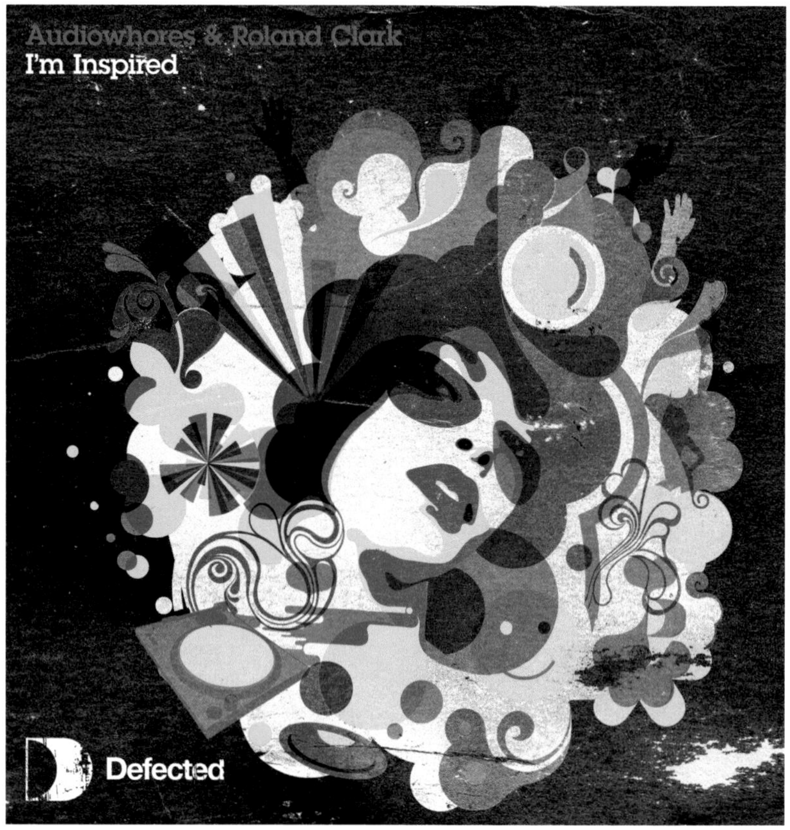

ZIP DESIGN, D.: NEIL BOWEN **for Copyright feat. Imaani** "I Pray", **for Copyright feat. Tasita D'Mour** "We Can Rise", **for Jose Burgos & Duce Martinez** "The Soul Creation Sessions" & **for Audiowhores & Roland Clark** " I'm Inspired" (12") *on Defected Records in 2006 - 2007 -* Dance -

ZIP DESIGN, D.: NEIL BOWEN **for Jason Hayes Jazz** "Pray For Love", **for Hanna Haïs** "(Je Ne Veux Plus Être) Ta Reine", **for Jamie Lewis & Michael Watford** "It's Over", **for Kathy Brown** "Get Another Love" & **for Ron Hall & The Mutherfunkaz feat. Marc Evans** "The Way You Love Me" (12") *on Defected Records in 2006 - Dance -*

GARY ST. CLARE for Robb Scott "Understanding" & "Anything You Like" (12") *on Sunshine Enterprises in 2005 & 2006* - Soul House Music -

GARY ST. CLARE for Robb Scott "Afro Odyssey" & "Revolution" (Vinyl)
on Sunshine Enterprises in 2006 - Soul House Music -

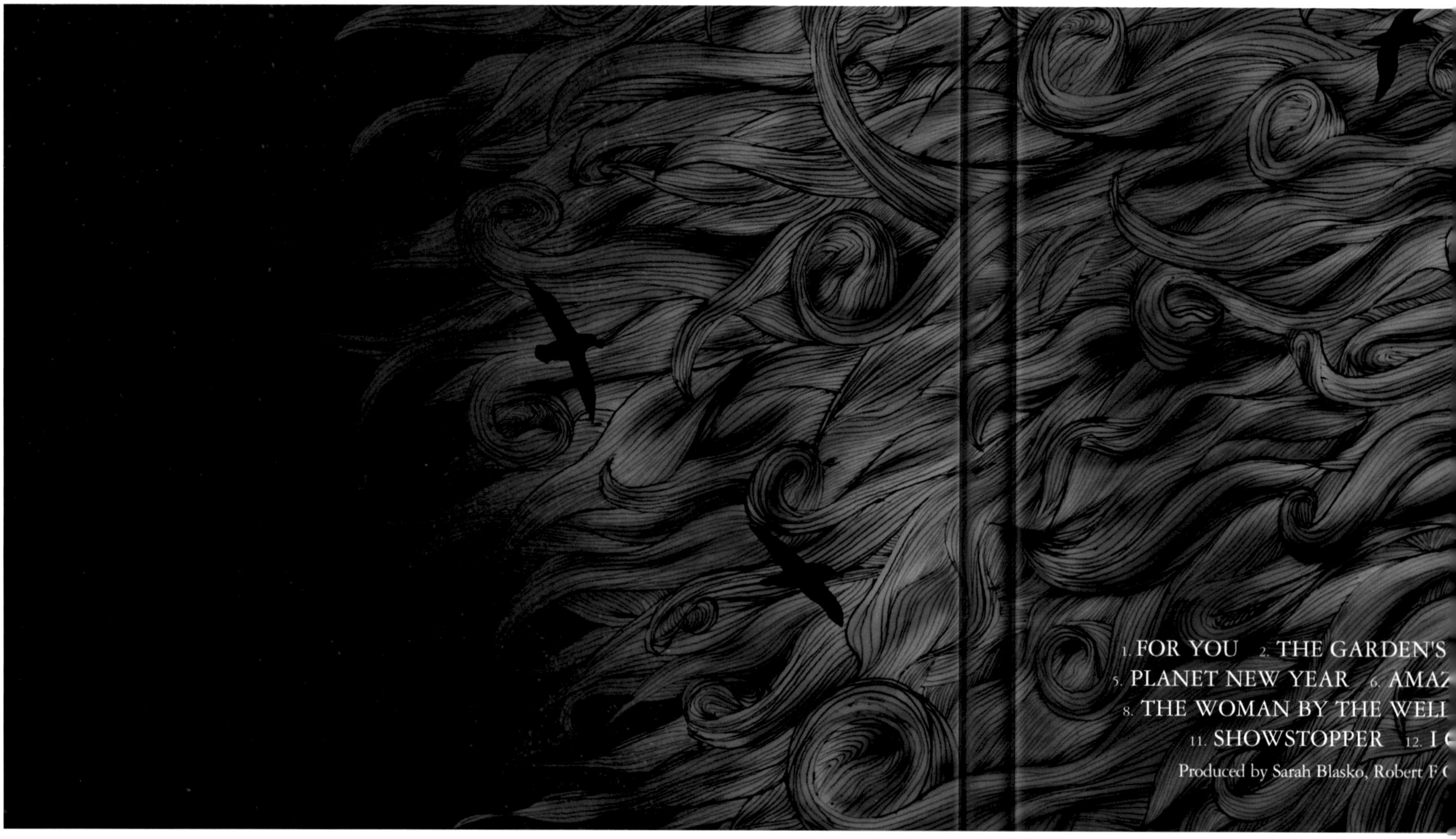

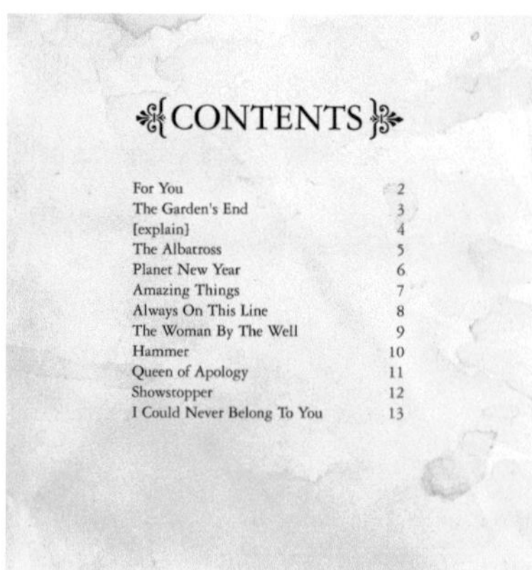

STYLOROUGE LTD, D.: SHARON CHAI **for Sarah Blasko** "What the Sea Wants, The Sea Will Have" (Special Edition digipak with spot UV varnish) *on Dew process in 2006* - Indie Rock -

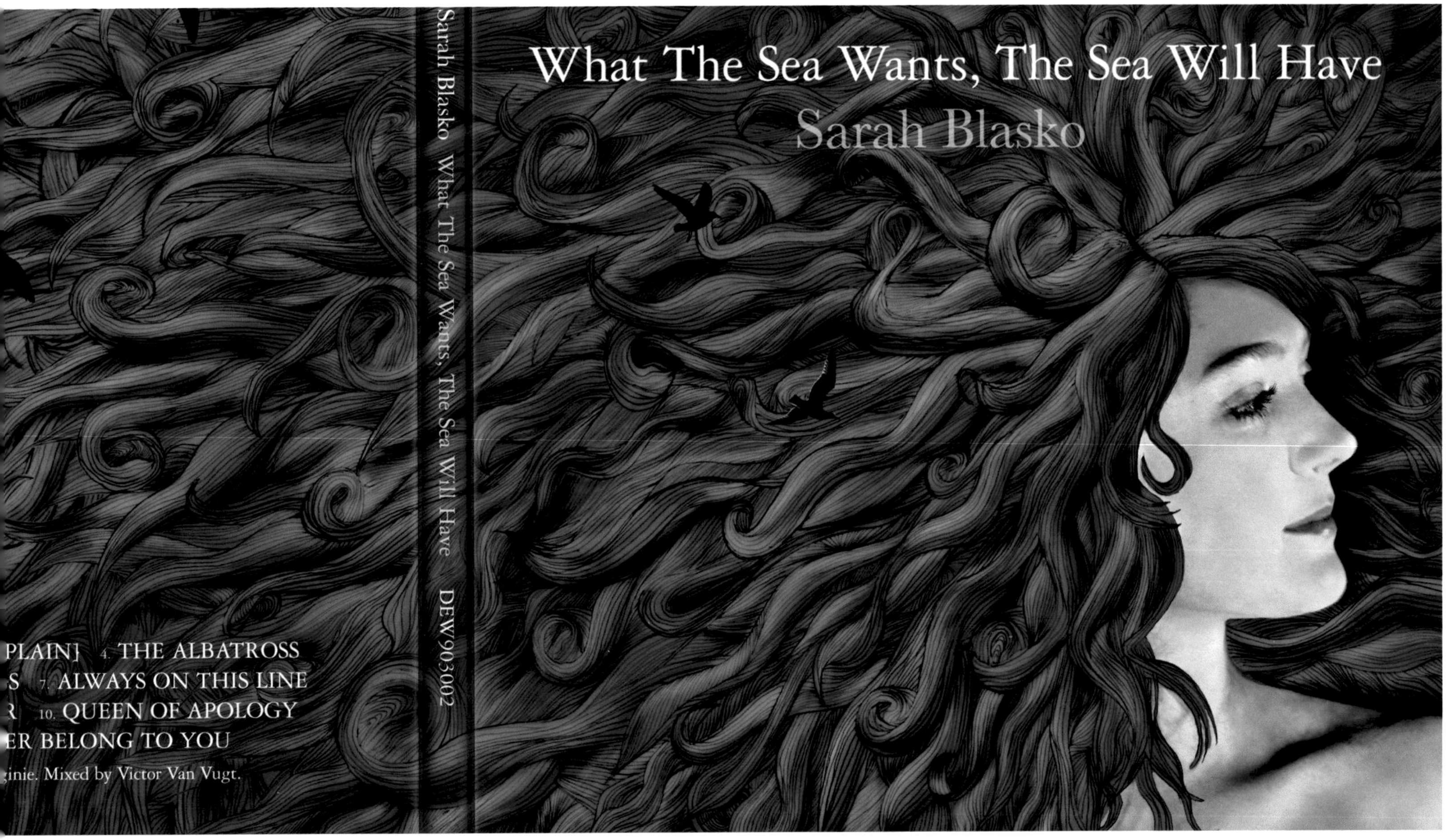
What The Sea Wants, The Sea Will Have
Sarah Blasko
Sarah Blasko What The Sea Wants, The Sea Will Have DEW903002
PLAIN] 4. THE ALBATROSS
S 7. ALWAYS ON THIS LINE
R 10. QUEEN OF APOLOGY
ER BELONG TO YOU
ginie. Mixed by Victor Van Vugt.

PLANET NEW YEAR

AMAZING THINGS

ALWAYS ON THIS LINE

THE WOMAN BY THE WELL

HAMMER

QUEEN OF APOLOGY

SHOWSTOPPER

I COULD NEVER BELONG TO YOU

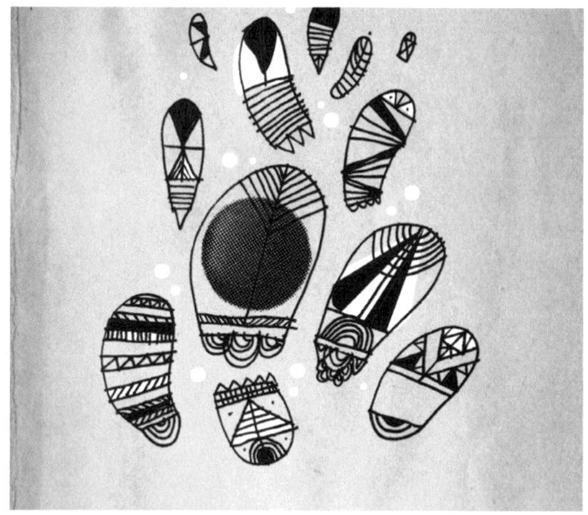

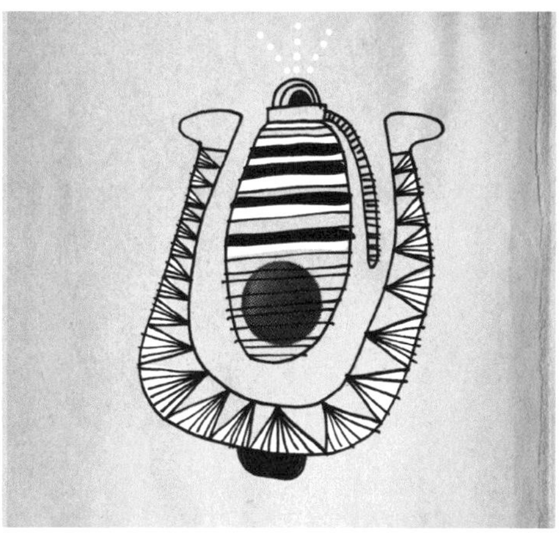

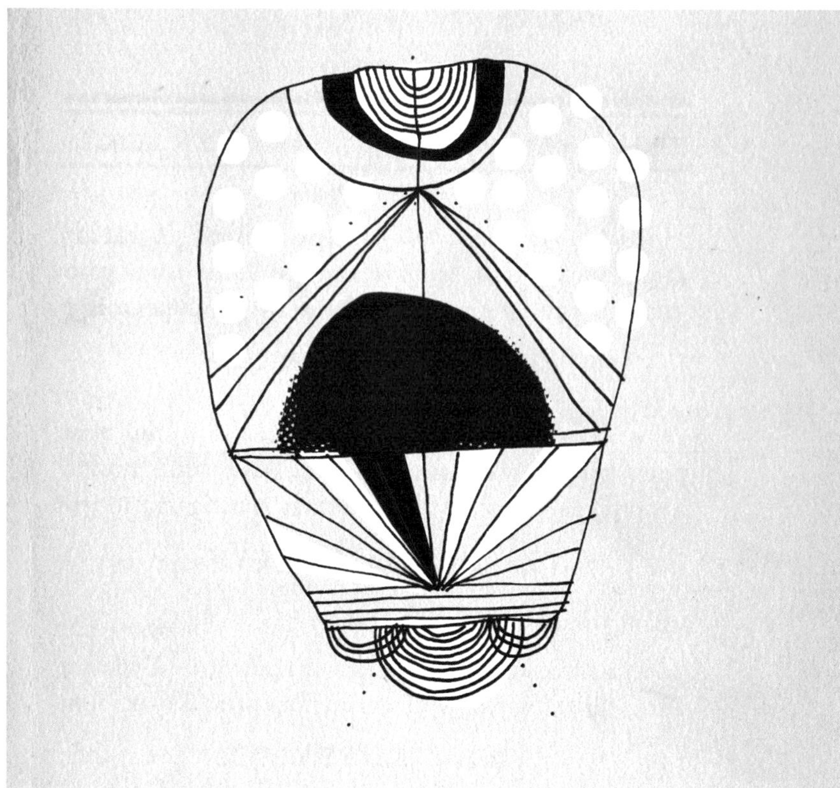

STRUGGLE INC. for The Berg Sans Nipple "Along the Quai" (CD) *on Team Love in 2007* - Abstract -

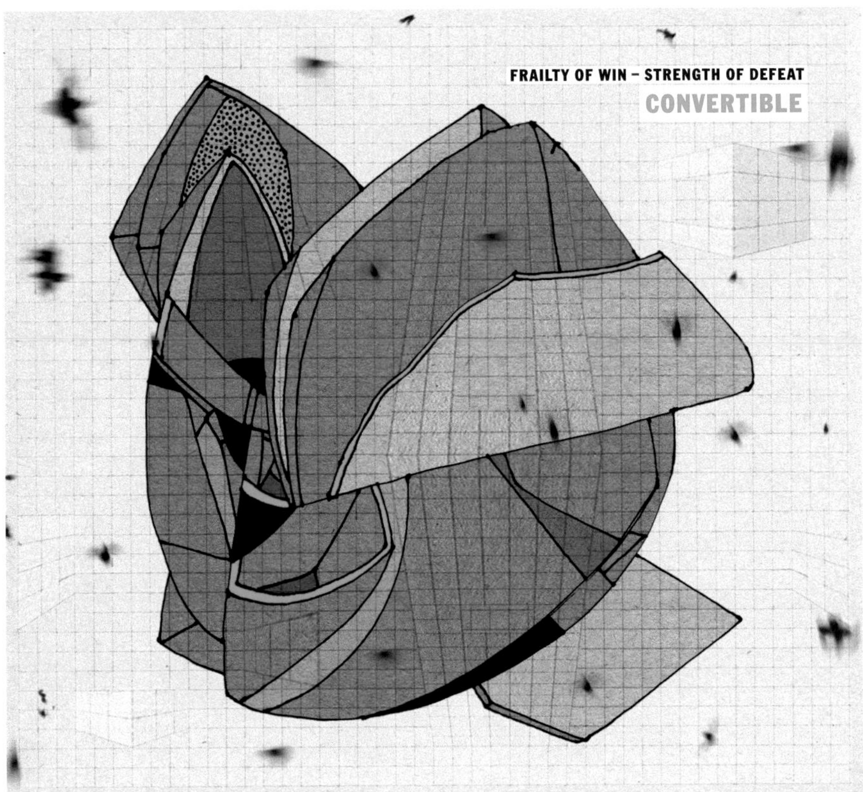

BUFFET FÜR GESTALTUNG for Convertible "Frailty of win - strength of defeat" (CD) *on Monkeymusic in 2005* - Indie -

CHRIS BOLTON for Lindstrom & Prins Thomas "Turkish Delight" & "Boney M Down" (12") & "Linstrom&Prins Thomas" (CD Foldout Poster/12" Gatefold)
on Eskimo Recordings in 2005 & 2006 - Electronic -

CHRIS BOLTON for Lindstrom & Prins Thomas "Mighty Girl" & "Sykkelsesong" (12")
on Eskimo Recordings in 2006 - Electronic -

INVISIBLE CREATURE, INC., D.: RYAN CLARK **for Haste The Day** "Pressure The Hinges" (CD) *on Solid State Records in 2007* - Metal -

SKIN DESIGN AS, D.: ARE KLEIVAN **for Amuelt** "Blessed & Cursed" (6 panel Digipack CD) *on Bitzcore in 2007* - Hardcore Punk -

BOOMPJE, D.: ROY GERRITSEN **for Refuse** "Need To" (Compact Disc.) *on Refuse in 2005* - Grunge Metal -

LA BOCA, D.: SCOT BENDALL **for Kelpe** "Sunburnt Eyelids" (12") *on DC Recordings in 2005* - Electronica -

kelpe
sunburnt eyelids

NIGEL PEAKE for Coldcut "Everything is Under Control" (7", 12", CD) *on Ninja Tune in 2005/6*

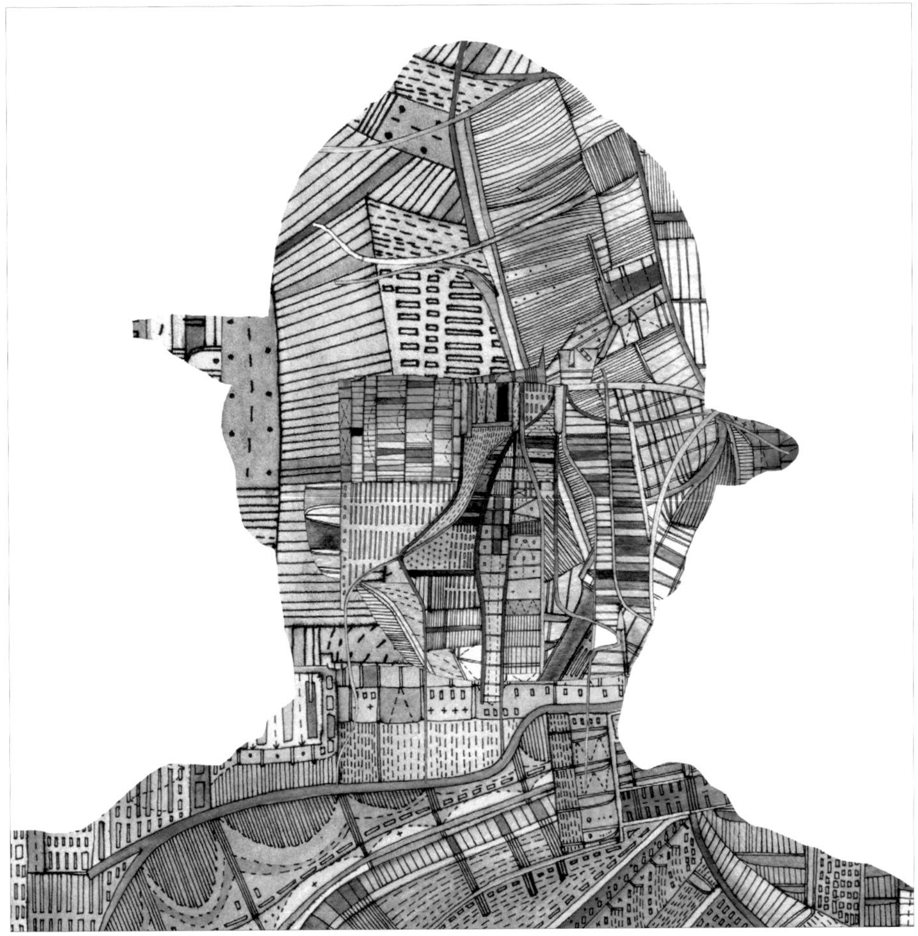

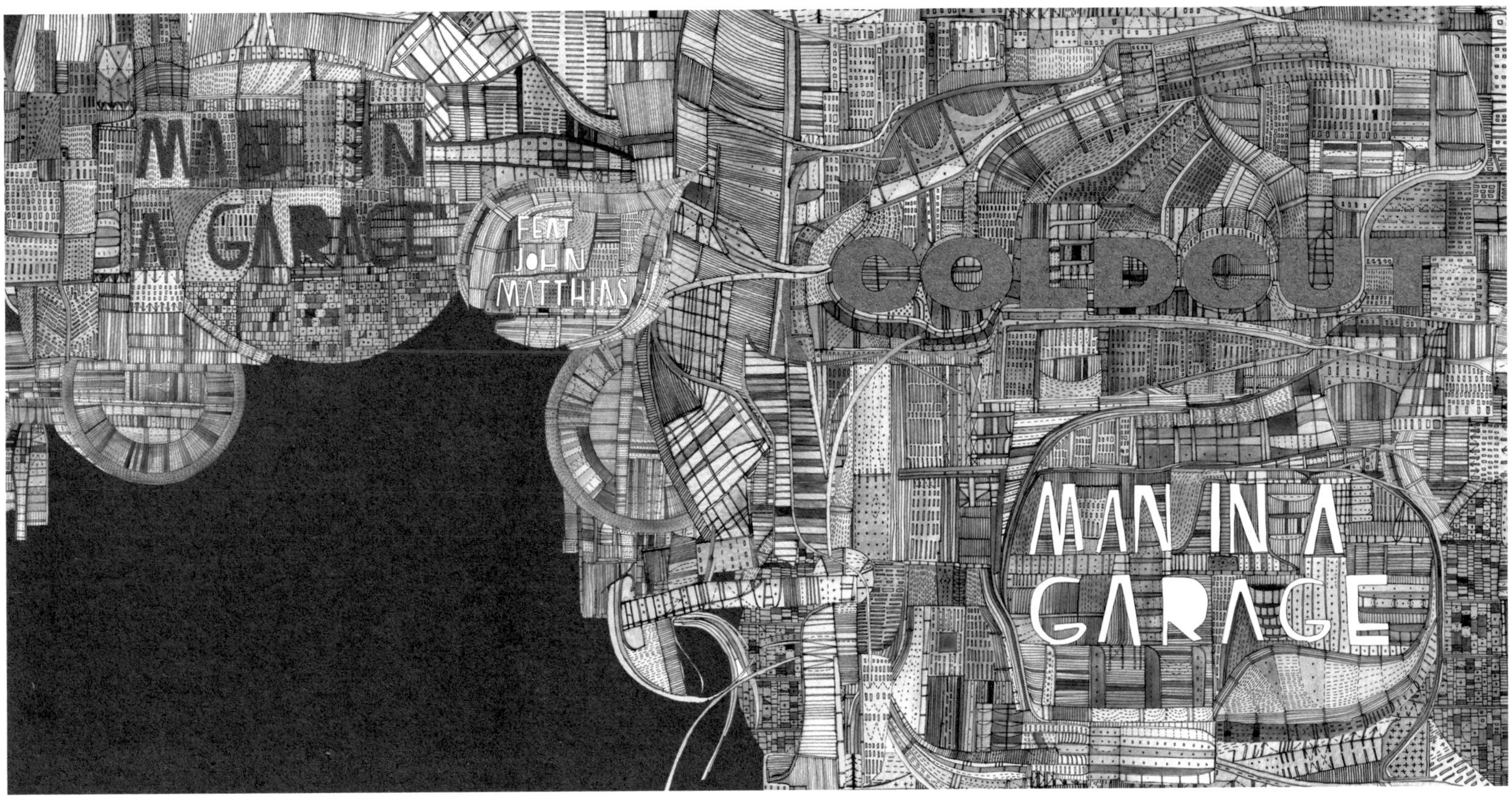

NIGEL PEAKE for Coldcut "Man in a garage" (7", 12", CD) *on Ninja Tune in 2005/6*

NIGEL PEAKE for Coldcut "Man in a garage" (7", 12", CD) *on Ninja Tune in 2005/6*

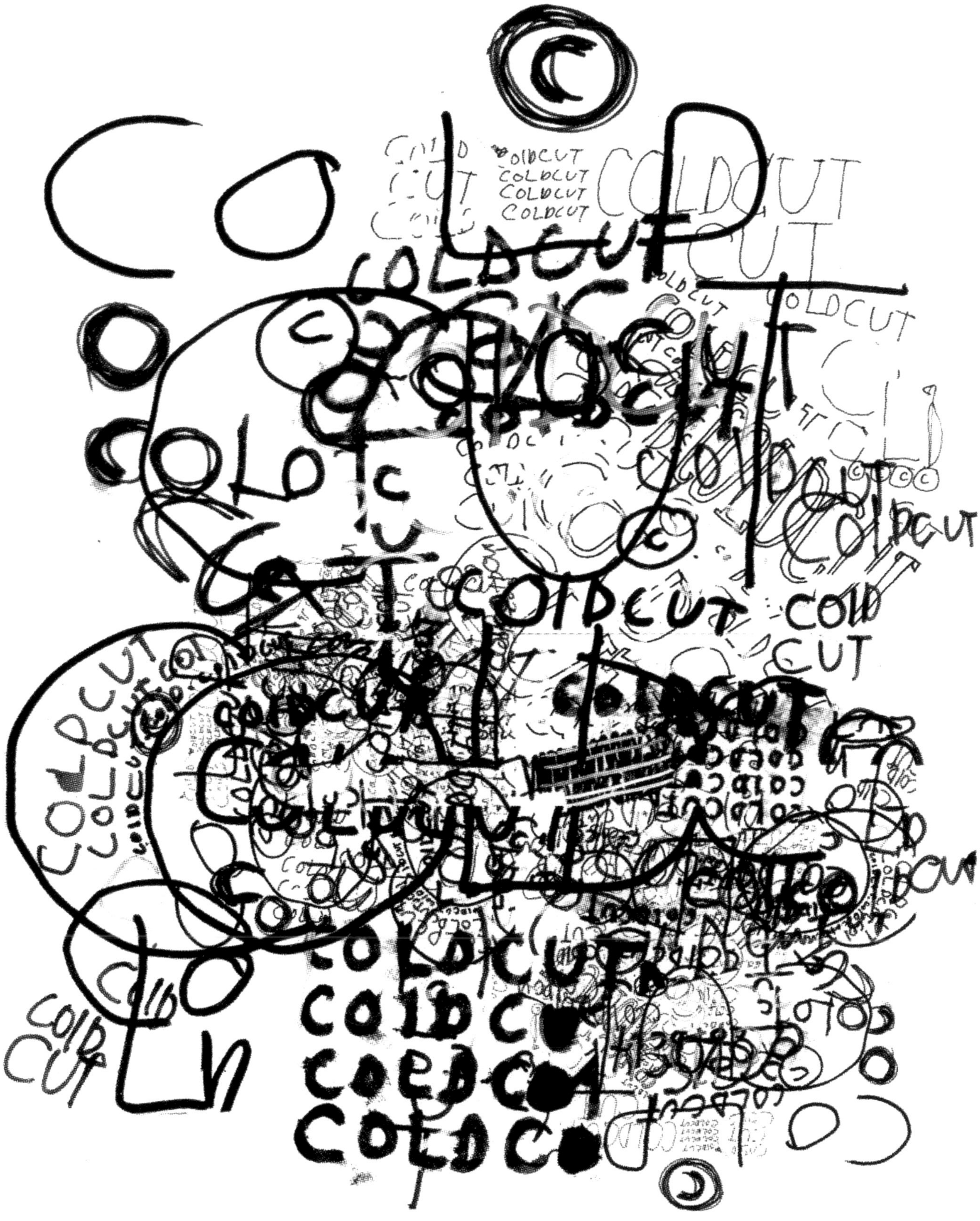

NIGEL PEAKE for Coldcut (Poster) *on Ninja Tune in 2005/6*

WARREN HEISE **for Dustin Cole / Try and Love Me** "Try and Love Me" (CD) *on Scratch Recordings in 2007*

ZIP DESIGN, D.: CHRISSIE ABBOTT **for BBC's Folk Britannia series and concerts at the Barbican** "Folk Britannia" (Branding and 14 x 14cm, 4pg booklet flyer) *on Barbican in 2005* - Folk -

SNASK, D.: MAGNUS BERG (A2 Gig Poster) *on Motivesounds Recordings in 2006*

JDK, D.: MIKE CARTER **for Dresden Dolls Show @ Higher Ground Music, October 27, 2005** (Hand screenprinted Poster) *in 2005*

MARTIN KVAMME / SVEIN KVAMME for The Ocean "Aeolian"
on Metal Blade in 2005 - Metal -

MARTIN KVAMME for Norwegian Chamber Orchestra Xenakis, Thommessen, Hegdal, Hvoslef "Corelli Machine" (CD) *on Aurora in 2006* - Contemporary -

HUMAN EMPIRE, D.: JAN KRUSE for B. Gibbard & A. Kenny "Home" (EP) *on Morr Music in 2005*

RINZEN for The Incredible Strand "The Name of this Band is" *on The Incredible Strand in 2005* - Pop -

THE BACK BURNER, D.: MATT WAGNER **for Emery Reel** "Second Story, Bloomington" (60x40 inch banner digitally printed on canvas) *on First Flight Records in 2006* - Instrumental Rock -

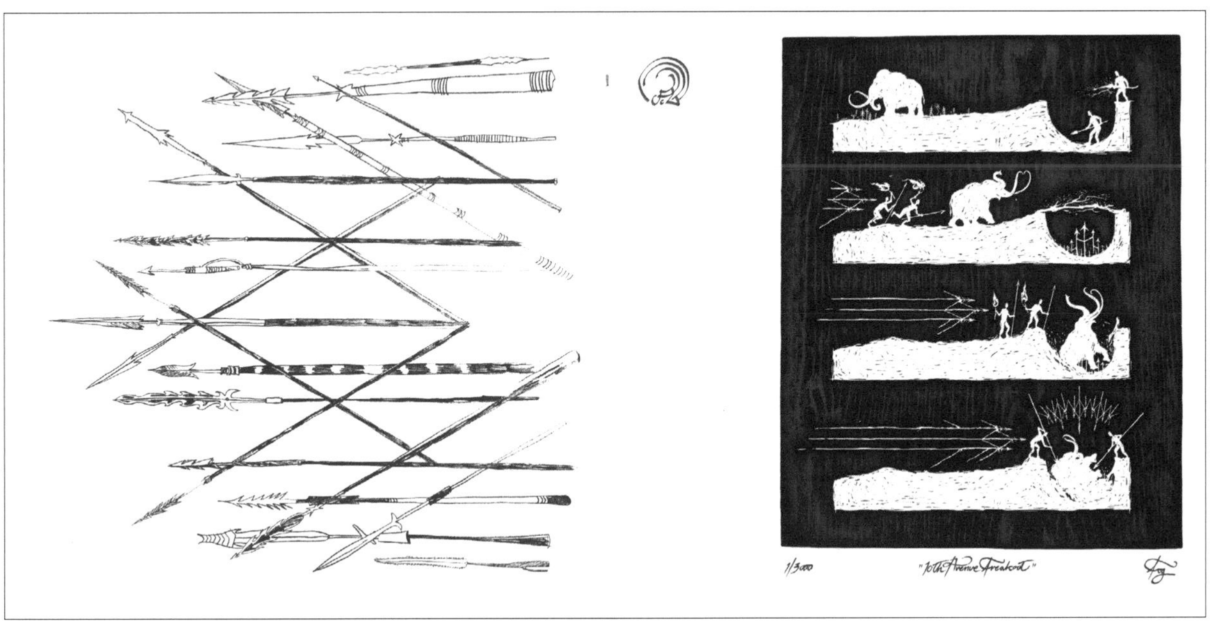

EHQUESTIONMARK for Fog "10th Avenue Freakout" (LP) *on Lex Records in 2005*

INVISIBLE CREATURE, INC., D.: DON CLARK **for Starflyer 59** "My Island" (CD) *on Tooth & Nail Records in 2006* - Indie -

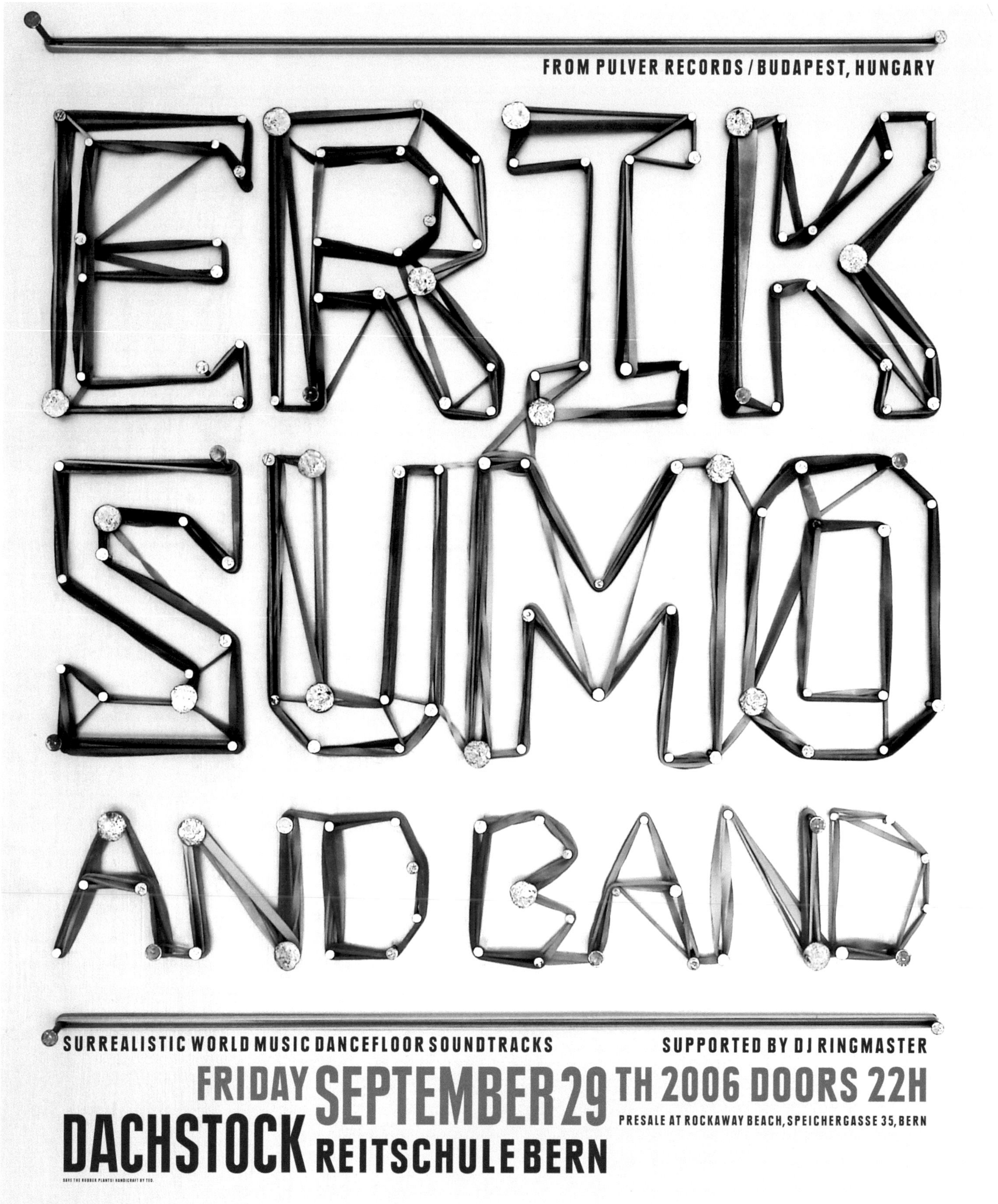

LORENZO GEIGER for Erik Sumo (Poster 42 x 52.5 cm) *in 2006*

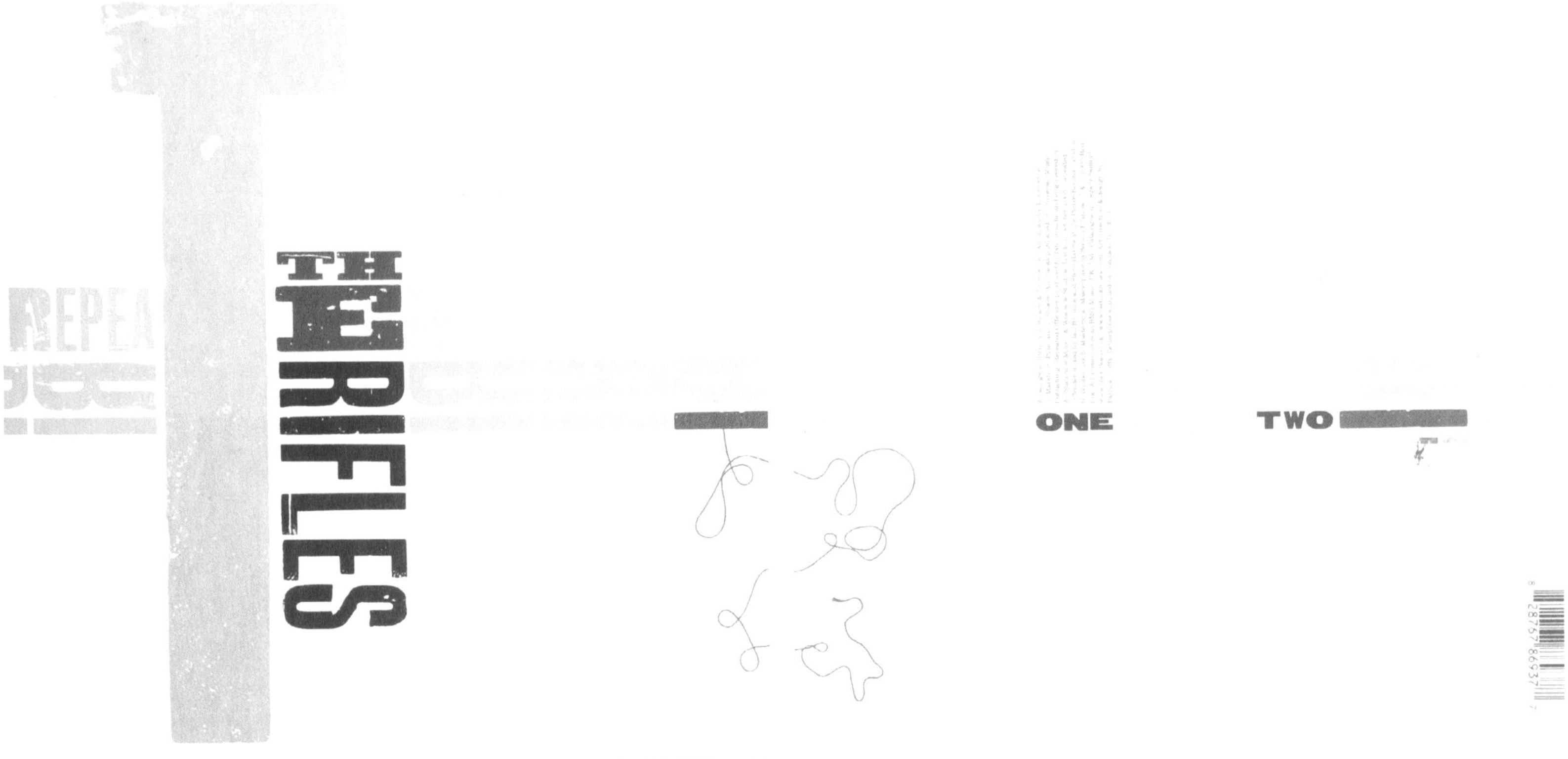

NO DAYS OFF, D.: PATRICK DUFFY **for The Rifles** "Repeated Offender" (Seven inch sleeve printed on uncoated board) *on Red Ink/SonyBMG in 2006*

NO DAYS OFF, D.: PATRICK DUFFY **for The Rifles** "Repeated Offender" (Seven inch sleeve printed on uncoated board) *on Red Ink/SonyBMG in 2006*

NO DAYS OFF, D.: PATRICK DUFFY **for The Rifles** "She's Got Standards" (Card wallet, printed on reverse board) *on Red Ink/SonyBMG in 2006* - Rock -

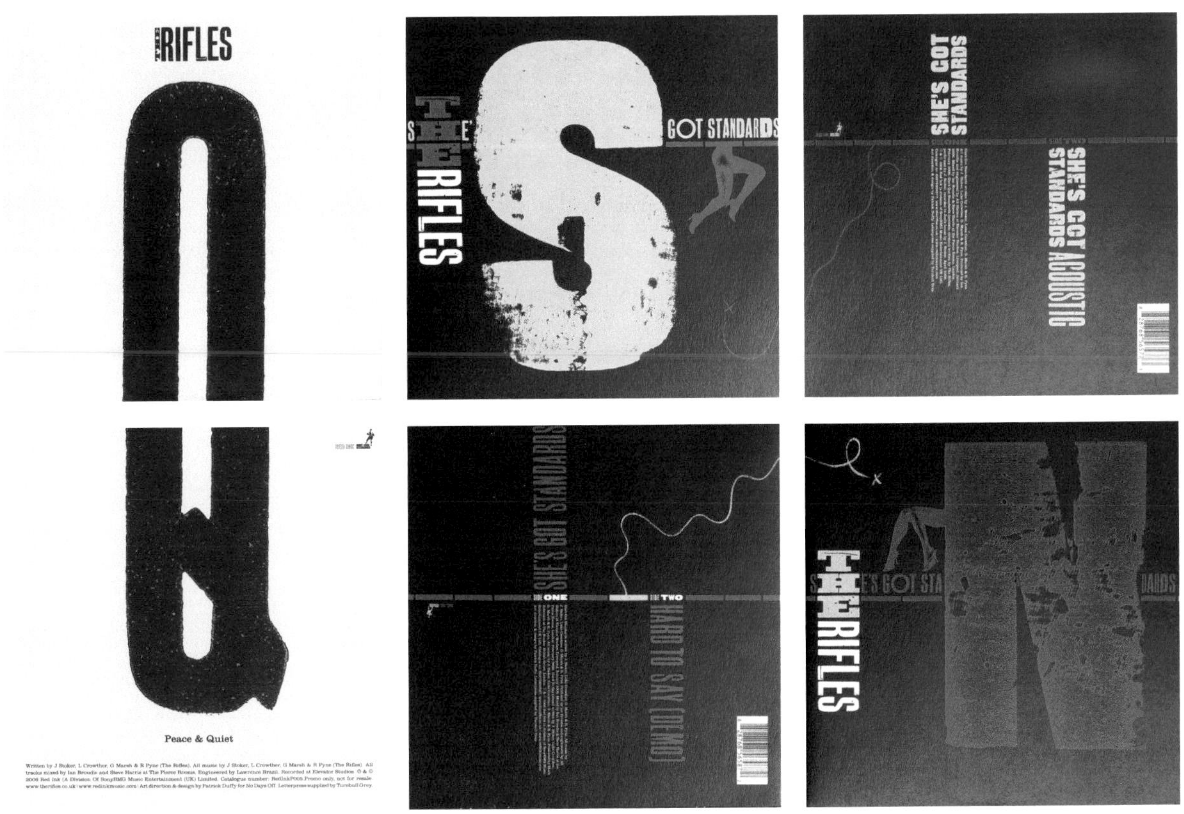

NO DAYS OFF, D.: PATRICK DUFFY **for The Rifles** "Peace & Quiet promo" (Card wallet printed on reverse board) & "She's Got Standards" (Seven inch sleeve printed on uncoated board) *on Red Ink/SonyBMG in 2006* - Rock -

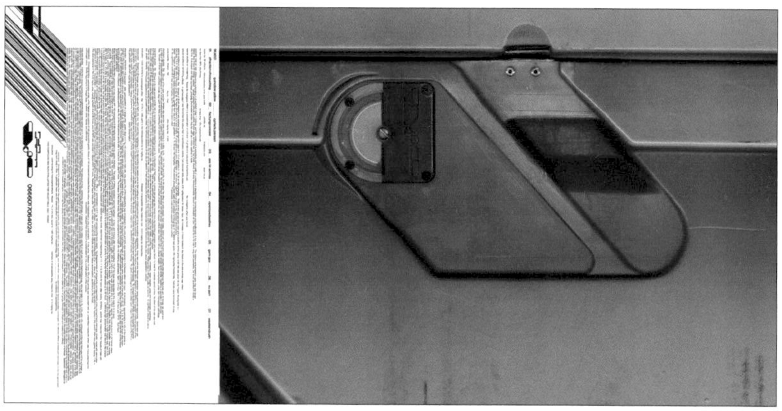

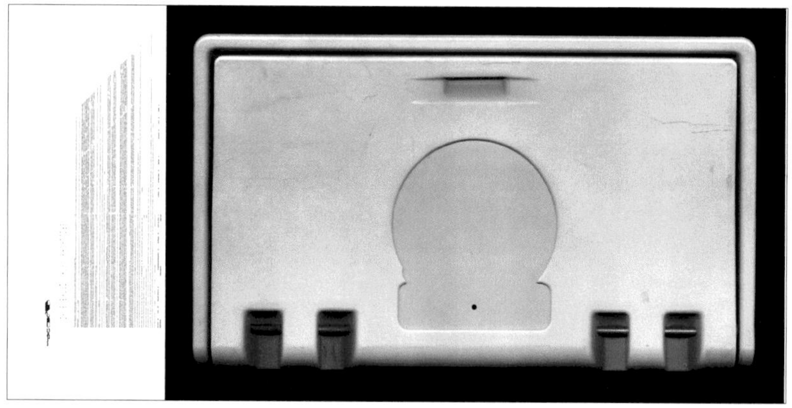

BHATOPTICS **for Quinoline Yellow** "Dol-goy assist" (LP) *on Skam in 2005*

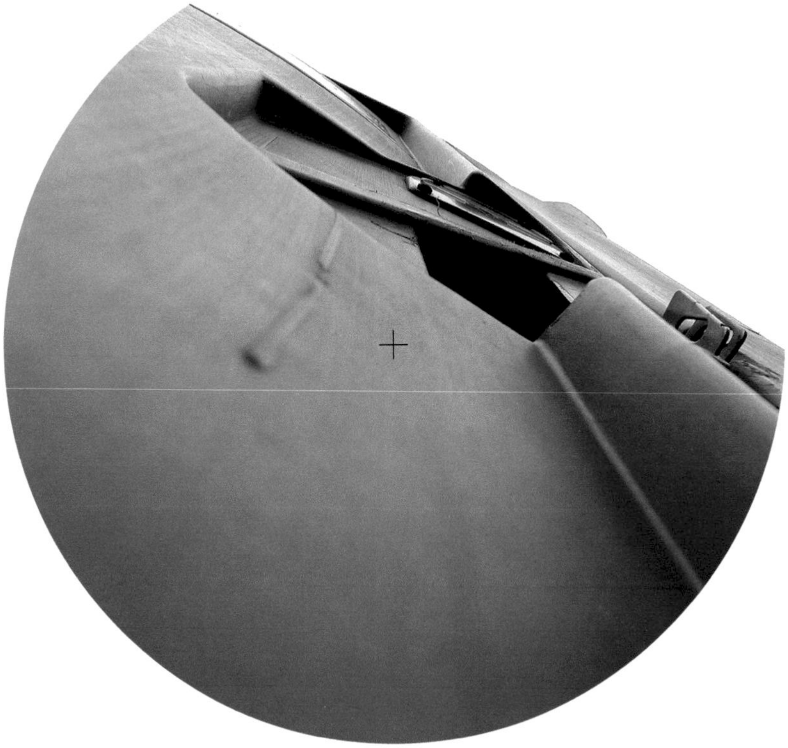

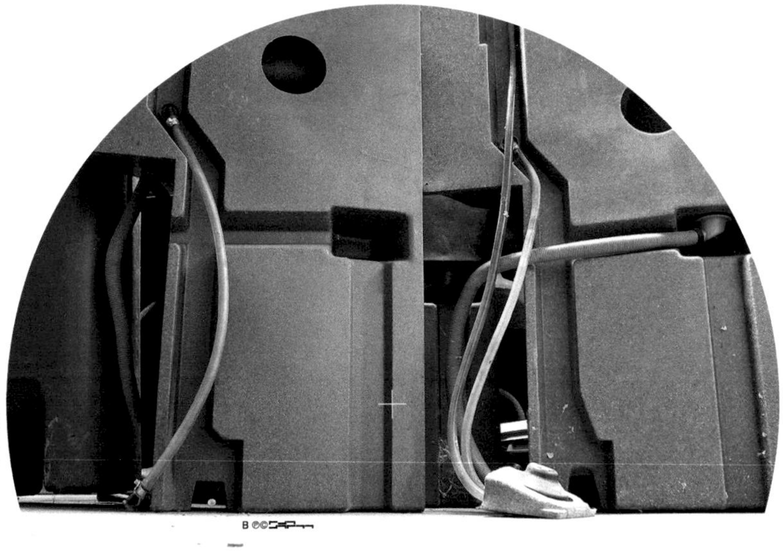

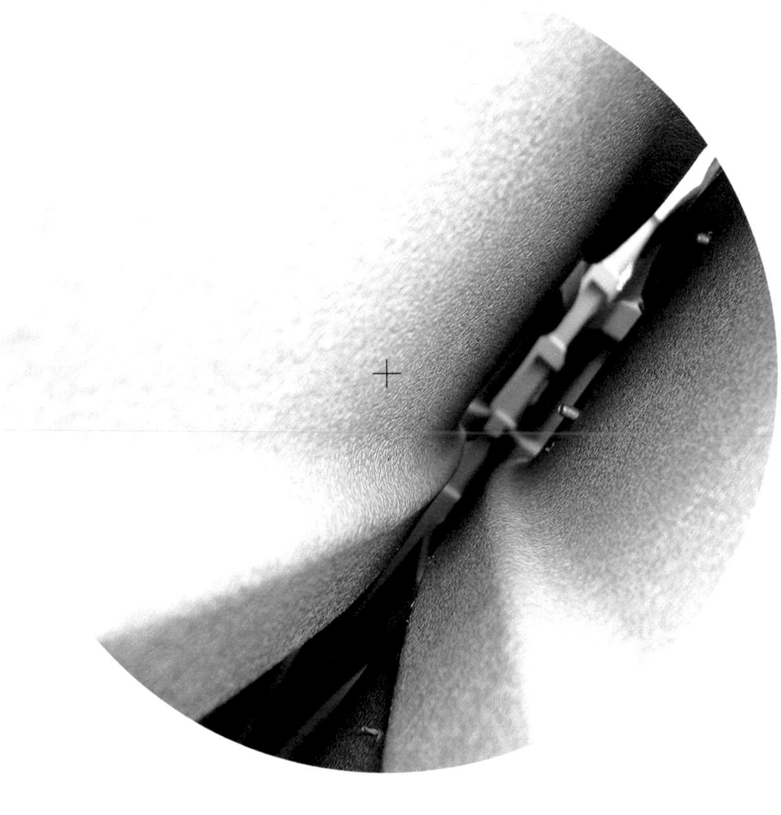

MARTIN KVAMME for Rolf Erik Nystrøm "Concepts of Sorrow & Dangers" (CD) *on Aurora in 2006* - Contemporary -

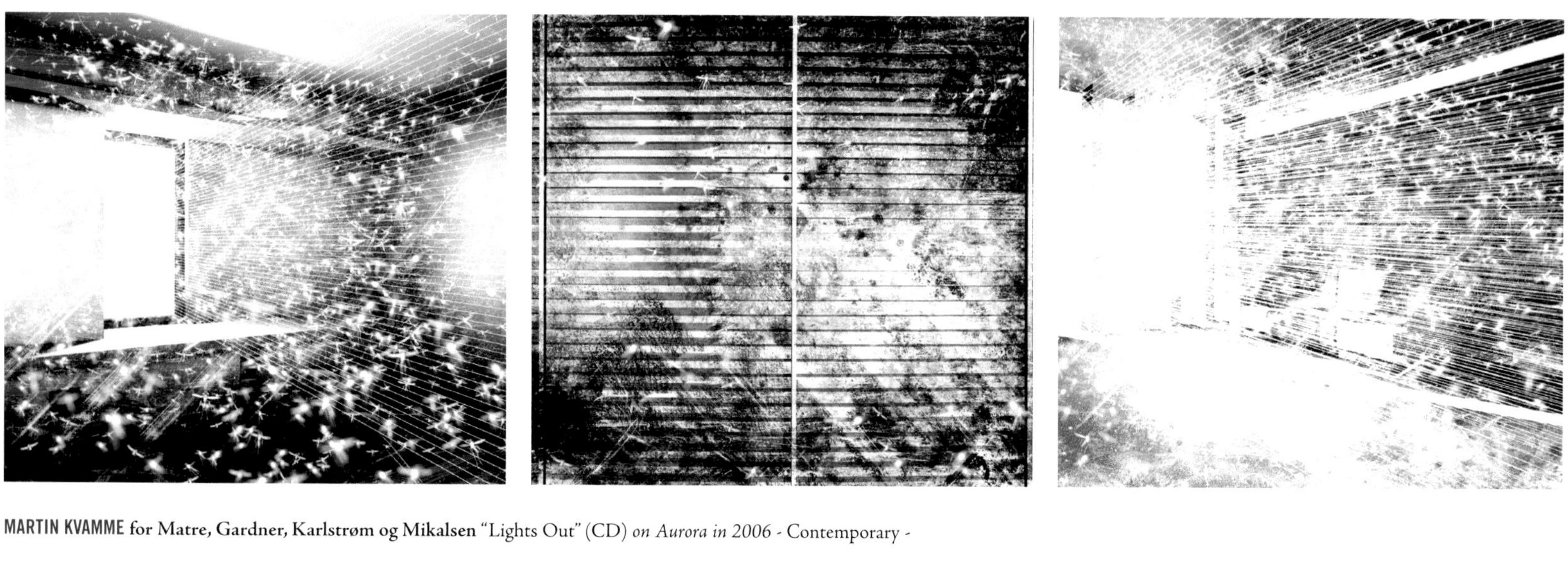

MARTIN KVAMME for Matre, Gardner, Karlstrøm og Mikalsen "Lights Out" (CD) *on Aurora in 2006* - Contemporary -

MARTIN KVAMME **for Rolf Erik Nystrøm** "Concepts of Sorrow & Dangers" (CD) *on Aurora in 2006* - Contemporary -

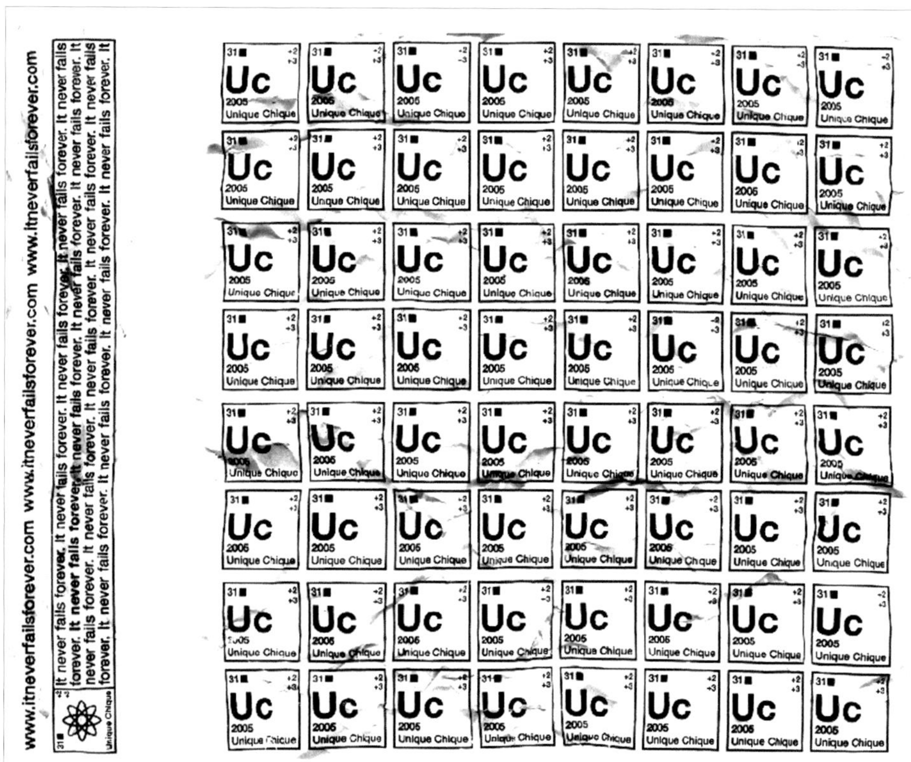

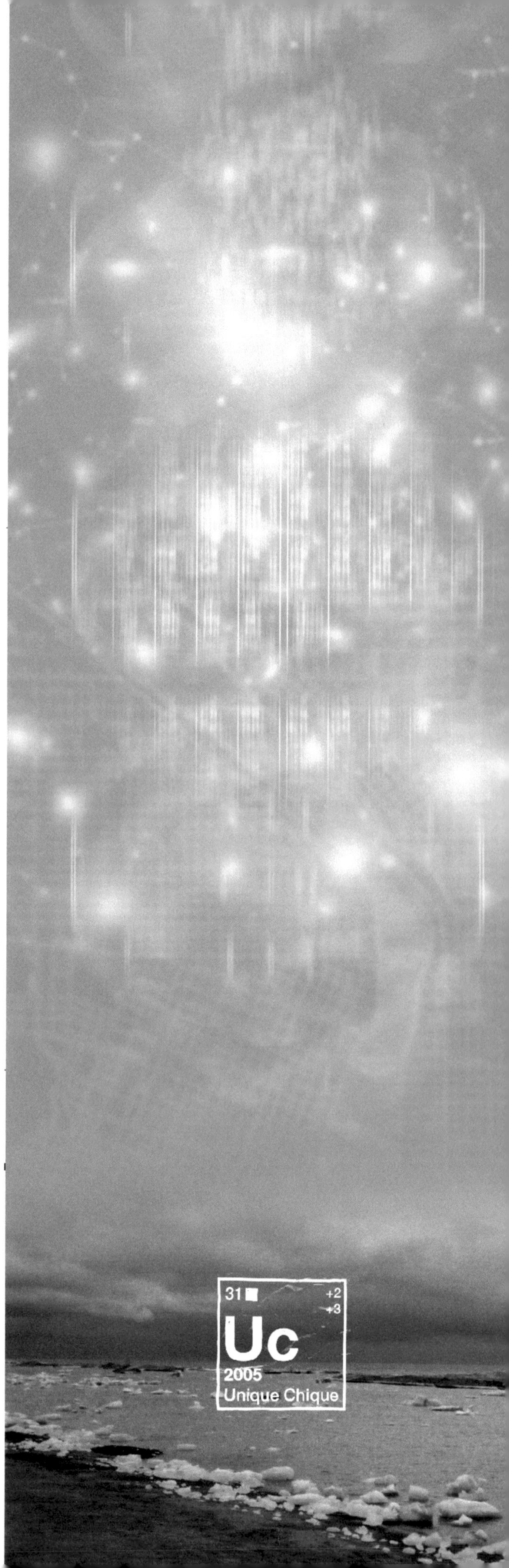

GREGG BERNSTEIN for Unique Chique "It Never Fails Forever" (CD)
on Alarm Clock Records in 2005 - Post-Punk -

GREGG BERNSTEIN for Mira Mira / Midnight for You "Midnight for You" (CD) *on Ickydog Music Group in 2006* - Chamber pop -

STYLOROUGE LTD, D.: MARK HIGENBOTTAM **for Undercut** "Singles- Delight, Soul Food Mother" (Commercial singles) *on Distiller Records in 2005* - Rock -

WEISSRAUM.DE(SIGN)°, D.: **BERND BRINK & LUCAS BUCHHOLZ** **for Energy 52** "Anthems 1.0 - Cafe Del Mar" & "Anthems 3.0 Cafe Del Mar" (Vinyl Cover) *on Grand Casino in 2004*

LAURA VARSKY **for Semilla** "Semilla" (CD) *on Surco – Universal Music in 2006* - Argentinean Folk-Rock -

MARTIN KVAMME for 120 Days/Serena-Maneesh (Poster 50x70) *in 2007* - Alternative -

STYLOROUGE LTD, D.: ANTHONY LUI **for JJ72** "Coming Home" (CD Single - Jewel Case & Poster) *on Lakota in 2005* - Indie -

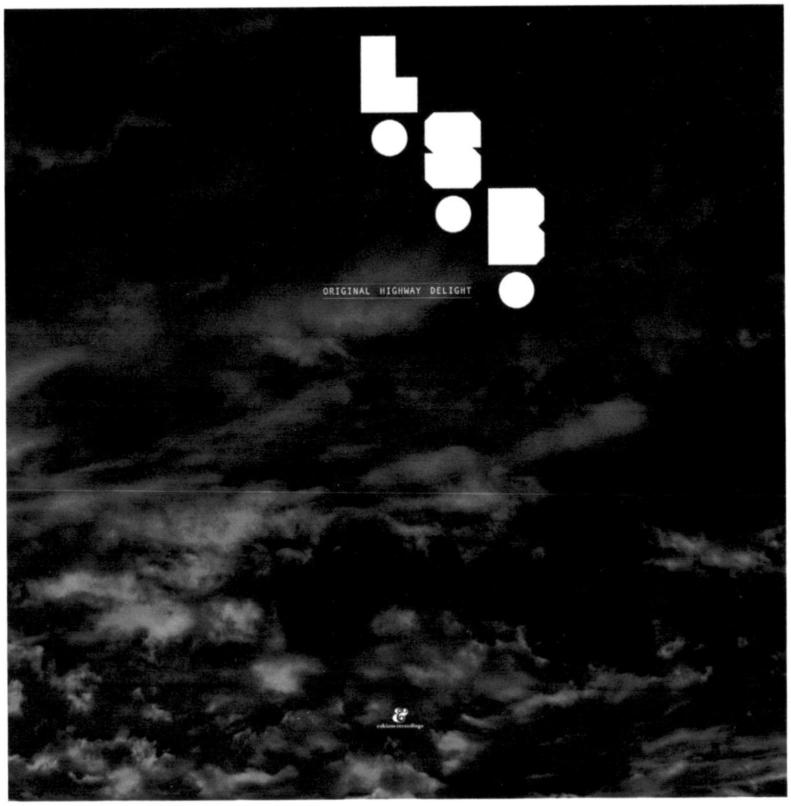

CHRIS BOLTON for **L.S.B.** "Original Highway Delight" (12") *on Eskimo Recordings in 2006* - Electronic -

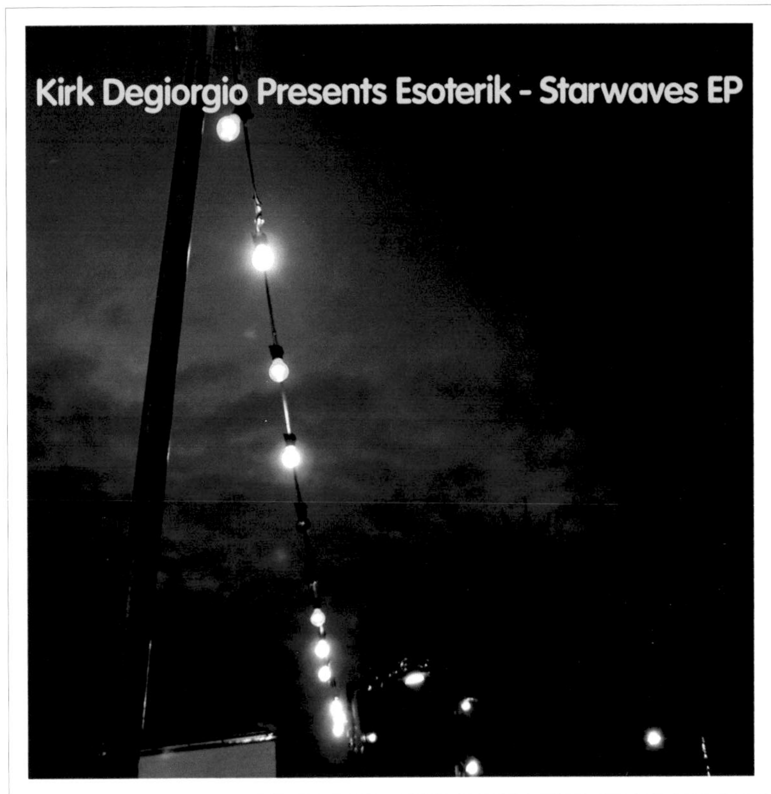

JAWA AND MIDWICH, D.: NILS DAVEY AND SIMON DOVAR for **Kirk Degiorgio** "Kirk Degiorgio Presents Esoterik – Starwaves EP" (12") *on Freerange Records in 2005* - House -

STYLOROUGE LTD, D.: SHARON CHAI for **Colin Towns & NDR Bigband** "Lend Me Your Ears" (CD) *on Provocateur Records in 2006* - Jazz -

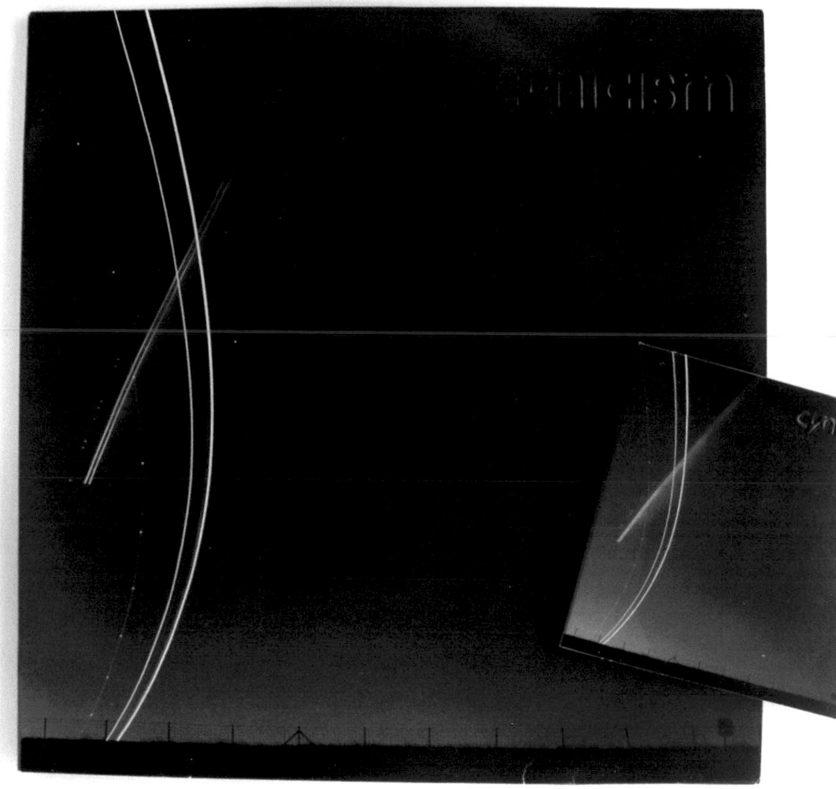

RED DESIGN for **Cynicism** "Cynicism" (LP, CD) *on Cynic Records in 2006* - Deep House -

MARTIN KVAMME / SVEIN KVAMME for The Ocean "Aeolian" *on Metal Blade in 2005* - Metal -

MARTIN KVAMME / SVEIN KVAMME for The Ocean *"Aeolian"* on *Metal Blade in 2005* - Metal -

BOOMPJE, D.: ROY GERRITSEN **for Camino Blue** "Ten Short Stories" (CD) *on Camino Blue Recordings. in 2006* - melodic atmposheric Drum n Bass -

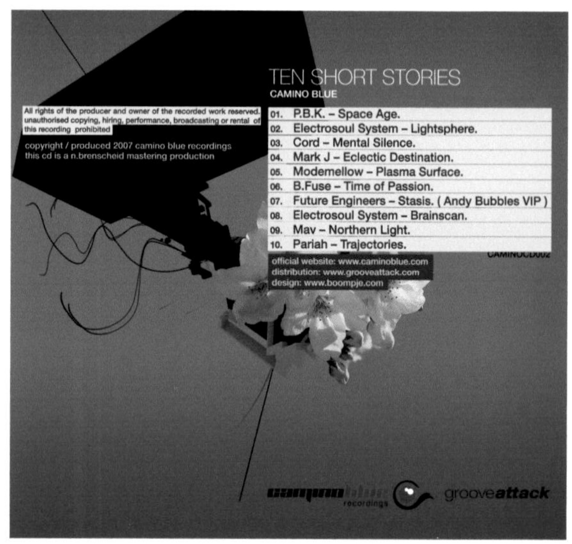

BOOMPJE, D.: ROY GERRITSEN **for Into the machines** (CD) *on Triple Vision in 2005* - Techno -

BOOMPJE, D.: ROY GERRITSEN **for MAV "Ocean Phantom", "Special Forces"** & "Chasm" (CD) *on Scientific Records in 2006* - Atmospheric Drum n Bass -

HANS SCHABUS for Naked Lunch "Military Of The Heart" (CD) *on Louisville Records in 2007*

WEISSRAUM.DE(SIGN)°, D.: BERND BRINK & LUCAS BUCHHOLZ for Trentemøller "The Last Resort" (Poster) *on Poker Flat Recordings in 2006* - Electronica -

BIANCA STRAUCH WITH JAN JELINEK for Jan Jelinek "Tierbeobachtungen" (CD) *on Scape in 2006* - Electronic -

HANS SCHABUS for Naked Lunch "This Atom Heart Of Ours" (CD)
on Louisville Records in 2007

VIVELETUNING, D.: **HELM PFOHL & CHRAGI FREI for Monochrome** "éclat" (12")
on Sticksister in 2006 - Pop -

INVISIBLE CREATURE, INC., D.: **RYAN CLARK for Fair** "The Best Worst-Case Scenario" (CD) *on Tooth & Nail Records in 2006* - Indie -

STRUGGLE INC. for Piano Overlord
"Aninha Mission" (LP) *on Chocolate Industries in 2007* - Abstract -

BIG ACTIVE for Vega 4 "You & Others" (Album) *on Sony/BMG in 2006. Art Direction: Richard Andrews & Gerard Saint @ Big Active, Design: Richard Andrews @ Big Active, Photography: Annabel Elson/Lindsay Milne.* - Pop -

RED DESIGN for Bonobo "Days To Come" (CD, 12") *on Ninja Tunes in 2006* - Soul / Trip Hop -

IO SZUDIO for Isolation Years "Sign, Sign" (CD)
on Stickman Records in 2007

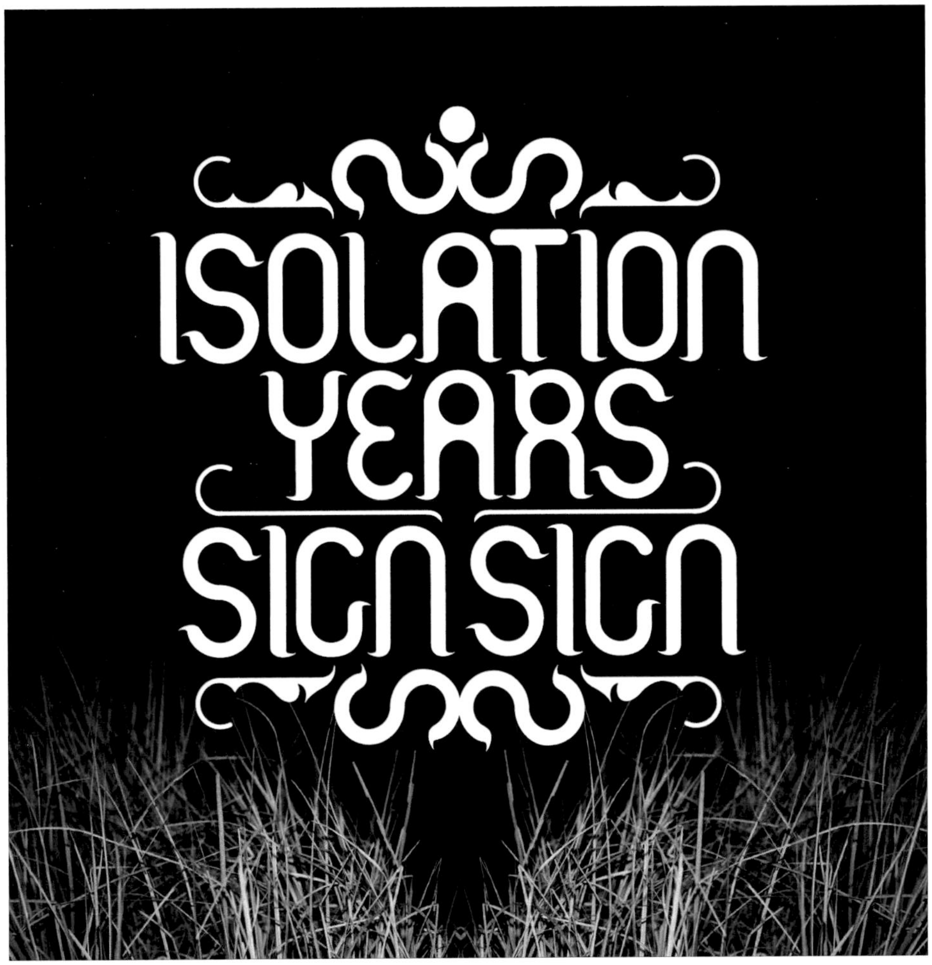

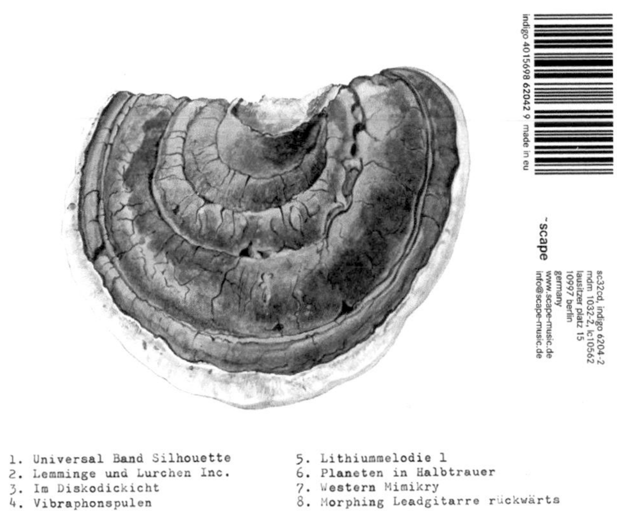

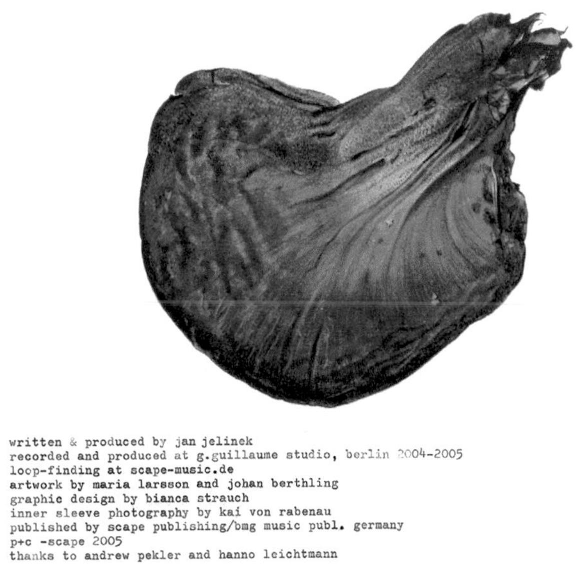

BIANCA STRAUCH for Jan Jelinek "Kosmischer Pitch" (CD/LP) *on Scape in 2005* - Electronic -

DIRK RUDOLPH for Virginia Jetzt! "Land unter" (CD) & "Mehr als das" (CD-Maxi) *on Universal in 2006; Photography by Harald Hoffmann & Dirk Rudolph, Thomas Kretzschmar* - Rock -

DIRK RUDOLPH for Phillip Boa & The Voodooclub "Burn All The Flags" & "Decadence & Isolation" (CD-Maxi) & "Decadence & Isolation" (CD) *on Motor Music in 2005; Photography by Olaf Heine* - Rock -

MULTIFRESH, D.: DAVID NAKAMOTO **for The Blow remixed by Strategy and Caro** "The love that I crave" (12") *on Audraglint & holocene music in 2006*

HUMAN EMPIRE, D.: JAN KRUSE **for Ms. John Soda** "Notes and the like" *on Morr Music in 2006*

JAWA AND MIDWICH, D.: NILS DAVEY AND SIMON DOVAR **for Shur-I-Kan** "Living Inside EP" (12") *on Freerange Records in 2006* - House -

WEISSRAUM.DE(SIGN)°, D.: BERND BRINK & LUCAS BUCHHOLZ **for Diverse** "Audiomatique - Volume 1.1" & "Audiomatique - Volume 1.2" (Vinyl Cover) *on Audiomatique in 2006* - Minimal Tech-House -

RINZEN for **The Scare** "Masochist Mimes" & "Vacuum Irony" (Digipak) *on Below Par Records in 2004 & 2005* - Rock -

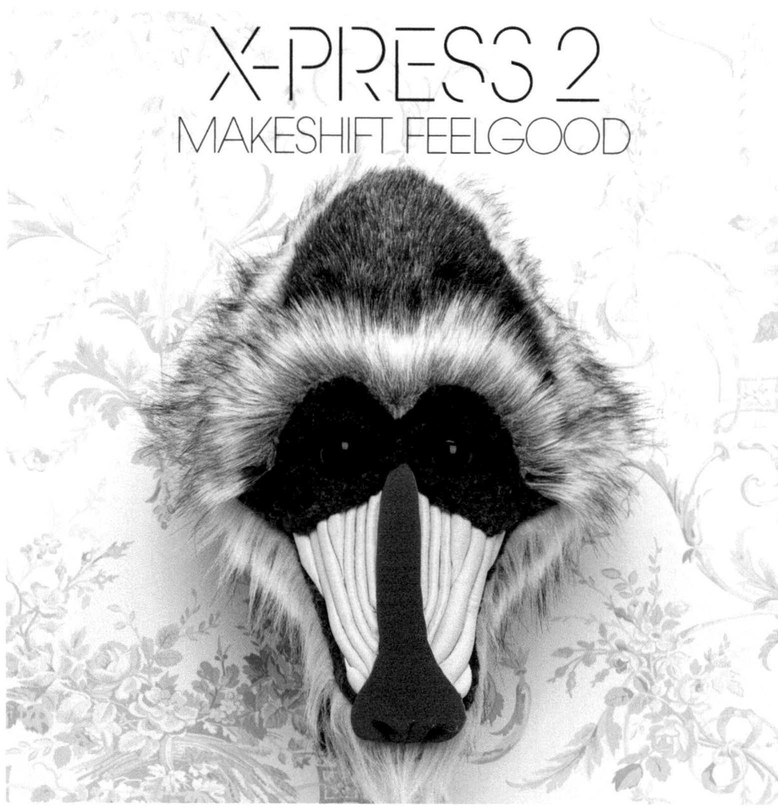

RED DESIGN for **Xpress 2** "Makeshift Feelgood" (CD) & "Kill 100" (7" / 12" / CD) *on Skint in 2006* - House -

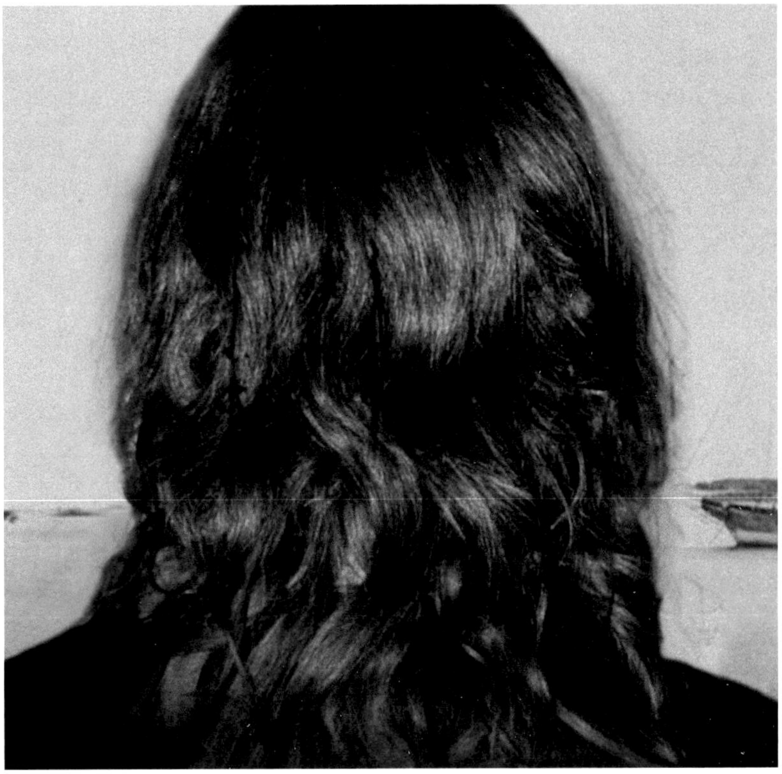

IO STUDIO for The Animal Five "The Animal Five E.P." (CD) *on Universal in 2007*

IO STUDIO for James Brown "Dynamite X" (CD) *on Couch Records in 2007*

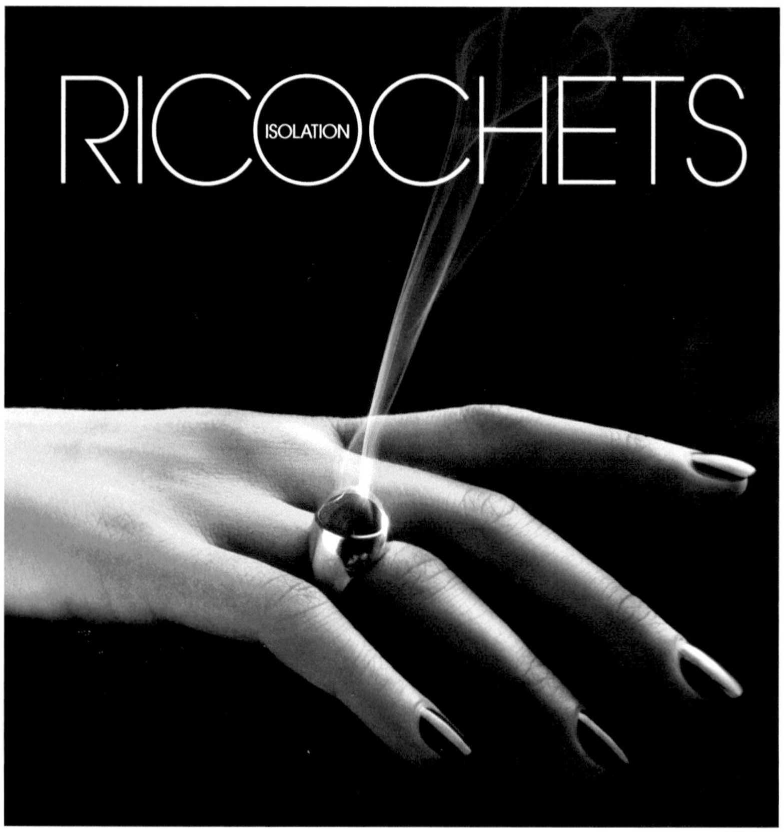

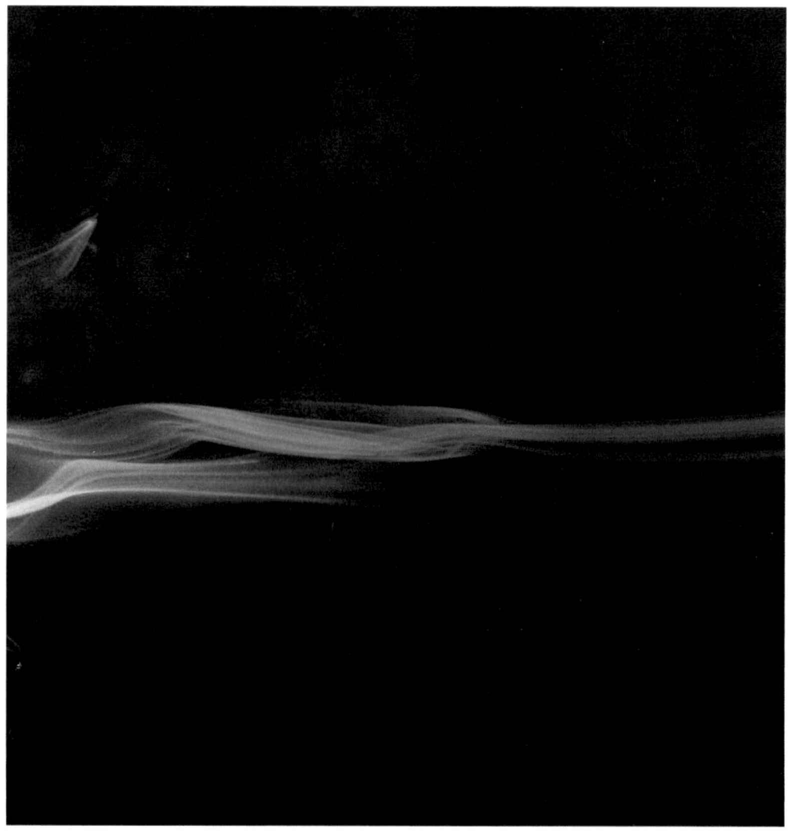

MARTIN KVAMME **for Ricochets** "Isolation" *on Kong Tiki in 2005* - Rock -

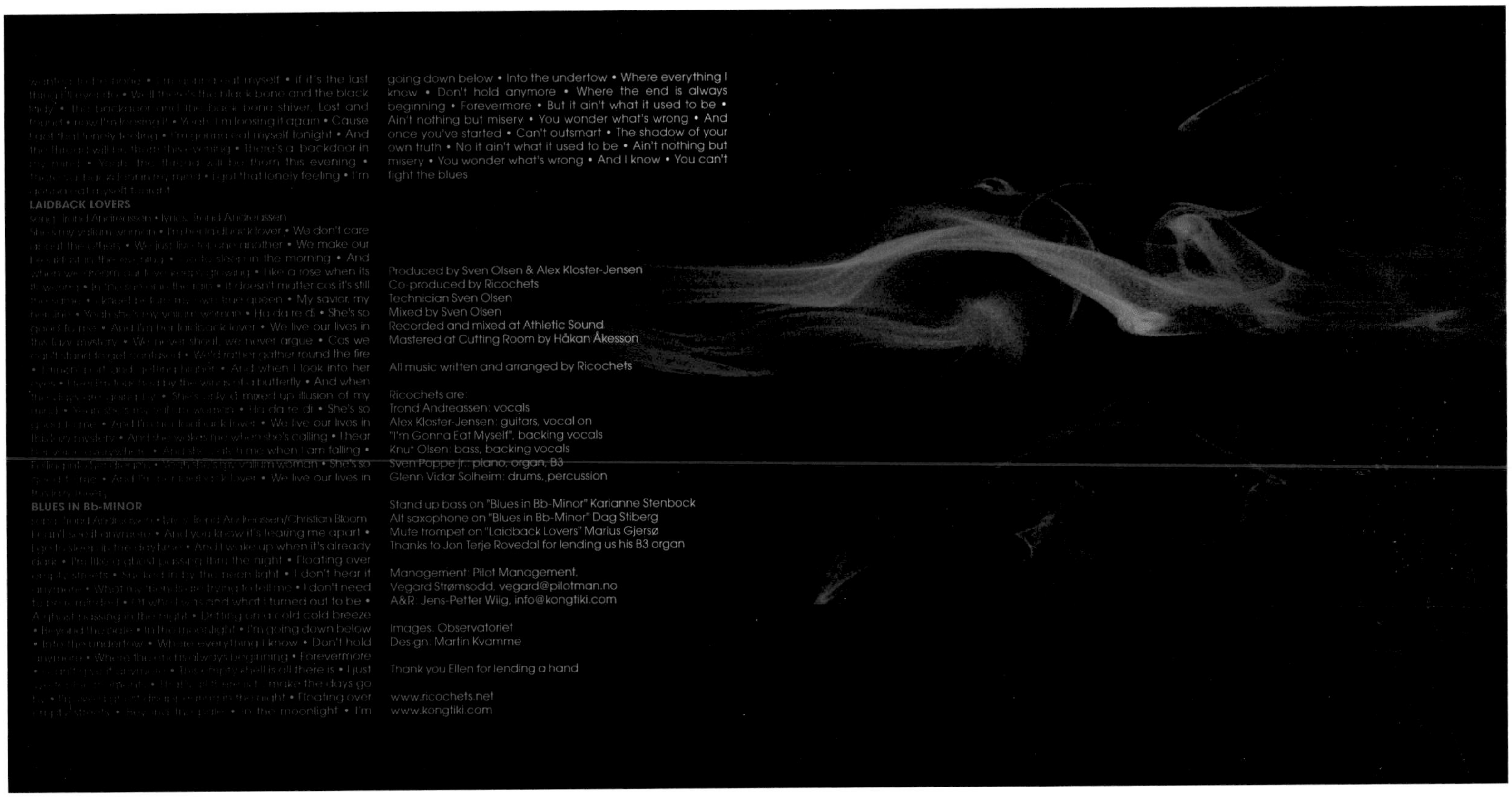
LAIDBACK LOVERS
BLUES IN Bb-MINOR
going down below • Into the undertow • Where everything I know • Don't hold anymore • Where the end is always beginning • Forevermore • But it ain't what it used to be • Ain't nothing but misery • You wonder what's wrong • And once you've started • Can't outsmart • The shadow of your own truth • No it ain't what it used to be • Ain't nothing but misery • You wonder what's wrong • And I know • You can't fight the blues
Produced by Sven Olsen & Alex Kloster-Jensen
Co-produced by Ricochets
Technician Sven Olsen
Mixed by Sven Olsen
Recorded and mixed at Athletic Sound
Mastered at Cutting Room by Håkan Åkesson
All music written and arranged by Ricochets
Ricochets are:
Trond Andreassen: vocals
Alex Kloster-Jensen: guitars, vocal on "I'm Gonna Eat Myself", backing vocals
Knut Olsen: bass, backing vocals
Sven Poppe jr.: piano, organ, B3
Glenn Vidar Solheim: drums, percussion
Stand up bass on "Blues in Bb-Minor" Karianne Stenbock
Alt saxophone on "Blues in Bb-Minor" Dag Stiberg
Mute trompet on "Laidback Lovers" Marius Gjersø
Thanks to Jon Terje Rovedal for lending us his B3 organ
Management: Pilot Management,
Vegard Strømsodd, vegard@pilotman.no
A&R: Jens-Petter Wiig, info@kongtiki.com
Images: Observatoriet
Design: Martin Kvamme
Thank you Ellen for lending a hand
www.ricochets.net
www.kongtiki.com

MARTIN KVAMME for Brut Boogaloo "When the dogs take over" (CD. 5 cards, dog on the one side, band member on the other.) *on Midnight Monkeys in 2006* - Rock -

Rocco

Henning

Otto

Borge

MIRKO BORSCHE for Süddeutsche Zeitung "Diskothek" (Poster, announcement for a discussion event tour about 50 years of pop music incl. live music) *in 2006* - Pop -

ON TOUR
SÜDDEUTSCHE ZEITUNG DISKOTHEK
DIE HERAUSGEBER DER POP-EDITION DER SÜDDEUTSCHEN ZEITUNG, JOHANNES WAECHTER UND PHILIPP OEHMKE, DISKUTIEREN ÜBER 1000 SONGS AUS 50 JAHREN: AN DER GITARRE UNTERSTÜTZT VON BERND BEGEMANN.
München, 9.6.2006, München, 9.6.2006, München, 9.6.2006, München, 9.6.2006, München, 9.6.2006, München, 9.6.2006, München, 9.6.2006, München, 9.6.2006, München, 9.6.2006, München, 9.6.2006, München, 9.6.2006, München, 9.6.2006, München, 9.6.2006, München, 9.6.2006, München, 9.6.2006, München, 9.6.2006, München, 9.6.2006, München, 9.6.2006, München, 9.6.2006,
SPECIAL GUEST BERLIN: ANNETTE HUMPE (2RAUMWOHNUNG)
MIT FREUNDLICHER UNTERSTÜTZUNG VON HUGENDUBEL, THALIA UND DER MEYERSCHEN BUCHHANDLUNG.

ON TOUR
SÜDDEUTSCHE ZEITUNG DISKOTHEK
DIE HERAUSGEBER DER POP-EDITION DER SÜDDEUTSCHEN ZEITUNG, JOHANNES WAECHTER UND PHILIPP OEHMKE, DISKUTIEREN ÜBER 1000 SONGS AUS 50 JAHREN: AN DER GITARRE UNTERSTÜTZT VON BERND BEGEMANN.
SPECIAL GUEST BERLIN: ANNETTE HUMPE (2RAUMWOHNUNG)
MIT FREUNDLICHER UNTERSTÜTZUNG VON HUGENDUBEL, THALIA UND DER MEYERSCHEN BUCHHANDLUNG.

ON TOUR
SÜDDEUTSCHE ZEITUNG DISKOTHEK
DIE HERAUSGEBER DER POP-EDITION DER SÜDDEUTSCHEN ZEITUNG, JOHANNES WAECHTER UND PHILIPP OEHMKE, DISKUTIEREN ÜBER 1000 SONGS AUS 50 JAHREN: AN DER GITARRE UNTERSTÜTZT VON BERND BEGEMANN.
SPECIAL GUEST BERLIN: ANNETTE HUMPE (2RAUMWOHNUNG)
MIT FREUNDLICHER UNTERSTÜTZUNG VON HUGENDUBEL, THALIA UND DER MEYERSCHEN BUCHHANDLUNG.

ON TOUR
SÜDDEUTSCHE ZEITUNG DISKOTHEK
DIE HERAUSGEBER DER POP-EDITION DER SÜDDEUTSCHEN ZEITUNG, JOHANNES WAECHTER UND PHILIPP OEHMKE, DISKUTIEREN ÜBER 1000 SONGS AUS 50 JAHREN: AN DER GITARRE UNTERSTÜTZT VON BERND BEGEMANN.
SPECIAL GUEST BERLIN: ANNETTE HUMPE (2RAUMWOHNUNG)
MIT FREUNDLICHER UNTERSTÜTZUNG VON HUGENDUBEL, THALIA UND DER MEYERSCHEN BUCHHANDLUNG.

STYLOROUGE *Answers by Rob O'Connor, Creative Director*

Set up by Rob O'Connor in the aftermath of punk, when small independent design agencies began to compete with the in-house departments of major record companies, London-based cross-media company and creative consultancy Stylorouge has weathered the vagaries of the music business since 1981 - no mean feat in a business that thrives on fickle styles and has seen more than a few radical format changes.
Quick to embrace new technologies and developments, Stylorouge was among the first music design agencies to branch out into web design and video production. And while the team has worked with a generous share of industry heavyweights, from Siouxsie and the Banshees to Blur, Morrissey and Paul Mc Cartney, it has always retained its sense of 'cheeky cynicism' and intuitive knack for 'subcultural plundering' – a stance that has served Stylorouge well for more than a quarter of a century.

Stylorouge has weathered the ups and downs of the music business for more than 25 years – how did you manage this rare and impressive feat?

We've always kept abreast of the changes in the various industries we are involved in and tried to react early on - without compromising our principles. One thing we've always had is a variety of opinions and skills and tastes in the company, the ability to be fairly versatile. We try and make it possible for any client to have what they want - if you become too snobby about that your workload might dry up altogether. On the other hand, we don't free pitch. Some people would think that's stupid, but in another way we retain our dignity; at least people who come to us know what we're worth and why they approach us.

Over the years, you've worked with quite a few big name artists. To what extent do artists, record companies, management etc. get involved in the design process?

It depends, really. Some of the bands and artists we work with are very design-conscious, others are only interested in the music. Then there's the celebrity culture, which has really grown because of reality TV. The last thing these would-be stars think about is how they're presented and perceived. That's quite distressing, really. In the current climate of throwaway celebrities, being young healthy and good-looking is simply not enough. So, it is our job to create something striking that represents their personality.
This is where it really helps if the artist himself has a strong opinion, like Damon Albarn or Mika, because then all the other potential decision makers takes a back seat. Surprisingly enough, the record companies don't mind an opinionated artist because it gives them one less thing to worry about. It may make the job a little less personal to the designer, but the result will be a more honest representation of the artist's actual personality.
Morrissey and Paul McCartney are very good examples of this. I always knew that Morrissey had an image of being in control – he basically art-directed his own shoot – so we only supported his efforts, really. Paul McCartney, on the other hand, does not come up with his own ideas, but has a very strong opinion about the final result. Working with major stars can actually be less stressful as the chain of command tends to be shorter and it's a lot easier to get it the budget approved if the artist himself supports the idea.

To what extent has the music and design business changed over the last few years?

This might sound like blasphemy, but I think that the best days of the record cover are over, not in creative terms, but in terms of overall relevance. Basically, the physical package is still the foundation from which everything else should emanate, but it does not hold quite the same magic any more.
When you think about it, artwork and design has always been in flux – why settle for a drawing if you can have a painting, why a painting if you can have a photograph, why monochrome if you can have colour, why a still when you can have a moving image? Don't get me wrong – this progression does not make the other, previous incarnations redundant, but it adds excitement to the mix. And now that everyone can publish their own work on the Internet, there is a lot more scope for interesting, experimental film-making again, for example.
For the music business, the change has been enormous. Not just the format, but the whole process of distribution and marketing has been turned on its head. Record companies have always relied too heavily on radio and high street retail. I am surprised by how many people and musicians out there still think that way, people who have difficulties embracing the Internet. Especially the majors are slow to catch on - you can always tell the difference between an independent website and one that has a large record company behind it, the latter is always more corporate. I mean, 99% per cent of all bands don't appear in magazines or ad campaigns, but use the Internet to build their own page, present their work, show pictures, videos etc. Effectively, they are building their own micro markets where the quality of presentation isn't that important as long as it represents the band.

And how does this shift towards digital releases and websites affect your work?

We've been doing websites for a very long time, much longer than most, and always knew that this shift from physical product to the web would happen at some point. Nevertheless, we didn't expect it to happen quite so soon and quite so fast. On the one hand, it's a positive development because it gives a lot more artists and smaller labels a chance to promote and sell their work around the world – I expect a boom of interesting independent labels - but on the other hand, they won't be able to spend the same amount of money on presentation and artwork and probably do it in-house.

STYLOROUGE LTD, D.: ANTHONY LUI *for*
Morrissey „Ringleader of the Tormentors"
(CD Special Edition) *in 2006*
- Alternative Rock -

Overall, the climate has changed quite a bit - years ago, record companies couldn't stop spending money and would consider 100,000 pounds for a video or 20,000 pounds for a sleeve design good investment. Nowadays, you often find yourself faced with impossible budgets.
Basically, the culture of the Internet has led people to believe that things should be cheap or free. It's the spirit of the moment, the zeitgeist, if you like. People are willing to share their work and expertise on the Net. This has affected the entire design landscape – and not necessarily in a bad way. When people discover the free graphics software preinstalled on their computer, you often you get some interesting results. Some people, on the other hand, can't spot the difference between inspired design and something that was simply cobbled together. Overall, the quality of music artwork has gone down quite a bit and prices have dropped to the point where talented people move out of music design because the fees are simply too low. I mean, you can't really compete with talented amateurs who are willing to work for free, at least not in financial terms. So, I have mixed feelings about this overall development - it's a great and exciting climate for young, independent designers, but much tougher for established with regular bills and overheads.

Any advice for up-and-coming designers?

Designing record covers is not exactly a lucrative long-term career prospect, so music enthusiasts should think a bit wider, consider other ways to indulge their love of music.

Don't get me wrong – I am not trying to revive the death of the album cover or CD vs. vinyl debate. I for one don't have that problem with CDs per se or the smaller size - some of the best designers in the world are renowned for designing stamps and you can't get much smaller than that. The current design and sales crisis is not one of canvas size, but of quality – when record companies switched from LP to CD, very little was done to adjust and improve the quality of the reproduction. If they had paid a bit more attention and money on imaginative, high quality packaging early on, we wouldn't be in this predicament now.
In a climate where all music is just a click away, even before it's official release, it has become a lot harder to make that experience of discovering new music as special as it was for previous generations, that terrible yearning for a new release or limited edition … so all we can do is keep up the quality, make sure that fans get very good value-added content when they buy a product.
For a glimpse of the future, Warner Music in America have recently set up a department for interactive album covers to rekindle an interest in the album as a body of work. When people can look forward to exclusive, interactive artwork with their purchase, e. g. an animated click-through of the booklet with links to exclusive videos etc., they might think twice about downloading individual tracks. I think that's definitely a path worth exploring.

RUNE MORTENSEN for Paal Nilssen-Love / Ken Vandermark "Seven" (CD) *on Smalltown Superjazzz in 2006* - Freejazz -

RUNE MORTENSEN for Cato Salsa Experience and The Thing with Joe McPhee "Two Bands and a Legend" (CD) *on Smalltown Superjazzz in 2007* - Garage / Freejazz -

NO MUSIC REQUESTS 1984 - 2004

Tittelen på denne denne plata henspeller på begynnelsen av nittitallet, en tid da noen plater rett og slett ble for populære for oss. Slett ikke dårlige, bare plagsomme for bartenderne. Løsningen på dette ble et beskjedent skilt med den imøtekommende påskriften NO MUSIC REQUESTS. Senere fikk t-skjortene til de ansatte samme trykk. Etter kort tid ble dette Last Train's varemerke, og har hengt ved stedet siden. Denne sunne vi-vet-best-holdningen er noe som bestandig har preget Last Train. Kombinert med troskap til et slags no-nonsense-no-concept-konsept, har det gjort at Last Train har overlevd alle sosiale og musikalske trender, alle tenkelige nedturer (og oppturer, for den saks skyld) og ikke minst alle "konkurrenter" de siste 20 åra.

Denne plata er ikke bare en feiring av Last Train. Den feirer også de hundrevis av artister og band som har spilt på stedet, helt siden bartender Tom booket TV Personalities til stedets første konsert, i mars 1990. Den feirer alle band og plateselskap som har oppstått og blitt oppløst på Last Train, alle ansatte og gjester som har vært med å gjøre stedet så bra, og selvfølgelig feirer den Oslo og musikkmiljøet her. Et miljø vi med denne plata beviser er landets absolutt beste.

Over 100 band og artister ble oppfordret til å levere bidrag til 20-års jubileet, og vi ble etterhvert sittende med den håpløse oppgaven å velge ut de 20 riktige. Vi valgte å prioritere uutgitt materiale, og mener at alle låtene på hver sine måter gjenspeiler historien, variasjonen og ikke minst kvaliteten som alltid har kjennetegnet miljøet rundt Last Train.

Hurra for oss!
Vi sees!
Last Train OSLO

SKIN DESIGN AS, D.: ARE KLEIVAN "No Music Requests - Last Train's 20th Anniversary CD" (CD, 32 pg Booklet. 2 Col Print Black + Gold) *on Peekaböö / Sonet in 2004* - Rock -

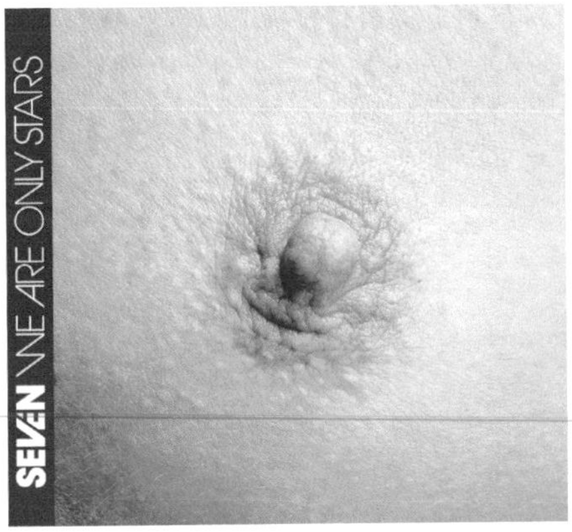

SKIN DESIGN AS for Seven "We are Only Stars" (50x70 cm) & "We are Only Stars" (CD) *on MTG in 2006* - Pop/Rock -

WEISSRAUM.DE(SIGN)°, D.: BERND BRINK & LUCAS BUCHHOLZ **for 2DJ'S & ONE** "I Engineer" & "I Engineer Remixes" (Vinyl Cover) *on Polydor/Zeitgeist in 2005* - Electro Pop -

STYLOROUGE LTD, D.: MARK HIGENBOTTAM **for Huron** "Love, Elation, Loss, Anger and Redemption" (Flyer) *on Como Park in 2005* - Electronic Rock -

MARTIN KVAMME for Kaada "Music for Moviebikers" (CD) *on Ipecac Recordings in 2006* - Alternative -

INVISIBLE CREATURE, INC., D.: DON CLARK **for Funeral For A Friend** "Hours" (CD) *on Atlantic Records in 2005* - Rock -

SURFACE for März "Wir sind hier" (CD) *on Karaoke Kalk in 2004* - Electronic -

SUPERLOW, D.: HALVOR BODIN **for White Lord Jesus** "White Lord Jesus" (CD) *on Kong Tiki Records in 2005* - Electronic -

BIG ACTIVE for **Athlete "Tourist"** (Album) *on EMI in 2005. Art Direction: Richard Andrews & Gerard Saint @ Big Active, Photography: Dan Tobin Smith, Set Design: Lyndsay Milne.* - Pop -

BIG ACTIVE for **Protocol** "Rules of Engagement" (Album) *on Polydorin 2006. Art Direction: Richard Andrews & Gerard Saint @ Big Active, Photography: Dan Tobin Smith, Set Design: Lyndsay Milne.* - Pop -

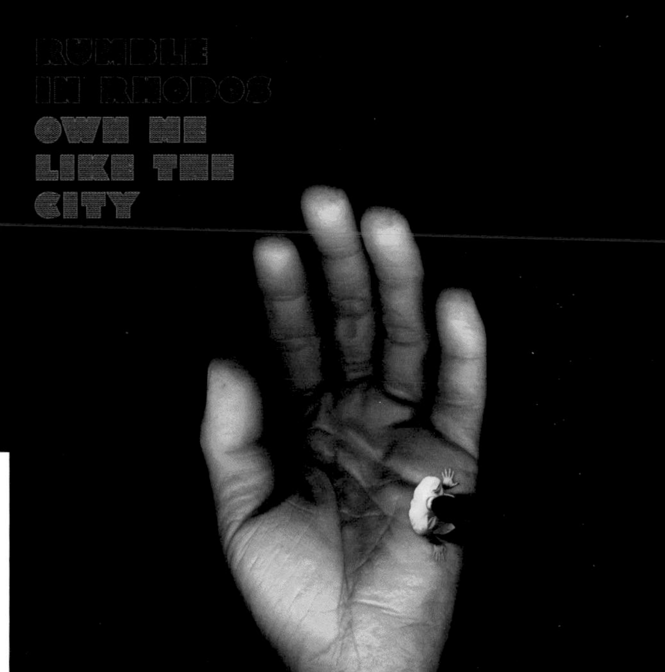

MADE for **Rumble in Rhodos** "Own me like the city" (12" album) *on Anomalie Records in 2006* - Indie Rock -

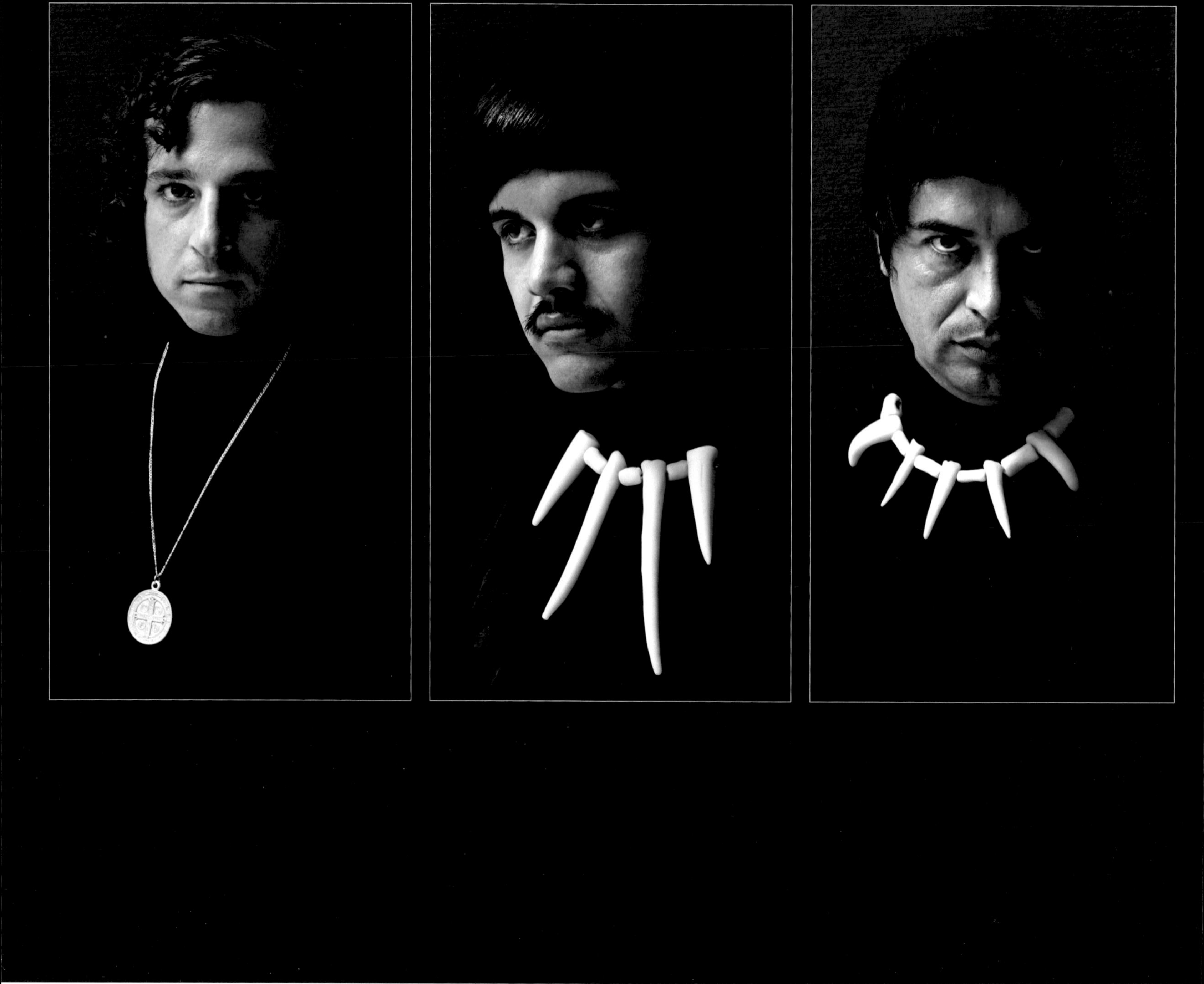

ROCK INSTRUMENT BUREAU, D.: JAVIER AUGUSTE **for Los Peyotes** "Los Peyotes - Cavernicola" (CD Interior)
on Rockaway Records in 2005

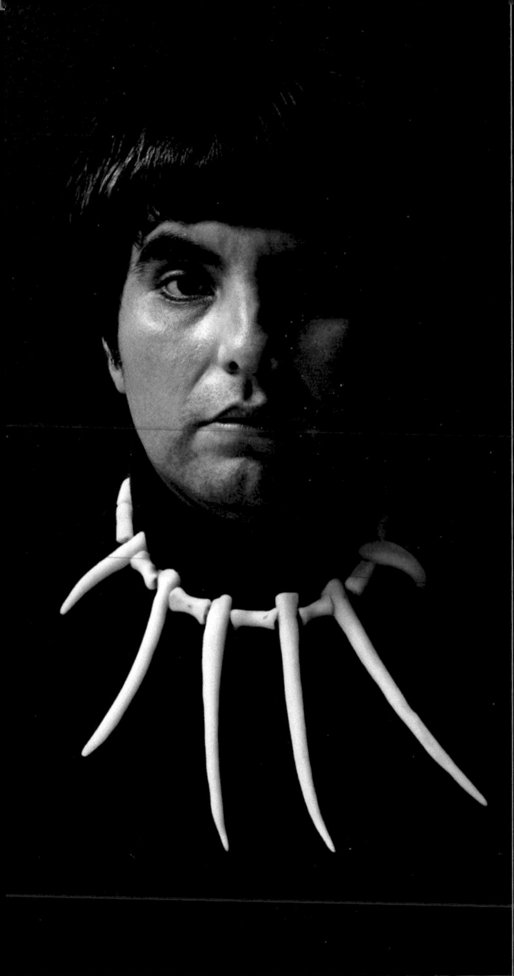

ROCK INSTRUMENT BUREAU, D.: ROY GARCIA **for Los Peyotes** (Rock Concert Poster) *on Rockaway Records in 2006*

INVISIBLE CREATURE, INC., D.: DON CLARK **for Mnemic** "Passenger" (CD)
on Nuclear Blast Records in 2006 - Metal -

MARTIN KVAMME **for Turbonegro** "Party Animals" *on Burning Heart in 2005* - Rock -

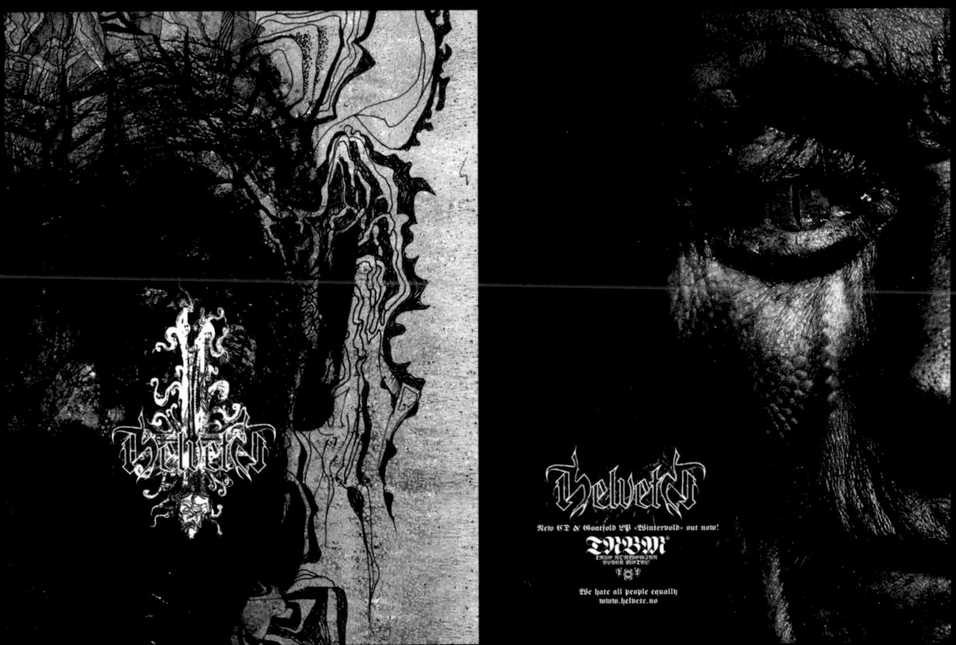

SUPERLOW, D.: **HALVOR BODIN** **for Helvete** "Wintervold" (Ad for album release)
on Memphis Only in 2005 - True Norwegian Black Metal -

MARTIN KVAMME / HALVOR BODIN **for Satyricon** "Now, Diabolical"
on Roadrunner *in 2006* - Black Metal -

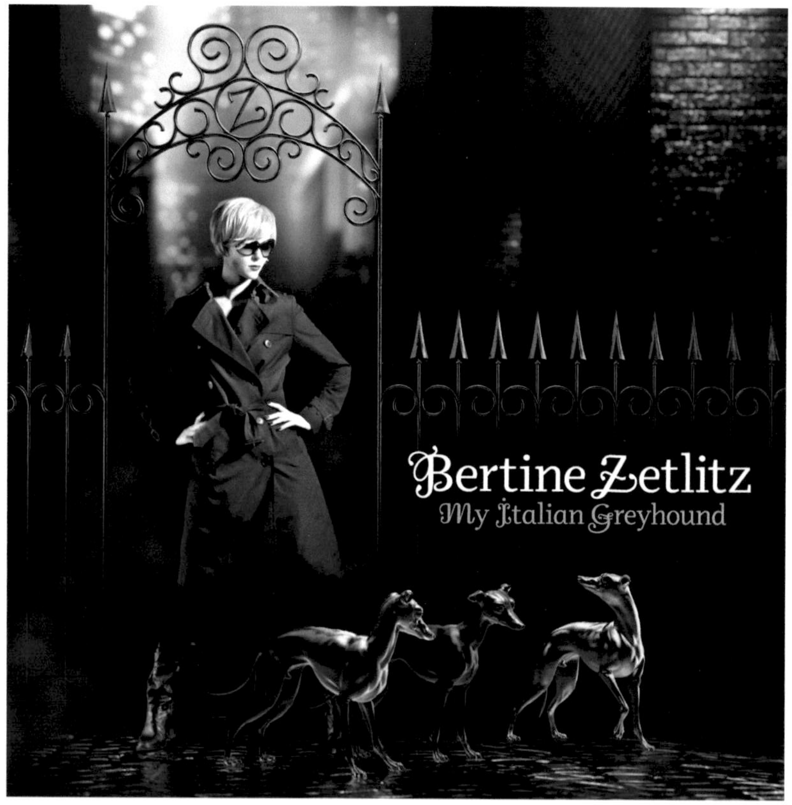

MARTIN KVAMME for Kaada "Music for Moviebikers" (CD)
on Ipecac Recordings in 2006 - Alternative -

MARTIN KVAMME for Bertine Zetlitz "My Italian Greyhound" (CD)
on Capitol Records Norway in 2006 - Pop -

DIRK RUDOLPH for **Kain** "Leben im Schrank" (CD) *on Universal* in 2006; *Photography by DerDehmel (Band), Stock-Photos, Dirk Rudolph* - Rock -

DIRK RUDOLPH for **Apoptygma Berzerk** "Shine On" (CD-Maxi/Digipak) *on Gun Records in 2005; Photography by Harald Hoffmann* - Rock -

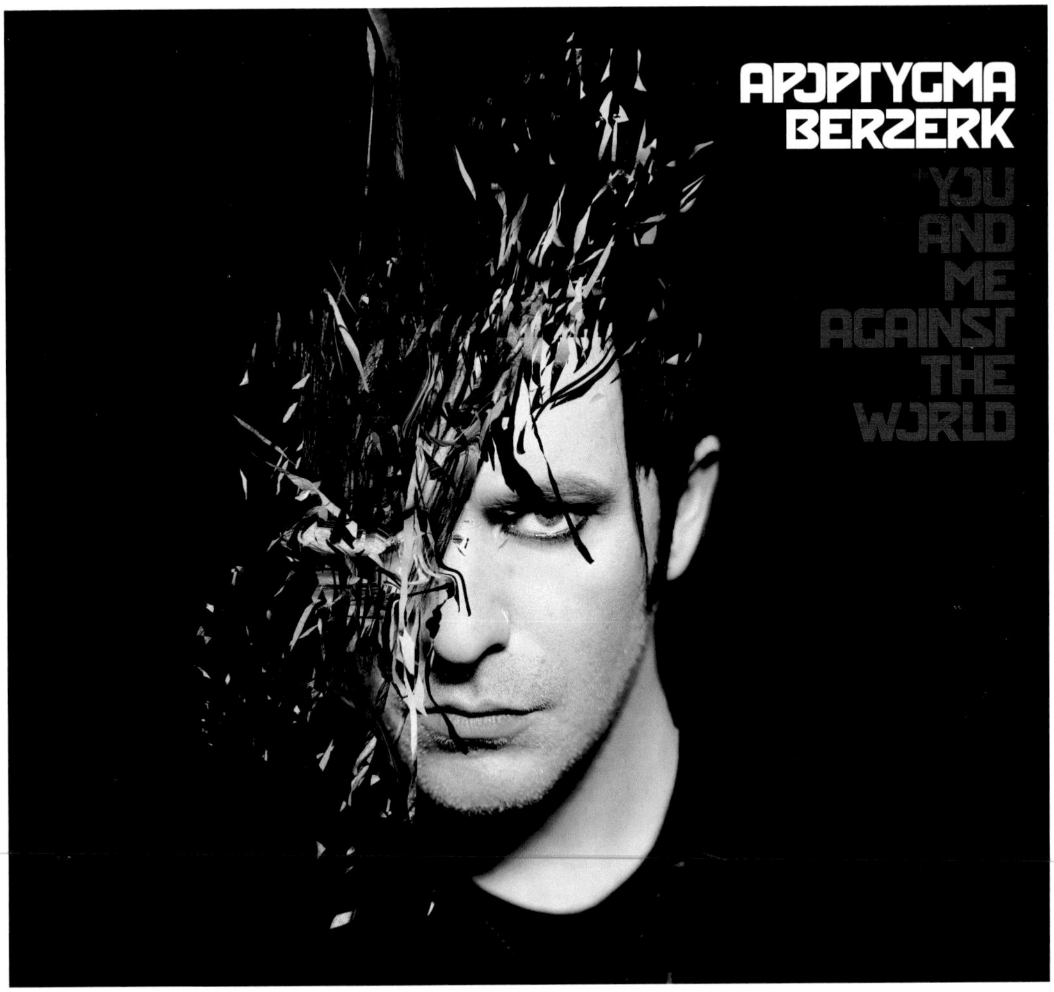

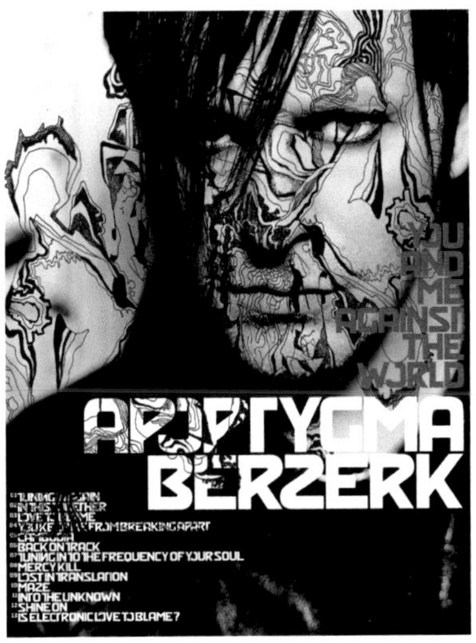

DIRK RUDOLPH for Apoptygma Berzerk "You And Me Against The World" (CD) *on Gun Records in 2005; Photography by Harald Hoffmann & Sebastian Ludvigsen* - Rock

DIRK RUDOLPH for Curse "Sinnflut" (CD) *on Premium Blend / Sony BMG Music Entertainment in 2005; Photography by Jens Boldt* - HipHop -

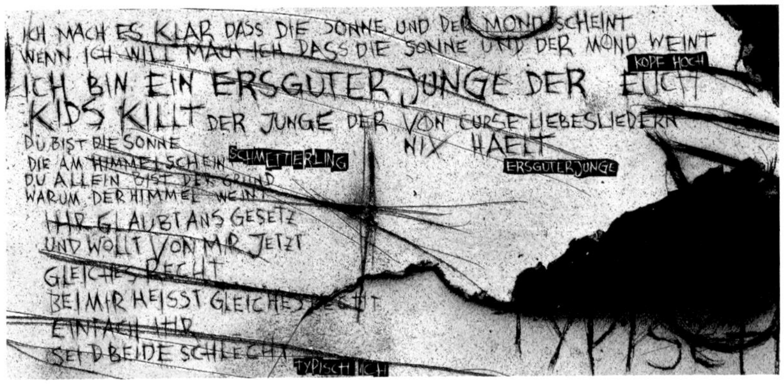

DIRK RUDOLPH for Bushido "Electro Ghetto" (CD) *on Universal in 2004; Photography by Kasskara* - HipHop -

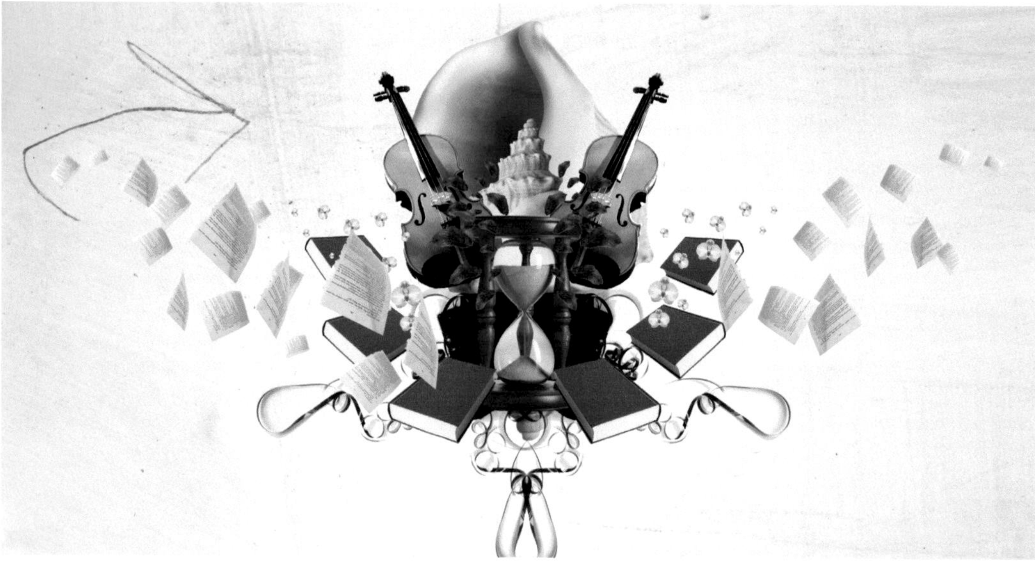

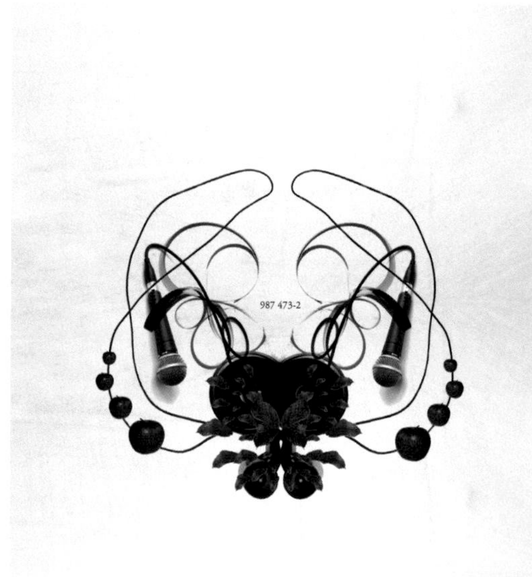

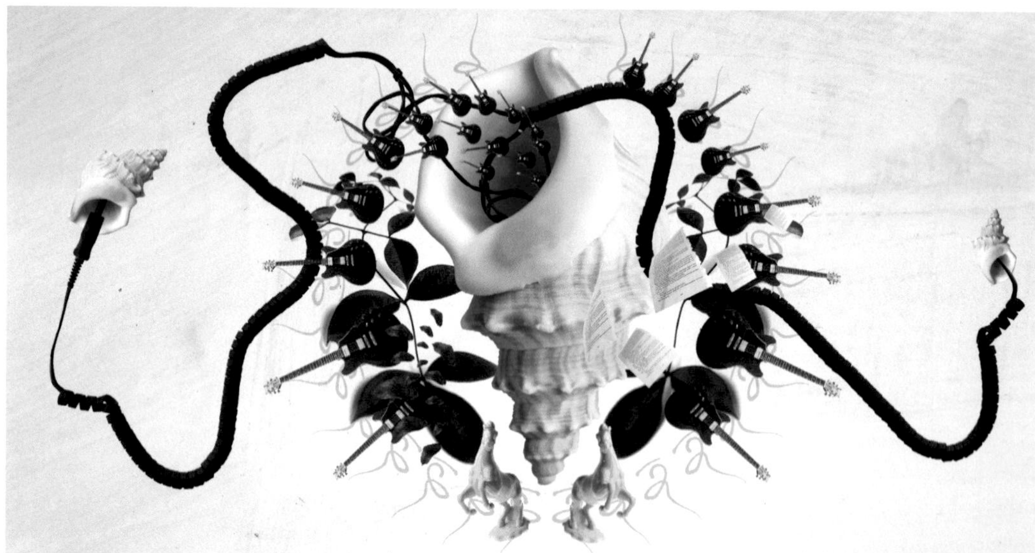

DIRK RUDOLPH for Ich + Ich "Ich + Ich" (CD) *on Universal in 2005; Photography by Olaf Heine & Kasskara (Band), Dirk Rudolph* - Rock/Pop -

MARTIN KVAMME for Saosin "Saosin" (CD) *on Capitol Records USA in 2006* - Rock -

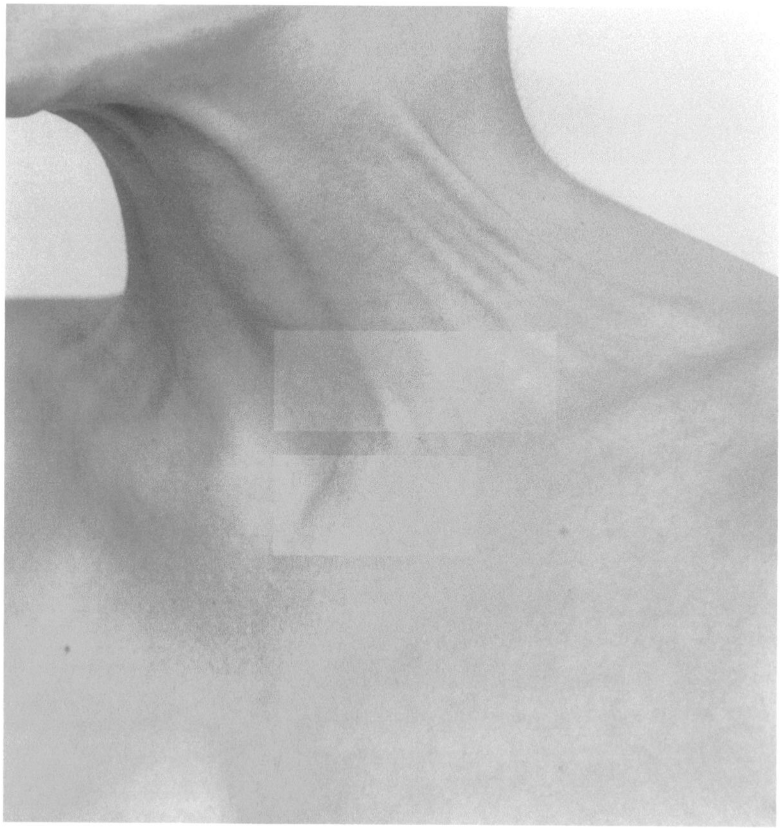

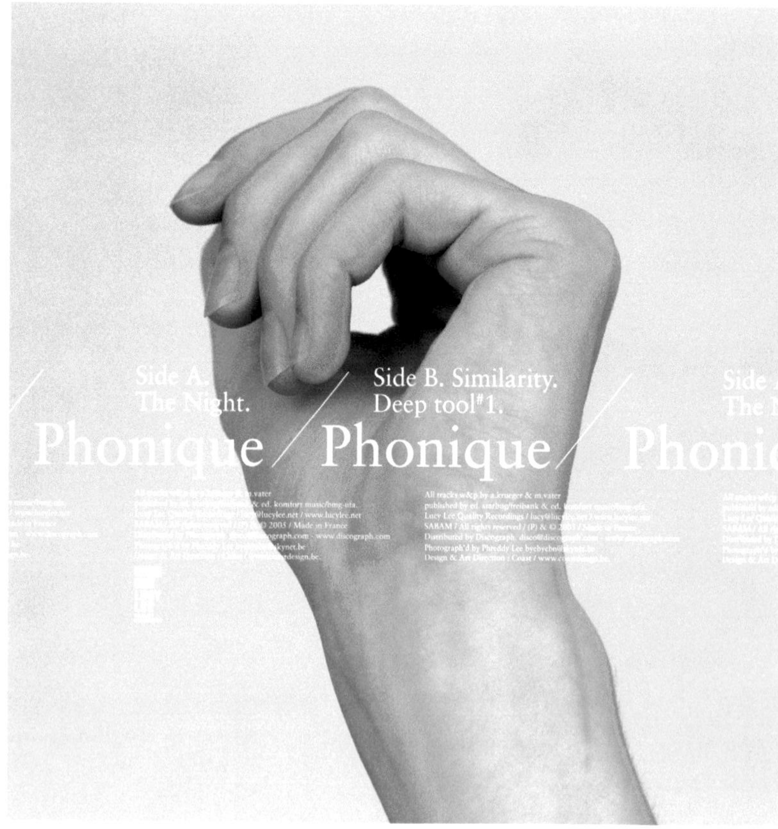

COAST DESIGN, D.: FRÉDÉRIC VANHORENBEKE **for The Penelopes** "Alice" (A2 Poster) *on lucy lee in 2006* & **for Phonique** "The Night" (12") *on Lucy Lee in 2006*

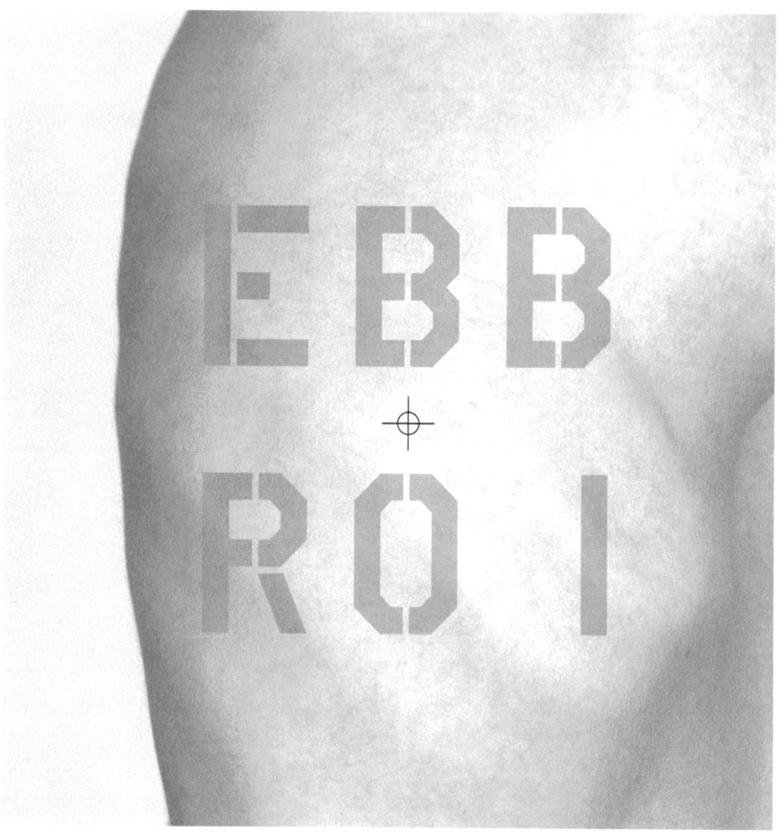

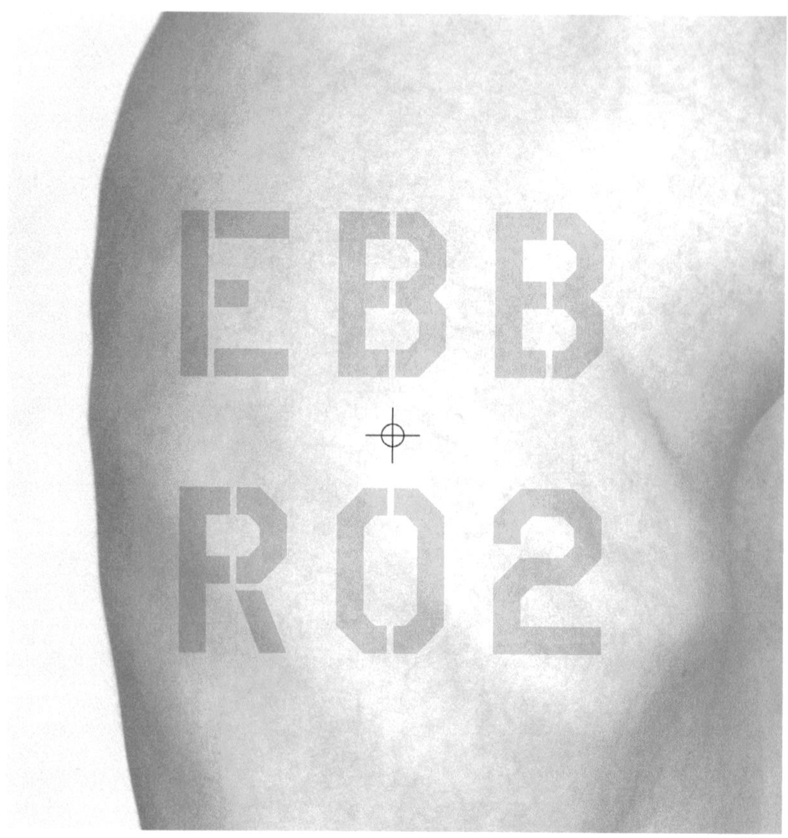

COAST DESIGN, D.: FRÉDÉRIC VANHORENBEKE **for Ebbro** "Uno" & "Duo" (12") *on Lucy Lee in 2007*

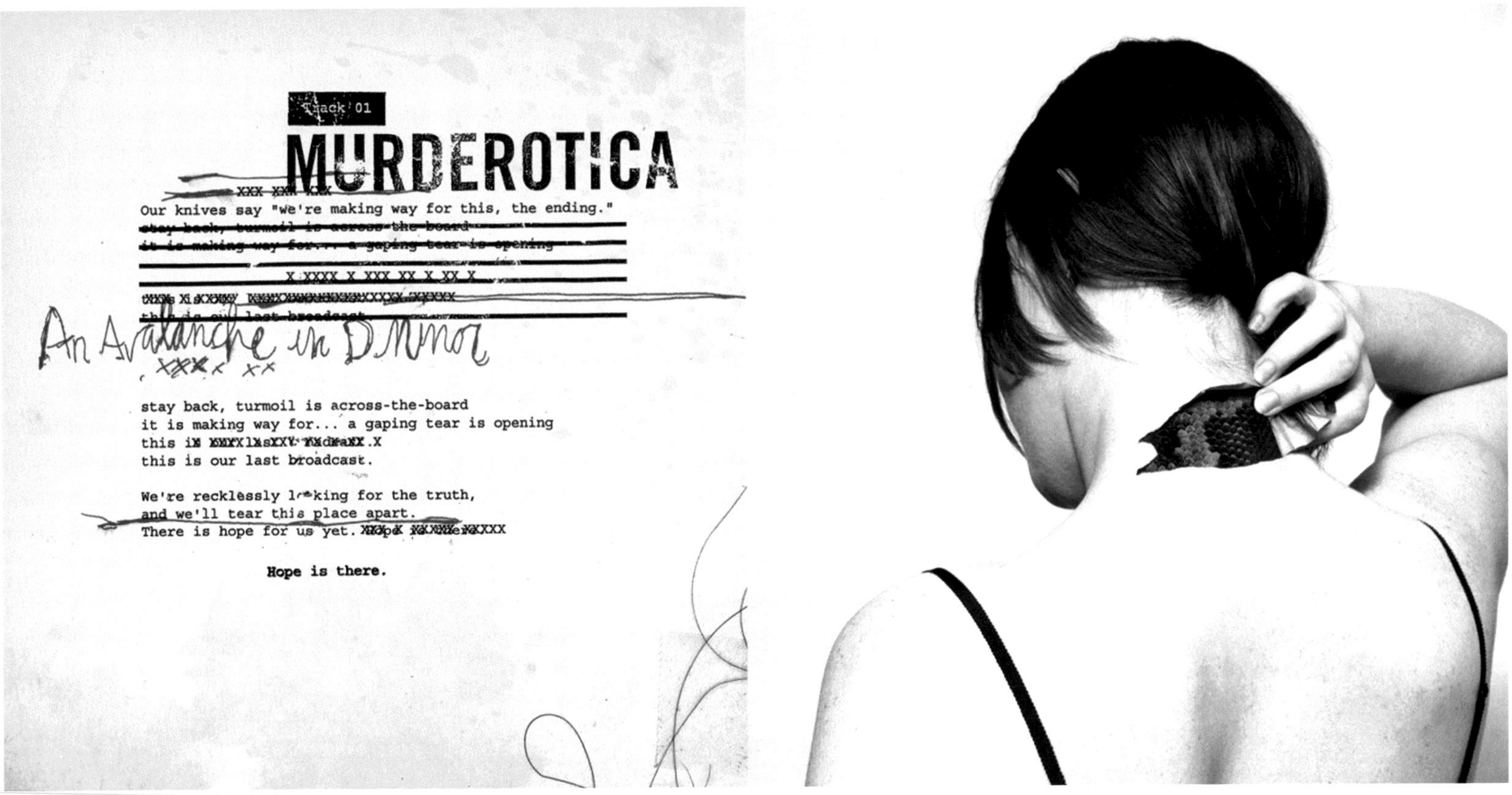

INVISIBLE CREATURE, INC., D.: RYAN CLARK **for Norma Jean** "O' God, The Aftermath (CD) *on Solid State Records in 2005* - Metal -

INVISIBLE CREATURE, INC., D.: RYAN CLARK **for Norma Jean** "O' God, The Aftermath (CD) *on Solid State Records in 2005* - Metal -

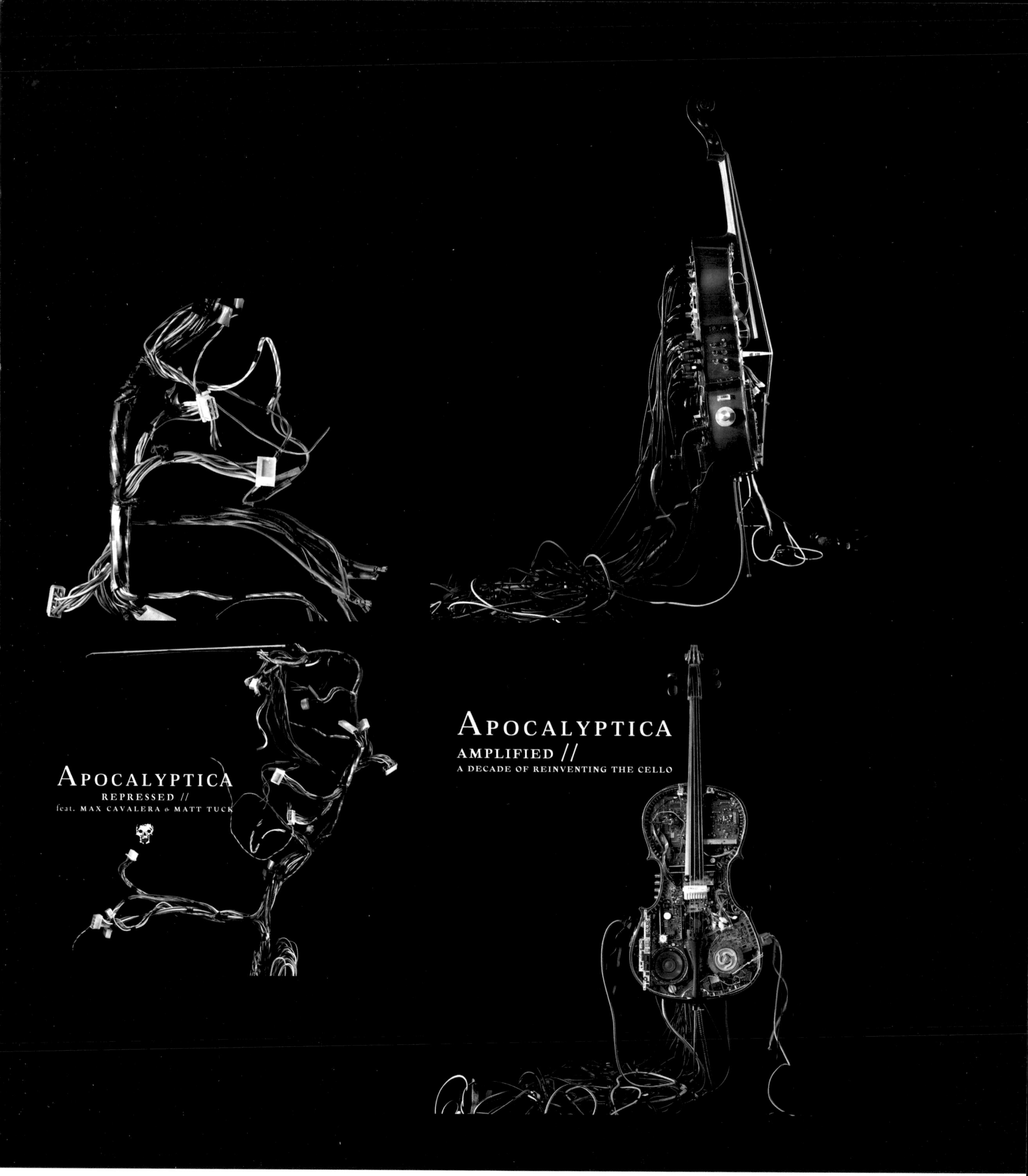

DIRK RUDOLPH for Apocalyptica "Amplified" (CD) *on Universal in 2006; Photography by Harald Hoffmann* - Rock -

DIRK RUDOLPH for Apocalyptica "Amplified" (CD) *on Universal in 2006; Photography by Harald Hoffmann* - Rock -

DIRK RUDOLPH for Valentine "Blue Merry-Go-Round" (CD) *on Capitol / EMI Music Germany in 2006; Photography by Kasskara* - Pop -

DIRK RUDOLPH for Somersault "Paper Walls" (CD) *on Sony BMG Music Entertainment in 2006; Photography by Jim Rakete* - Rock/Pop -

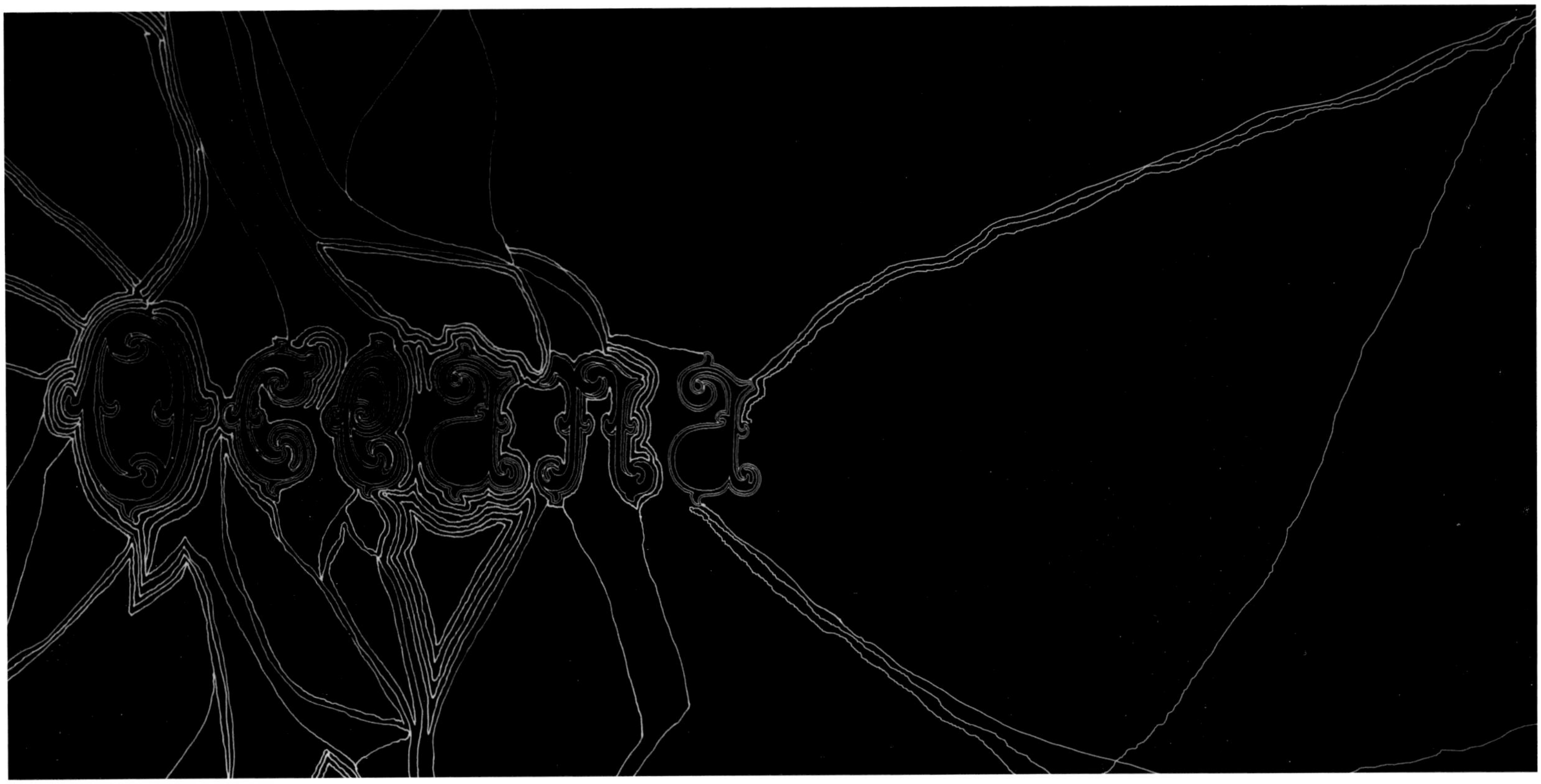

DIRK RUDOLPH for Till Brönner "Oceana" (CD) *on Bam Bam Music / Universal Classics & Jazz in 2006; Photography by Jim Rakete, William Claxton* - Jazz -

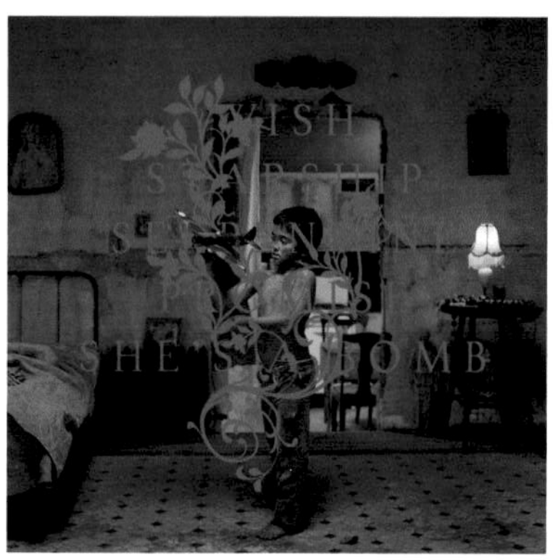

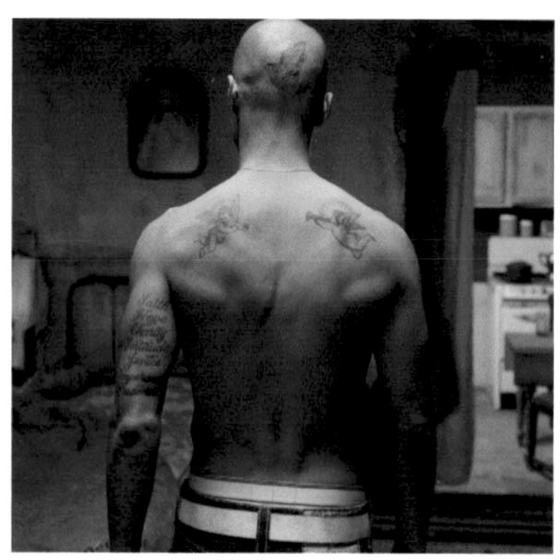

DIRK RUDOLPH for Reamonn "Wish" (CD) *on Universal in 2006; Photography frontcover: Christof Schulte, Band by Olaf Heine* - Rock -

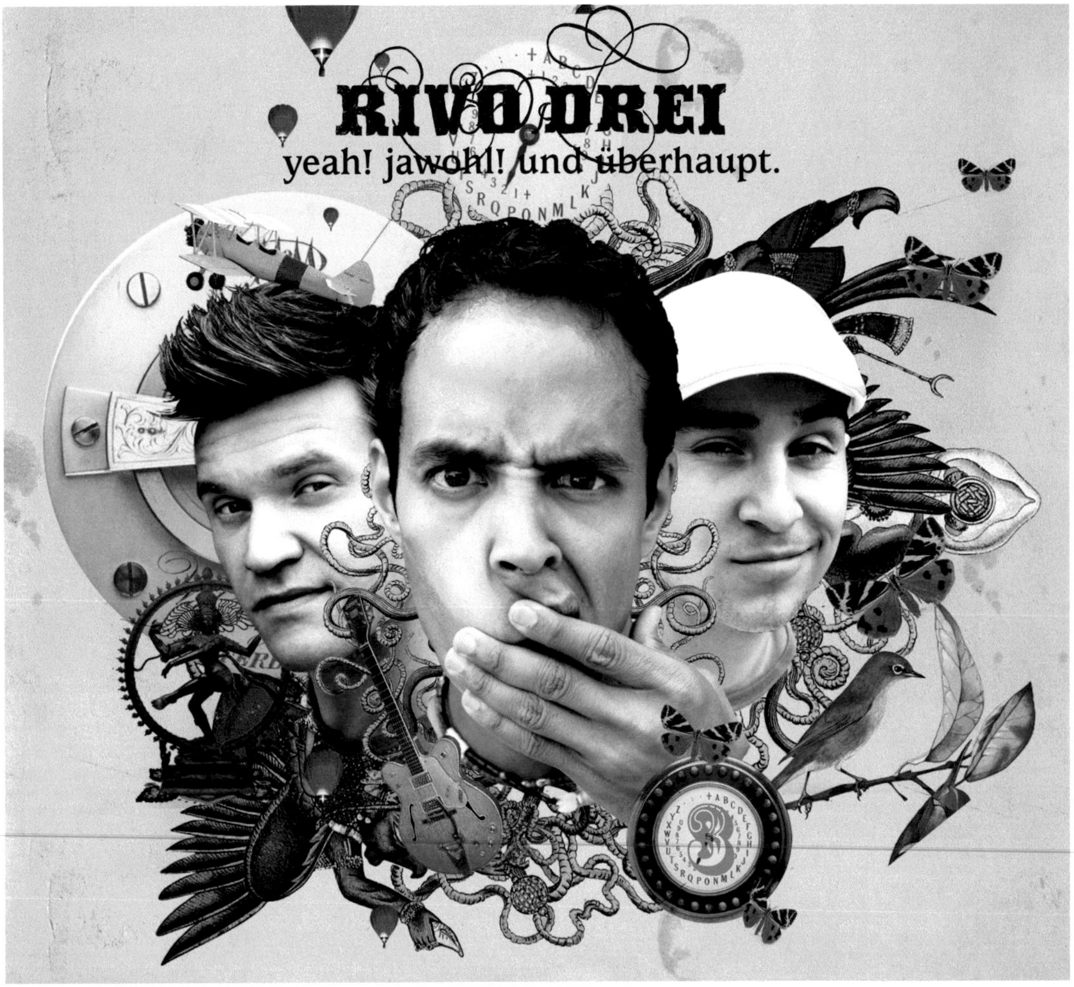

DIRK RUDOLPH for Rivo Drei "Yeah" (CD) *on Sony BMG Music Entertainment in 2005; Photography by Katja Kuhl* - Rock/Pop -

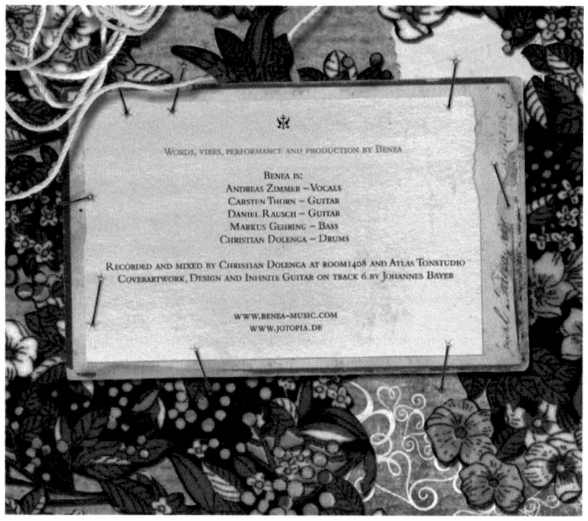

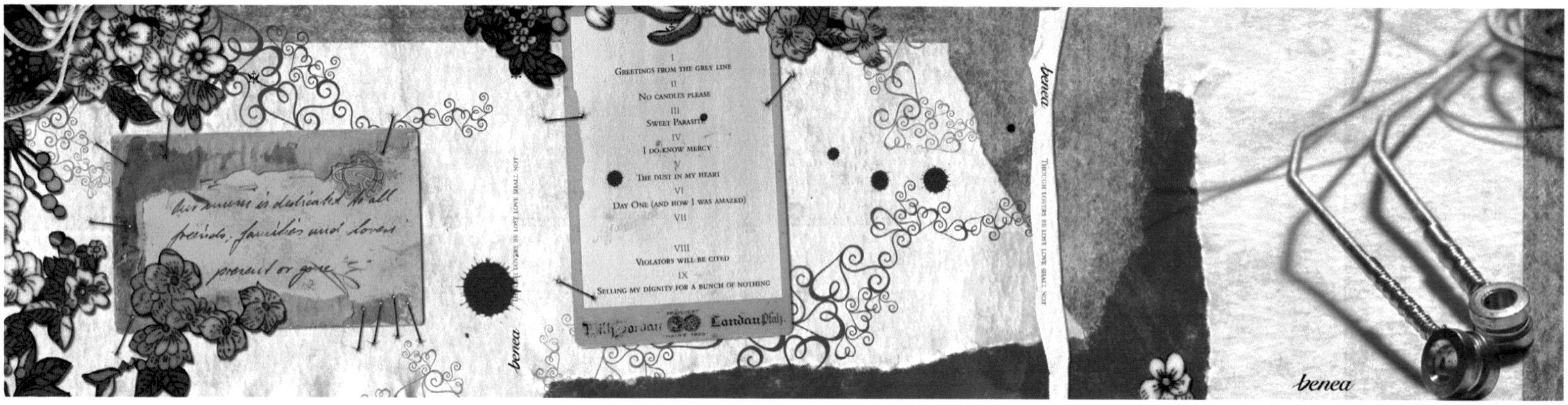

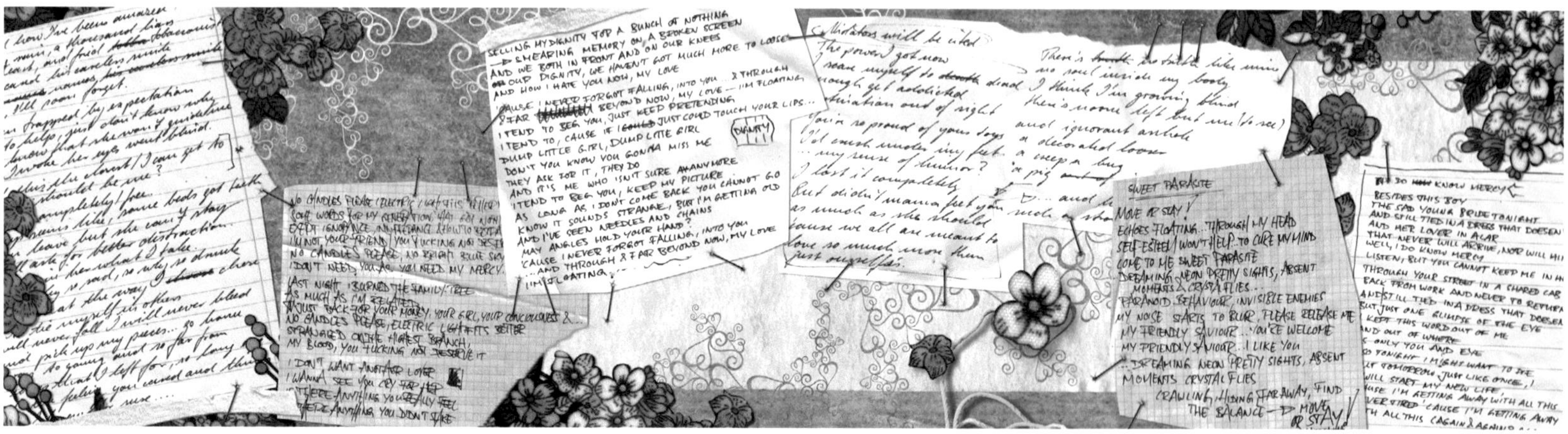

JOTOPIA | VISUAL NOISE, D.: JOHANNES BAYER **for Benea** "Though lovers be lost love shall not" (CD) *in 2007* - Alternative -

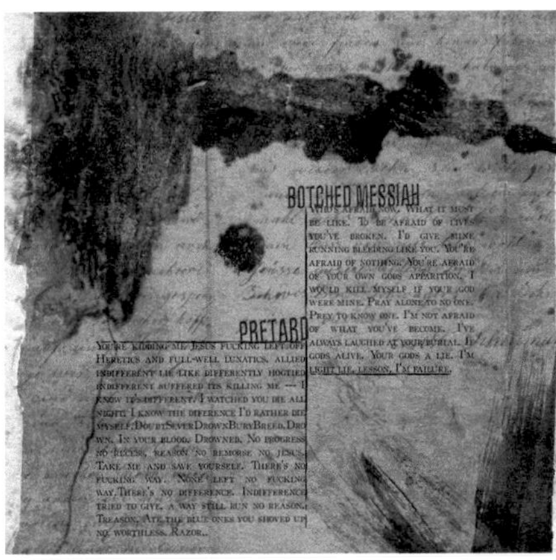

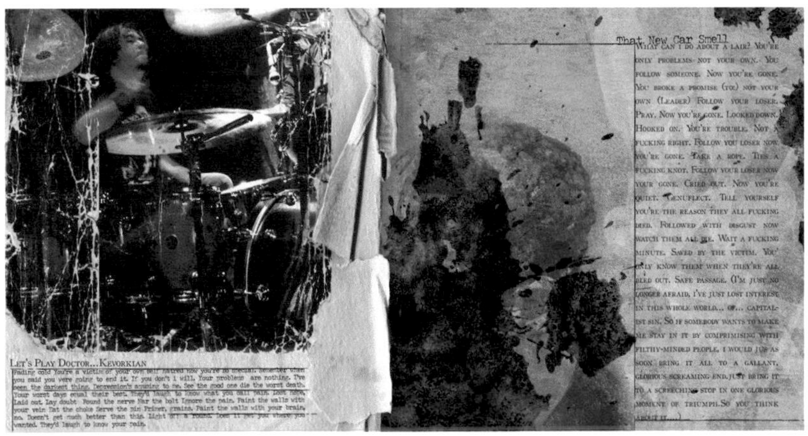

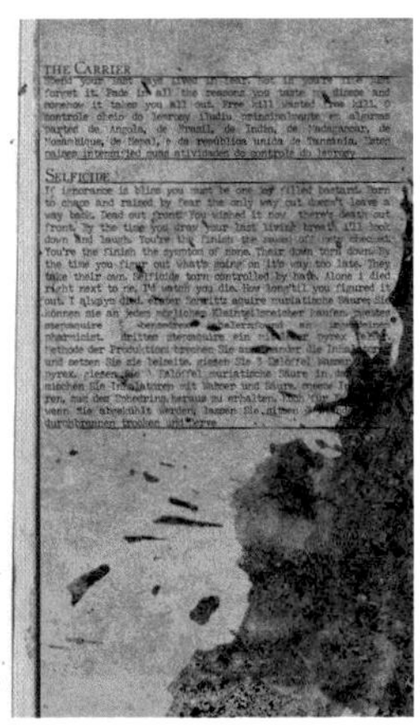

APT13, D.: PHILLIP DWYER **for Blessing The Hogs** "The Twelve Gauge Solution" (CD) *on Goodfellow Records in 2006* - Hardcore/Metal -

ULTRABAZAR, D.: MÄRT INFANGER **for Jolly & the Flytrap** "Electric Polka" (A2) *on Noman Records in 2004* - Global Rock'n'Roll -

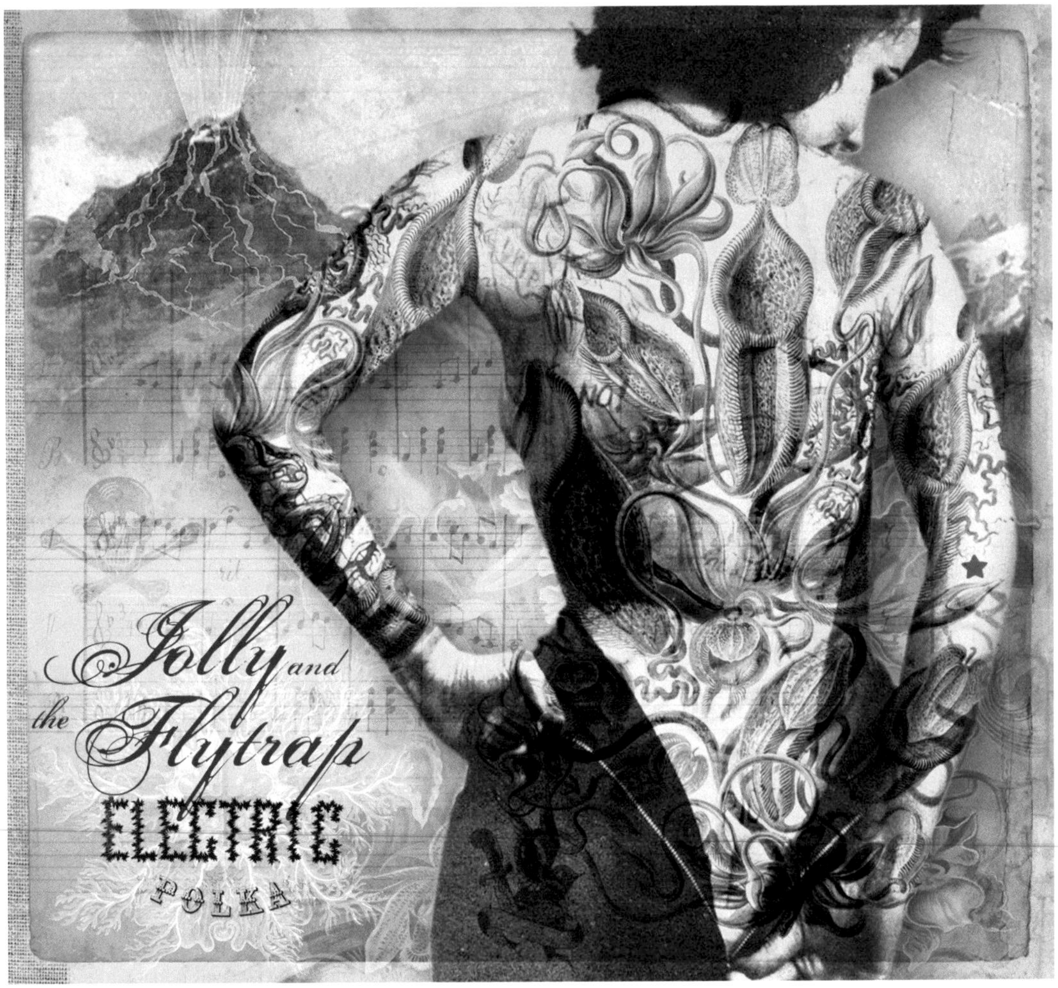

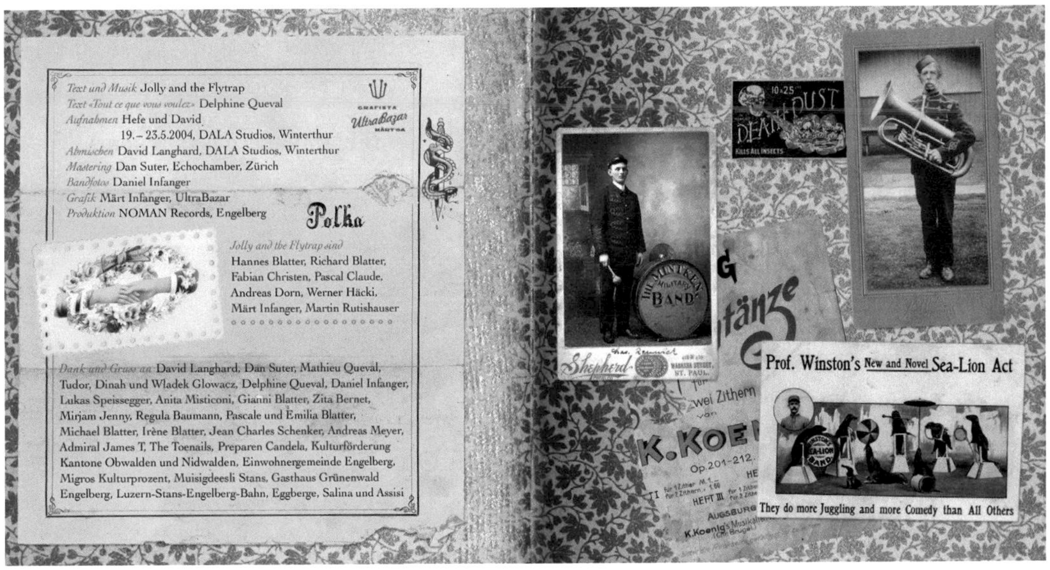

ULTRABAZAR, D.: MÄRT INFANGER **for Jolly & the Flytrap** "Electric Polka" (CD) *on Noman Records in 2004* - Global Rock'n'Roll -

MARTIN KVAMME for Magnet "The Tourniquet" (CD) *on Atlantic in 2005* - Alternative -

MARTIN KVAMME for JR Ewing "Maelstrom" (CD) *on SonyBMG in 2005/2006* - Alternative Rrock -

MARTIN KVAMME for Magnet "Hold On" & "Fall at your feet" (7" Vinyl) *on Ultimate Dilemma in 2005* - Alternative -

MONE MAURER for DJ Hell "Best of Album: Größenwahn 1992-2005" + Remix Album "Monotonie durch Automation" (Double CD & Poster. Uncoated paper and special effects such as blind embossing & uv varnish) *on International Deejay Gigolo Records in 2005* - techno -

SUPERLOW, D.: HALVOR BODIN **for Red Harvest** "A Greater Darkness" (Digipak)
on Season of Mist in 2006 - Metal -

KIM HIORTHØY for Moha! "Raus Aus Stavanger" (CD) *on Rune Grammofon in 2005*

KIM HIORTHØY for Susanna and The Magical Orchestra "Melody Mountain" (CD) *on Rune Grammofon in 2006*

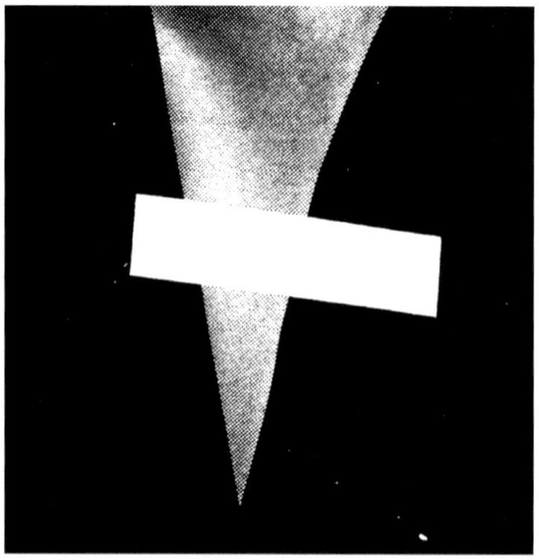

KIM HIORTHØY for Free Fall "Amsterdam Funk" (CD) *on Smalltown Superjazzz in 2005*

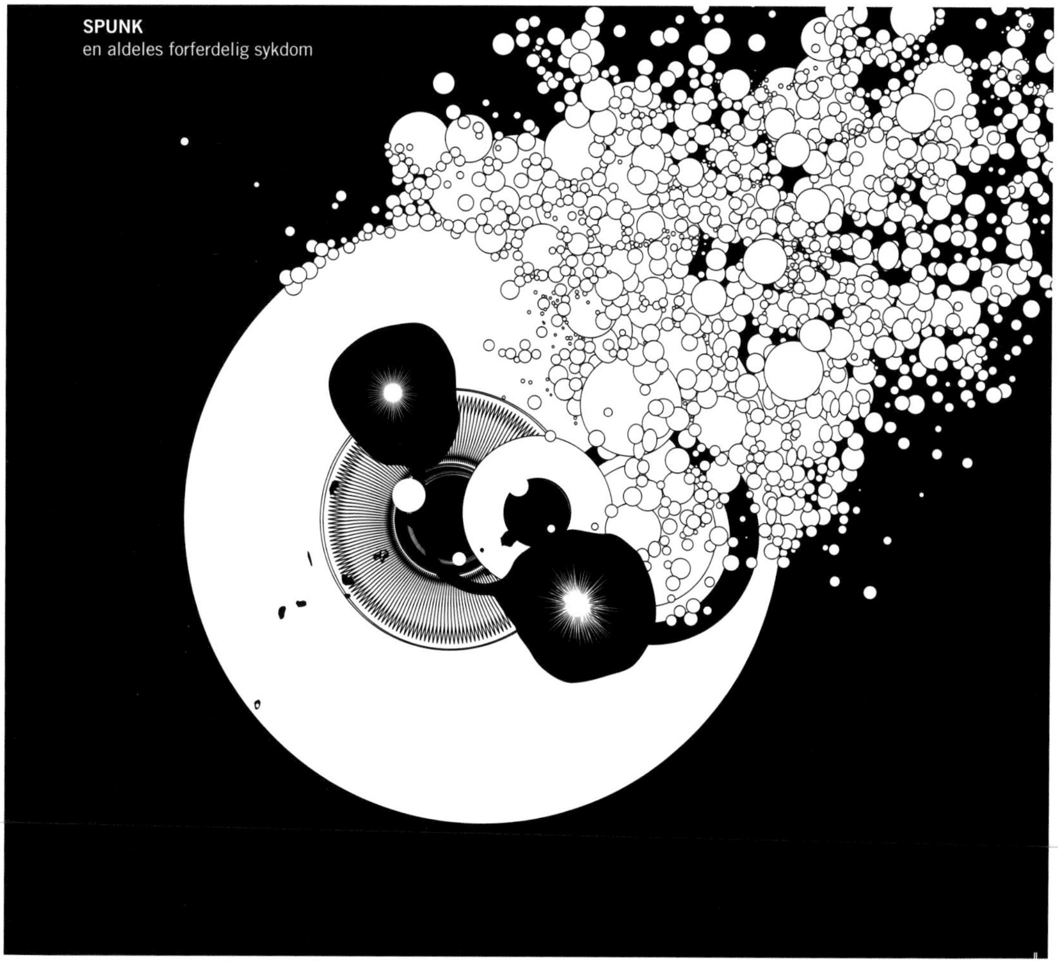

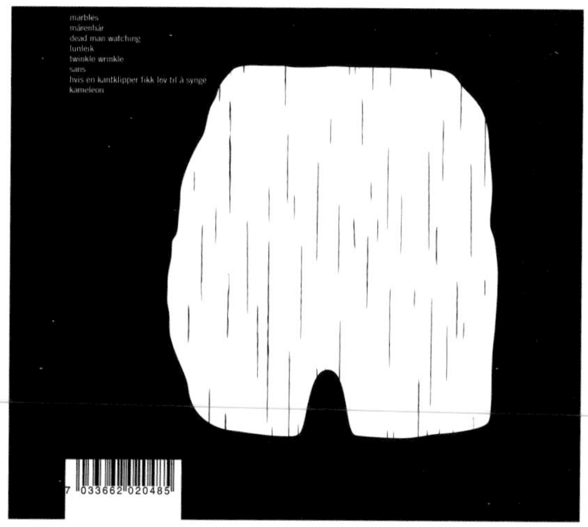

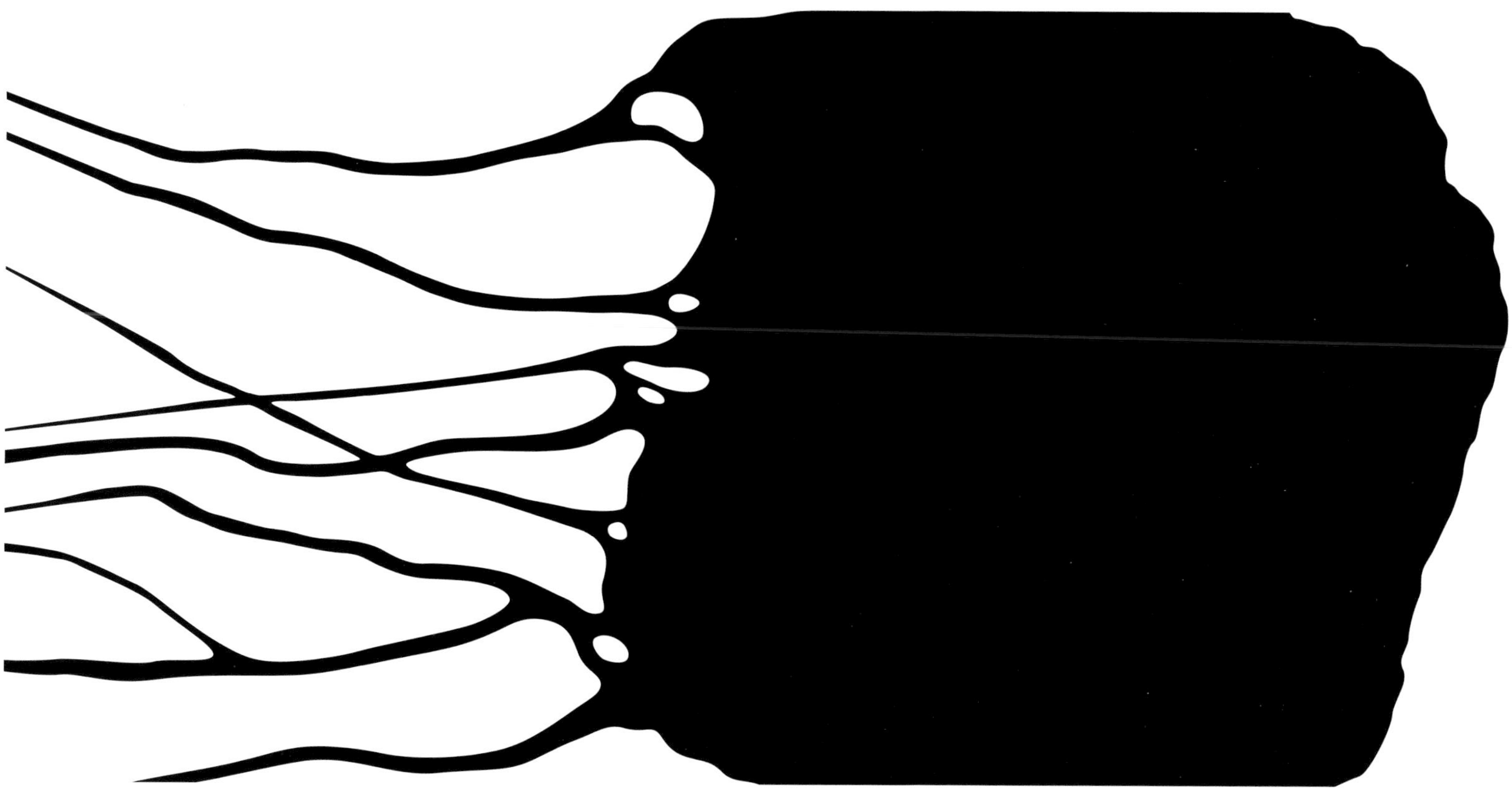

KIM HIORTHØY for Spunk "En aldeles forferdelig sykdom" (CD) *on Rune Grammofon in 2005*

KIM HIORTHØY for Motorpsycho "Black Hole/Blank Canvas" (LP) *on Stickman Records in 2006*

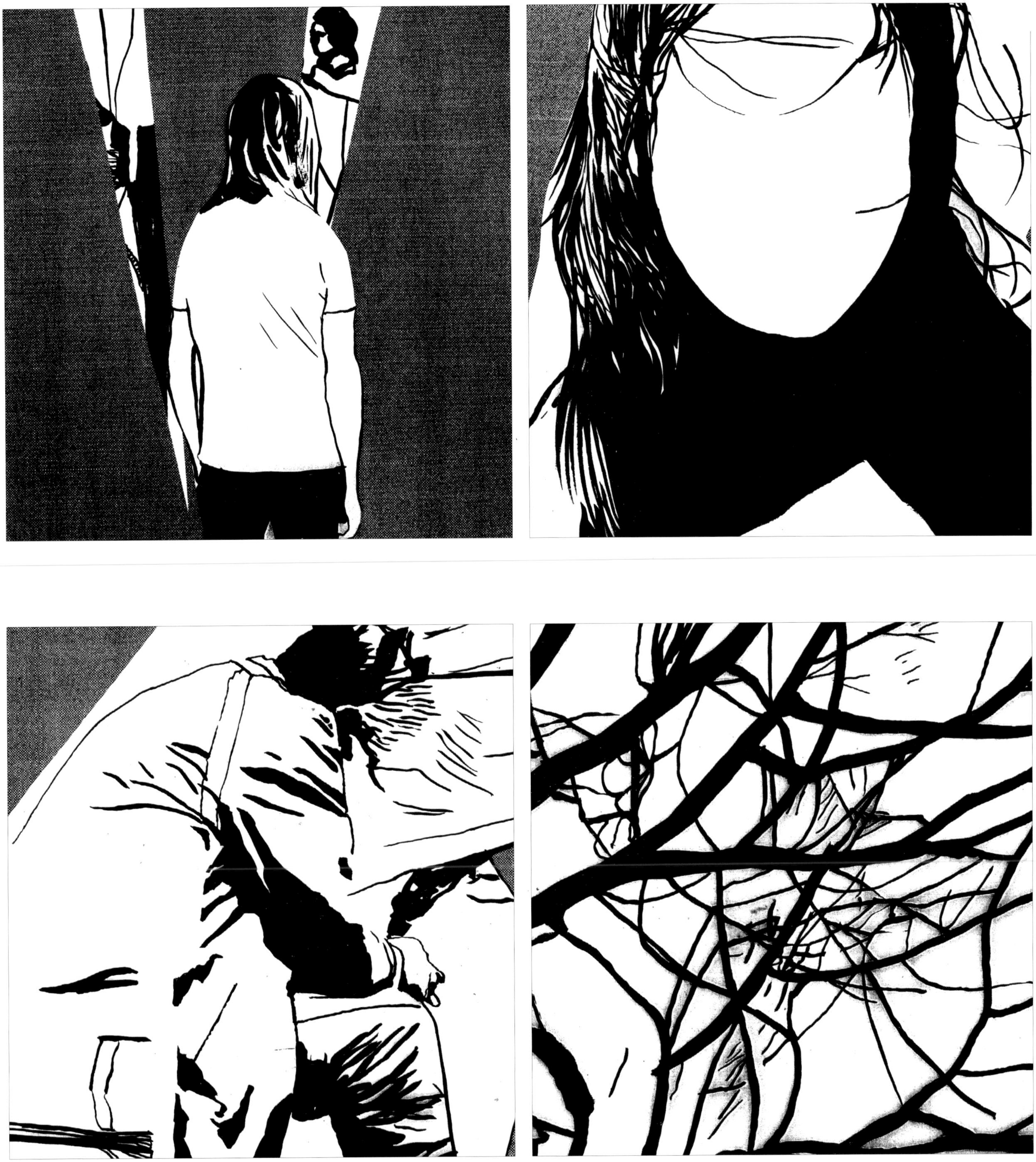

KIM HIORTHØY for Motorpsycho "Black Hole/Blank Canvas" (LP) *on Stickman Records in 2006*

PAUL FLACK & NON FORMAT for Lo Editions presents "Tummy Touch" (CD)
on BMG Zomba / Lo Recordings in 2006

PAUL FLACK for Michael Garrick Trio "Moonscape" (Limited Set of 3 Posters - A1)
on Trunk Records in 2007 - Rare British Jazz -

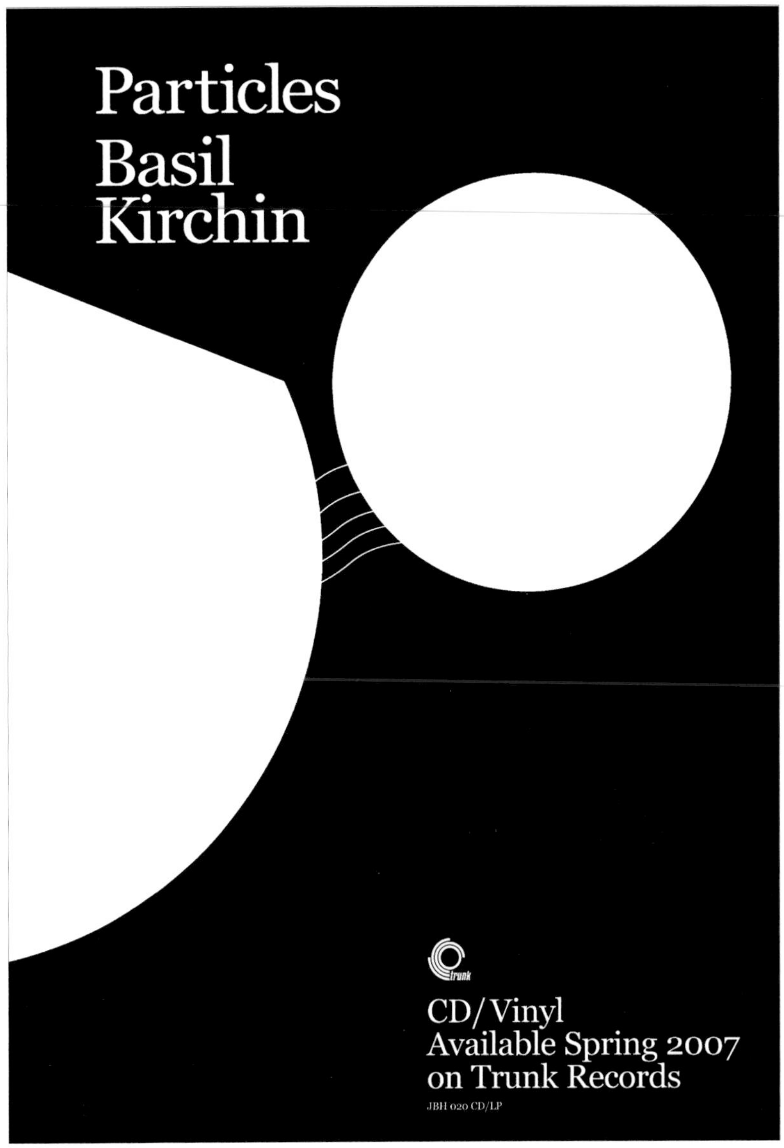

PAUL FLACK for Basil Kirchin "Particles" (Limited Edition Promotional Poster - A1)
on Trunk Records in 2007 - Obscure British Jazz -

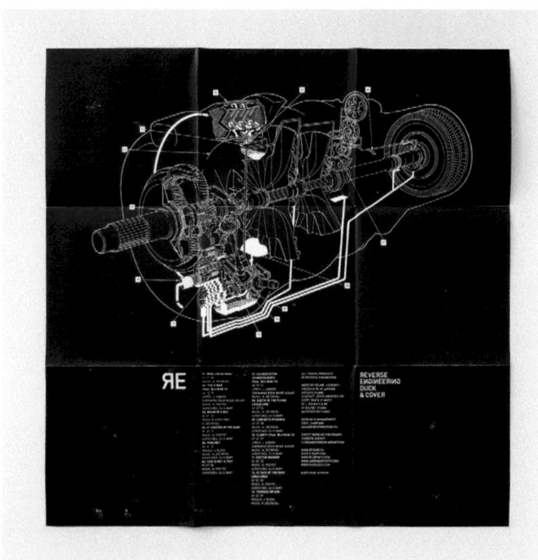

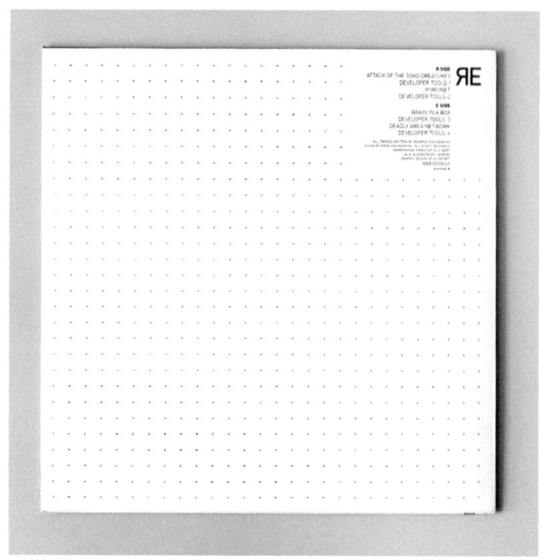

SÉBASTIEN VIGNE, D.: JULIEN NOTTER **for Reverse Engineering** "Duck & Cover" (Pocketpack), "Reverse Engineering feat. Blu Rum 13" (Vinyl) & "RE" (Vinyl) *on Jarring Effects in 2004 - 2006* - Abstract Hip Hop -

ANGELA LORENZ for Son Of Clay "Two Abstract Paintings" (CD/LP, prints, sound installation, realtime visuals)
on Mitek in 2005 (ongoing) - Soundscape -

JOT for Blown "Promo CD" (CD) *on Condor Records in 2004* - Metalcore -

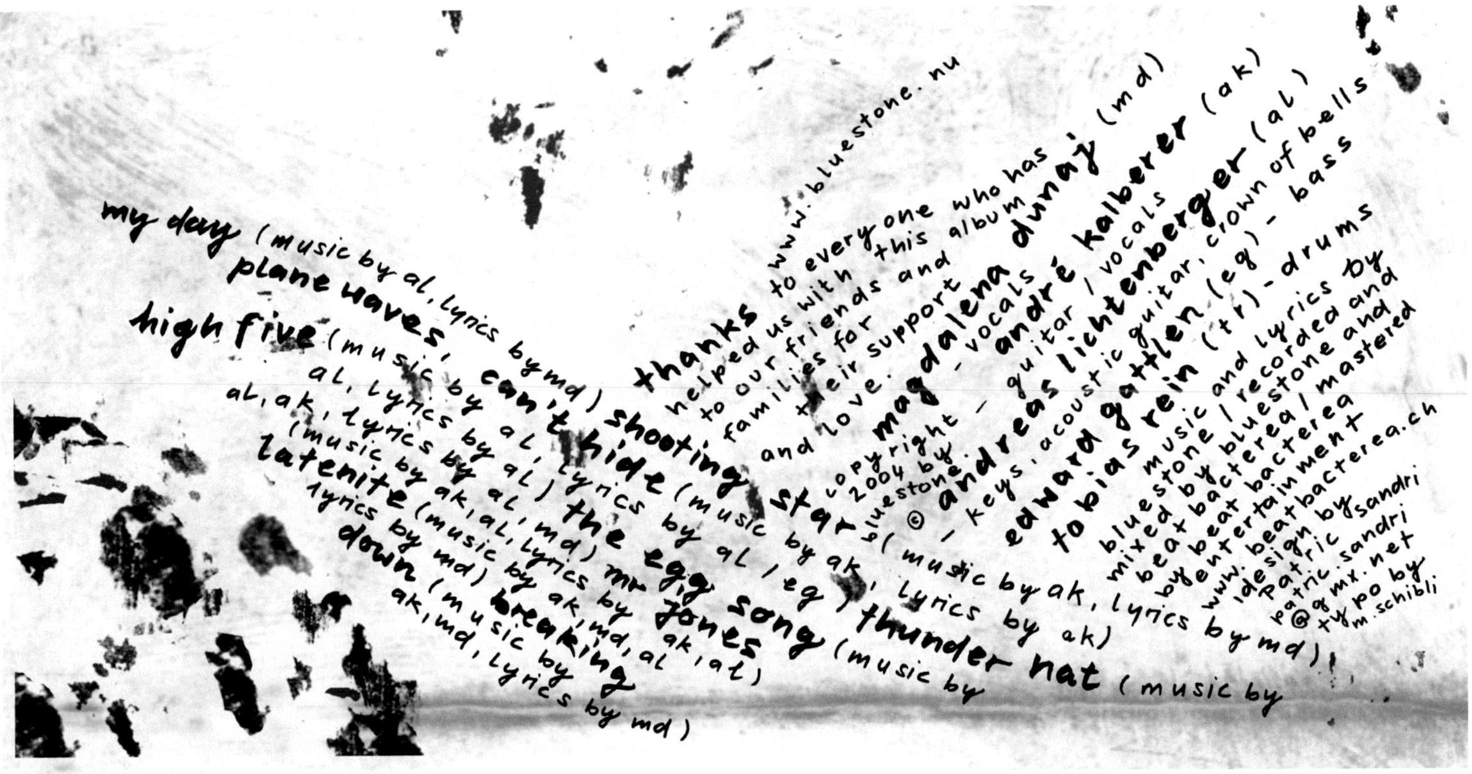

PATRIC SANDRI for Bluestone "Bluestone, Latenine" (CD) *in 2005* - Rock -

PRECIOUS | ART DIRECTION & DESIGN for Giardini di Mirò "North Atlantic Treaty Of Love, Part 2" (12") *on 2nd rec in 2006* - Postrock / Electronica -

PRECIOUS | ART DIRECTION & DESIGN for Giardini di Mirò "North Atlantic Treaty Of Love" (CD) *on 2nd rec in 2006* - Postrock, Electronica -

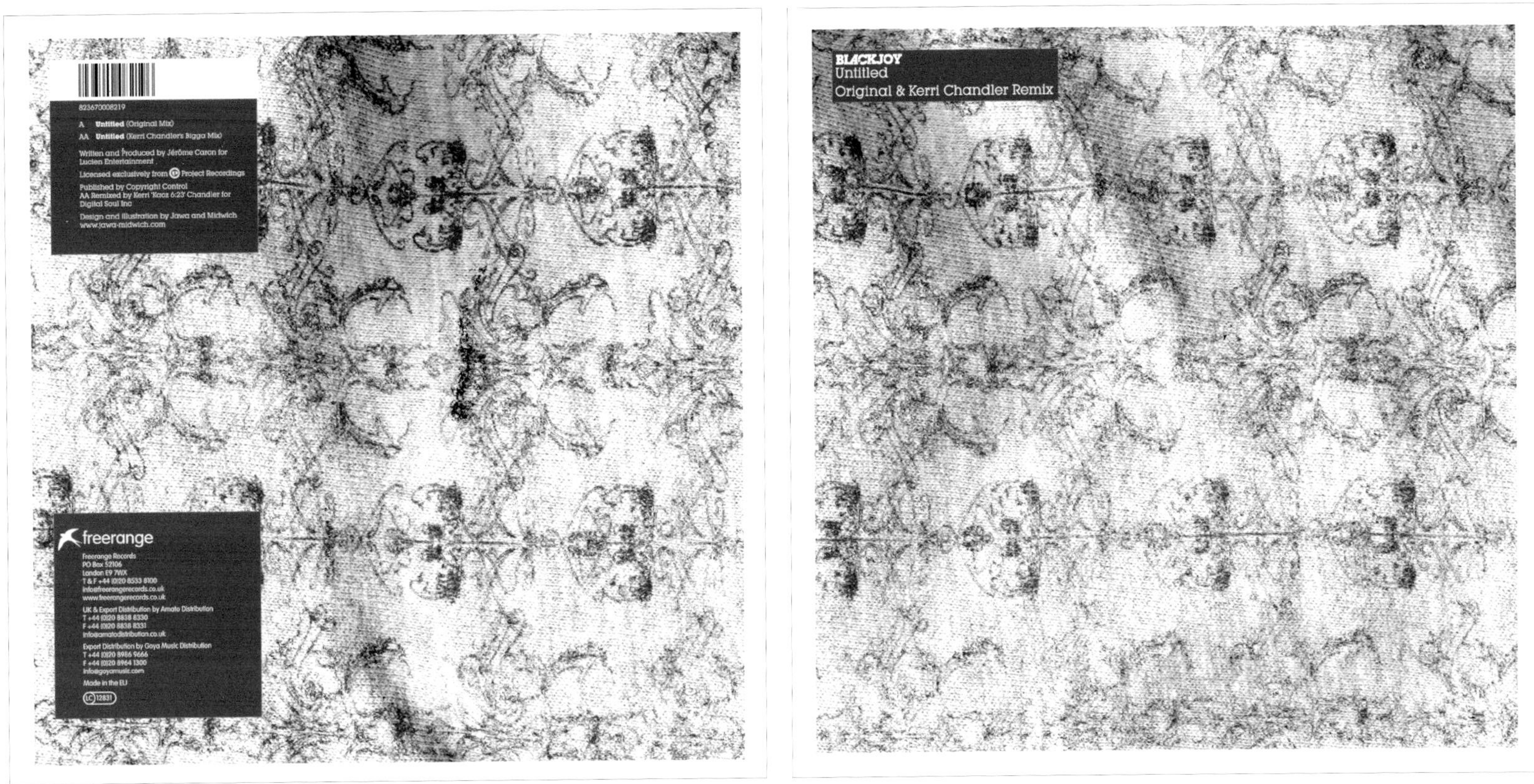

JAWA AND MIDWICH, D.: NILS DAVEY AND SIMON DOVAR **for Black Joy** "Untitled" (12" Slipcase) *on Freerange Records in 2006* - House -

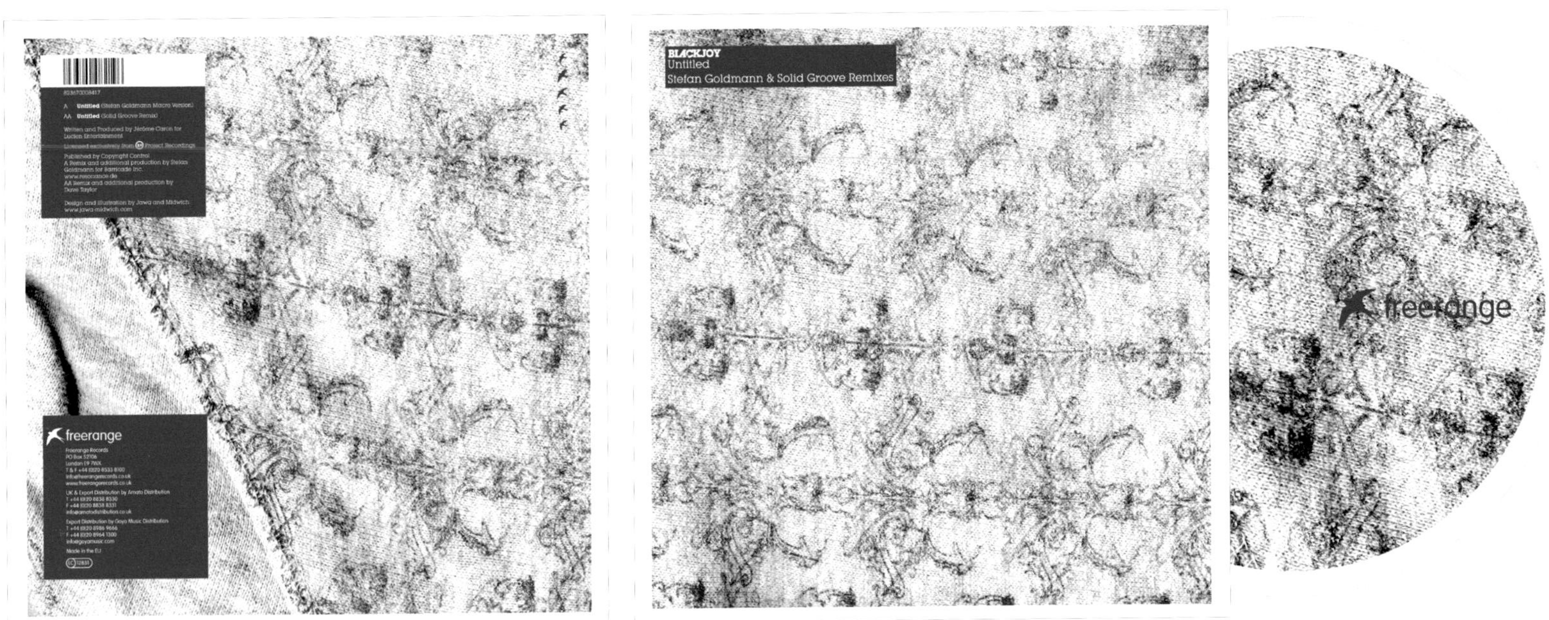

JAWA AND MIDWICH, D.: NILS DAVEY AND SIMON DOVAR **for Black Joy** "Untitled Remix" (12" Slipcase) *on Freerange Records in 2006* - House -

KIM HIORTHØY for Mats Gustafsson and Yoshimi "Words On The Floor" (CD) *on Smalltown Superjazzz in 2007*

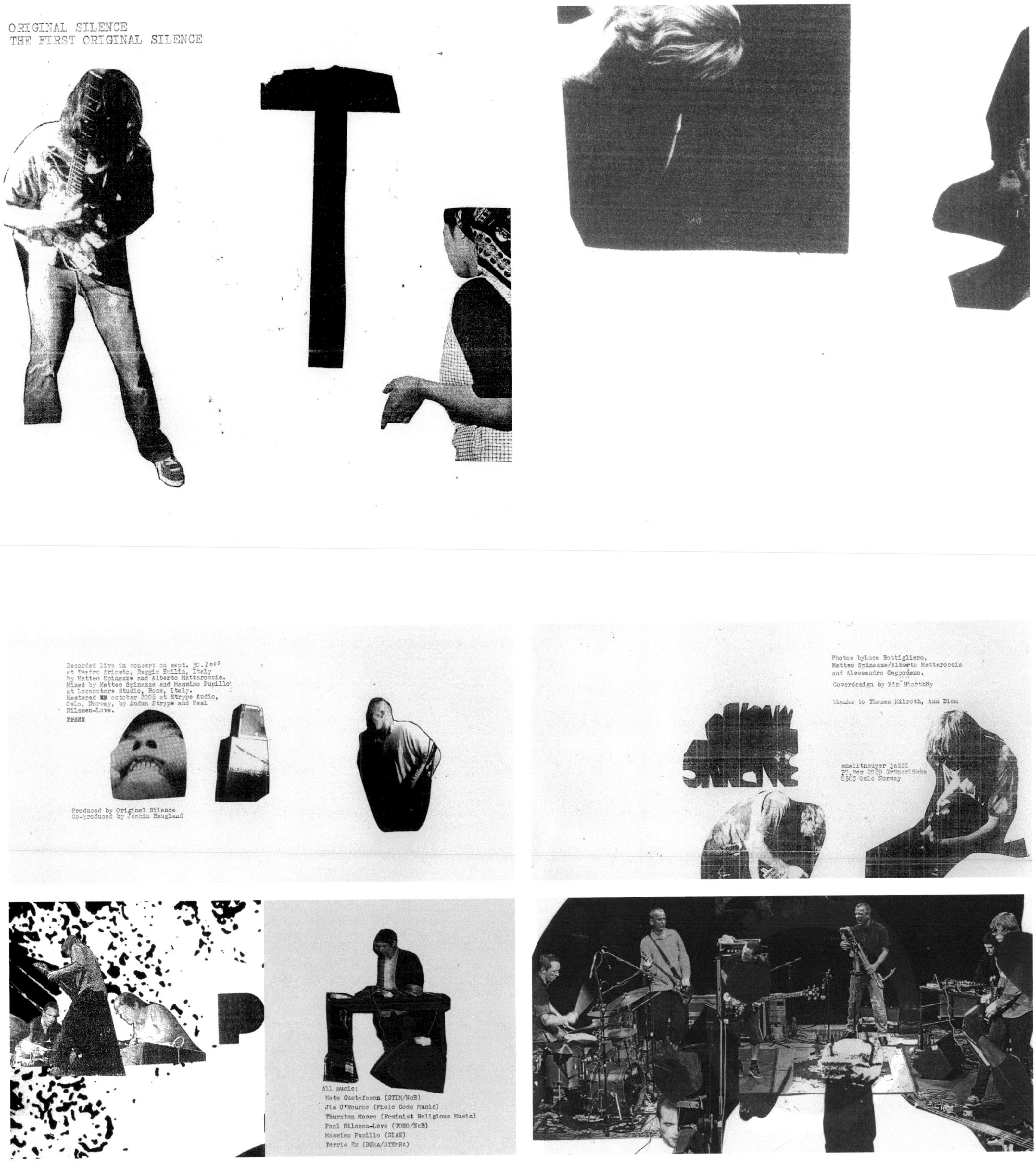

KIM HIORTHØY for Original Silence "The First Original Silence" (CD) *on Smalltown Superjazzz in 2007*

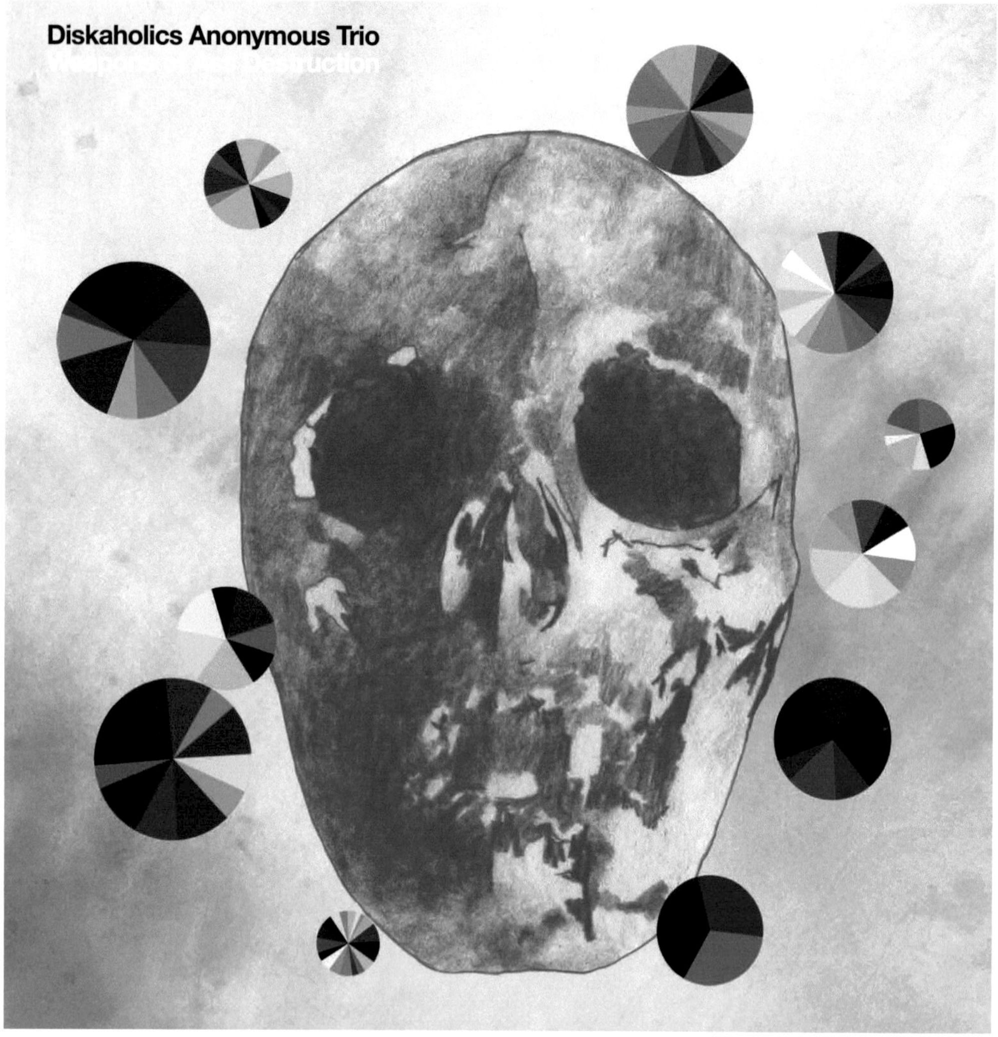

KIM HIORTHØY for Diskaholics Anonymous "Weapons of Ass Destruction" (LP) *on Smalltown Superjazzz in 2005*

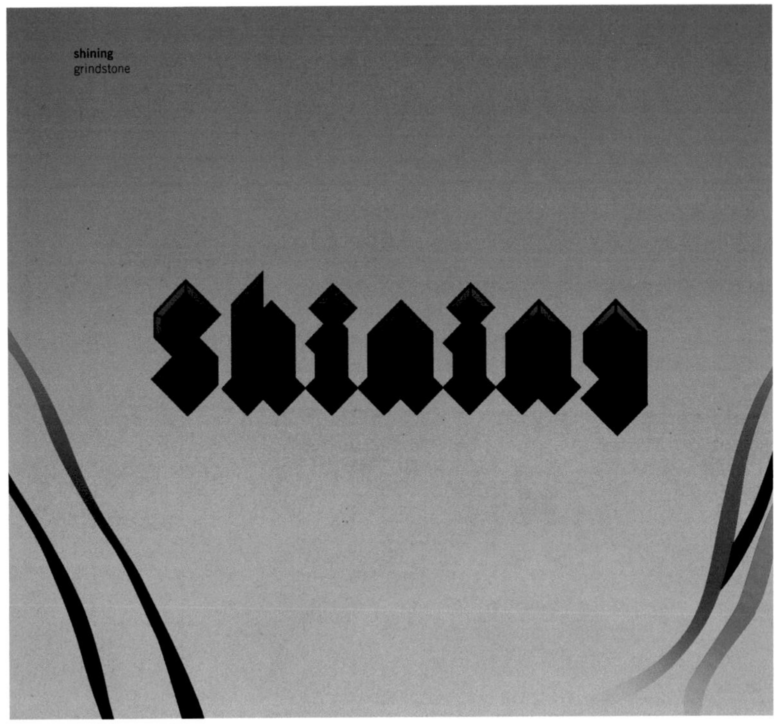

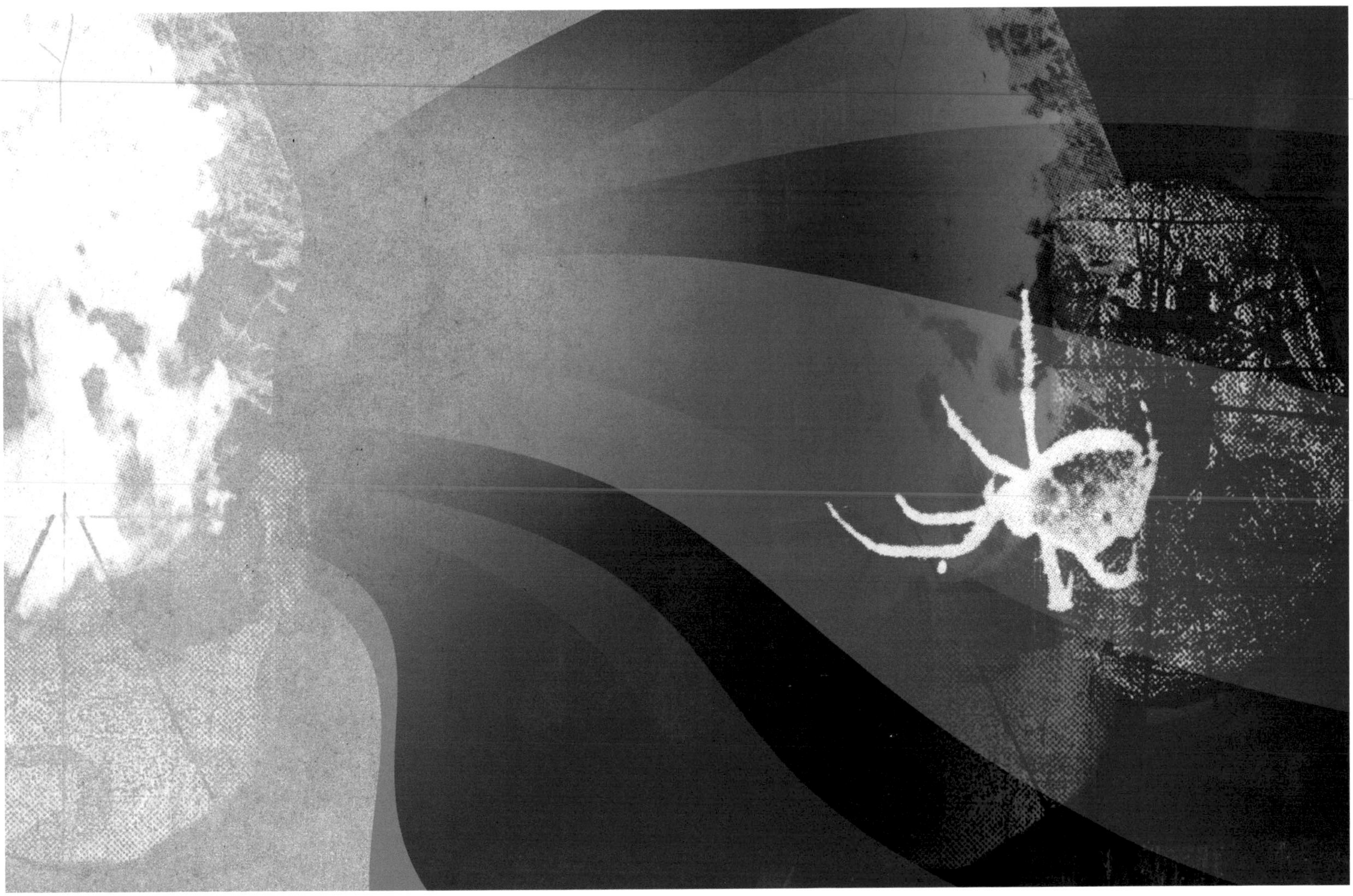

KIM HIORTHØY for Shining "Grindstone" (CD) *on Rune Grammofon in 2006*

YOKOLAND, D.: ASLAK GURHOLT RØNSEN **for Center of the Universe** "Anachronisma" (CD-R) *on Metronomicon Audio in 2006*

YOKOLAND, D.: ESPEN FRIBERG, CHRISTIAN BRANDT & ASLAK GURHOLT RØNSEN **for Magnus Moriarty™ vs. Center of the Universe** "Did U order a Radar?" (CD-R) *on Metronomicon Audio in 2006* -Folk Rock/Mash-up -

YOKOLAND, D.: ASLAK GURHOLT RØNSEN & ESPEN FRIBERG **for Magnus Moriarty™** "Sky-fi Beatitude" (CD-R) *on Metronomicon Audio in 2005* - Lo-fi/Sci-fi -

YOKOLAND, D.: ASLAK GURHOLT RØNSEN & ESPEN FRIBERG **for Täppas Strepens** "The Great American Brainkiller" (CD-R) *on Metronomicon Audio in 2005*

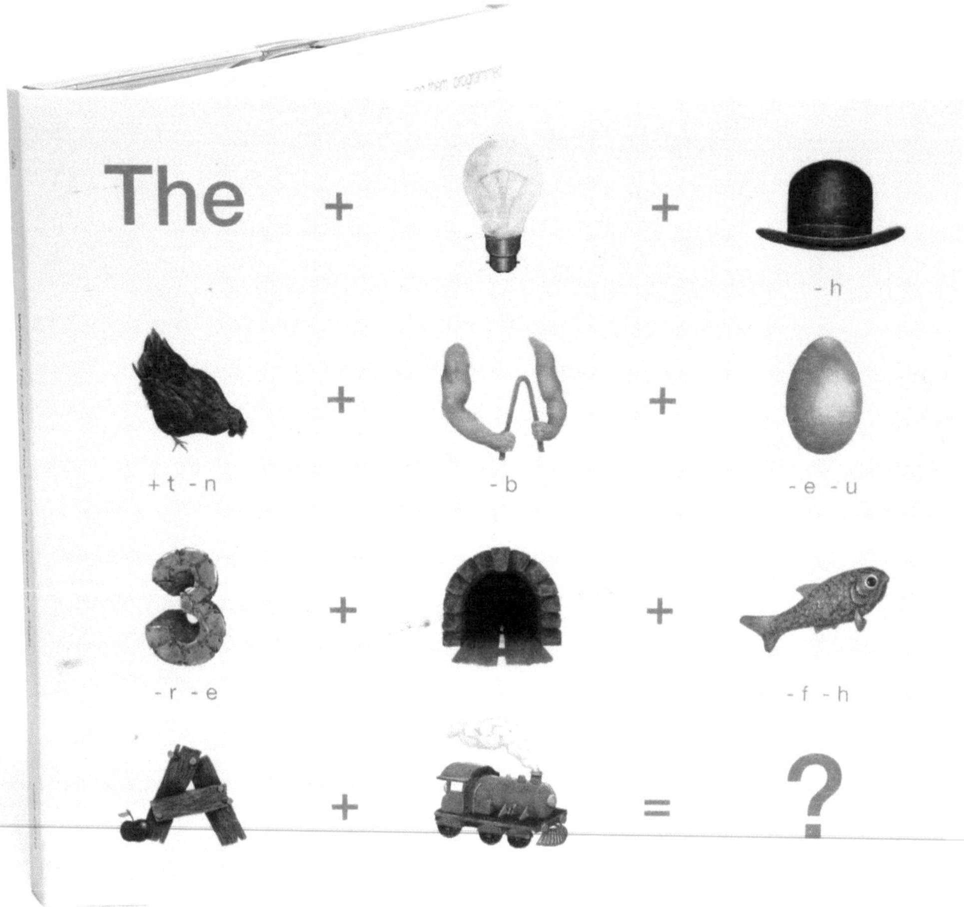

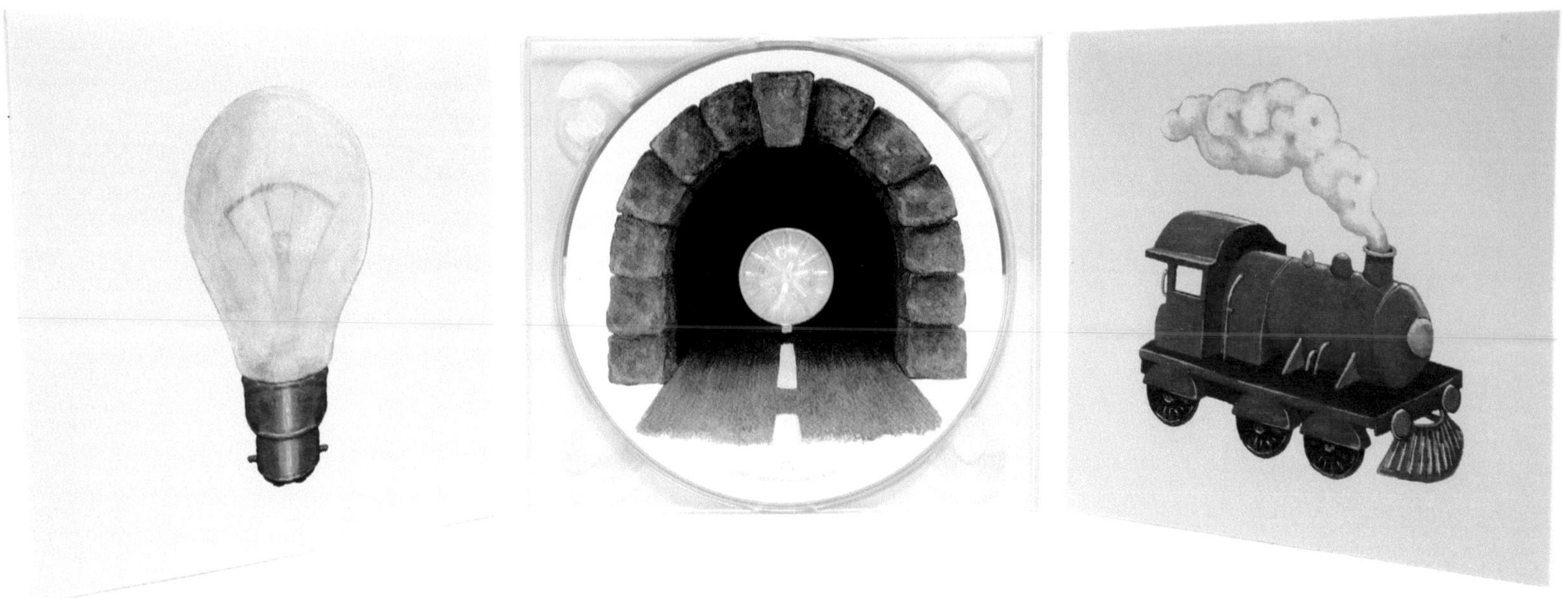

PATRICK DUFFY for Whitey "The Light At The End Of The Tunnel Is A Train" (6 panel digipak printed 4 col on uncoated stock) *on 1234 Records in 2005 - Electro Rock -*

STYLOROUGE LTD D.: SHARON CHAI **for The Cooper Temple Clause** "Make This Your Own" (Special limited edition 12" vinyl (& CD jewel case also to be uploaded) with die-cuts & 2 inserts - Paper Sculptures - Richard Sweeney Photography - Mikkel Lundsager Hansen, Richard Sweeney, Sharon Chai Live band photography - Ami Barwell Group band photography - Ellis Parrinder) *on Sequel Records, 2007*

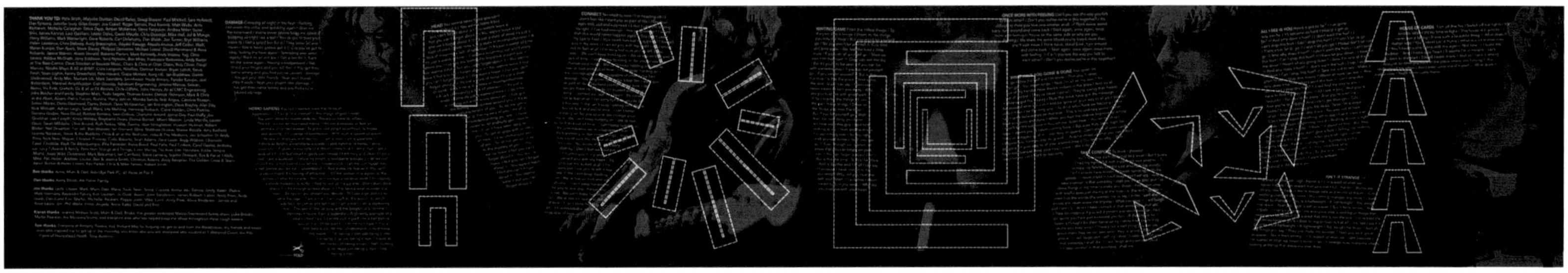

THE
COOPER
TEMPLE
CLAUSE
MAKE THIS YOUR OWN

VIVELETUNING, D.: HELM PFOHL / CHRAGI FREI **for Wheel** "Destination Anywhere" (CD) *on (self produced record) in 2005* - Rock -

FROM ME. HEY, YOU BROWN-EYED BARMAID. TAKE A REST AND COME WITH ME. I'LL SHOW YOU THE COLOUR OF THE OCEAN. I'LL SHOW YOU THAT LIFE IS FREE. .: **FAR FROM HEAVEN** :. I'M MISSING YOU. AND TO KISS WITH YOU. I SEE YOUR FACE. ON ANOTHER PLACE. I WANNA BE WITH YOU. I WANNA TRUST TO YOU. JUST TELL ME WHY. IT MAY NEVER BE. I'M FAR FROM HEAVEN. I'M FAR FROM HOME. I SHOULD TAKE ANOTHER TRAIN TO COME. I'VE GOT A ONE WAY TICKET. THERE IS NO RETURN. THIS TRAIN'S TOO FAST. MY SOUL ALREADY BURNS. I'M TRYING TO CATCH YOU. I'M TRYING TO SEE YOU. BUT THERE ARE TOO MANY PEOPLE WHO LOOK LIKE YOU. IT SEEMS TO ME, YOU'RE NOT EVEN REAL. I'M FIGHTING A GHOST FROM ANOTHER WORLD. .: **KLEBSTOFF** :. MY WORDS DON'T MAKE A SENSE. THEY ARE JUST HELPLESS SELF-DEFENCE. NO LANGUAGE CAN BE STRONG ENOUGH TO TELL YOU. TO TELL YOU WHAT'S UP. I SEE MY DREAMS FALLING APART. NO GLUE CAN HEAL MY BROKEN HEART. YOUR FACE BEHIND MY CLOSED EYES. IT HEARTS MY HEART SO MANY TIMES. I'M INCAPABLE TO DESCRIBE THE PAIN. IT WILL NEVER BE THE SAME. THE PASSING DAYS ARE GREY LIKE STONE. WITHIN ALL THOSE PEOPLE I'M STILL ALONE.

TUNNEL :. EVERYBODY, EVERYBODY'S TELLING ME STORIES. HISTORIES ABOUT MYSTERIES OF LOVE. SO I'M ASKING MYSELF: WHY IS EVERYBODY RUNNING AWAY OR PUSHING AWAY THE REALITY? IT'S JUST A TUNNEL. A CRAZY FUNNEL. AN UNCONTROLLABLE SWITCHBOARD PANEL. A TUNNEL OF DARKNESS. THE LIGHT IS TOO FAR AWAY. YOU'LL NEVER SEE A SUNNY DAY. IT'S JUST A GAME OF EVOLUTION. YOU'VE GOT NO CHANCE FOR REVOLUTION. YOU'RE A POOR SLAVE OF YOUR OWN. YOU'RE LIKE A ROLLING STONE. YOU KNOW YOUR DESTINATION WELL. DESTRUCTION. IT'S NO NEED TO TELL. HER CHEMISTRY WILL BRING YOU DOWN. AND TURN YOUR HEART. AGAINST YOUR BRAIN. I'M TRYING TO SAIL AGAINST THE WIND. I'M LIKE A FOOL. COMPLETELY BLIND. I LOST MY WAY AND TRY TO FIND. A HOTEL IN A DESERT PLAIN. .: **BLUES BEIN** :. I'M WALKING DOWN THE SEDWYEON STREET. LOOKING FOR A PLACE TO STAY. ELWOOD AND THE BLUES ARE CALLING. THE BLUES BEIN IS OPEN AGAIN! HEY, YOU BROWN-EYED BARMAID. DON'T YOU KNOW THERE'S ANOTHER LIFE. YOU'RE WORKING EVERY DAY AND NIGHT. THE WORLD IS AS BEAUTIFUL AS YOU ARE! A PLACE IS ONLY AS GOOD AS YOU FEEL. THIS MAY BE THE REASON FOR ME. CAUSE I FEEL GOOD AND I FEEL FREE. THE SADNESS HAS FALLEN OFF

BIANCA STRAUCH for Thomas Fehlmann "Honigpumpe" (Do LP Cover) *on Kompakt in 2007* - Electronic -

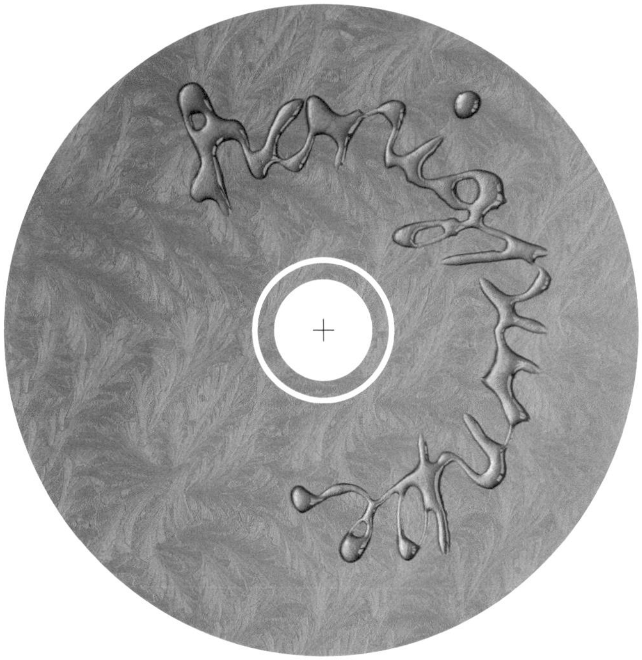

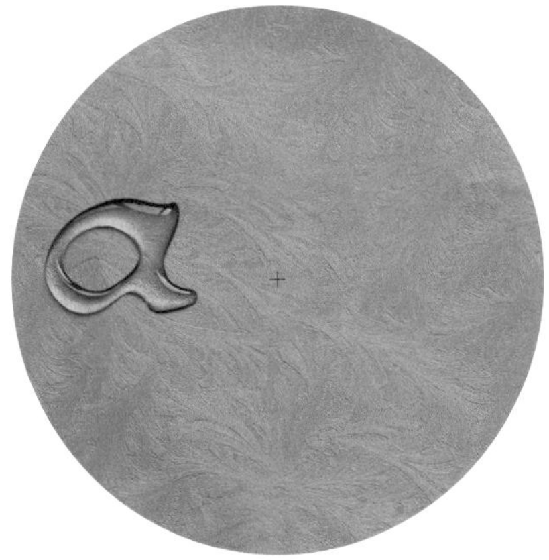
a

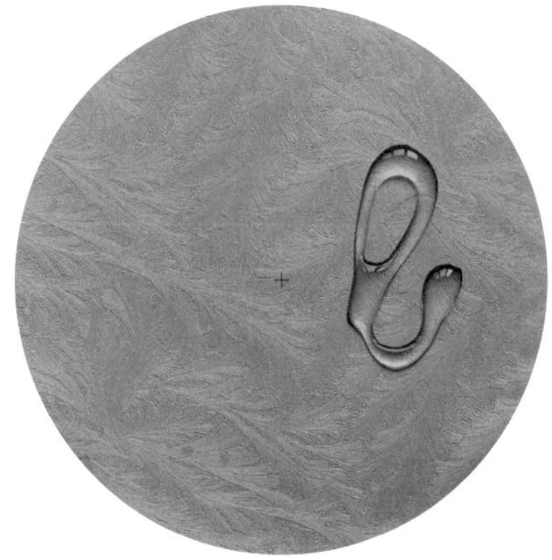
b

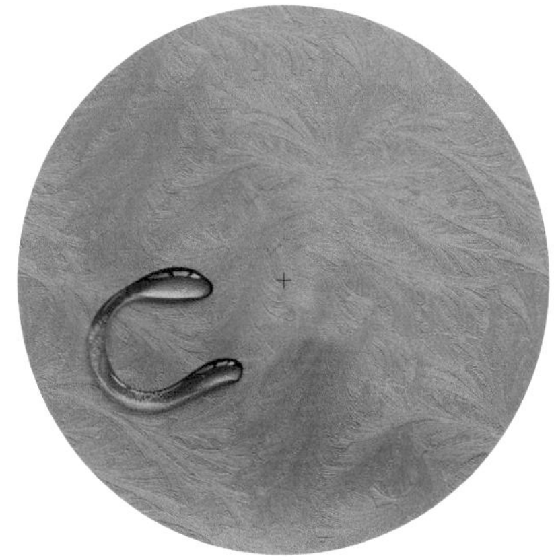
c

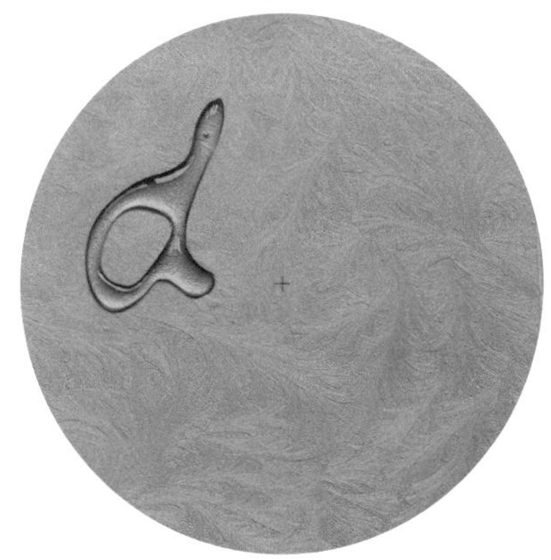
d

1. strahlensatz
2. soziale wärme
3. atlas 4. schaum
5. little big horn (liegend)
6. bienenkönigin
7. I.R.N.I.I.F.
8. 100 bäume
9. arbeitstitel 10. atlas 2
11. dusted with powder
12. with oil
8 80319 03092 5
●KOMPAKT SCHALLPLATTEN WERDERSTRASSE 15-19 D-50672 KÖLN FON+49/221-94995-0 FAX-150 WWW.KOMPAKT-NET.DE MADE IN GERMANY GEMA LC 12012
●KOMPAKT CD 59

STYLOROUGE LTD, D.: SARAH FOLEY **for The Subways** "Young for Eternity" (10" vinyl & CD)
on Infectious records in 2005 - Rock -

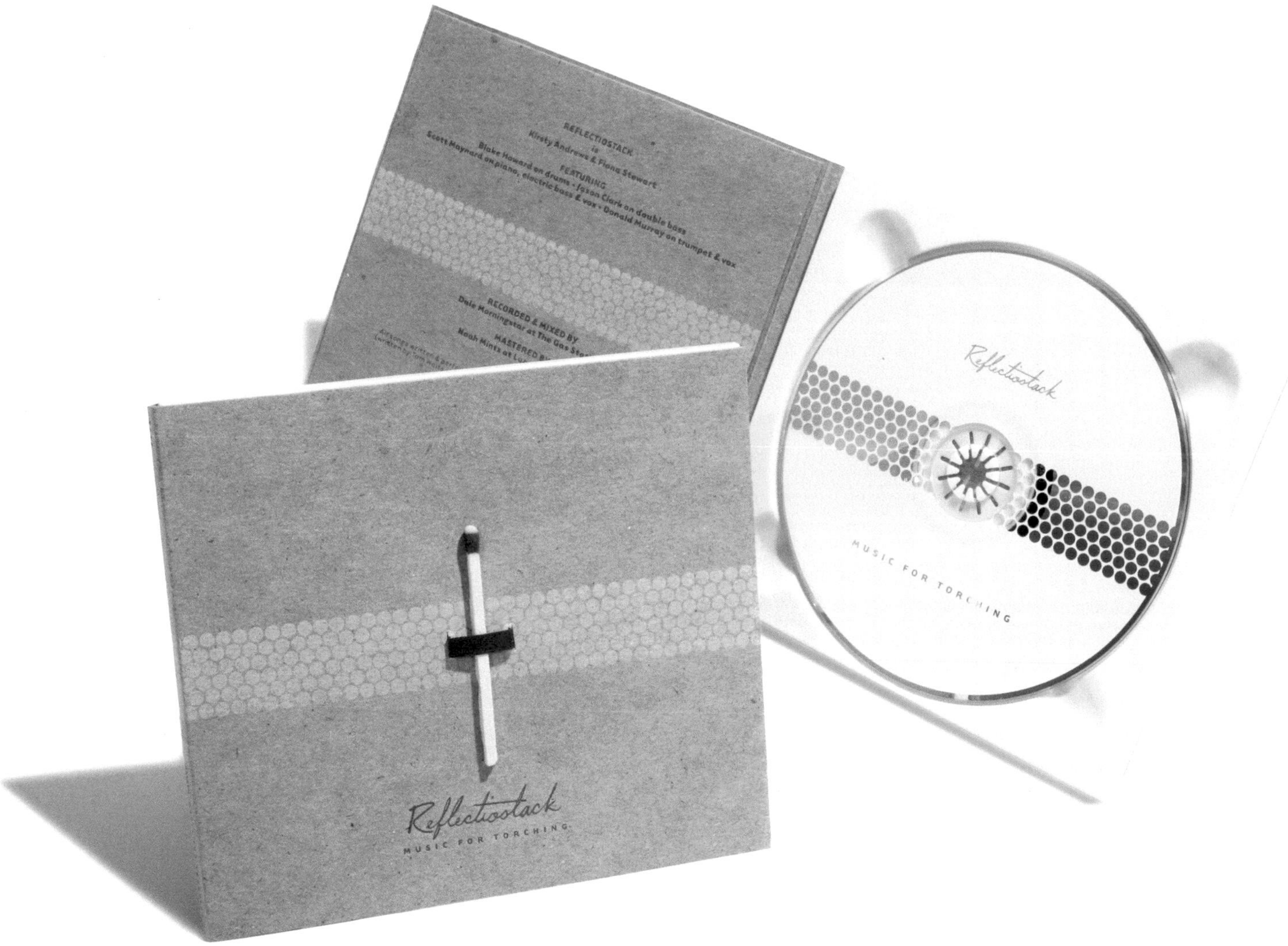

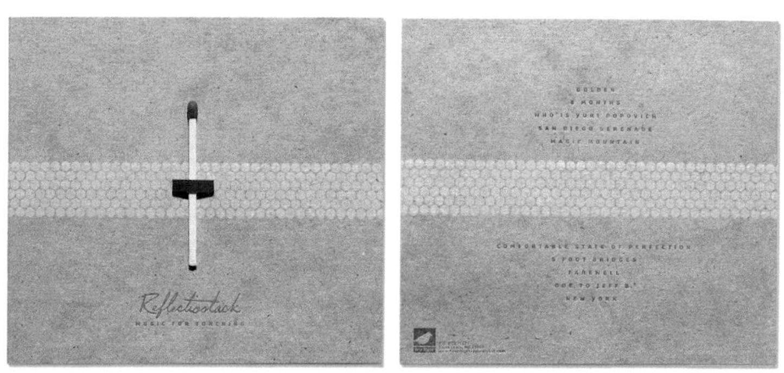

THE BACK BURNER, D.: JESSE SOUTHERLAND **for Reflectiostack** "Music for Torching" (Letterpress, hand-assembled, each package contains single match handplaced and strapped to cover.) *on First Flight Record Label in 2006* - Indie -

SNASK, D.: MAGNUS BERG **for Manatees-Untitled** (Digi Pack: Black matte papper, Black spot varnish on Front, Gold foiling on inside) *on Motivesounds Recordings in 2006*

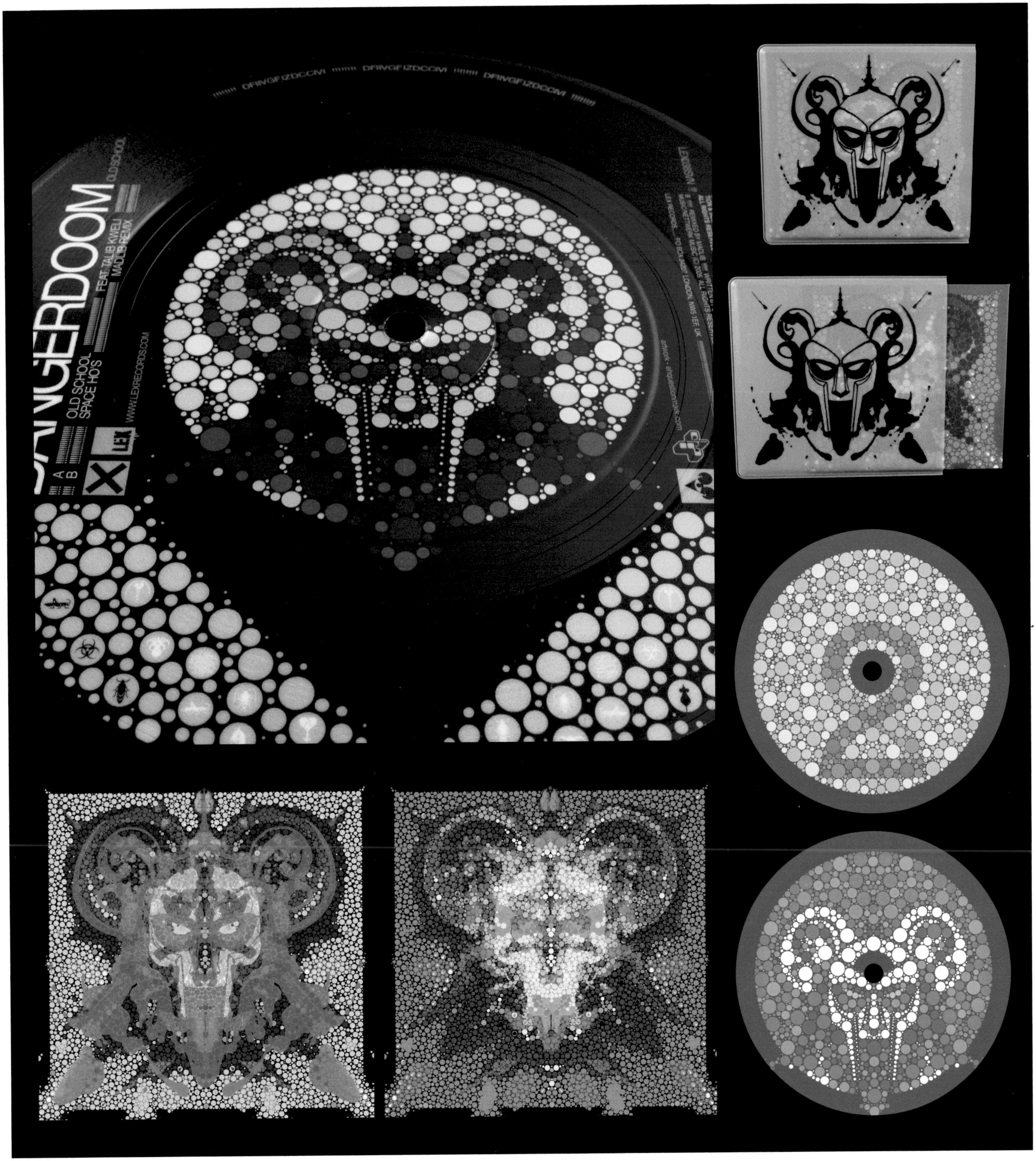

EHQUESTIONMARK for Dangerdoom "Old school" & "The mouse and the mask" (EP, 7", LP) *on Lex Records in 2005 & 2006*

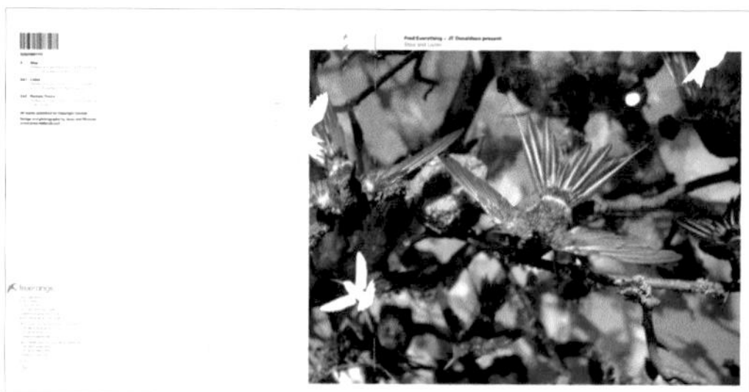

JAWA AND MIDWICH, D.: NILS DAVEY AND SIMON DOVAR **for Fred Everything + JT Donaldson** "Stop and Listen" (12") *on Freerange Records in 2006* - House -

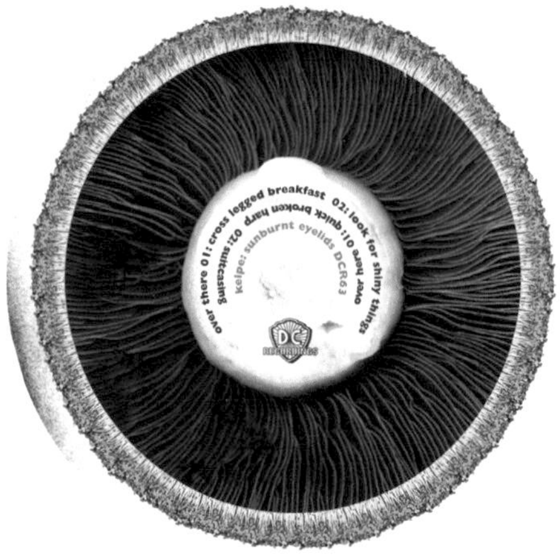

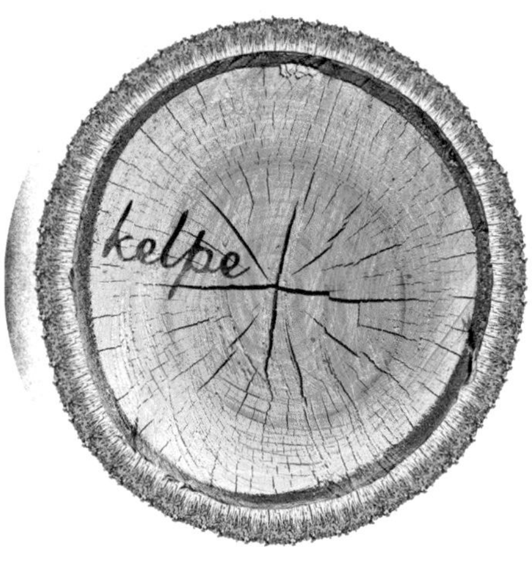

LA BOCA, D.: SCOT BENDALL **for Kelpe** "Sunburnt Eyelids" (12") *on DC Recordings in 2005* - Electronica -

ROBERT SAMSONOWITZ for various artists "Jazzflora 2 - Scandinavian Aspects of Jazz" (CD) *on Dealers of Nordic Music in 2005* - Jazz, Nu-jazz, Electronic -

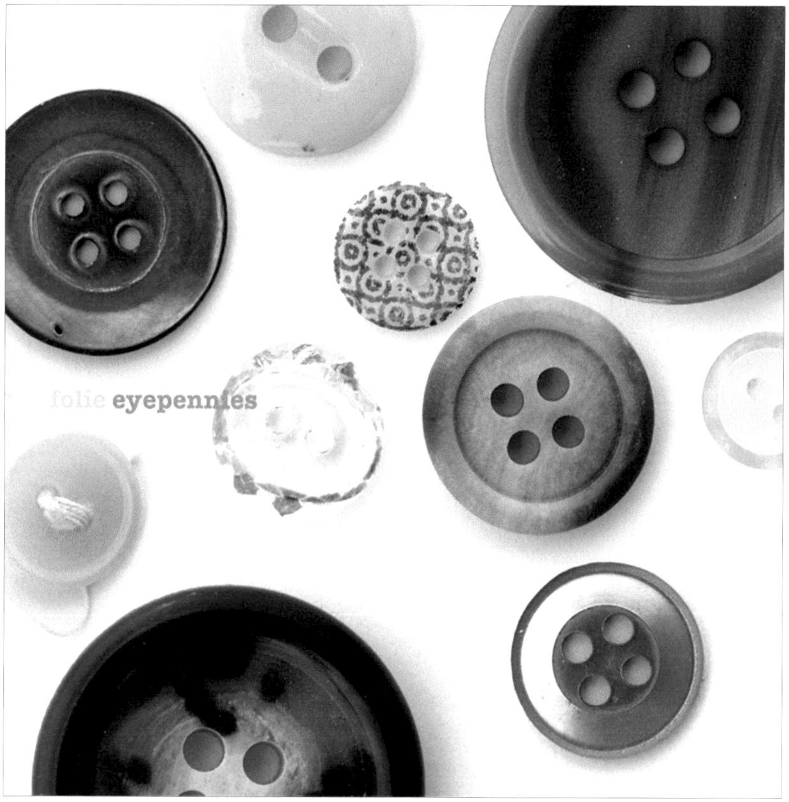

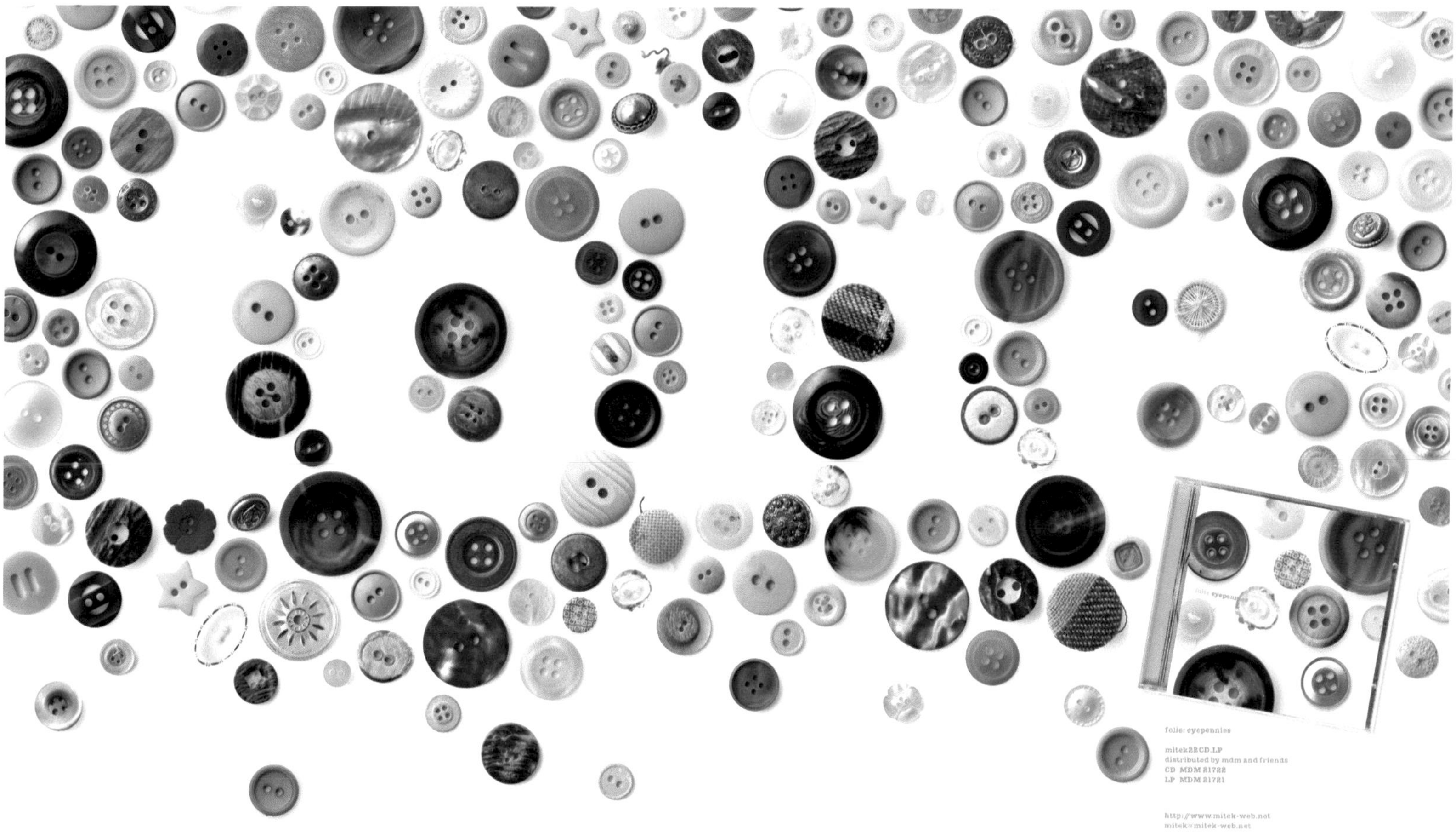

ANGELA LORENZ for Folie "Eyepennies" (Tour/sales Poster, DIN A2) *on Mitek in 2005* - Electronic -

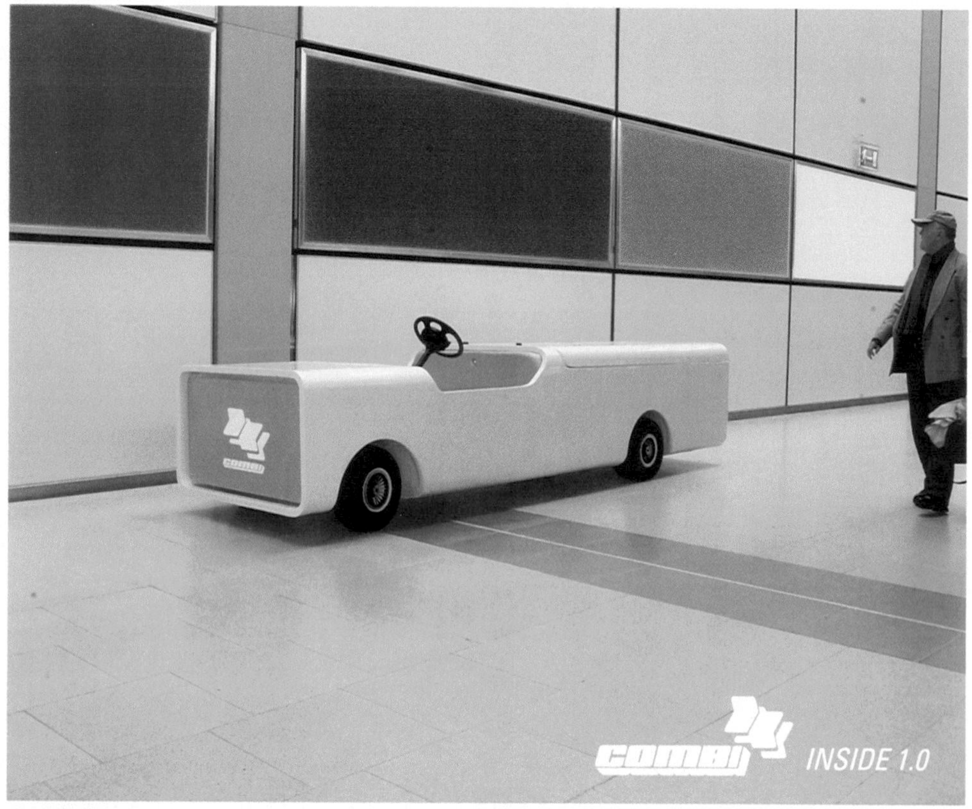

WEISSRAUM.DE(SIGN)°, D.: BERND BRINK & LUCAS BUCHHOLZ **for Combi** (Flyer *on Danced Records in 2005* - Tech-House -

YOKOLAND, D.: ASLAK GURHOLT RØNSEN & ESPEN FRIBERG **for Center of the Universe** "Staying up all night with the Center of the Universe" (CD-R) *on Metronomicon Audio in 2003* - Electronica/Pop/Breakbeats -

YOKOLAND, D.: ASLAK GURHOLT RØNSEN & ESPEN FRIBERG **for Cover for Metronomicon Audio's third compilation record** "3.0" (CD) *on Metronomicon Audio in 2006* - Various Alternative Music -

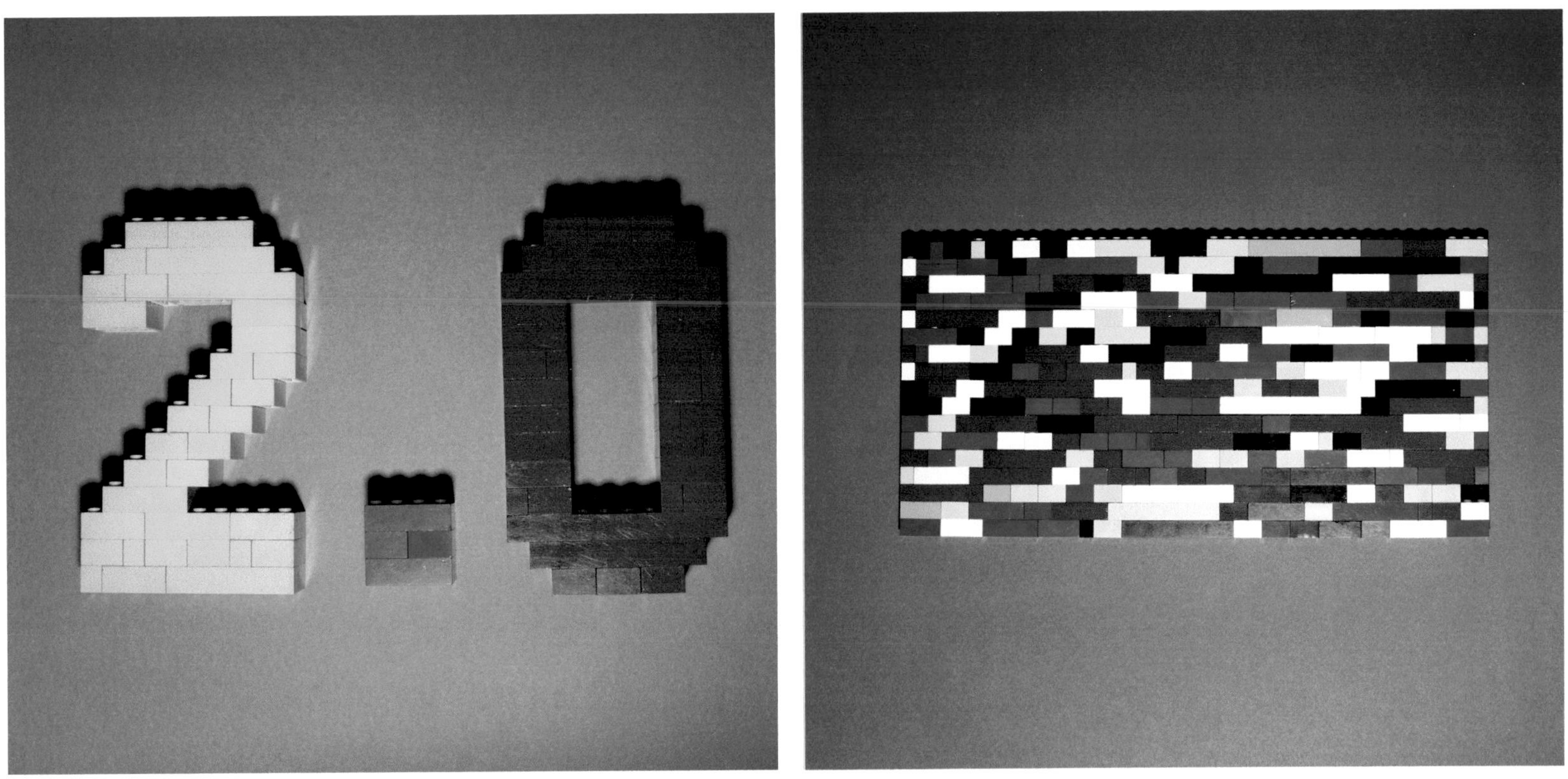

YOKOLAND, D.: ASLAK GURHOLT RØNSEN & ESPEN FRIBERG **for Metronomicon Audio's second compilation record** "2.0" (Recordcover for CD-R) *on Metronomicon Audio in 2005* - Various Alternative Music -

RINZEN for Farrah "Cut-out & Keep" (CD) *on Lojinx in 2006*

DIRK RUDOLPH for Marius Jung „Schau einfach nicht hin" (CD) *on Tacheles!/Roof Music GmbH in 2006; Photography by Christian Liepe* - Kabarett -

DIRK RUDOLPH **for Rufus Wainwright**
"Yellow Lounge" (CD) *on*
Deutsche Grammophon in 2007

TEA TIME STUDIOS, D.: SEBASTIAN LITMANOVICH **for Cineplexx** "Posologia" (CD) & "Pequeños accidentes domésticos" (mini CD)
on Caipirinha Music in 1999 & 2004 - indie electronic -

ASHI & OFFICE GREMINGER for "Cheers britain vol.4 the curfew protest!", "Cheers britain vol.1 ale right" & "Cheers britain vol.3 sparkling hits a go-go" (LP) *on primroose music in 2006*
- Typical Pub Tunes From Britain -

ZION GRAPHICS for **The Ark** "The Worrying Kind" (CD single) *on Roxy Recordings in 2007* - Pop -

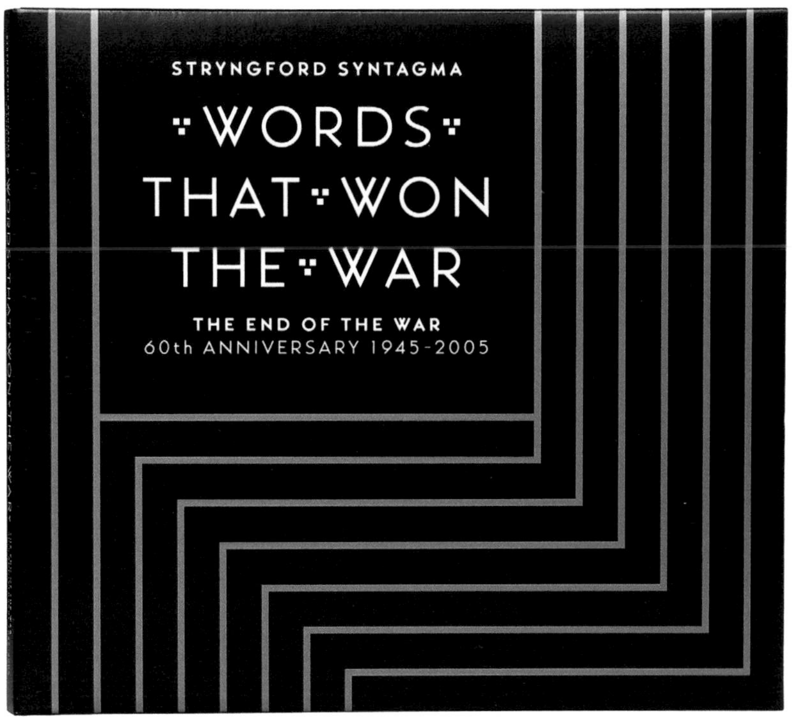

ZION GRAPHICS for **Stryngford Syntagma** "Words That Won The War" (CD)
on Stryngford Syntagma Records in 2005 - Electronic -

EHQUESTIONMARK for **Goove** "#103/No12" (CD)
on Groove Compilation in 2006

HUMAN EMPIRE, D.: JAN KRUSE for The Year Of "Slow days" (LP) *on Morr Music in 2006*

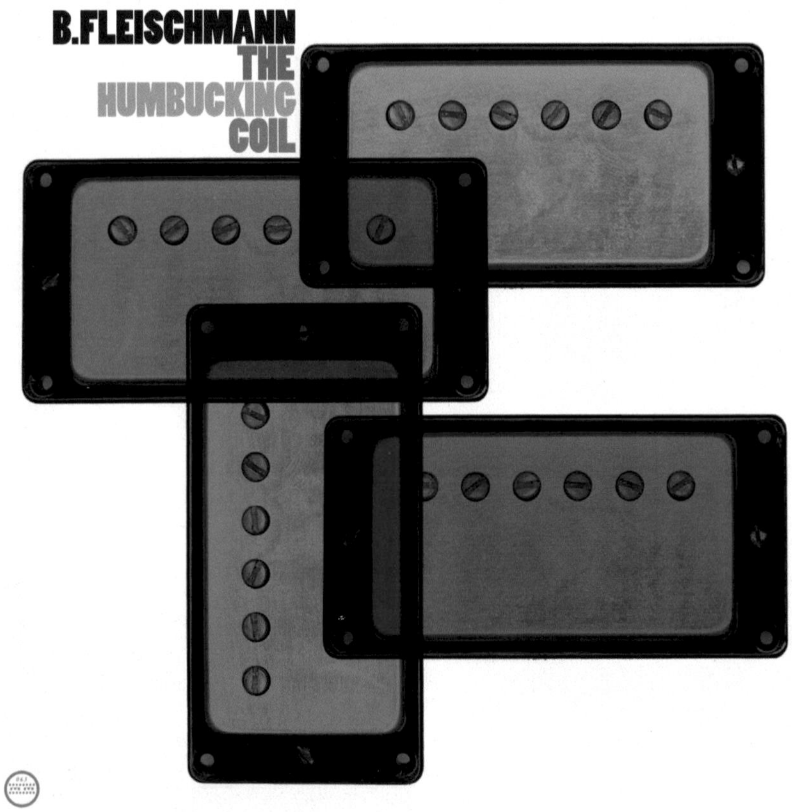

HUMAN EMPIRE, D.: JAN KRUSE for B. Fleischmann "The humbucking coil" (LP) *on Morr Music in 2006*

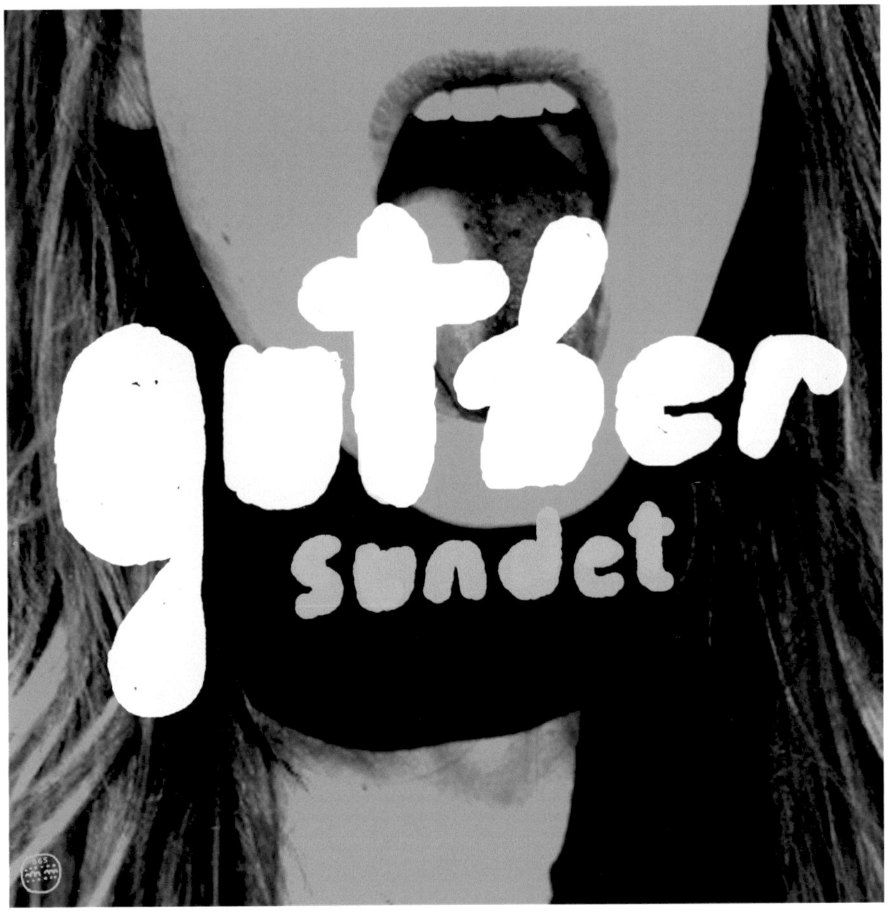

HUMAN EMPIRE, D.: JAN KRUSE **for Guther** "Sundet" (LP) *on Morr Music in 2006*

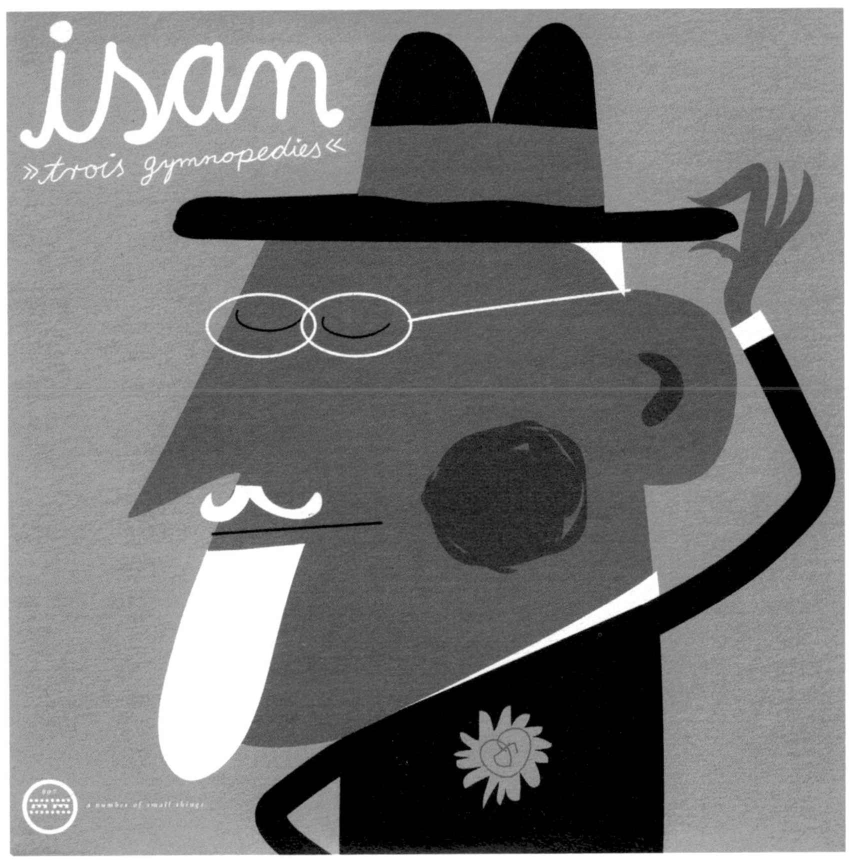

HUMAN EMPIRE, D.: JAN KRUSE **for Isan** "Trois Gymnopedies" (7") *on Morr Music in 2006*

JDK, D.: MIKE CARTER **for Wolf Parade April 18, 2006,** (Hand screen printed Poster) *in 2006*

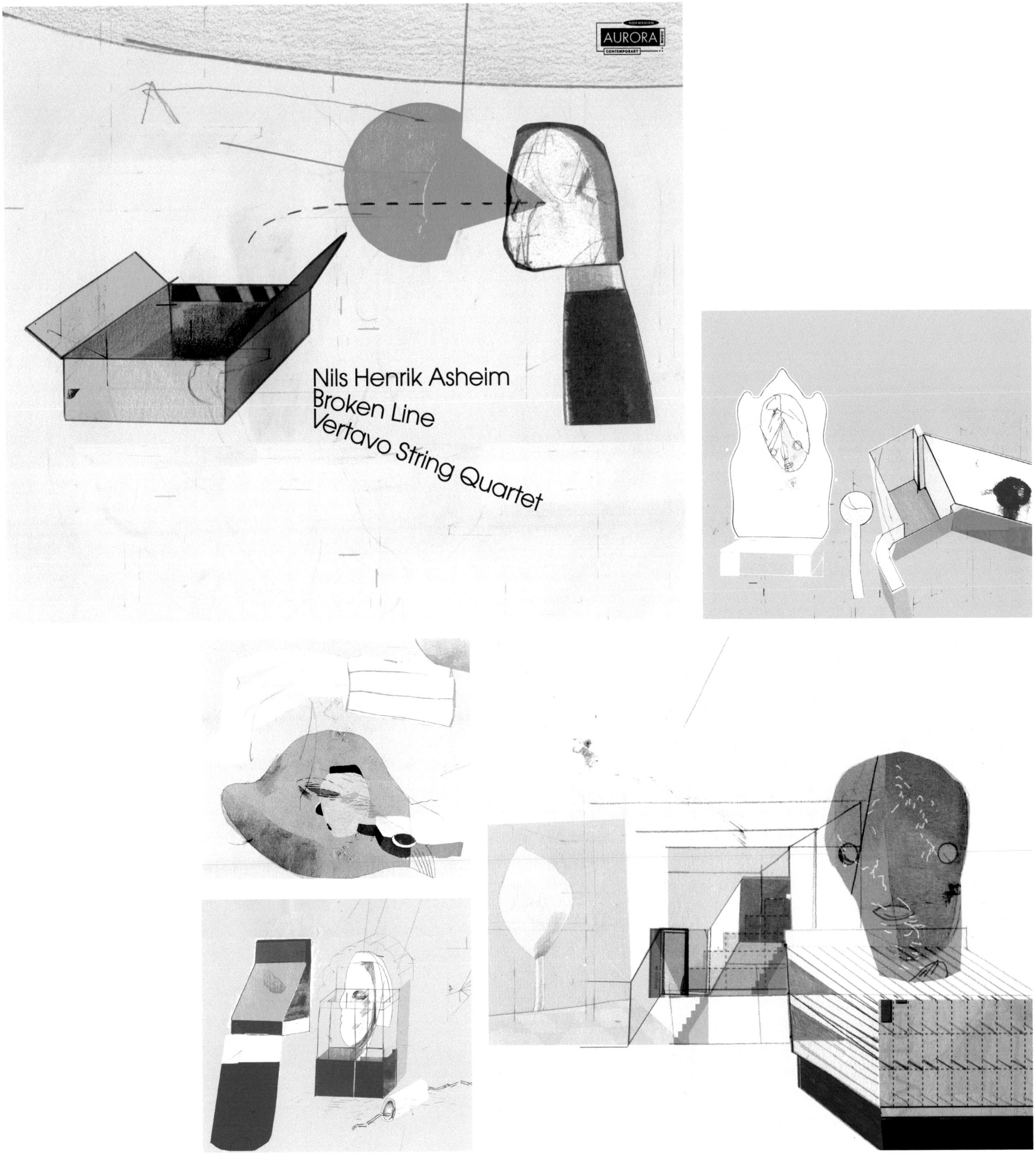

MARTIN KVAMME for Nils Henrik Asheim Vertavo String Quartet "Broken Line" (CD Digipak) *on Aurora in 2007* - Contemporary -

DIRK RUDOLPH for Russian Philharmonic Orchestra, Thomas Sanderling: Dmitri Shostakovich "Balda: Suite from Lady MacBeth" (CD)
on Deutsche Grammophon GmbH in 2006; Photography by AKG - Klassik -

DIRK RUDOLPH for Sergei Leiferkus, Russian Philharmonic Orchestra, Thomas Sanderling "Dmitri Shostakovich - Songs And Waltzes" (CD)
on Deutsche Grammophon GmbH in 2006; Photography by AKG - Klassik -

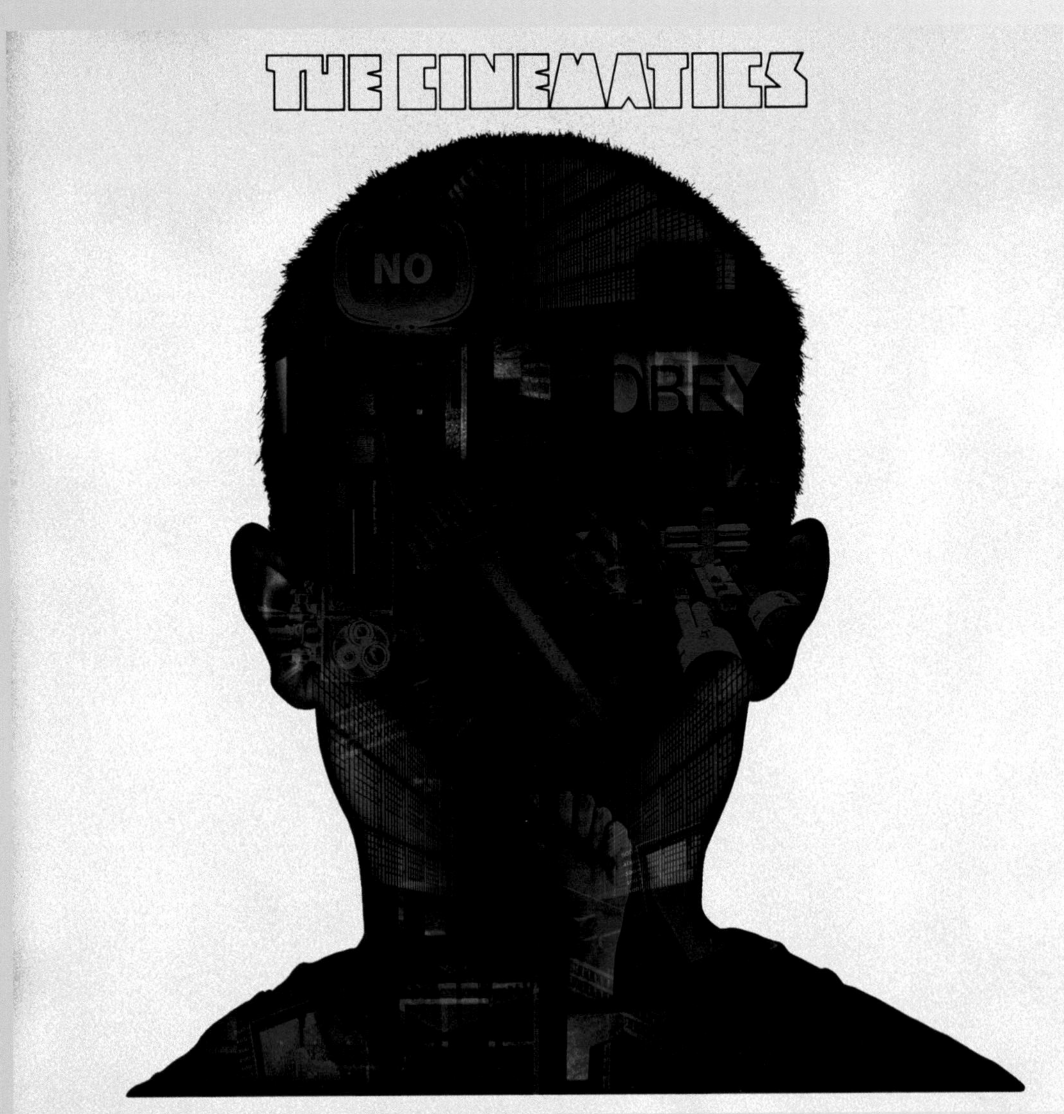

INSECT, D.: LUKE INSECT **for The Cinematics** "A Strange Education - Sleeve concept" (CD album / 12" vinyl) *on TVT in 2006* - Rock and Pop -

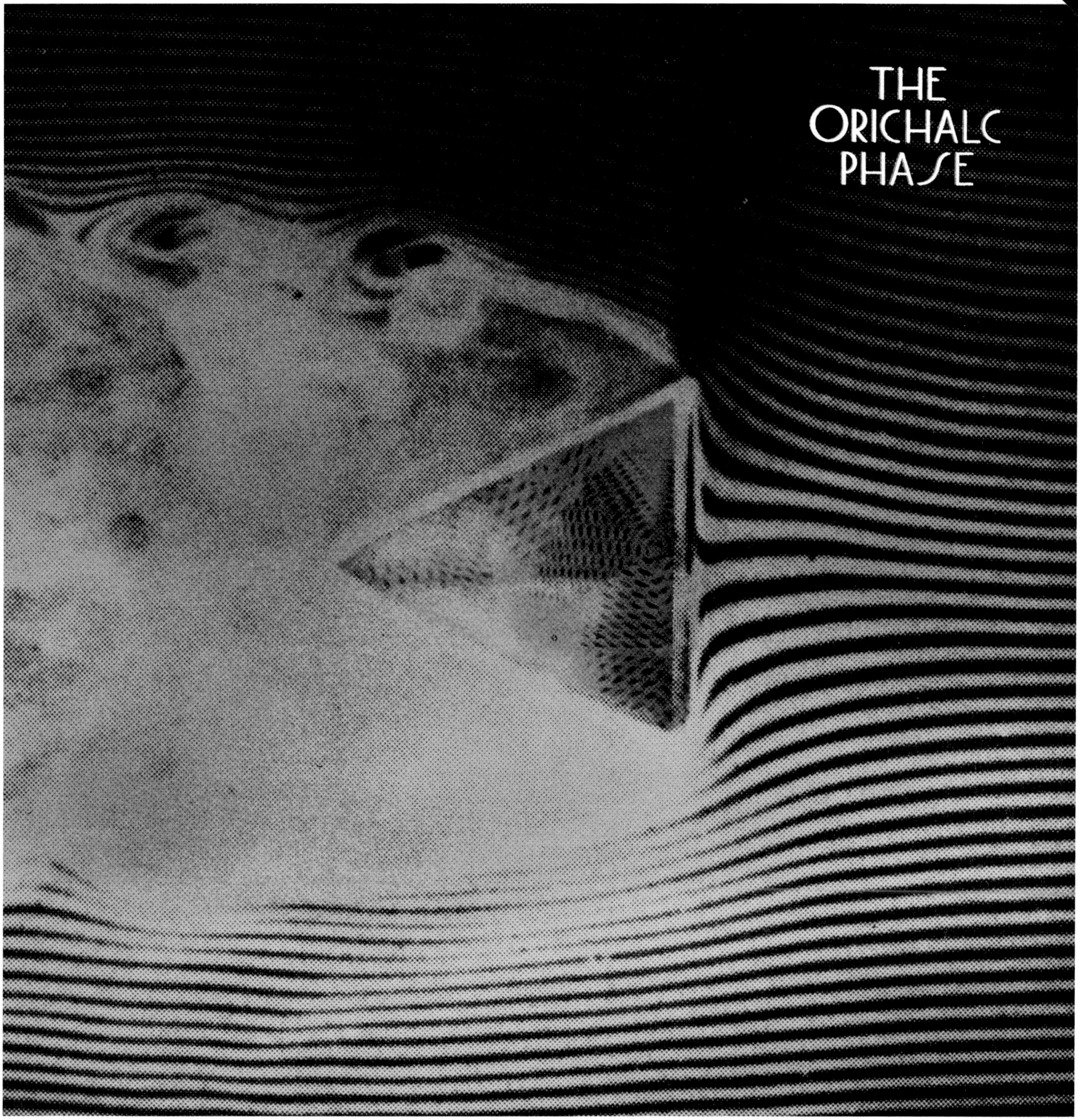

LA BOCA, D.: SCOT BENDALL **for The Orichalc Phase** "Violations" (12") *on DC Recordings in 2006* - Electronica -

MARTIN KVAMME, MIKE PATTON AND LADY T **for Peeping Tom** “Peeping Tom” (Burgopak packaging. CMYK + UV gloss) *on Ipecac Recordings in 2006* - Pop/Rock/Electronica/Hip Hop -

FIVE SECONDS
FEAT. ODD NOSDAM
MOJO
FEAT. RAHZEL & DAN THE AUTOMATOR
DON'T EVEN TRIP
FEAT. AMON TOBIN
GETAWAY
FEAT. KOOL KEITH
YOUR NEIGHBORHOOD SPACEMAN
FEAT. JEL & ODD NOSDAM
KILL THE DJ
FEAT. MASSIVE ATTACK
CAIPIRINHA
FEAT. BEBEL GILBERTO
CELEBRITY DEATH MATCH
FEAT. KID KOALA
HOW U FEELIN?
FEAT. DOSEONE
SUCKER
FEAT. NORAH JONES
WE'RE NOT ALONE (REMIX)
FEAT. DUB TRIO
Ipecac Recordings
℗& © 2006 IPECAC RECORDINGS • P.O. BOX 1778 • ORINDA • CA 94563 • USA • WWW.IPECAC.COM • INFO@IPECAC.COM
MANUFACTURED AND DISTRIBUTED BY CAROLINE DISTRIBUTION • BARCODE: 689230007722 • IPC 77

ALL MUSIC WRITTEN BY MIKE PATTON AND PUBLISHED BY MAL DI GOLA (ASCAP) EXCEPT «GETAWAY» WRITTEN BY MIKE PATTON AND KEITH THORNTON, PUBLISHED BY MAL DI GOLA (ASCAP) AND
REVEREND TOM MUSIC/KOHAW MUSIC, INC./NOTTING HILL MUSIC LTD. C/O THE BIC YCLE MUSIC COMPANY. RECORDED BY MIKE PATTON AT VULCÁN, SF AND S. HUSKY HOSKULDS AT SOUND FACTORY, LA
MIXED BY S. HUSKY HOSKULDS AT THE MUTE MATRIX, LA • MASTERED BY GAVIN LURSSEN AT THE MASTERING LAB, HOLLYWOOD • ARTWORK/LAYOUT BY MARTIN KVAMME, MIKE PATTON AND LADY T
NORAH JONES APPREARS COURTESY OF BLUE NOTE • AMON TOBIN AND KID KOALA APPEAR COURTESY OF NINJA TUNE • DUB TRIO APPEARS COURTESY OF ROIR •
MASSIVE ATTACK APPEARS COURTESY OF VIRGIN • KOOL KEITH APPEARS COURTESY OF HIS OWN DAMNED SELF • DOSE, ODD AND JEL APPEAR COURTESY OF ANTICON
BEBEL GILBERTO APPEARS COURTESY OF ZIRIGUIBOOM/CRAMMED DISCS • DALE CROVER APPEARS COURTESY OF IPECAC RECORDINGS

THANKS: GREG WERCKMAN, HOWIE KLEIN, JENNIFER JUSTICE, Q, JOSEPH YOON, LADY T, THE ANTICON FAMILY, RHYNA THOMPSON,
TOMMY MANZI, JON ROSNER, TONI ISABELLA, MARC PICKEN, MICHAEL BULL, ANDRE MORAES, MIGUEL DEPEDRO, DALEK,
AHMED ABDUL-MALIK, DIRT STYLES, FUTURE PRIMITVE SESSIONS, BILL LASWELL, RICHARD DEVINE, AND MUGGS.
I WOULD LIKE TO SEND EXTRA SPECIAL GOODNESS TO ALL THE MUSICIANS, PRODUCERS AND FRIENDS WHO HELPED BRING THIS MUSIC TO LIFE.
MAKING THIS RECORD WAS AN EXERCISE IN CONSTIPATION AND YOU WERE MY EX-LAX. MUCH LUV N RESPECT. MP '06

LA BOCA, D.: SCOT BENDALL **for Padded Cell** "Signal Failure" (12") *on DC Recordings in 2005* - Electro -

LA BOCA, D.: SCOT BENDALL **for Padded Cell** "Are You Anywhere?" (12") *on DC Recordings in 2006* - Electro -

CRUSH DESIGN & ART DIRECTION
for Freestylers (div. 12") & **for Krafty Kuts** (div. 12") *on Against the grain in 2006* - Break Beat -

BASS PHENOMENON

BASS PHENOMENON

featuring Yolanda
TELL ME HOW YOU FEEL REMIXES

featuring Yolanda
TELL ME HOW YOU FEEL
BASKETBALL JAM

Freestylers feat. Pendulum
PAINKILLER
REMIXES

Freestylers feat. Pendulum
PAINKILLER

INSECT, D.: LUKE INSECT **for White Noise Club Night** "Club Night Promotional Poster" (A2 Poster) *in 2006* - Psychedelic -

INSECT, D.: LUKE INSECT **for The Laughing Windows** "Opel Hair / Growing Pains" (7") *on Battered Ornaments in 2006* - Experimental / Psychedelic -

INSECT, D.: LUKE INSECT **for The Sessions - EP 1** "What Is This Feeling" (7")
on Poptones in 2007 - Rock and Pop -

INSECT, D.: LUKE INSECT **for The Sessions - EP 2** "What Is This Feeling" (7")
on Poptones in 2007 - Rock and Pop -

INSECT, D.: LUKE INSECT **for Wolf People** "October Fires / Black Water" (7")
on Battered Ornaments in 2006 - Folk Rock / Psychedelic -

INSECT, D.: LUKE INSECT **for Spinning Jenny Club Night** "Club Night Promotional Poster" (A2 Poster) *on in 2006* - Folk / Psychedelic -

HUMAN EMPIRE, D.: JAN KRUSE **for Populous** "Breathes the best" (7") *on Morr Music in 2006*

HUMAN EMPIRE, D.: JAN KRUSE **for B. Gibbard &A. Kenny** "Home" (EP) *on Morr Music in 2005*

HUMAN EMPIRE, D.: JAN KRUSE **for Electric President** "You have the right to remain awesome: vol.1" (7") *on Morr Music in 2006*

HUMAN EMPIRE, D.: JAN KRUSE **for Morr Music label Poster** (200 x 100 cm) *on Morr Music in 2006*

BÜRO DESTRUCT, D.: LOPETZ **for Ellen Allien & Apparat Live** "Orchestra of Bubbles Concert Poster" (42x42cm Poster, CMYK) *in 2006* - Techno -

BÜRO DESTRUCT, D.: LOPETZ **for Mandingda** (CD) *on Swixx in 2006* - World Music -

HUMAN EMPIRE, D.: JAN KRUSE for Morr Music compilation for PNG magazine (CD)
on Morr Music in 2006

HUMAN EMPIRE, D.: JAN KRUSE **for Morr Music Poster** "New Releases Spring 2006" (Morr Music Poster) *on Morr Music in 2006*
& **for Morr Music label night** "Morr Music label night" (Poster 40 x 60 cm) *in 2007*

SLANGINTERNATIONAL.ORG for **DJ Rupture** "Special Gunpowder" (CD) *on Tigerbeat6 in 2005*

HUMAN EMPIRE, D.: AUDUR JORUNDSDOTTIR & JAN KRUSE for **Benni Hemm Hemm** "Kajak" (LP) & for **Benni Hemm Hemm & Jens Lekman** "Skvavars" (7") *on Morr Music in 2006*

HUMAN EMPIRE, D.: AUDUR JORUNDSDOTTIR & JAN KRUSE **for Benni Hemm Hemm** "Beginning End" (7") *on Morr Music in 2006*

HUMAN EMPIRE, D.: JAN KRUSE **for Electric President** "s/t" (LP) *on Morr Music in 2006* **& for Click Click Decker** "Nichts für Ungut" (LP) *on Audiolith Records in 2006*

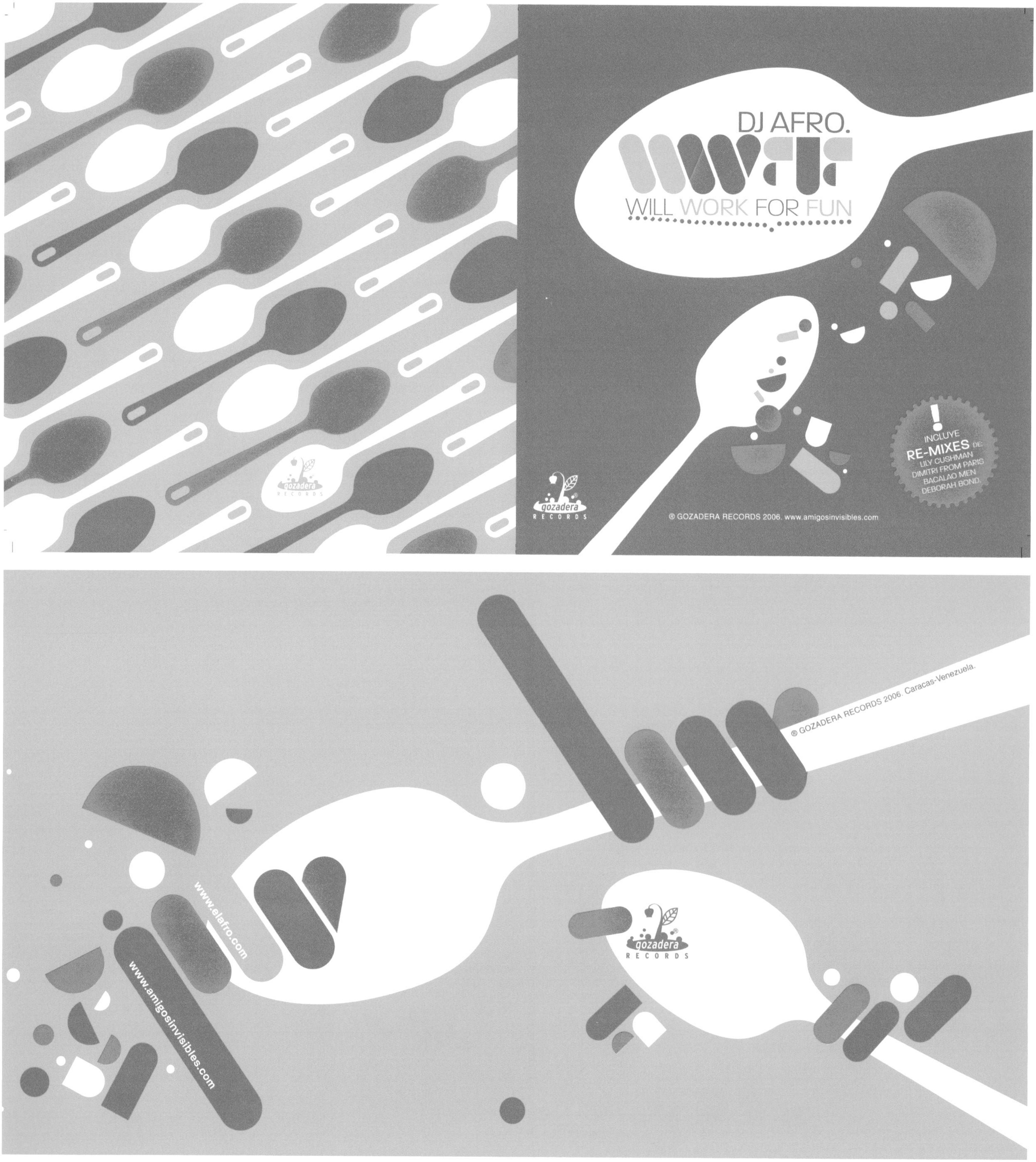

MASA for DJ Afro "Will Work For Fun" (CD) *on Gozadera Records in 2007* - Dance -

MARTIN KVAMME for **Helge Sunde** "Rotations" (CD) *on Aurora in 2006* - Contemporary -

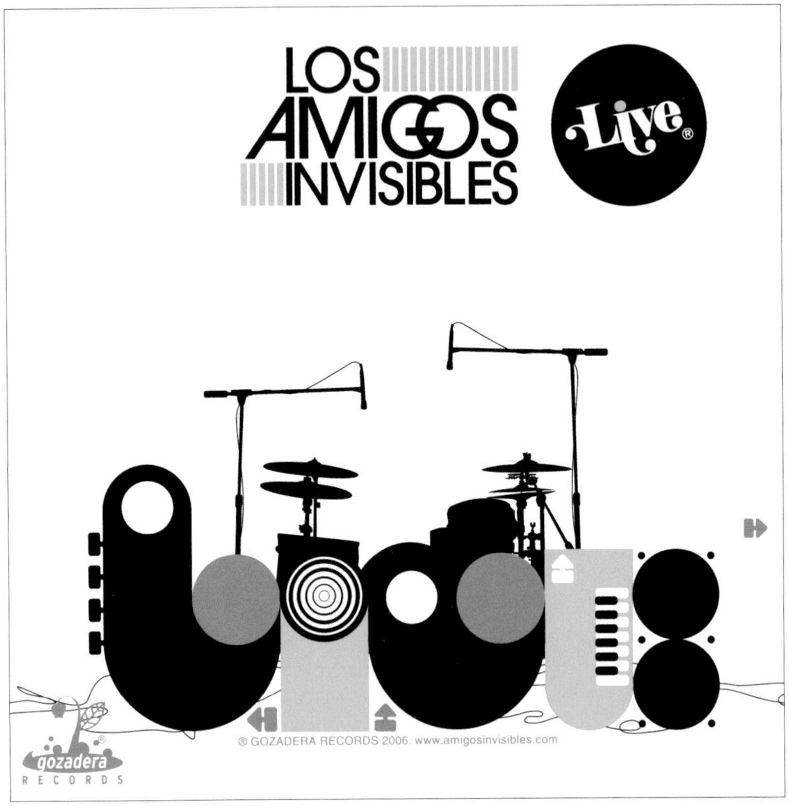

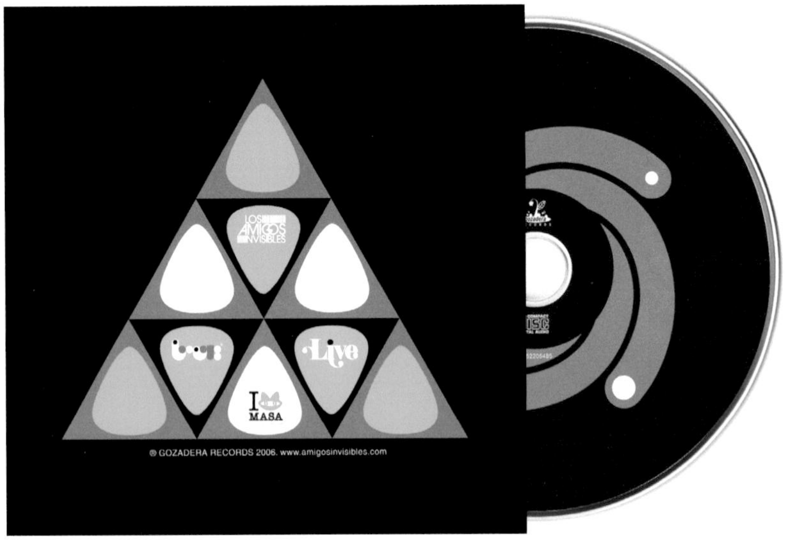

MASA for Los Amigos invisibles en Vivo! "LAI Live!" (CD) *on Gozadera Records in 2007* - Acid Jazz - Dance -

GEBOREN FÜR DICH: Hast mich gefragt, ob ich weiß, ob es auch anders geht / ob das Ziel im Weg ist und uns die Stunde schlägt / Ist das Schicksal, Dummheit oder Erfüllung? / Durch Kampf im Spiel das Glück zu finden / um dann wieder unvorbereitet daran zu erblinden / Ist das Schicksal, Dummheit oder Erfüllung? / Ich bin geboren für dich / Du bist geboren für mich / Hast mich gefragt, warum ich tu', was ein Mann tun muss / wie ein Junkie ohne Angst vor dem goldenen Schuss / Ist das Wahrheit, Wahnsinn oder Bestimmung? / Ich weiß, du wirst gehen, bevor es dunkel wird / konntest es nie gut sehen, wenn etwas stirbt / Ist das Wahrheit, Liebe oder Verwirrung? / (Vergiss nie) / Ich bin geboren für dich / Du bist geboren für mich / Durch Kampf im Spiel das Glück zu finden / um dann wieder unvorbereitet daran zu erblinden / Ist das Schicksal, Dummheit oder Erfüllung? / Ich bin geboren für dich / Du bist geboren für mich.

Musik & Text: Thorsten Wingenfelder
Bass: Volker Rechin
Drums: Lutz Sauerbier
Gesang, Gitarre: Thorsten Wingenfelder
Hammondorgel: Ecki Hüdepohl
Omnichord, Percussion: Tom Ripphahn

VON ANFANG AN ZU ENDE: In der Kälte der Nacht warst du kaum zu bezähmen / Zwei Herzen schreien auf, zu laut um zu verstehen / Wir waren Funken in einer erfrorenen Winternacht / und dann hast du gesagt / "Jedes Ende ist auch als neuer Anfang gedacht" / Gestohlene Stunden malen auf nackter Haut / kryptische Zeichen nur der Zukunft vertraut / Und ich kann dir nicht sagen, ob es richtig ist / dass du jetzt gehst und alles vergisst / Wir waren die Wahrheit in einer verlogenen Winternacht / und dann hast du gesagt / "Jedes Ende ist auch als neuer Anfang gedacht" / Aber wir waren von Anfang an am Ende / Von Anfang an zu Ende.

Musik & Text: Thorsten Wingenfelder
Bass: Volker Rechin
Drums: Lutz Sauerbier
Gitarren: Tom Ripphahn
Gesang, Gitarre: Thorsten Wingenfelder
Hammondorgel: Ecki Hüdepohl
Gitarre, Tambourin: Tom Ripphahn

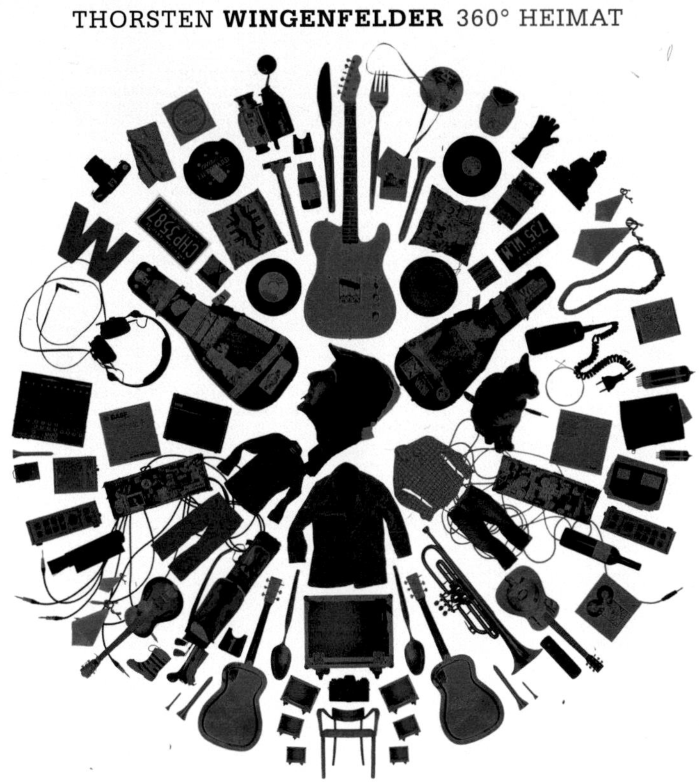

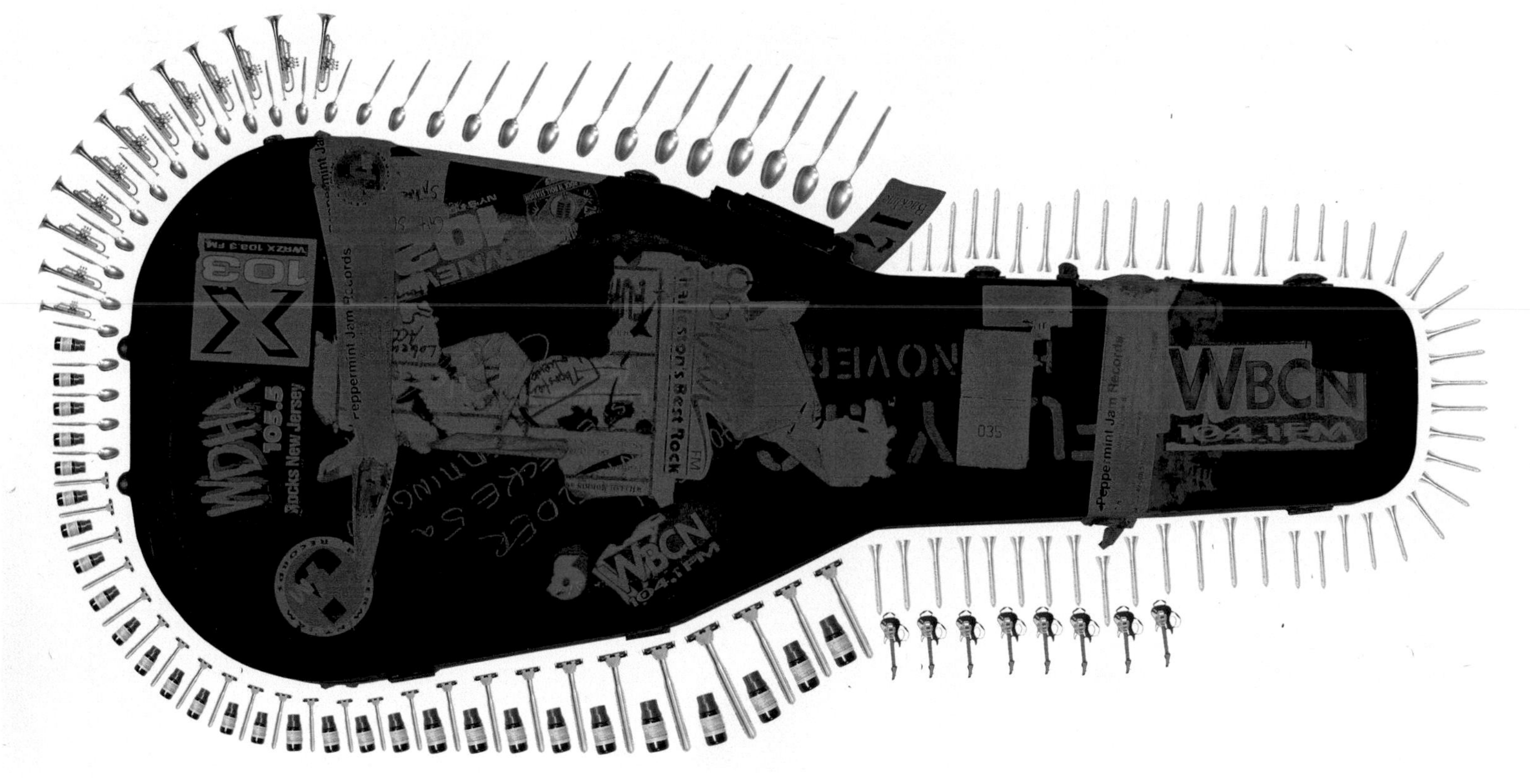

DIRK RUDOLPH for Thorsten Wingenfelder "360 Grad Heimat" (CD) *on Sony BMG Music Entertainment in 2006; Photography by Andreas "Bär" Läsker, Christof Schulte* - Rock -

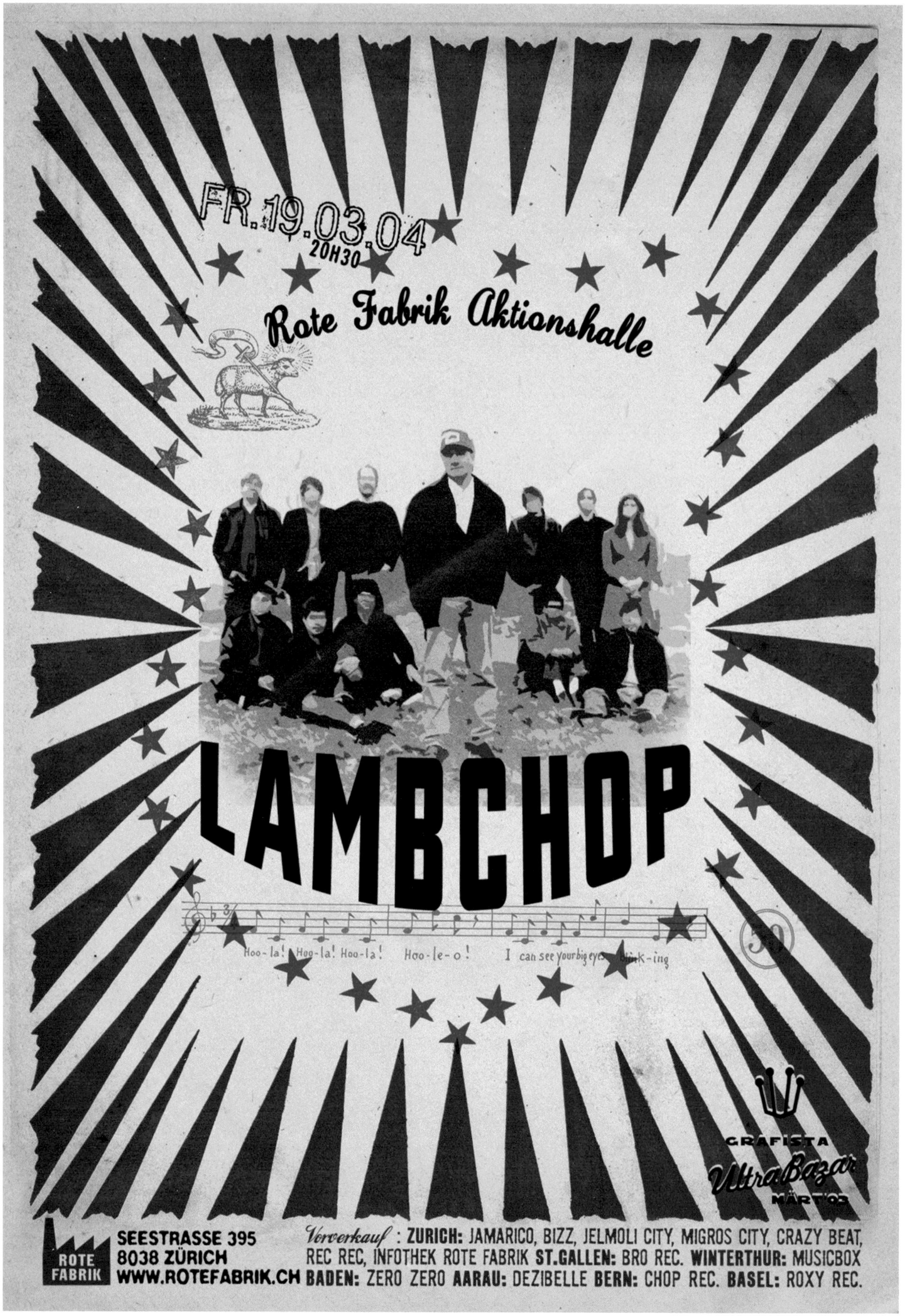

ULTRABAZAR, D.: MÄRT INFANGER for Lambchop for Rote Fabrik, Zurich (A3) *in 2004* - Folk -

ULTRABAZAR, D.: MÄRT INFANGER for Lupo. (Subkulturaustausch Luzern-Potsdam) (A2) *in 2004* - Div. -

VOODOO RHYTHM RECORDS, D.: BEAT-MAN **for Reverend Beat-Man** "Your Favorite Position Is On Your Knees" & "Get On Your Knees" , **for** C. W. Stoneking "King Hokum"
on Voodoo Rhythm Records in 2004-2006 - Industrial Blues Trash, Blues Trash, 20's 30's Pre WW2 Jazz Blues -

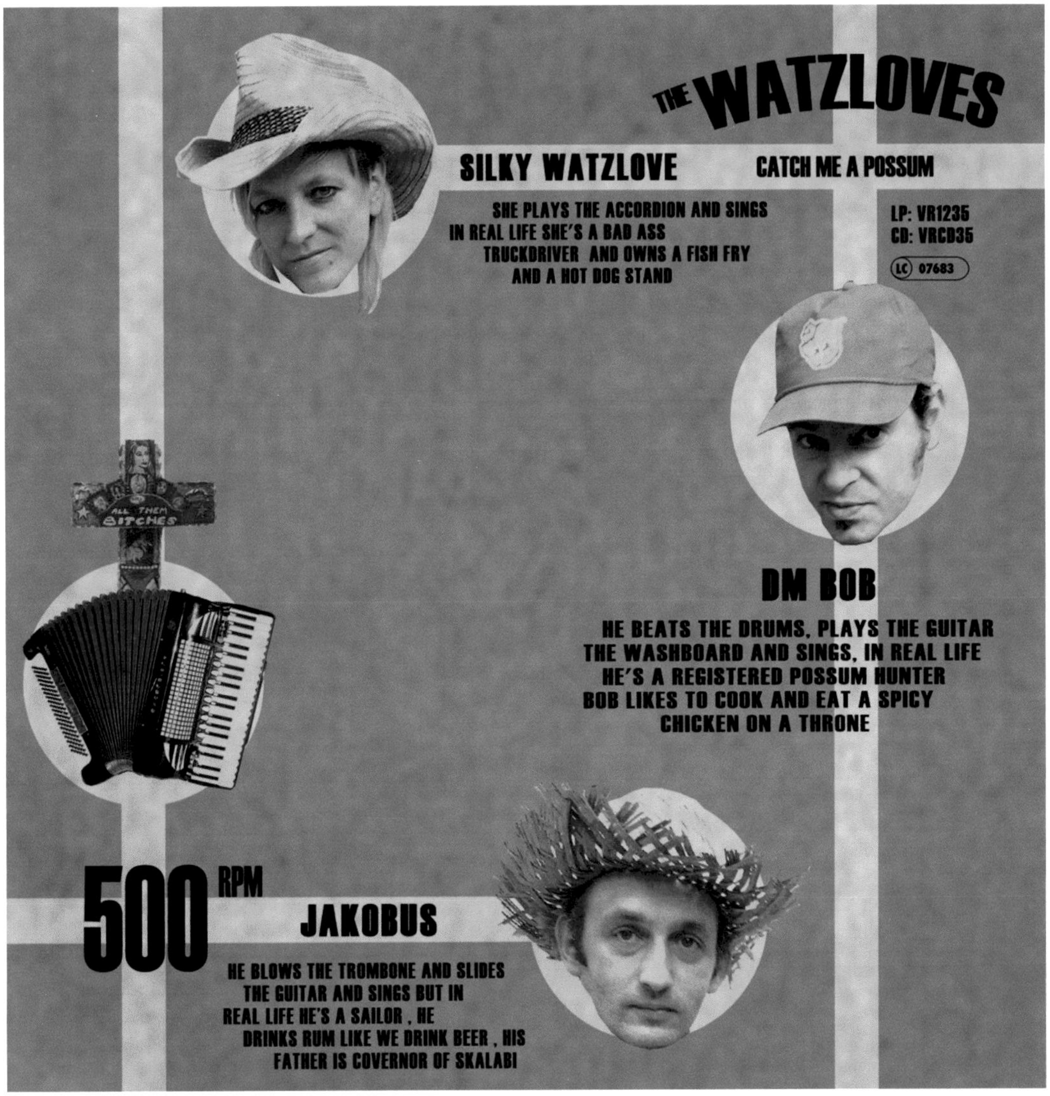

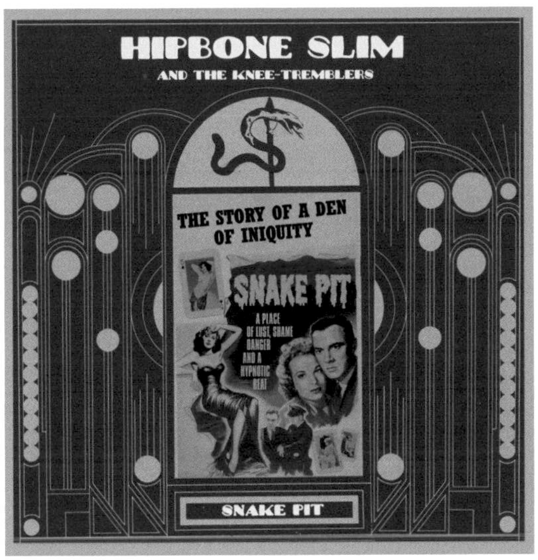

VOODOO RHYTHM RECORDS, D.: BEAT-MAN **for Hipbone Slim And The Knee Tremblers** "Snake Pit" , **for The Watzloves** "Catch Me A Possum" & **for Zeno Tornado And The Boney Google Brothers** "Dirty Dope Infected Blue Grass Hillbilly Hobo XXX Country Music" *on Voodoo Rhythm Records in 2003-2006* - Delinquent Rock'n'Roll, Cajun Tex Mex, Dirty Blue Grass Hillbilly -

VOODOO RHYTHM RECORDS *Answers by Reverend Beatman*

Almost 30 years ago, the mountainous idylls of Switzerland spawned a small, but thriving Trash and Garage scene. (In)famous for its inspired mix of 'three parts Trash and Garage, four parts Voodoobilly', this tight-knit community and congregation has been delving into the dirty underbelly of Rock'n'Roll since the early 1980s. Their self-appointed leader: Gospel Blues Trash evangelist Reverend Beatman - amateur wrestler, member of seminal band the Monsters and proprietor of Voodoo Rhythm Records, Switzerland's only haven of bona fide Rock'n'Roll and ,records to ruin any party'.

Lo-fi to the core in both music and design, Voodoo Rhythm serves up platters of primitive Rock'n'Roll 'by bands no one has ever heard of before' and champions a strong DIY ethic in both music and design. From straight-laced copies of corner store bargain bin favourites to insidious takes on tacky disco covers and classic pin-ups, flaws and all, the label's artwork is as charmingly ramshackle, raw and improvised as the music itself – and a visual blueprint of what Rock'n'Roll is all about.

You seem to have dedicated your entire life to Garage, Trash and Rock'n'Roll – what got you hooked in the first place?

Most of all, it was the music's amazing immediacy, its no frills, in-your-face attitude, about to erupt at any moment - that thrilling tightrope walk between unsavoury and repulsive, its unfettered ferocity ... when a record was truly great, the artwork, too, would reflects this elation and restlessness.

What about the very first record you spent your hard-earned cash on?

That must have been the Bay City Rollers – it came in this fancy gatefold sleeve with profiles on the musicians and removable cutouts ... I loved the idea and simply had to have it. Oh damn, come to think about it, I might have actually stolen that one! Back in those days I spent endless hours scanning thrift stores and flea markets. Most of the records I only bought for their sleeves – the music inside was usually a pile of trash. With my own label, I wanted to do something different: great sleeves with equally great content.

So, what makes a good Poster or sleeve?

I mean, beauty is in the eye of the beholder, but many sleeves by star designers are such a pile of crap and artsy trash that I would never in a million years be able to guess what they are on about. I like covers that are direct, in your face. When I enter a record shop, it's my eye that makes the decision, and the graphics should reflect the music. If you like it or not - a fly Poster needs to be an eyecatcher, it should get you off the couch and into the gig. That's especially important for unknown bands. When you design something for an artist who is already well-known, you can be more abstract in what you show or don't show.

In a way, most of your sleeves are a mix of nostalgic references – are you never worried about plagiarism?

I draw inspiration from junk graphics from the early 20th century. Nostalgia does not really come into that. All my designs are firmly rooted in the present, even when they have this deliberate faux-vintage look.

And what defines your own spirit and aesthetics?

We go on tour, enjoy our booze and get into trouble with our ladies. All this chaos shapes the way we do things. Most of it is ironic, but never dumb. I try to uphold a certain standard, but I'm not always sure how high it should be ...

What about the bands on your label? Do any of them ever veto your artwork?

Sure, many of them are pretty shocked by my suggestions and reject them outright, so then I have to call them up and explain the underlying concept. So far, I've always managed to convince them and in the end they really love the result. Sometimes, the artwork needs to contradict the music for the final product to make sense. For example, I really love the Zeno Tornado Dirty Dope album. If I saw that in a shop, I would buy it unheard. The cover really says it all.

And what about the fans? What's their reaction?

We don't have fans, just enemies, ha ha ha ...

Considering Voodoo Rhythms obvious Rock'n'Roll heritage. Why would a clean, picturesque country like Switzerland spawn a label and scene that is more American than Texas?

Oh no, it's the other way around! While America is still out there chasing a dream, we have long woken up from that dream and arrived in reality. Our country's favourable social and financial background gives us all the leeway we need to do whatever we want. We are what America would love to be!

VOODOO RHYTHM RECORDS, BEAT-MAN "Bottles" (Voodoo Rhythm Merchandise)

Fast-forward to the future – how did you end up where you are today? It's obviously a labour of love …

No idea, when I get up in the morning, I simply have to pick up my guitar, go to the office and put out records nobody buys – I have to. Don't ask me why! We are lucky enough to live in a time where literally anything and everything is possible. I have always played music 24-7, designed Posters in my spare time, drawn comic strips, so it seemed more of a natural progression when I shifted from working on building sites to doing music and illustrations fulltime. I am pretty proud that I actually did it, I definitely didn't choose the easy path.

Seems like music and artwork weren't enough, though - what about those forays into wrestling we've been hearing about?

When I went to LA in 1990, I got totally obsessed with Mexican wrestling. Naturally, I wanted to try it myself, but I am not much of an athlete. I wasn't about to give up on the idea, though, so I went to one of those specialist shops, bought a mask and took it back to Switzerland. I had this vision of crossing Rock'n'Roll with wrestling, so I thought – why not a one-man wrestling band? I toured all of Europe armed with just my guitar, a distorted mike and a wrestling mask, staging show fights against myself, so I'd always come out victorious. I used this mask for absolutely everything, did the craziest merchandise imaginable and had a blast.

Now that you mention it – we've noticed your slightly eccentric range of spin-offs: satchels, bags, pennants, water bottles, even household utensils. What is that all about?

Ah, that's just an evil money-making scheme. I buy cheap junk on flea markets, paint it or slap a sticker on, then sell it for a whopping profit. That's how the economy works today. Just making the most of today's economics. Soon we are going to be very rich - then we will buy Venus, hire a million space shuttles and start a whole new universe where people see the light and worship primitive Rock'n'Roll and Blues Trash. We would have go-go dancers with six different tit sizes and hot rods only roaming the streets …

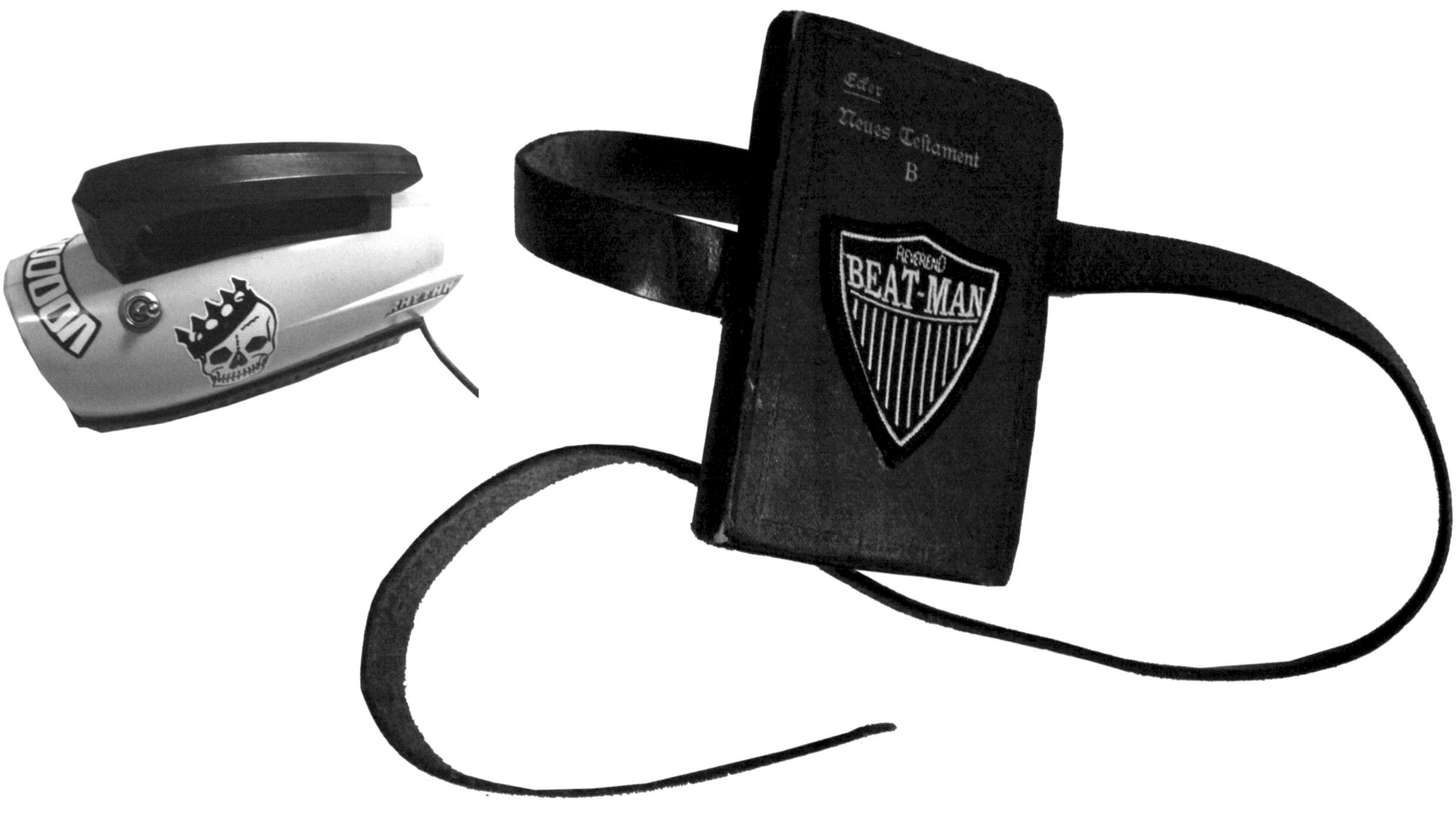

VOODOO RHYTHM RECORDS, BEAT-MAN Lightning Beat-man Flag, Table Hoover & Bible Belt (Voodoo Rhythm Merchandise)

VOODOO RHYTHM RECORDS, BEAT-MAN Candy Box , Suitcase & Nail Polishing Set (Voodoo Rhythm Merchandise)

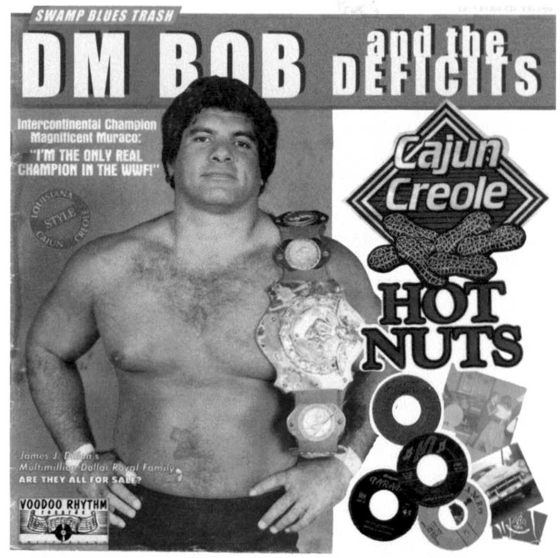

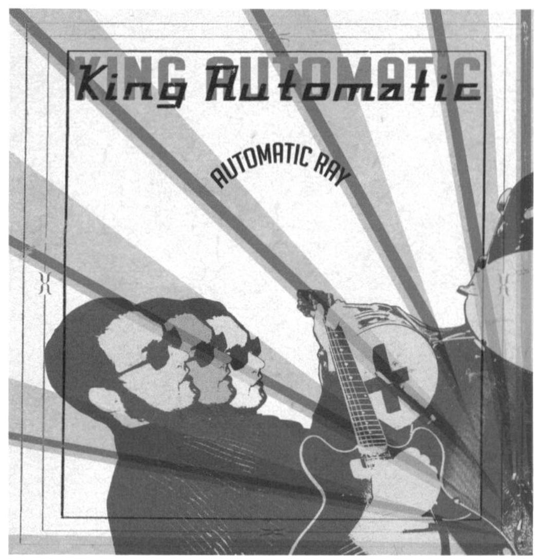

VOODOO RHYTHM RECORDS, D.: BEAT-MAN **for The Monsters** "I See Dead People", **for Dm Bob And The Deficits** "Cajun Creole Hot Nuts", **for The Dead Brothers** "Day Of The Dead" & **for King Automatic** "Automatic Ray" *on Voodoo Rhythm Records in 2001-2005* - Chanisaw Massacre Garage Punk, Swamp Blues, Funeral Music Java Gipsy Jazz Country, Elektro Blues -

VOODOO RHYTHM RECORDS, BEAT-MAN **for Wau Y Los Arrghs** "Canetan En Espanol", **for The Dead Brothers** "Dead Music For Dead People", **for Lightning Beat-Man** "Apartment Wrestling Rock'n'Roll", **for The Monsters** "Garage Punk From Bern Switzerland 1986-2006" *on Voodoo Rhythm Records in 1998-2006* - Garage Punk, Funeral Music, Wrestling Rock'n'Roll -

ULTRABAZAR, D.: MÄRT INFANGER for Halt auf Verlangen Festival 2006 Gasthaus Grünenwald, Engelberg (A3)
in 2006 - Div. -

ULTRABAZAR, D.: MÄRT INFANGER for Concert Poster for the Guilty Hearts/John Schooley One Man Band by Memphisto Produktion (450 x 645 mm) *in 2005* - Trash R'n'R -

ULTRABAZAR, D.: MÄRT INFANGER for the Delilahs by Gasthaus Grünenwald (A3) *in 2006* - Rock -
& for the Fe Fi Fo Fums/the Suspicions Memphisto Produktion (450 x 645 mm) *in 2006* - Trash R'n'R -

ULTRABAZAR, D.: MÄRT INFANGER for the Monsters by Memphisto Produktion (450 x 645 mm)
in 2005 - Trash R'n'R -

BUFFET FÜR GESTALTUNG for Spezialmaterial & Zukunft (Flyer series) *in 2006*

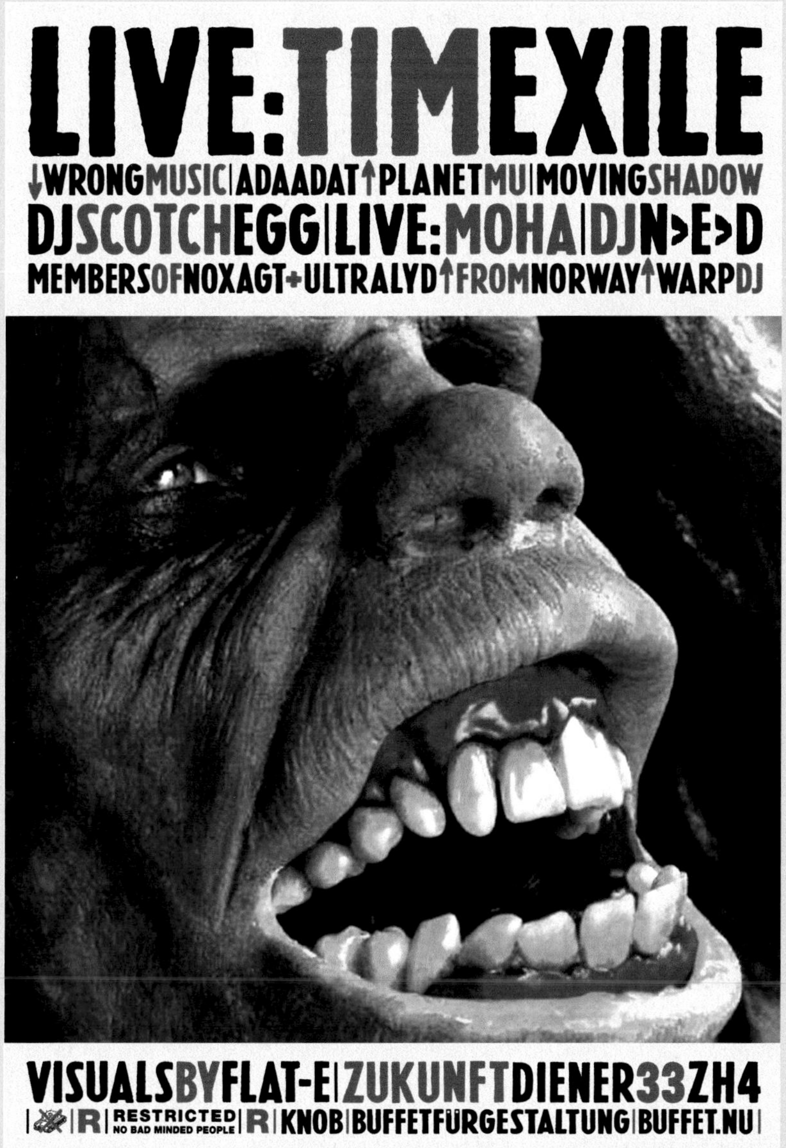
LIVE:TIMEXILE
WRONGMUSIC|ADAADAT PLANETMU|MOVINGSHADOW
DJSCOTCHEGG|LIVE:MOHA|DJN>E>D
MEMBERSOFNOXAGT+ULTRALYD FROMNORWAY WARPDJ
VISUALSBYFLAT-E|ZUKUNFTDIENER33ZH4
R RESTRICTED NO BAD MINDED PEOPLE R KNOB BUFFETFÜRGESTALTUNG BUFFET.NU

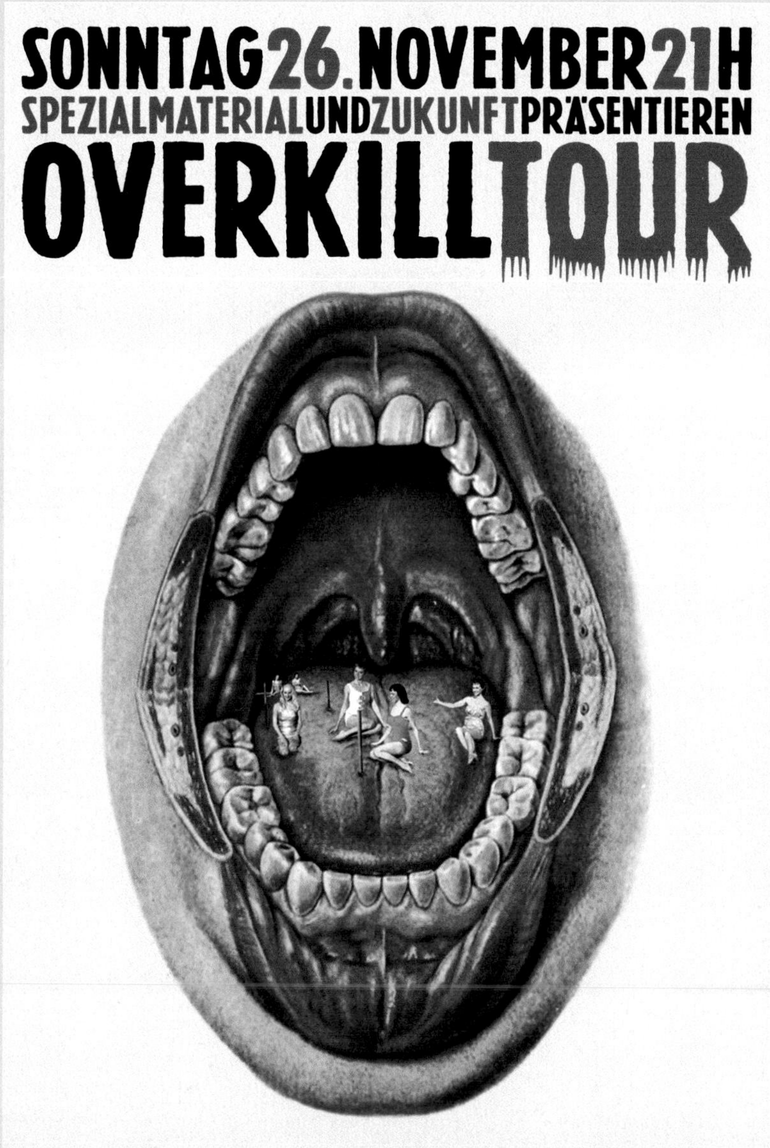
SONNTAG26.NOVEMBER21H
SPEZIALMATERIALUNDZUKUNFTPRÄSENTIEREN
OVERKILLTOUR

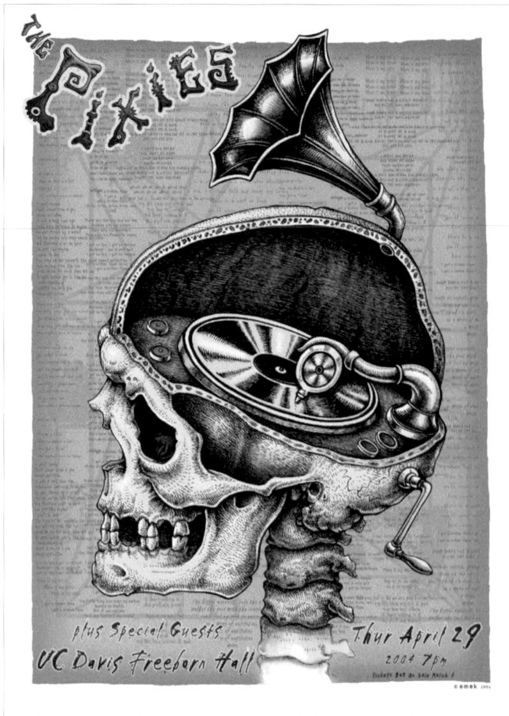

EMEK STUDIOS, INC. for Pixies "Pixies "PhonoSkull"" (Silkscreen) *in 2004* - Alternative -

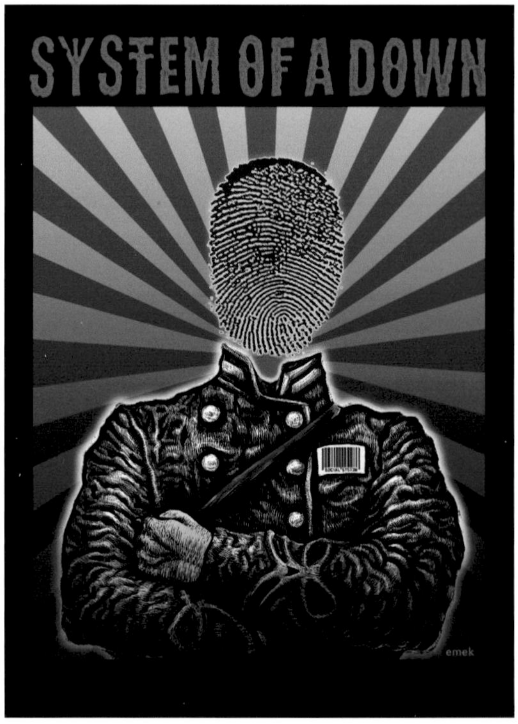

EMEK STUDIOS, INC. for The Decemberists (11 color silkscreen) *in 2007* - Alternative -
& for System of a Down (Silkscreen) *in 2005/2006* - Metal -

EMEK STUDIOS, INC. for Ween and the Flaming Lips (12 Color Glow In the Dark Silkscreen) *in 2006* - Alternative -

EMEK STUDIOS, INC., EMEK & GAN **for Coheed & Cambria** (Silkscreen) *on Sony Music in 2006* - Hard Alternative -

EMEK STUDIOS, INC., for PJ Harvey "PJ Harvey" (12 Color Silkscreen) *in 2004* - Alternative -
& **for Audioslave** "Black Hole Sunblock: Audioslave in LA" (Silkscreen) *on Interscope in 2005* - Heavy Indie -

EMEK STUDIOS, INC., EMEK & GAN **for Erykah Badu** (Silkscreen) *on Control Freaq Records in 2005-2006* - Soul -

EMEK *The Thinking Man's Poster Artist*

Revered by the US poster cognoscenti, Emek's limited edition silkscreen prints clash 60s imagery with 90s post-industrial iconography and a generous dash of daring, surrealist humour and social commentary.

Populated by endearingly morbid characters and flitting between styles and ideas like there's no tomorrow, these fleeting noir sketches come with a striking mix of fact and fiction, of printing techniques and band reference, yet always carry his unmistakeable fingerprint – often literally.

Almost too good to be true, and definitely too good for a basic concert reminder, his experimental creations and have attracted a sizeable following among gig goers and art fans alike.

Do you still remember what brought you to illustration in the first place?

All my family are professional artists – mom, dad, brother and sister. We were raised in a wonderfully eclectic art studio, basically, the whole house was a giant art studio and there was also my dad's studio in the backyard.

One day, when we were very little, my parents threw out the TV and said, "Whatever you want to create, we will help you with it!" - so we started to experiment with any techniques imaginable, from crayon drawings and printing etchings to sculpting and welding, and we got to meet a lot of cool artists who dropped in for a visit. Of course, it wasn't all fun and games. When my dad sold his art, we ate, when he didn't, it was tough, but there were always plenty of books and art supplies. Sometimes my mom would read us a story and we would illustrate parts of it or they would read us the newspaper and we would get ideas from that ... but most of all, we loved monsters and stories from mythology. One day, my parents decided to splash out on clean white paper and we were stumped. Faced with this 'good' paper, I got artist's block, when it was scrap paper, we never cared or thought twice about it, we just started drawing. We had so much fun that I would always get my friends gifts of art supplies - paints, brushes, markers and good paper. But as I got older, I noticed that my 'presents' no longer met with much enthusiasm. „Gee, mom, Emek got me a bunch of blank paper – wtf?"

Your website calls you 'The thinking man's poster artist'. That's quite a claim to live up to …

Since 1994, most of my art has been concert posters. Some people have called me the „thinking man's poster artist" because I care too much about what I do. It's just a poster, who cares? Today's disposable culture paves the way for tomorrow's collectible nostalgia … For poster artists, striving for artistic integrity is an everyday struggle. On the one hand, it's one of the most burgeoning creative fields in art right now, but to a lot of critics it's still just a ghetto of lowbrow trash. I never really cared about what other people thought, I just wanted to draw what made me happy and challenged me.

Have you never been tempted to switch to a more 'permanent' medium like record sleeves or book jackets?

Besides the posters, I also paint for private commissions and do some album covers and illustrations for Rolling Stone and Wired, but concert posters remain the biggest thrill, always fresh and exciting because I can do whatever I want. I never run out of ideas, every project gives me more ideas, and the music inspires me as well. Record sleeves and book covers, while they might be more 'permanent' to some, are small items that end up on a shelf and disappear. My work, on the other hand, is done in the tradition of fine art, it is meant to hang on a wall and grab your attention. Of course, it also serves a real function, to advertise a tribal gathering.

How do you approach your commissions?

Every project starts with a concept. In order to create an image, I need a story that inspires me. The bands and record companies usually give me free reign – "do something cool our fans will like …" and that freedom keeps every project fresh and exciting. I guess more and more companies are looking for street cred, so they want a unique, heartfelt and hand-done look by someone who is obviously passionate about their art.

All my concert posters are silkscreen prints (or 3D experiments), mostly hand drawn in black and white, coloured by cutting out layers of film and then printing one colour at a time for the limited editions. The process is very labour intensive, but pretty cool. Sure, computers are also involved – I mean, would you still travel everywhere by horse and carriage? I think an artist should know and use all tools available to him, but never rely on them too heavily. But whatever I do, I'm trying to stretch the art form. It's about trying to be true to what a rock poster is supposed to be, and yet do something that hasn't been done before. A rock poster relies on a few Simple Truths, i. e. name of the band, show date, place, time … so, after hundreds of posters, I wanted to add dimension to a medium that has traditionally been flat. And how can I make it different? Cut it, scratch it, sculpt, cast, BURN it!, rip, melt, cook, weave, emboss, embroider, recycle. After all is said and done, I have stretched the medium to three dimensions while keeping the poster's Simple Truths.

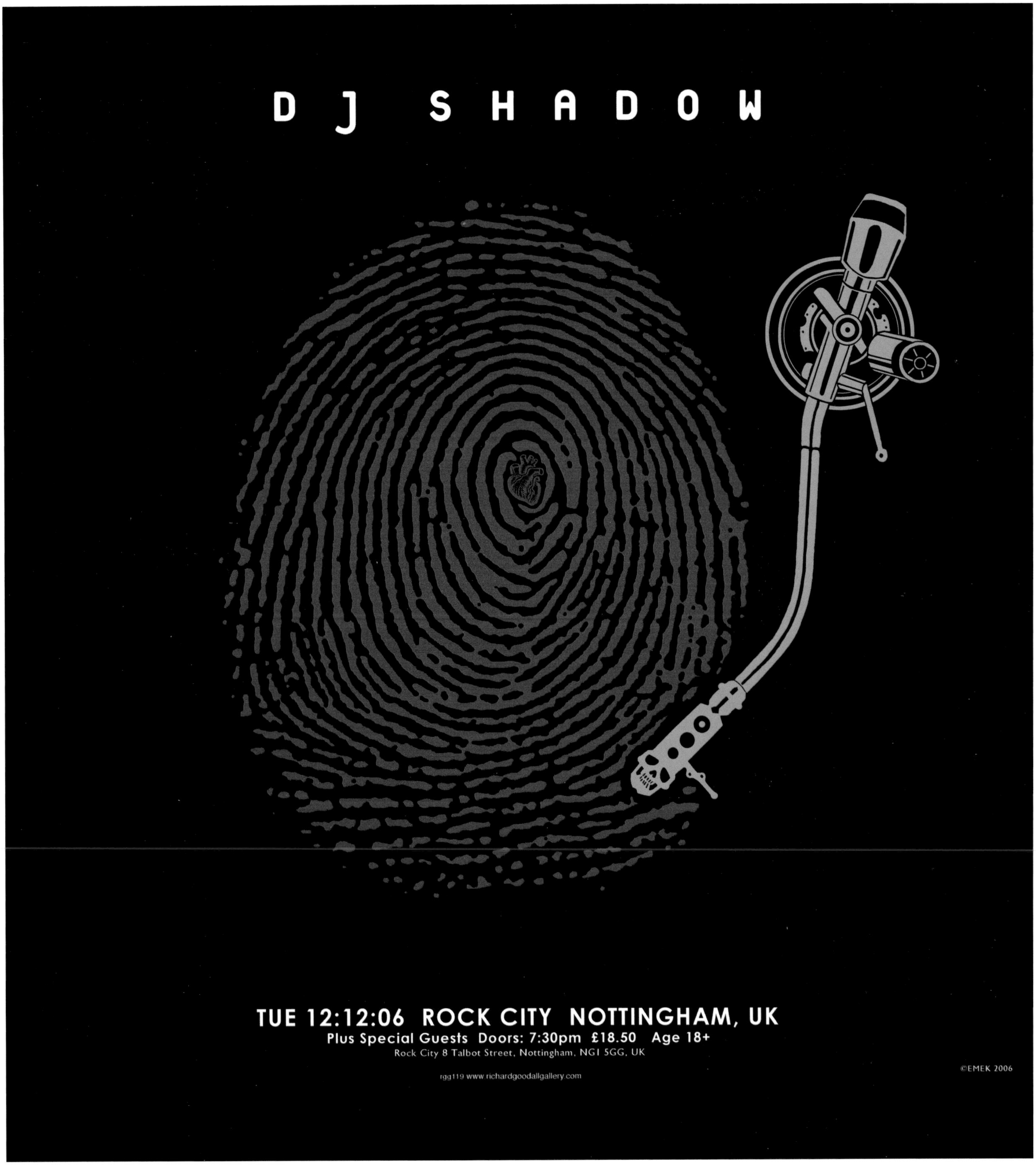

EMEK STUDIOS, INC. for DJ Shadow "DJ Shadow" (Silkscreen) *in 2006* - Trip Hop -

So, how long does it usually take you to finish an artwork?

No matter how long I have, I will always work right down to the last second. That's part of my motivation - the challenge is to come up with my own concept, submit a sketch, draw the art, colour the layers, print it, sign and number each piece, then pack them up and ship them off to the bands... every step has to be done with utmost care.

It's always a love-hate thing, really. So much time goes into each piece that it always feels like a birth. Once it's done and out in the world, the immediate feeling is: If only I had one more day, it could have been a lot better, I am not happy with the composition or the way this colour is printed ... Once the bands have seen and liked it and some time has passed, then I think it's not so bad any more and move on to the next project.

Sounds like a lot of work for what is basically a functional, transient reminder of a band or gig ... why all this effort and limited editions?

I get a kick out of the fact that a certain percentage of my work is stapled up somewhere. And a lot of collectors go nuts when they see a bunch of my posters stapled to a wall. I even get e-mails from people who only go to the concerts to buy the posters - I am not sure what to make of that, but it's amusing. I am very meticulous about my work; every poster should look like a piece of art worthy of hanging on my wall, even though a certain number of them are put up or tossed out. I gear every poster toward the vibe of the band. It's still a rock poster, but it's also so much more - made to last and stand up to the impermanence of its origins and using all the experiences I had growing up.

Another irony of creating 'rock poster art', besides the intrinsic dichotomy of trying to give permanence to the impermanent medium of temporary advertising with an obvious expiration date printed right on the artefact, is that posters are meant to be displayed in public for a social gathering. Yet the process involved in creating this art is very anti-social. The artist needs to be holed up in his dark studio, alone with his thoughts. So it is very important to regularly reconnect with the outside world for inspiration. Reading all kinds of books and poetry is great for ideas, lots of brain stimulation, just watching the world around me, current events and politics, going to galleries and museums, art books are great, but going out and seeing other people's art in person just makes me want to work harder, and do research on what their influences were. I want to know who my heroes' heroes were. As far as ideas go, I always liked dark images, but with a light at the end of the tunnel ... I've always been intrigued by monsters - maybe they can't help it, it's just their outward appearance ... and what made them monsters in the first place? I also like the idea of the mechanics of the body, the idea that beneath every living, breathing, beautiful thing there is blood and guts and bones. I was never into „blood and gore", but I love the mechanics of muscle and skeletons, the amazing engineering inside of our bodies. When you think about it, bones are always inside us, and they are all that are left when we are gone ... So, some artwork should be confrontational, to remind us of our fears and show us a reality that lies beneath the surface.

Have your goals and aims changed over time?

When I started in the business many years ago, I said I would retire once I created posters for my favourite artists, artists I thought had a lot of soul and creative integrity - people like Bob Dylan, Leonard Cohen, Björk, Radiohead, Henry Rollins, Nick Cave and Cesaria Evora. So now, having crossed quite a few of those off my list and hundreds and hundreds of posters later, I just like working with bands that appreciate what I do, that let me do my thing. My phone keeps ringing, so I must be doing something right.

EMEK STUDIOS, INC. for Weezer "Make Believe" (Silkscreen) *in 2005* - Alternative -

EMEK STUDIOS, INC., GAN & EMEK for Fantomas & the Melvins "Rockin' Uranus" (Glow in the Dark Silkscreen) *in 2006* - Alternative -

EMEK STUDIOS, INC. for High On Fire

"I wanted to do something that called into question the impermanence of Rock Posters as an artform.. their origin is that they were designed to be seen in public spaces and grab one's attention, but maybe next week they are torn down and replaced by something else, and as a paper artifact, a carelessly tossed match and its all just a memory anyways..I also like the idea of a lot of negative space of the clean white paper marred by random chaos (each piece is hand burned). I also like this 'Low Tech' solution to this Poster. Clean design meets down and dirty rock and roll...and finally, the long horizontal nature of the piece recalls something else that is smoking to get one."

(Hand Burned Silkscreen, Edition of 150) *in 2006* - Metal -

METHANE, D.: ROBERT LEE for **Black Keys/Black Angels** (4 color Screen Print) *in 2006* - Indie Rock -

METHANE, D.: ROBERT LEE for **Electric Six** (screen print) *in 2006 & 2007* - Indie Rock -

METHANE, D.: MARK MCDEVITT **for Dave Matthews Band** (silkscreen Poster) *in 2006* - Rock -
& **for Camera Obscura** (4 color screen print) *in 2007* - Indie Rock -

METHANE, D.: ROBERT LEE **for Clap Your Hands Say Yeah** (3 Color screen print) *in 2006* - Indie Rock -

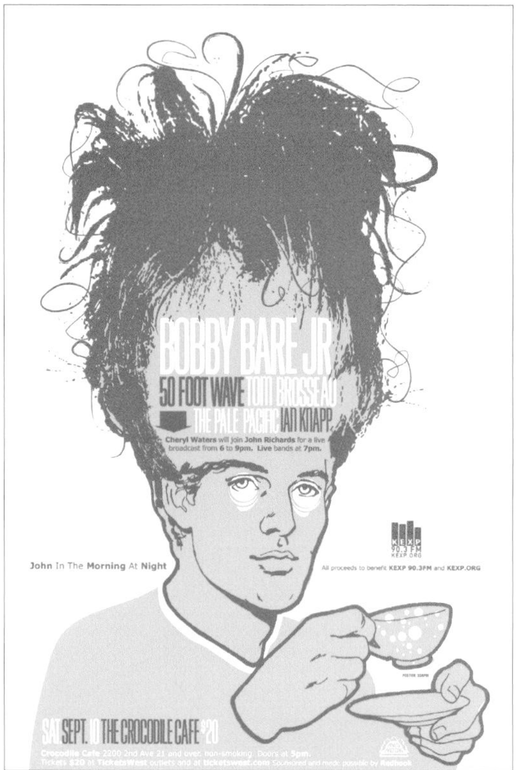

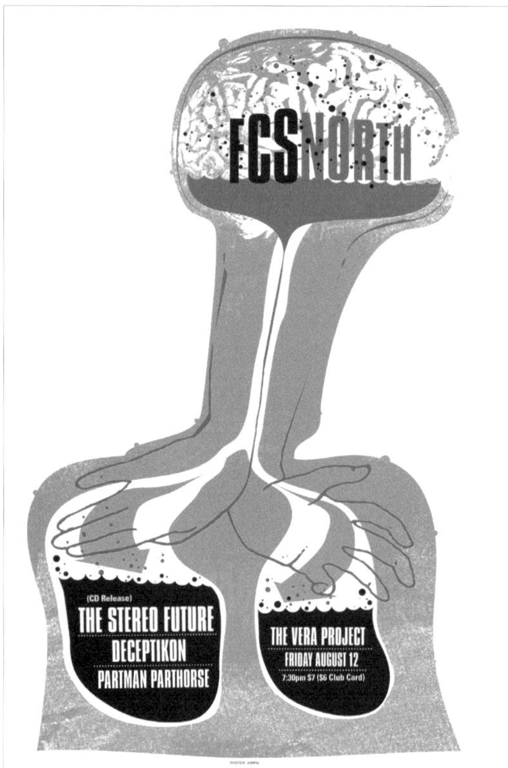

ANDRIO ABERO | 33RPM for FCS North (12"x18" 3-color screen print) *in 2005* - Electronic -

ANDRIO ABERO | 33RPM for John in the Morning at Night (13"x19" 2-color screen print) *in 2006*

SASHA BARR for North Mississippi All Stars and Lucero, New Year's Eve 2007 Poster, Memphis, TN
(Two color Screen-print, 19" x 25") *in 2006*

ANDRIO ABERO | 33RPM for The Glasses (17"x11" 2-color screen print) *in 2006* - Indie Rock -

ANDRIO ABERO | 33RPM for Live from the Morniing Alternative (CD package) *in 2006*
& for Velella Velella tour Poster (24"x18" 2-color screen print) *in 2006* - Electronic -

INVISIBLE CREATURE, INC., D.: DON CLARK for Pinback "Detective" (poster) *in 2006* - Indie -

ANDRIO ABERO | 33RPM for And You'll Know Us By The Trail Of Dead (24"x 15" 3-color screen print) *in 2006* - Rock -

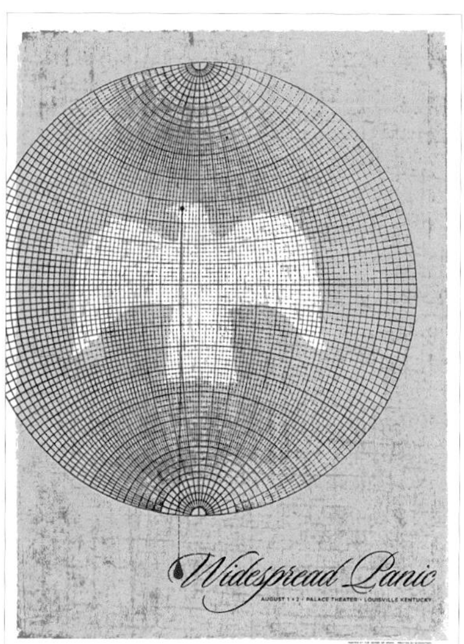

THE HEADS OF STATE, D.: **DUSTIN SUMMERS** for Widespread Panic Poster & for Bill Riccini Record Release Poster(18"x 24") *in 2005 & 2006*

SASHA BARR for Broken Social Scene Poster, Ann Arbor, MI & for Giant Bear Poster, Memphis, TN (Three Color Screen-print 19"x 25") *in 2006* - Rock -

TODD SLATER for Cat Power (Silkscreen Poster)
in 2006 - Rock -

TODD SLATER for Of Montreal (Silkscreen Poster) *in 2006* - Rock -

METHANE, D.: ROBERT LEE for THE SUBMARINES
(3 color screen print) *in 2007* - Indie Rock -

TODD SLATER for Pretty Girls Make Graves
(Silkscreen Poster) *in 2006* - Rock -

TODD SLATER for Interpol (Silkscreen Poster) *in 2004* - Rock -

TODD SLATER for **Death Cab for Cutie** (Silkscreen Poster) *in 2006* - Rock -

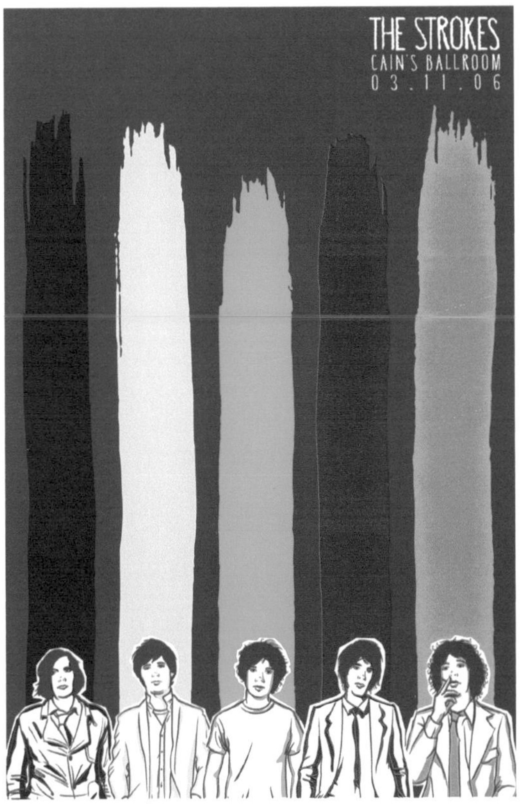

TODD SLATER for **The Strokes** (Silkscreen Poster) *in 2006* - Rock

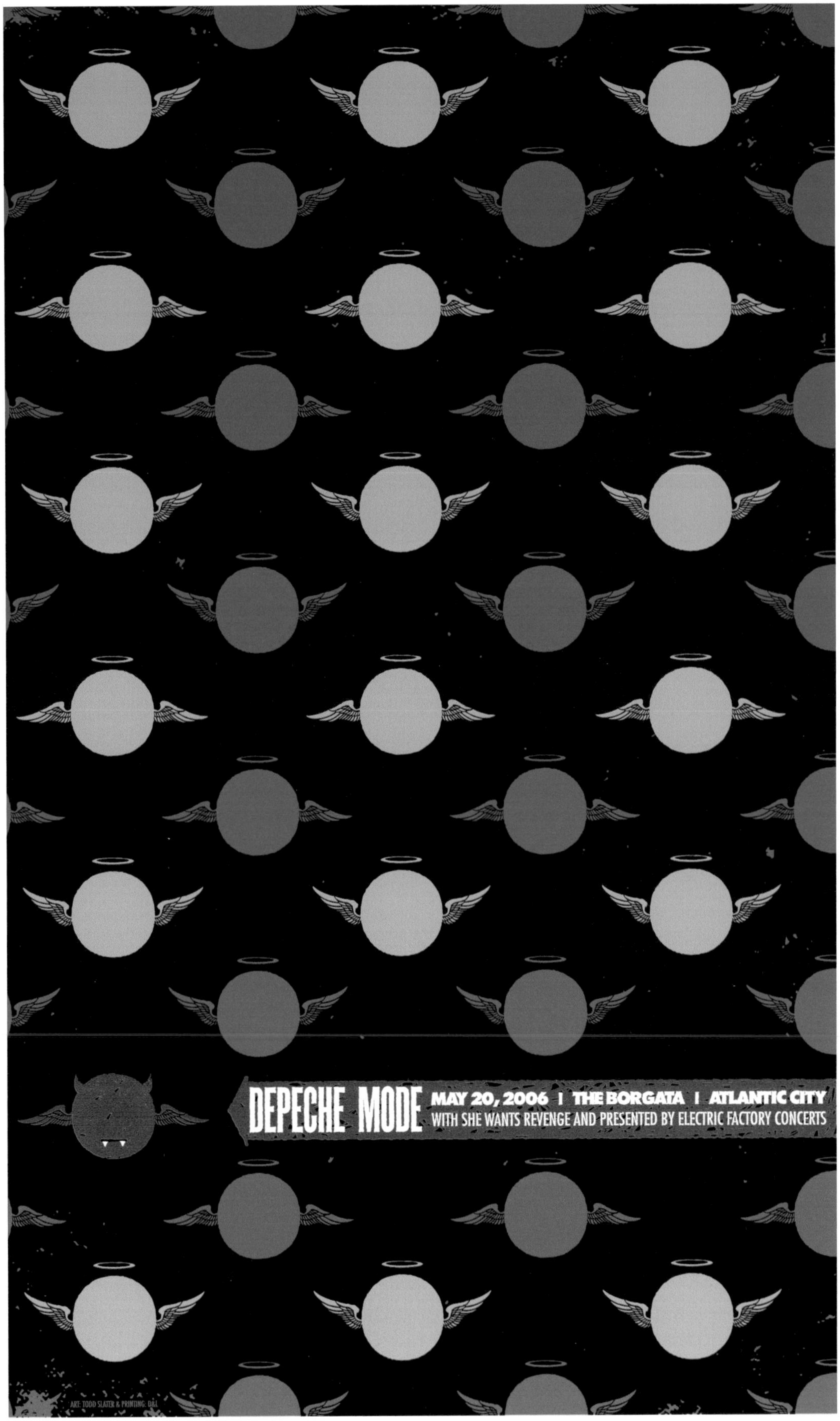

TODD SLATER for **Depeche Mode** (Silkscreen Poster) *in 2006* - Rock -

ANDRIO ABERO | 33RPM for Thievery Corporation (18" x 24" 3-color screen print) *in 2006* - Electronic -

THE HEADS OF STATE, D.: DUSTIN SUMMERS for R.E.M. Poster (16 x 24 silkscreen) *in 2005*

THE HEADS OF STATE, D.: DUSTIN SUMMERS for Gomez / Concert Poster (15 x 24 Silkscreened) *in 2007*

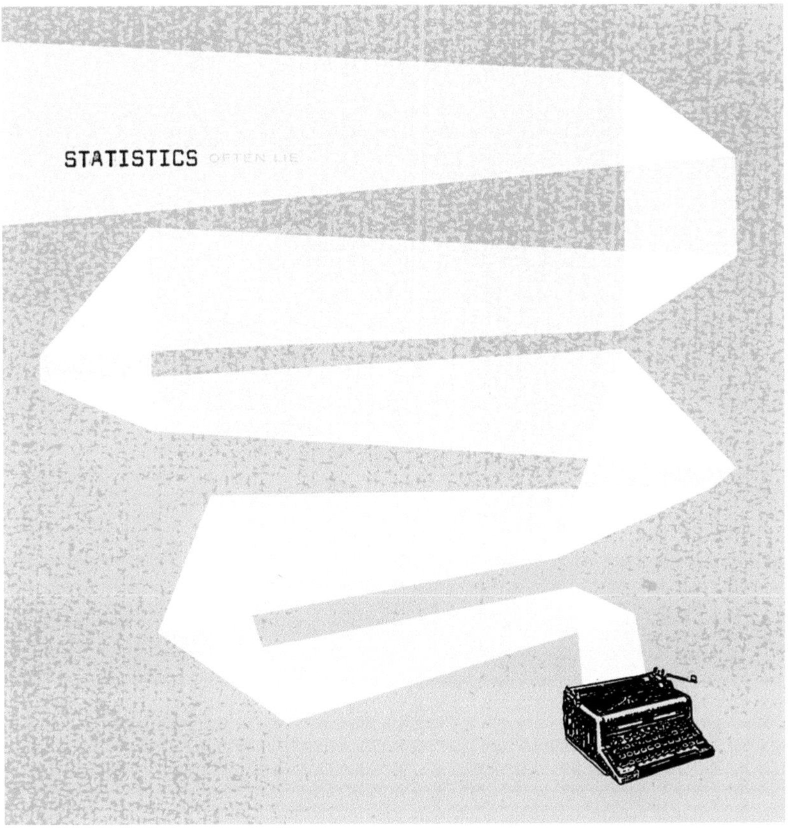

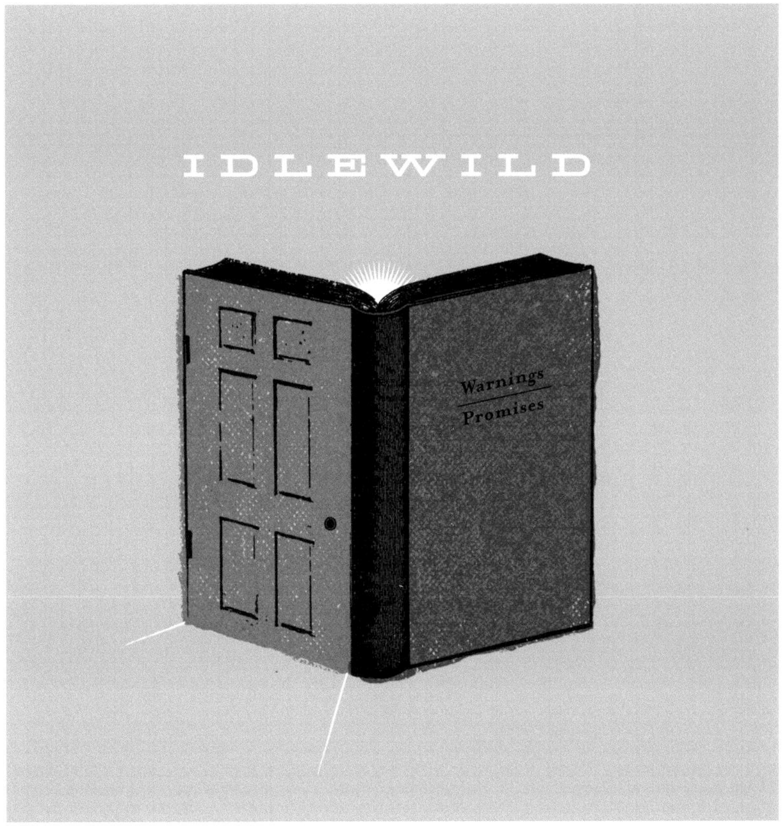

THE HEADS OF STATE, D.: **DUSTIN SUMMERS, JASON KERNEVICH for Statistics** "Often Lie" (Jewel Case) *on Jade Tree in 2006*
& for Idlewild "Warnings / Promises" (Jewel Case) *on parlophone in 2006*

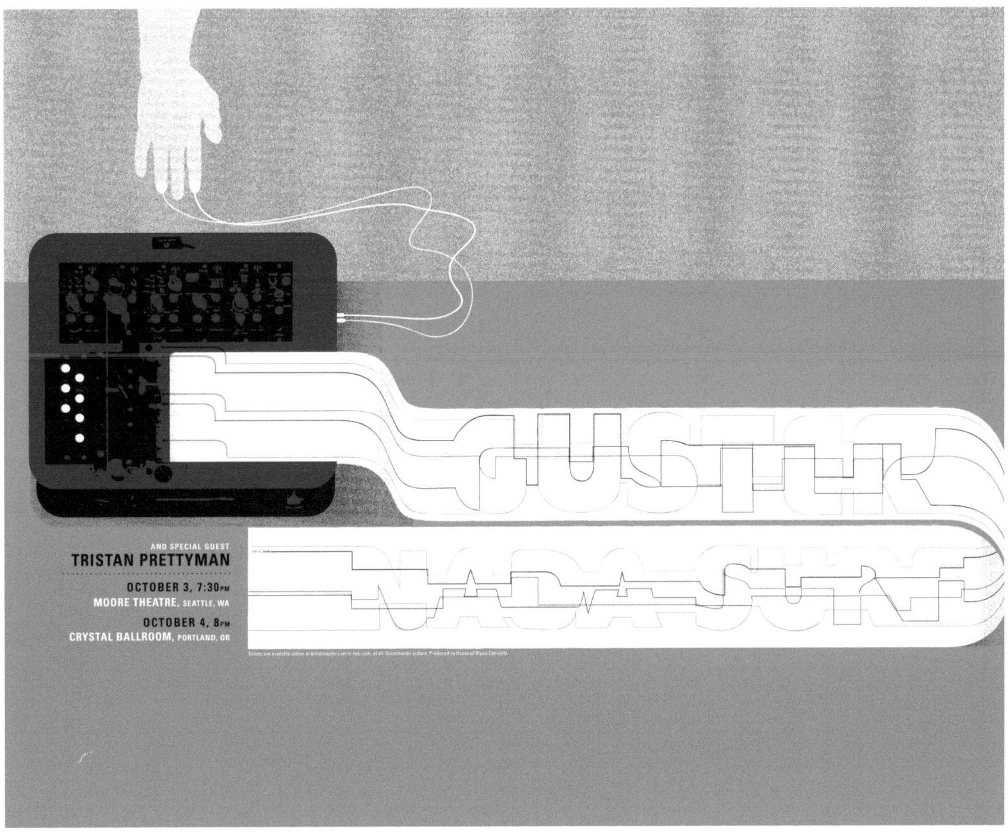

ANDRIO ABERO | 33RPM for My Morning Jacket (18" x 24" 3-color screen print) *in 2006*
& for Guster/Nada Surf (24" x 18" 2-color screen print) *in 2006*

SASHA BARR for Ray LaMontagne Poster, Detroit, MI *in 2006*

SASHA BARR for Death Cab For Cutie Poster, Memphis, TN *in 2006*

SASHA BARR North Mississippi All Stars and Lucero, Memphis, TN *in 2007*

SASHA BARR for Jeff Tweedy Poster, Nashville, TN (Three Color Screen-Print, 16" x 25") *in 2007*

SASHA BARR for Skyscraper Music Magazine #22 Cover Illustration *in 2006*

TODD SLATER for Fantomas (Silkscreen Poster) *in 2004* - Rock -

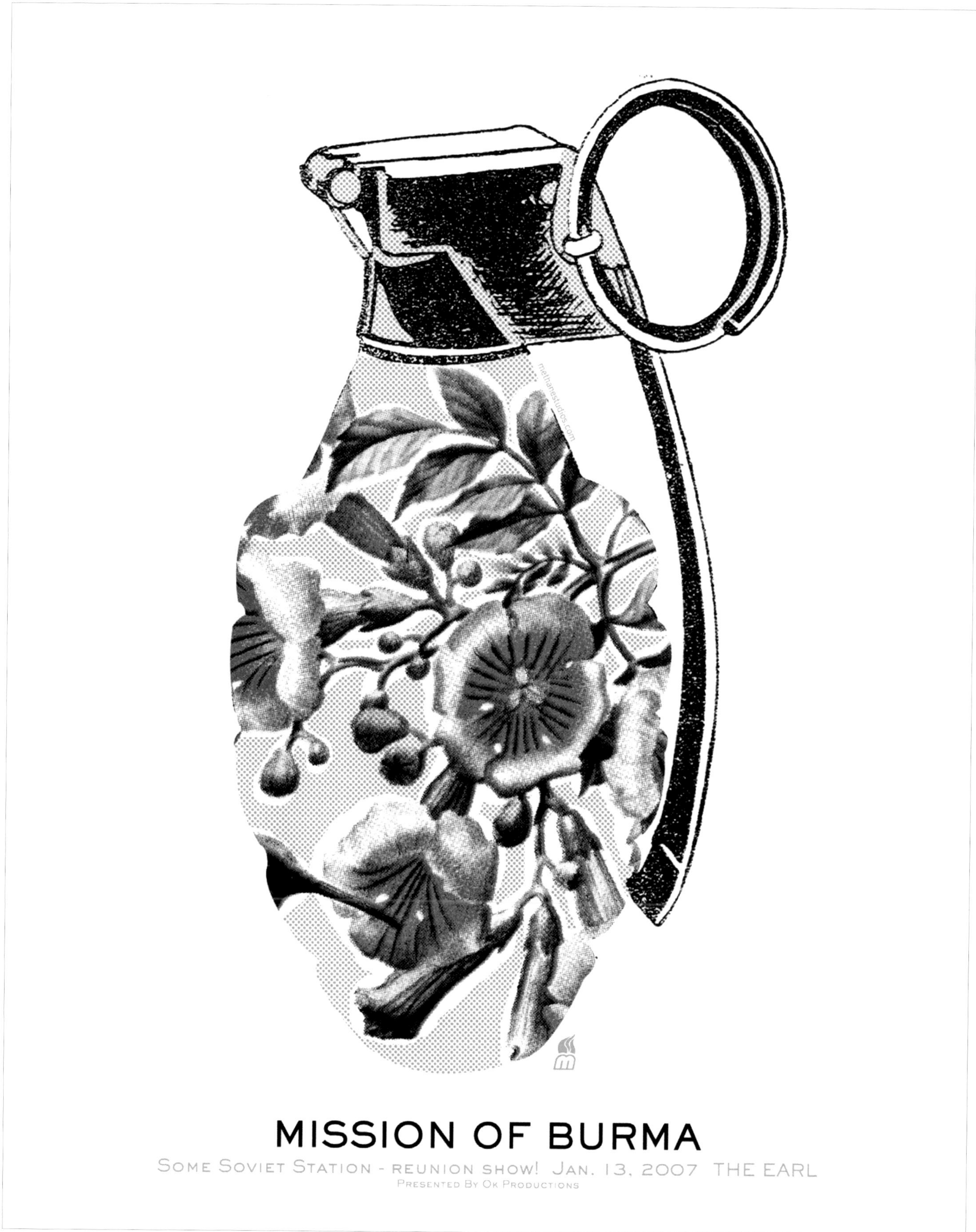

METHANE, D.: MARK MCDEVITT **for Mission of Burma** (silkscreen Poster) *in 2007* - Indie -

THE HEADS OF STATE, D.: DUSTIN SUMMERS for Bright Eyes (24x18 silkscreen) *in 2005*

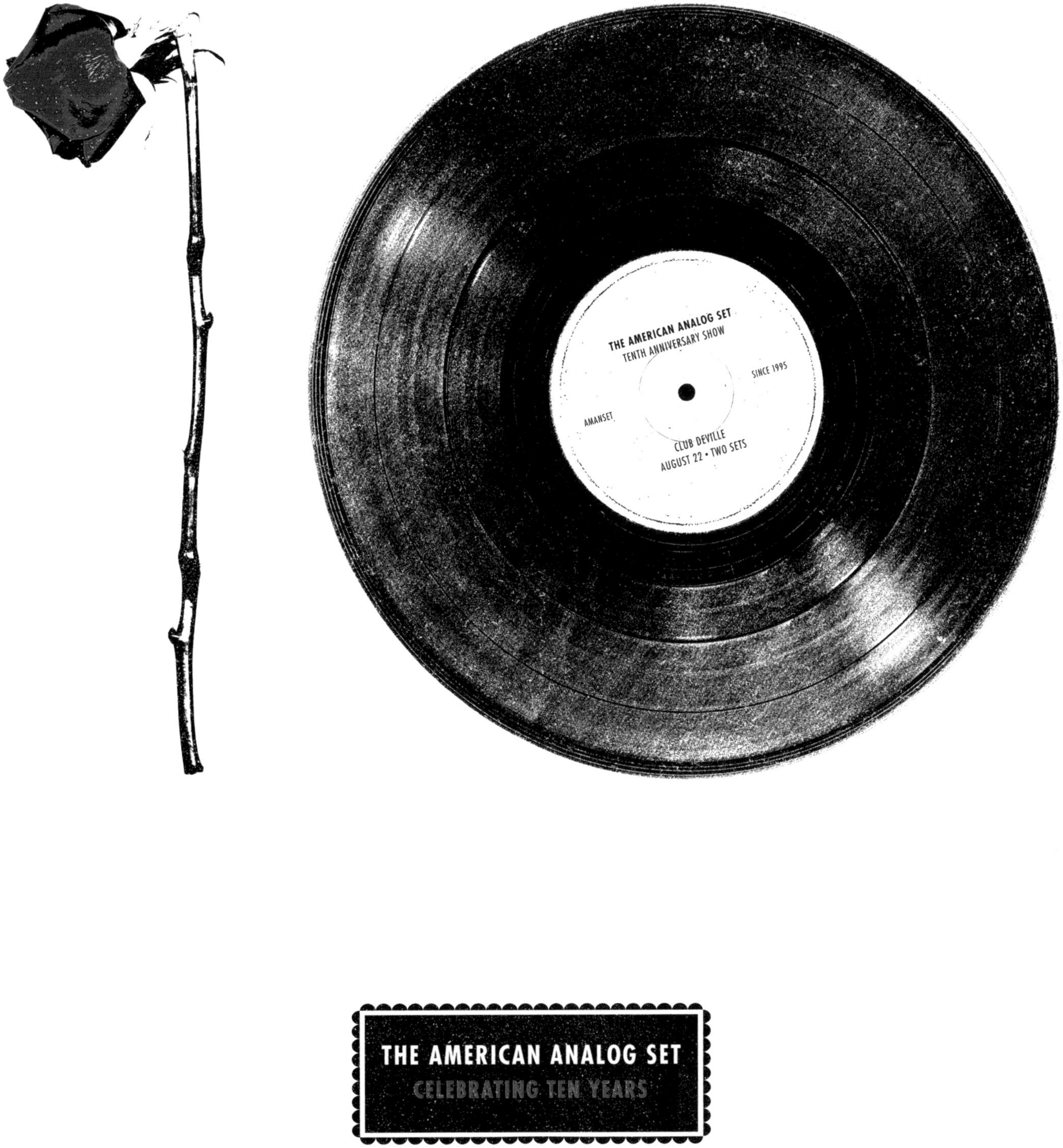

JASON MUNN / THE SMALL STAKES for The American Analog Set "10th Anniversary Poster" *on arts and crafts in 2005* -Independent -

JASON MUNN / THE SMALL STAKES for José González "José González Concert Poster" (poster) *in 2006* - Independent -

JASON MUNN / THE SMALL STAKES for Bonnie "Prince" Billy & or Mark Kozelek "Midwest Tour Poster"(poster) *in 2006* - Independent -

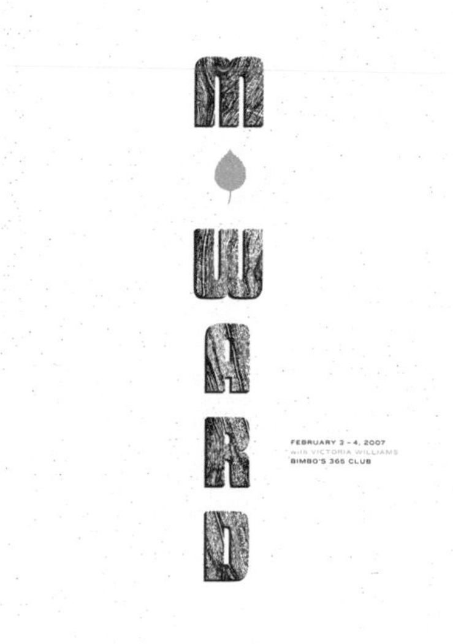

JASON MUNN / THE SMALL STAKES, for **Sufjan Stevens** *on Asthmatic Kitty*, for **The Shins**, for **M. Ward** *in 2007 &* for **The Walkmen** (Concert Poster) *in 2005* - Independent -

JASON MUNN / THE SMALL STAKES for The Wrens (Concert Poster) *on Absolutely Kosher in 2005* - Independent -

JASON MUNN / THE SMALL STAKES for Matt Pond PA (Tour Poster) *in 2006* - Independent -

JASON MUNN / THE SMALL STAKES for Calexico, for Mark Kozelek, for Neko Case & for Tag Team Media - 5th Anniversary with Broken Social Scene (Concert Poster) *in 2006* - Independent -

JASON MUNN / THE SMALL STAKES for The Flaming Lips (Concert Poster) *in 2006* - Alternative - & **for Deerhoof** "Deerhoof Concert Poster" (poster) *in 2007* - Independent -

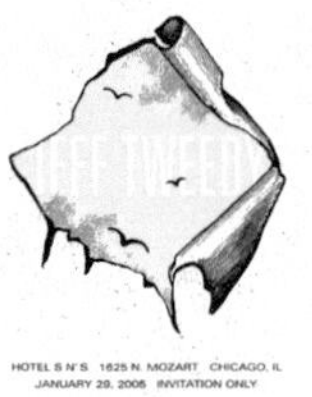

JASON MUNN / THE SMALL STAKES for Jeff Tweedy, for The Books, for Mission of Burma & for Stellastarr* (Concert Poster) *in 2005 & 2006* - Independent -

JASON MUNN / THE SMALL STAKES for Nouvelle Vague "Fall 2006 Tour Poster" *on V2 in 2006* - Independent -

JASON MUNN / THE SMALL STAKES for **Josh Ritter**
"Fall Tour 2006 Poster" *in 2006* - Independent -

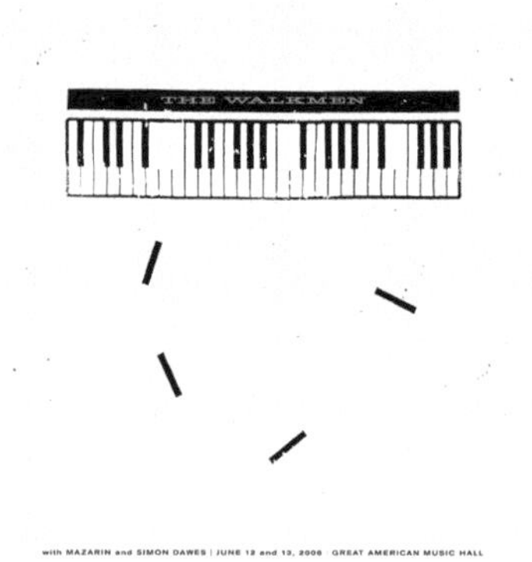

JASON MUNN / THE SMALL STAKES for **The Walkmen** (Concert Poster) *in 2006* - Independent -

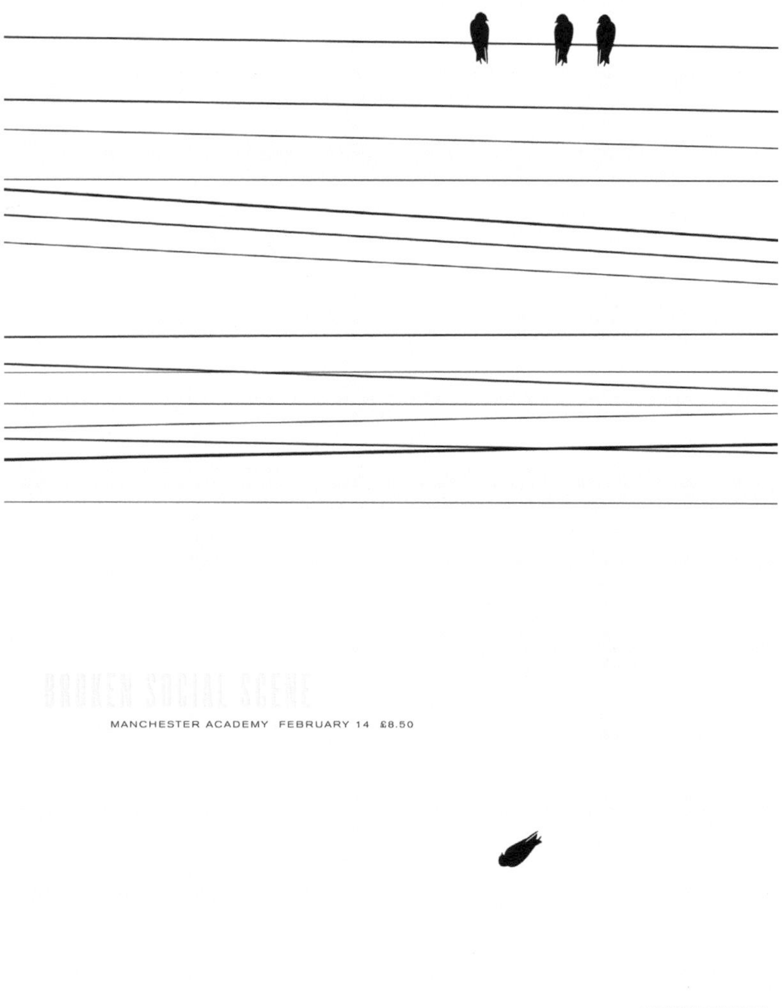

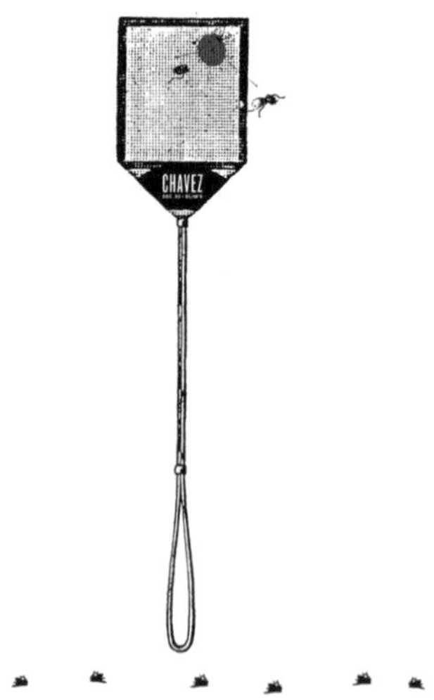

JASON MUNN / THE SMALL STAKES for **Chavez** & for **The Constantines** (Concert Poster) *in 2006* - Independent -

JASON MUNN / THE SMALL STAKES for **Broken Social Scene** (Concert Poster) *on Arts & Crafts in 2006* - Independent -

JASON MUNN / THE SMALL STAKES for Mark Kozelek "West Coast Tour Poster" (poster) *in 2006* - Independent -

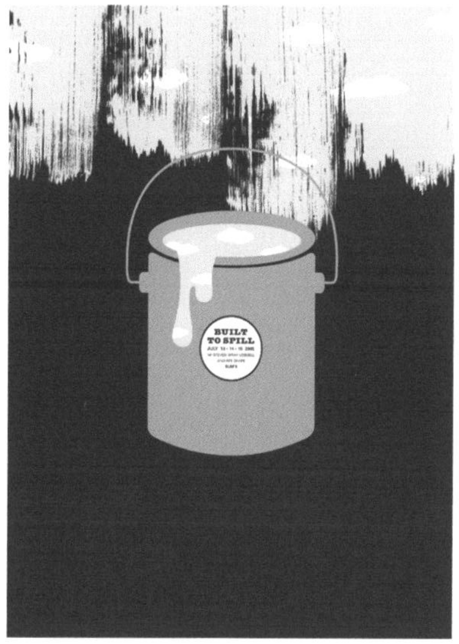

JASON MUNN / THE SMALL STAKES for Built to Spill (Concert Poster) *in 2005* - Independent -

JASON MUNN / THE SMALL STAKES for Death Cab for Cutie "Hurricane Katrina Benefit Concert" (Poster) *in 2005* - Independent - & **for Sufjan Stevens** "San Francisco Concert Poster" *on Asthmatic Kitty in 2005* - Independent -

JASON MUNN / THE SMALL STAKES for Rogue Wave (Concert Poster) *in 2005* - Independent -

INVISIBLE CREATURE, INC., D.: RYAN CLARK **for Fear Factory** "Factory Of Fear Poster" (Poster)
in 2006 - Metal -

THE HEADS OF STATE, D.: DUSTIN SUMMERS **for Iron and Wine Poster & for Jeff Tweedy Tour Poster** "" (18x24 Silkscreen) *in 2006*

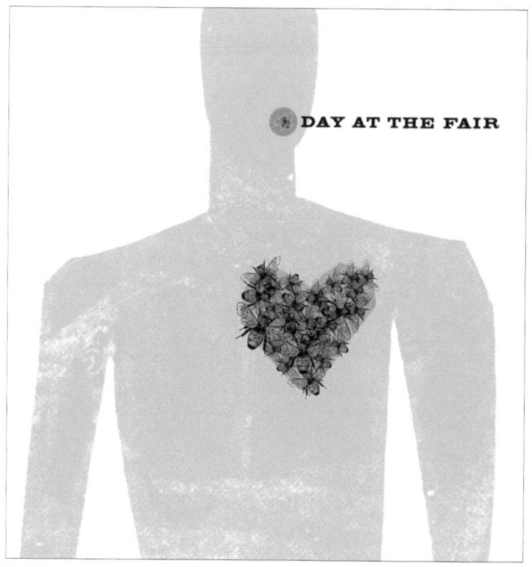

METHANE, D.: MARK MCDEVITT **for Band Of Horses** (Silkscreen Poster) *in 2006* - Indie -

THE HEADS OF STATE, D.: DUSTIN SUMMERS **for Edison Glass** "A Burn or a Shiver" (Jewel Case) *on Credential Recordings in 2006* - Indie - & **for Day at the Fair** "The Rocking Chair Years" (Jewel Case) *on Drive Thru in 2006*

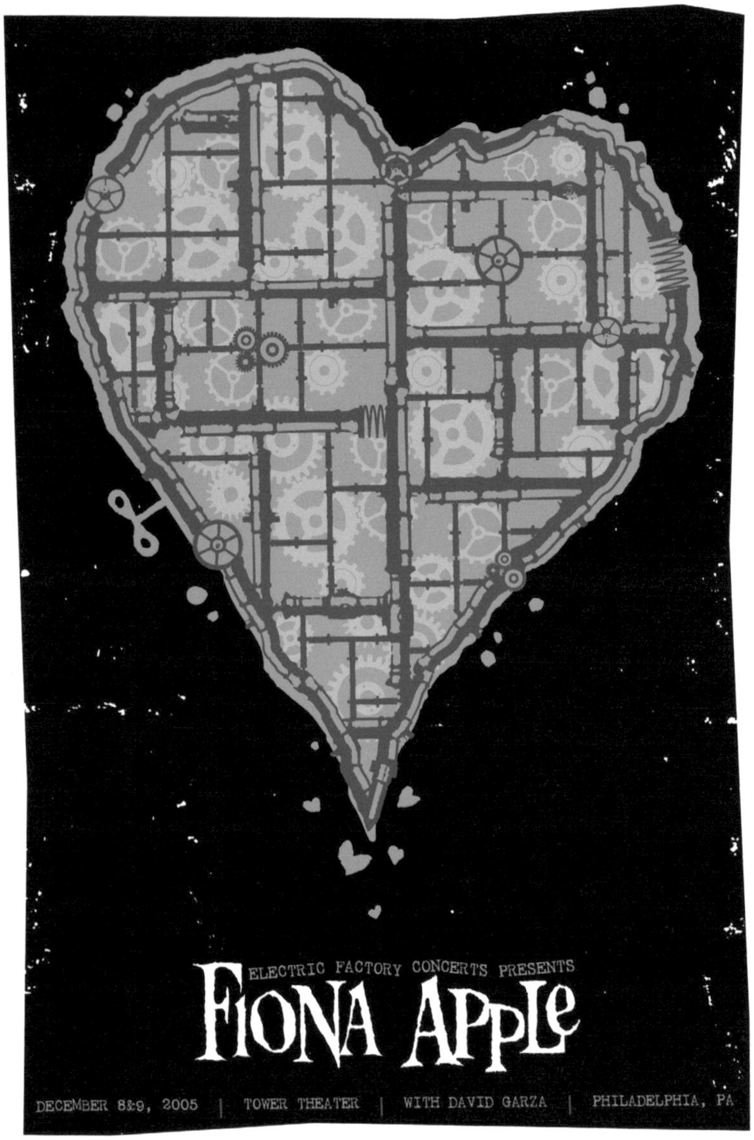

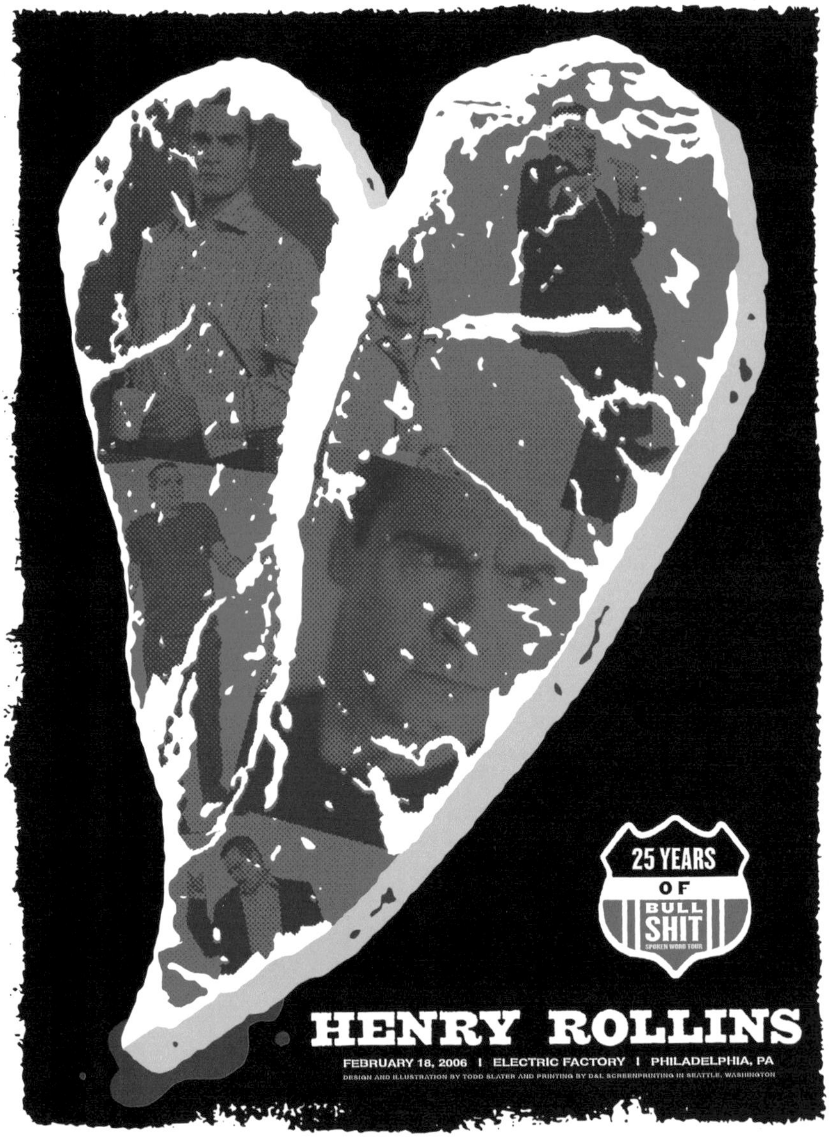

TODD SLATER for **Fiona Apple** & for **Henry Rollins** (Silkscreen Poster) *in 2006* - Rock -

METHANE, D.: ROBERT LEE, MARK MCDEVITT for **Dave Matthews Band** "Cheesy Goodness" (4 color screen print) & for **Silver Jews** *in 2006* - Rock, Indie -

JASON MUNN / THE SMALL STAKES for **Mates of State** (Poster) *on Barsuk Records in 2006* - Independent -

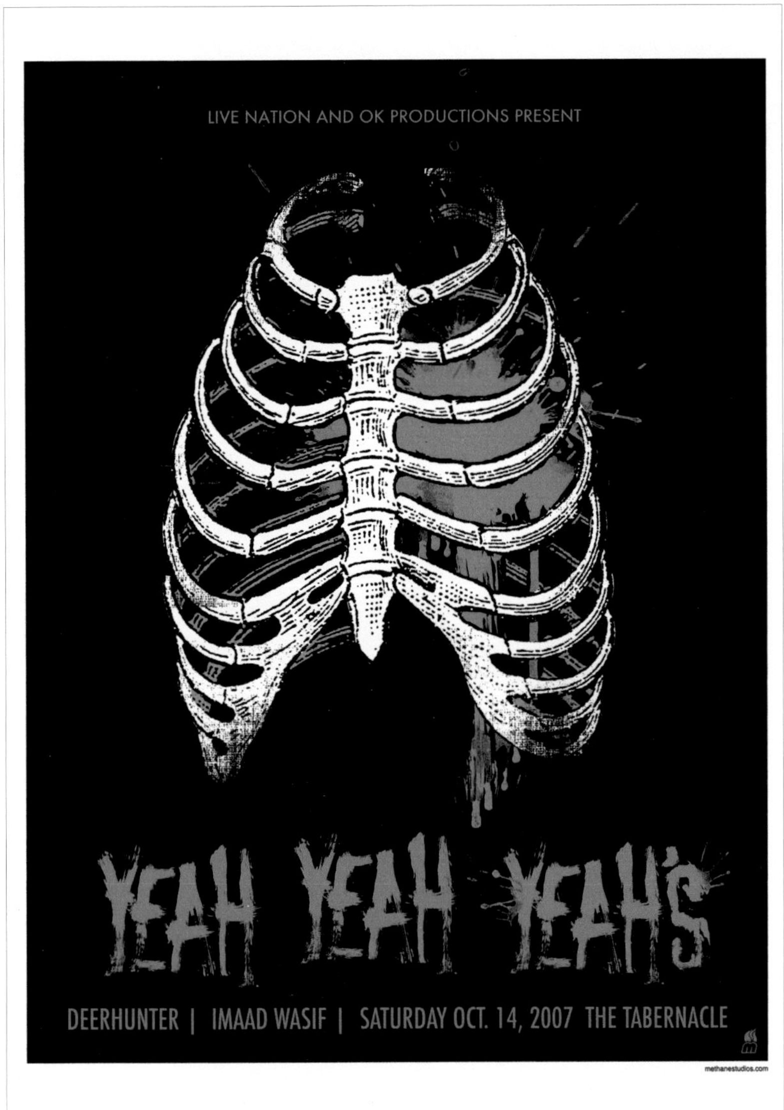

METHANE, D.: MARK MCDEVITT **for Yeah Yeahs Yeah's** & **for Heavy Trash** (silkscreen) *in 2006* - Alternative Rock -

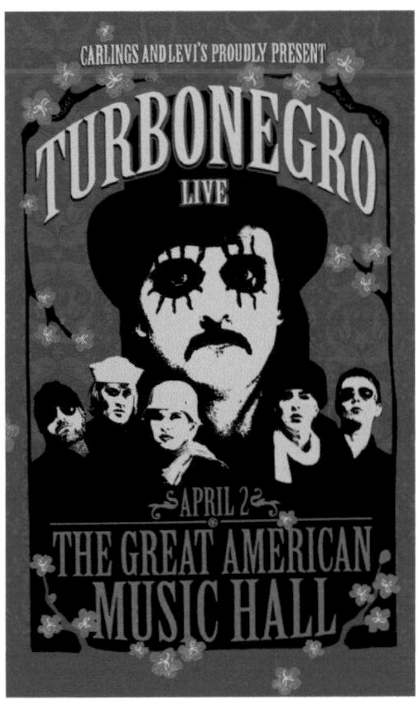

SKIN DESIGN AS, D.: ARE KLEIVAN **for Turbonegro** (45 x 70 cm) *on Venue Great American Music Hall, SF* - Deathpunk -, **for Ween** (40 x 70 cm) *on Venue: Södra Teatern* - Rock - & **for Gluecifer** "Royally Stuffed" (DVD Jewel Case) *on SVP & Columbia/SonyBMG in 2005* - Rock -

BENJAMIN GÜDEL for Sexo y Droga "Dog Monkey Man" (7") on A9 Records in 2006 - Garage Rock -

BENJAMIN GÜDEL for various artists "Tribute do Davie Allen - Evil Fuzz" (CD) *on Omom Records in 2004* - Surf - & **Sexo y Droga** "Woman Man Pain" (7", neon glow colour on white card board: white at daytime, glowing at nighttime), "Sexo y Droga" (LP) on A9 Records in 2005 - Garage Rock -

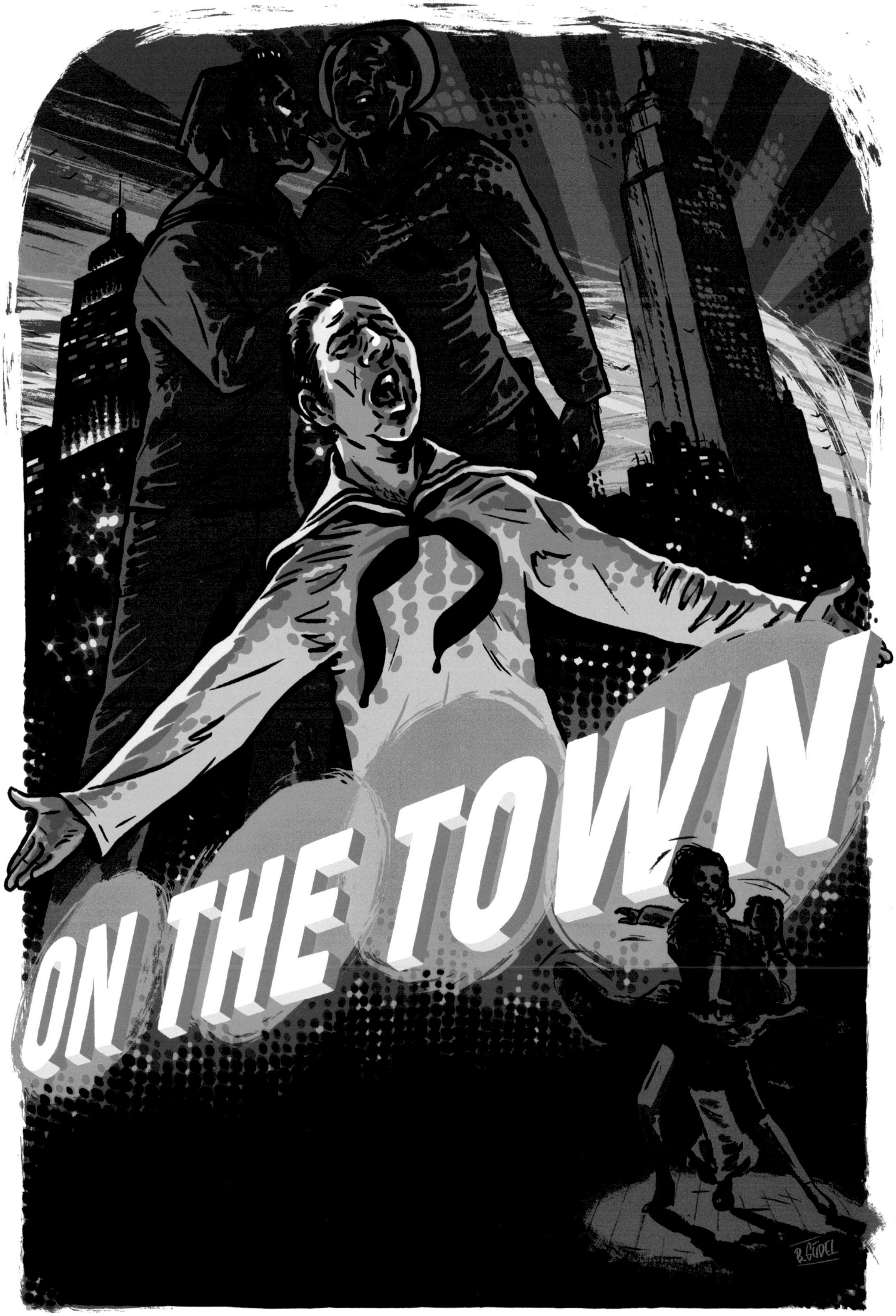

BENJAMIN GÜDEL **for Theater Basel** "On The Town" (90x120 cm) *in 2006* - Musical -

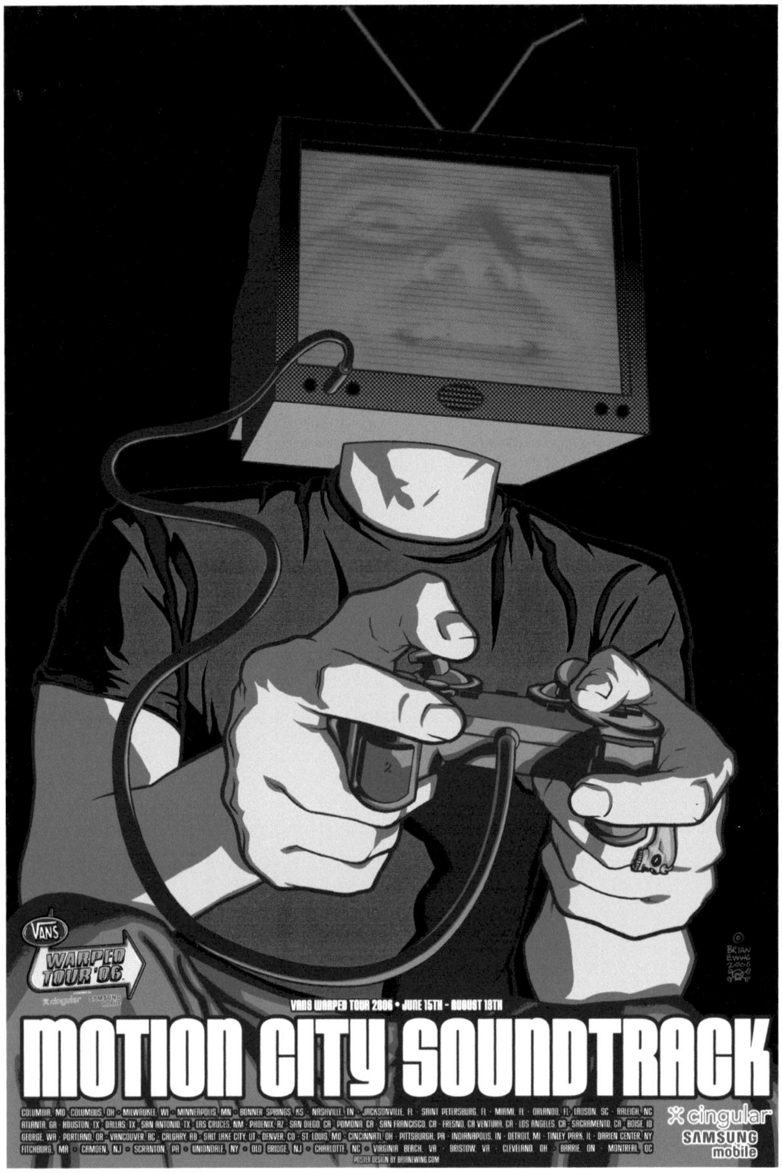

BRIAN EWING for Samsung and Cingular "Motion City Soundtrack Tour Poster" & "Vans Warped Tour Poster" (13" x 19" offset Poster) *in 2006* - Rock -

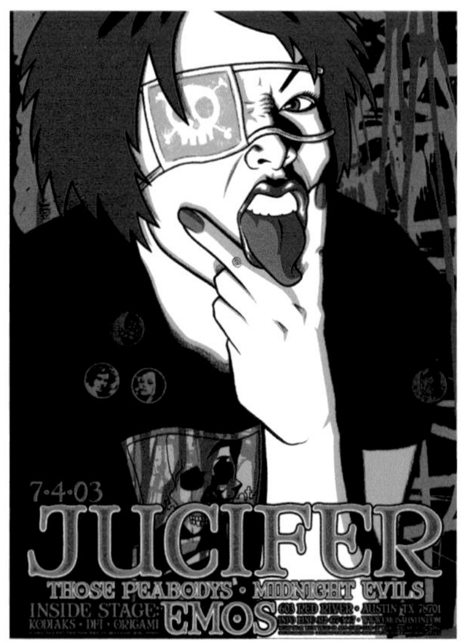

BRIAN EWING for Channel 4 Creative "The We're Not Communicating All That Well Tour" *in 2006*
& for Emos "Jucifer" (18" x 24" screen printed Poster limited to 300 pieces) *in 2003*

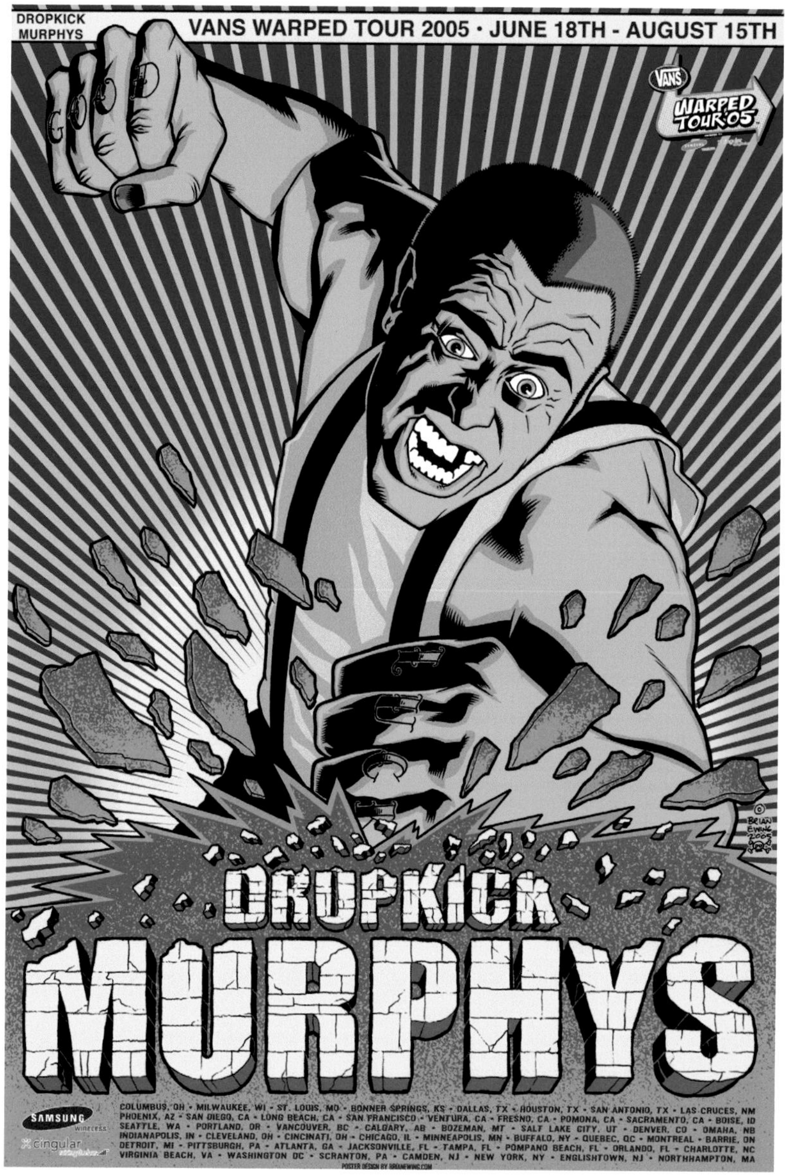

BRIAN EWING for **Samsung and Cingular** "Less Than Jake Tour Poster" & "Dropkick Murphys Warped Tour Poster" (13" x 19" offset Poster) *in 2005 & 2006* - Ska, Punk Rock -

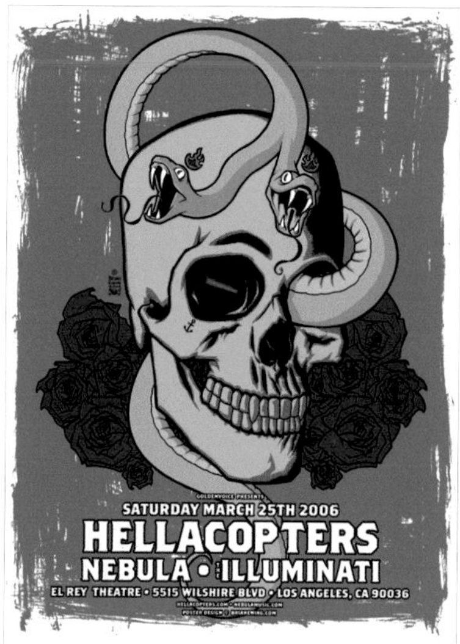

BRIAN EWING **for Zebrahead/ Mind Driver** (18" x 24" Poster) *in 2007* - Rock -, **for Fall Out Boy** (18x24 offset Poster limited to 50 pieces) *on Clearchannel in 2006* - Rock -, **for Hellacopters** (18" x 24" offset Poster limited to 300 pieces) *on Goldenvoice in 2006* - Rock - & **for The Fire Theft** (18" x 24" screen printed Poster limited to 300 pieces) *in 2004* - Alternative -

BRIAN EWING for Jimmy Eat World (18" x 24" screen printed Poster limited to 300 pieces) *in 2004* & for Punk Rock Social "Jucifer" (11" x 17" Poster) *in 2003*

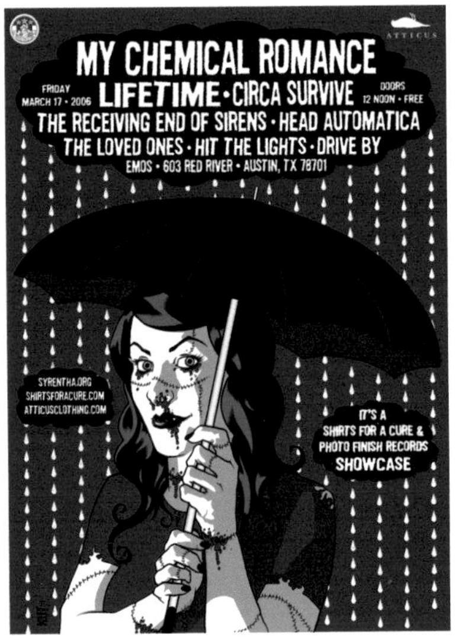

BRIAN EWING for Senses Fail (18" x 24") *on Vagrant Records in 2005*, for My Chemical Romance (13" x 19") *in 2006* & for Distort Entertainment "Listen Harder Tour Poster" (13" x 19") *in 2006*

BRIAN EWING for Electric Factory "N.E.R.D. & Black Eyed Peas Poster" (18" x 24") *in 2004* - Pop/ Hip Hop -

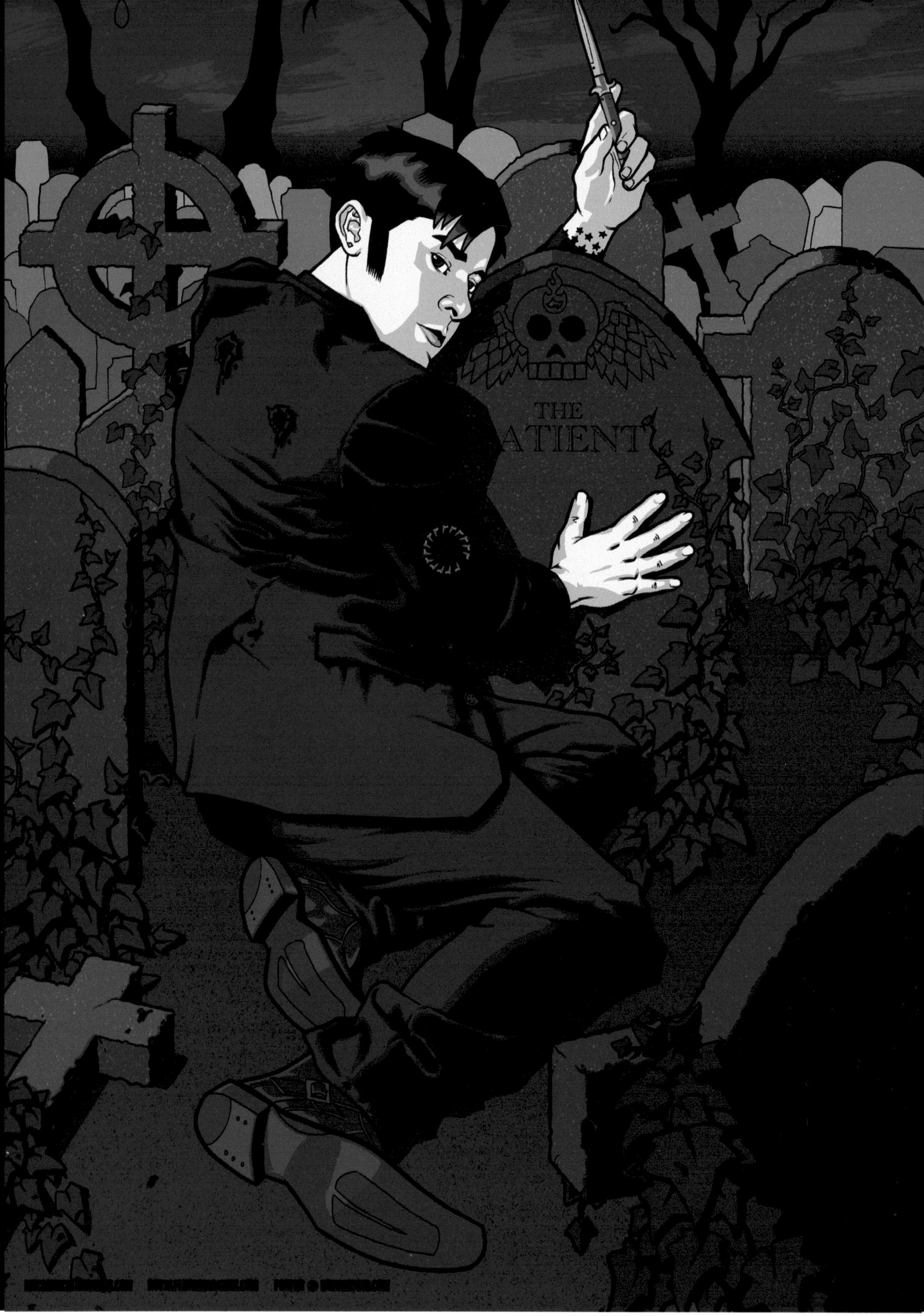

BRIAN EWING for My Chemical Romance (10" x 15" offset Poster for Royal Flush Magazine)
in 2006 - Rock -

BRIAN EWING for Senses Fail (18" x 24" litho Poster, Limited to 500 pieces. This was given out free to people that signed up for Vagrant's fan club) *on Vagrant Records in 2006* - Rock -

DESIGNER-INDEX

INTERVIEWS

Interviews by Sonja Commentz

LABEL-INDEX

SUPERSONIC *Visuals for Music*

Edited by Robert Klanten & Hendrik Hellige
Project management by Hendrik Hellige

Layout by Matthias Hübner for dgv
Interviews by Sonja Commentz, www.simpeltext.de
Production management by Janni Milstrey for dgv

Printed by Artes Graficas Palermo, Madrid

This book was printed according to internationally accepted standards for environmental protection.
These include ISO 14001, which specifies requirements for an environmental management system, and certification from the Forest Stewardship Council, which ensures that the products used do not contribute to global forest destruction.

Published by Die Gestalten Verlag, Berlin 2007
ISBN: 978-3-89955-186-0

Bibliographic information published by the Deutsche Nationalbibliothek.
The Deutsche Nationalbibliothek lists this publication in the Deutsche Nationalbibliografie; detailed bibliographic data is available on the Internet at http://dnb.d-nb.de.

None of the content in this book was published in exchange for payment by commercial parties or designers; dgv selected all included work based solely on its artistic merit.

For more information please check: www.die-gestalten.de

Respect copyright, encourage creativity!